Labour's International Policy

The Labour Party in the 1930s

Labour's

International Policy

The Labour Party in the 1930s

JOHN F. NAYLOR

State University of New York at Buffalo

WEIDENFELD AND NICOLSON

5 Winsley Street London W1

SBN 297 17781 8

Printed in Great Britain
by Ebenezer Baylis & Son Limited
The Trinity Press, Worcester, and London

Contents

Preface

Research at Labour Party Headquarters, Transport House, London, was made possible by a grant from the Graduate School of Arts and Sciences, Harvard University; I wish to express my gratitude to that institution. The staff of the Labour Party Library were most helpful in providing me with printed materials and in affording me the use of their valuable collection of press clippings. The party authorities were kind enough to give me access to the unpublished material of the International Department and the Advisory Committee on International Questions and to permit me use of those materials in this book.

I am also indebted to a number of Labour Party members who granted me interviews, which provide part of the fascination of the study of recent events. The late Hugh Gaitskell gave freely of time from his crowded schedule to discuss the parliamentary tactics of opposition, with which he was, alas, all too familiar; Lord Citrine provided insights concerning those trade union activities over which he presided with distinction for several decades. Two Members of Parliament, George Strauss and Michael Foot, recounted with conviction the efforts of the Labour left; Roy Jenkins, MP, spoke of general tendencies in the period, and kindly read my first efforts, for which I am particularly grateful. Leonard Woolf detailed the workings of the Advisory Committee on International Questions, which he saw from his post as secretary to that body.

This book originated as a doctoral dissertation prepared under the kindly supervision of the late Professor David Owen of Harvard University, whose gentle arts of persuasion succeeded in shortening the length first of the dissertation and subsequently of the book, for which its readers no less than I ought to be grateful. Professor Henry Winkler of Rutgers supplied pertinent

vii

criticism in a gracious manner. Professor James Joll of the London School of Economics provided helpful comments and encouragement in a fashion which all who know him have come to expect and appreciate all the more. Mr Philip Rich drew upon his skills as an editor in a way which far exceeded the call of duty. Of course the traditional caveat – that none of these helpful people is in any way responsible for infelicities of style or content – must apply; I would like, however, to express my gratitude for their share in whatever success may be the fortune of this book.

I wish to thank Mrs Joyce Klein and Miss Mary Ann Janiga of the State University of New York at Buffalo for their careful typing of the final draft.

Above all, I am greatly indebted to my wife Maiken, who examined successive drafts with a critical eye and a detached judgment; hers was a labour of love, if not a love of Labour. To her I dedicate this book.

J.F.N.

Eagle Crag Lake, New York

July 1968

1   The roots of Labour's international policy

Lord Randolph Churchill once commented that the business of the Opposition was to oppose everything, propose nothing and turn out the Government.[1] Judged by these standards, the Labour Party proved a singular disappointment in its long years of opposition during the 1930s. By no means did they oppose everything, though they certainly resisted the direction of the foreign policy pursued by the National Government, which held office from August 1931 until well after the outbreak of war. Nor did Labour propose nothing: during these years they took care to advance, both within and outside Parliament, recommendations in matters of international relations and defence. Unfortunately, their recommendations could never be implemented, since the party was quite unable to overcome the heavy parliamentary majorities which Ramsay MacDonald, Stanley Baldwin and Neville Chamberlain in turn invoked to sustain the governments which they headed.

Was the record of the Labour Opposition in the 1930s therefore one of complete futility? Some might quickly assent, for the party was badly divided throughout the decade and rarely presented the country with a unified appearance. Yet few could agree with Lord Randolph's negative formulation of the role of the Opposition: greater responsibility is expected of parliamentary critics of the government, and the Labour Party obviously cannot be censured for offering advice to the government, but must rather be judged with regard to the content of that counsel. Labour *claimed*, in these years, to be offering a comprehensive foreign and defence policy which would spare Britain both the scourge of war and the disgrace of appeasement. Was that policy in fact a viable alternative to the policy undertaken by the National Government?

A*

Though the students of that government's policy are legion, scant attention has been paid to Labour's alternative proposals. Perhaps the fresh perspective afforded from following the fortunes of the Opposition will provide insights into the theory and practice of appeasement. Certainly we will be able to assess the validity of Labour's claim to responsible opposition. Did the party come to speak with one voice by the time of Munich? What role did the Labour Party and its leaders play in these years in the political wilderness between 1931 and 1939? Of what stuff were the future innovators of the Welfare State made?

In the sphere of international relations, the party's views were shaped by the very nature of recent events, but Labour's own history also served as an important determinant of policy. To neglect either influence is to miss the interplay between the two and the subtlety of Labour attitudes.

Labour's international policy was, not surprisingly, affected decisively by the war of 1914–18, although its specific form was hammered out gradually in the first post-war decade.[2] To be sure, certain tenets of Labour policy predated the war, though the party was not then greatly concerned with foreign policy. Yet in response to the war experience, the Labour Party developed strong views in four areas bearing directly upon the conduct of foreign policy.

First among these were the question of the Treaty of Versailles and the related question of the League of Nations. Though the party assailed the Versailles settlement for fully a decade and a half, Labour throughout that period advocated strenuously the cause of the League of Nations, after some initial disappointment with that body. The party's criticism of the peace terms was in part rooted in its pre-war opposition to imperialism, but those terms poured fuel upon a long-smouldering antipathy. Similarly Labour's pre-war commitment to internationalism disposed it in favour of a league of nations. In such ways did the events of the war reinforce and extend older Labour beliefs.

In the third place, the war strengthened pacifist positions subscribed to by many within the party. Pacifism ran deep in Labour ranks, touching several of the party's leaders as well as the membership generally. Finally, Labour's post-war advocacy of

2

disarmament reflected in large measure a desire to escape another senseless carnage.

In sum, these four concerns – the peace treaty, the League, pacifism and disarmament – played a significant role in shaping Labour's post-war international policy. The war to end all wars had been won: the task now was to preserve the peace.

To place these four concerns in their proper context one must understand the nature of the forum within which Labour resolved its policy. Twice in the post-war years the Labour Party assumed the tasks of government, briefly in 1924 and again from 1929 to 1931. In both instances Labour served as a minority government, dependent upon Liberal support for continued survival in the House of Commons. In these administrations of Ramsay MacDonald, no radical socialist measures were secured; likewise at the Foreign Office, which MacDonald also presided over in his first government and which Arthur Henderson conducted in the second, traditional policies and practices were for the most part maintained. The parliamentary leaders, together with their colleagues on the party executive, Labour's own governing body, once each year submitted their policies for approval to the party as a whole, meeting in Conference. Because representation at those gatherings was scaled to membership, the trade unions exercised a predominant voice in Conference; the local Labour parties and the non-trade union socialist bodies who were affiliated to the Labour Party were given a smaller voice, though often this proved more politically articulate.

The policies adopted by the Labour governments were not called into question to any embarrassing degree by Conference in the 1920s: the trade union leaders were not disturbed by the reformist policies of Labour's parliamentary leaders, and the political activists of the local parties were sympathetic to the Labour government's minority plight. Matters of foreign policy did not divide the Labour Party: only the events of the 1930s drove the political activists – but by no means all of them – into sharp disagreement with official policies approved by Conference. The revival of dissent in the 1930s constitutes an important aspect of the role which the party attempted to play in the maintenance of peace.

3

To turn then to the first of the party's four major post-war concerns in the sphere of international policy, Labour had from the first announcement of terms opposed the Paris settlement, which it regarded as an unjust and undemocratic peace. All sections of the party combined in denouncing in bitter language the harsh provisions.[3] In this opposition the Labour Party was very much influenced by a small but talented group of men, members of the Union of Democratic Control, ' . . . in whose judgment the Treaty bore out the suspicions which they had entertained throughout the war of the purity of the Allied intentions'.[4] Most of the UDC group, who eventually joined the Labour Party, had until the outbreak of the war been Liberals; radicals in matters of foreign policy, their interest in the Labour Party other than as a forum for their ideas is dubious.[5] Norman Angell, Charles Trevelyan, Charles Roden Buxton, Arthur Ponsonby and their colleagues were, however, able propagandists who captured the attention of the rank and file. In their contemporary denunciation of the war the UDC had joined forces with the more numerous members of the Independent Labour Party, a component of the Labour Party which throughout the war had been the main anti-war political organization in Britain. The ILP numbered as members such stalwarts as Ramsay MacDonald and George Lansbury; though the Labour Party refused to endorse the ILP position, the latter remained affiliated throughout the war. Their anti-war attitude made possible the liaison through which the ex-Liberals came to influence a party which had to this time rather neglected foreign policy: ' . . . the socialism they came to profess as a result of their association with the ILP . . . was defined in terms of internationalism, open diplomacy and the democratic control of foreign affairs . . .'[6] With this merger a traditional radical attitude was infused into Labour, namely that of an over-readiness, especially when in opposition, to put all possible blame for whatever was wrong in the world upon the British government.[7]

Charles Trevelyan's criticism of the Versailles Treaty typifies the certainty felt by those who had opposed the war that their advice should be heeded: 'It was exactly as we had prophesied. The imperialist war had ended in the imperialist peace. We had been wrong in nothing except that we had failed to evoke in war time, the opinions which alone can extinguish war. *We* had been right; not the worthy optimists who had chattered about a war to end war.'[8] The trade union elements of the party were less outspoken in their denunciation, for they had supported the war effort, albeit reluctantly in some cases. However, they and their leaders shared the radicals' view that Germany had been treated too harshly.[9] At the Labour Party Conference which met in June 1919 the Treaty was denounced for failing to treat the defeated powers with justice.[10] With the subsequent addition of John Maynard Keynes' criticism, the scorn of the economist at the insanity of Versailles' provisions reinforced the radicals' complaint of the settlement's iniquity.[11] Labour's deeply-held strictures against Versailles contributed to the party's pro-German reputation in the 1920s. That reputation was ill-founded, for Labour's position reflected a much more basic attitude:

> The strong stand against the treatment which was meted out to Germany by the victorious Powers was the natural outcome of an ideological revolt against the War and its purposes . . . The postwar criticism of the Versailles settlement stemmed from the glaring contrast which Labour came to perceive between its own high-minded idealism and the performance of Allied statesmen at the Peace Conference.[12]

The severity of the terms, Labour held, ended hopes of a period of peace and stability; consequently Labour advocated revision, not to strengthen German nationalism, but rather to bolster democracy against those nationalist forces through a revised settlement which German opinion could accept. Labour consequently opposed (this was to prove ironic) placement of the Sudetenland in Czech hands, as well as the settlement of the Polish frontier.

The Labour Party Conferences of 1920–3 passed resolutions favouring treaty and frontier revision, but the short-lived Labour government of 1924 made no direct attempt to secure revision; instead they pursued the more practical economic approach for German recovery incorporated in the Dawes Plan.[13] As the passage of time hardened the frontier settlements, and as the treaties signed at Locarno in 1925 promised to initiate a new and more secure era of European relations, official Labour paid less attention to the territorial provisions of Versailles. Hugh Dalton, shortly to serve under Henderson at the Foreign Office, reflected this new attitude when he argued in 1928 that the frontiers should be regarded as settled; Labour should work, not for their revision, but for their obliteration.[14] Another factor in the evolution of a more conciliatory Labour approach to foreign policy was the concentration of the party's energies upon the General Strike of 1926: in the wake of the failure of working-class pressures to secure their domestic ends there followed a weakening of the militant spirit in foreign policy which had characterized the trade union approach earlier in the decade.[15] By the late twenties, frontiers had lost primacy of place in Labour's criticism of Versailles; the attempted revision of other aspects of the Treaty, however, continued well into the next decade.

These objections to the Treaty of Versailles dictated Labour's initially ambivalent attitude to the League of Nations, whose very covenant was a part of that document. The concept of such a league accorded well with the internationalist aspirations of the Labour Party. Indeed, Arthur Henderson had in 1918 looked to a league of nations as the world's hope of deliverance from war: the establishment of such a league, which would make the world 'safe for democracy', was one of Labour's principal war aims. Such a league was a prerequisite as well for the attainment of Labour's domestic goals: 'Neither national reconstruction nor international conciliation is possible so long as the people are preoccupied with the menace of foreign aggression, and Governments are forced to spend huge sums yearly upon the means of national self-defence.'[16] The party maintained that unless an international system which would prevent wars were established, the peoples would have lost the struggle of 1914–18, regardless of which side won. From the first Henderson associated with such a league the concept of compulsory arbitration; its member states would have recourse to the imposition of military or economic sanctions upon those who refused to keep the covenant of peace. What would appear a pragmatic approach was somewhat weakened by Henderson's implication that complete democratization of all member nations would be required if the league were to function at all. Only then could the league supersede the arbitrary powers, e.g. armaments manufacturers or the methods of secret diplomacy, which had hitherto held in thrall the choice between peace and war. Labour's league would be one of peoples rather than one of agreement among governments.

6

The League of Nations created at Paris was manifestly not one of peoples; rather, in Labour's view, it seemed the creation of statesmen pursuing the pre-war concept of balance of power, anxious to use the League to serve their own national purposes. The Labour Party, in Winkler's succinct words, ' . . . was disappointed with the league's membership, its structure, and its proposed functions'.[17] The League of Nations was not rejected out-of-hand by official Labour, as it was by the radical ex-Liberals now within its ranks, but it was not regarded as possessing much value in its existing form. Arthur Henderson played the major role in bringing the Labour Party to the view that, although the League fell far short of genuine internationalism, a reformed and strengthened League could be made to work in the interests of European conciliation and international peace.[18] Henderson was able gradually to modify Labour's initial criticism of the League as a disguise for a coalition of the Allies desirous of maintaining their predominance. By 1922 he had adumbrated ideas which three years later bore fruit in the Geneva Protocol; he recognized relatively early that disarmament, arbitration and the use of the League to promote peaceful settlement all depended upon the willingness of the member states to commit themselves to the task of enforcement of the Covenant. To achieve that enforcement, in the form of compulsory and binding arbitration, Henderson approved of the use of sanctions. In 1924 he specified that the League might have to resort to the use of force, if the international order were to be maintained.[19]

The Labour Party as a whole did not move as quickly as Henderson. Not until 1929 was he able to secure the party's acceptance of his League-centred policy. Other men assisted, notably J.R.Clynes and the majority of the Labour Party's Advisory Committee on International Questions. Hugh Dalton stood forthrightly for sanctions in 1928: 'If a high moral tone is to be the League's only weapon against the material force of an aggressor, its bluff will soon be called . . . To think, as some sentimentalists appear to do, that we can build a new international order without any sanctions whatever, is not to think at all.'[20]

Though Labour evolved its attitude towards the League, the party continued to emphasize hopes for the peaceful revision of Versailles through the League, rather than means for enforcing

7

that settlement. Thus the party's primary concern was to remove the likelihood of challenge, not to provide a mechanism of response. In this attitude, the party reflected the view of collective security which was prevalent in Great Britain at the time of Locarno:

> The very idea that there existed any need for an organized system of guarantees of mutual assistance against aggression ran counter to convictions deep-rooted in the traditions of British liberalism. It appeared to imply that fear and distrust were the sentiments which the peoples of different countries would necessarily and normally entertain towards one another . . . It was indicative of the wrong attitude of mind in the search for peace . . . The best guarantee of peace lay in the determination of men of all nations to prevent the recurrence of war.[21]

Philip Snowden expressed in a phrase the Labour Party's concept of the League of Nations as 'an instrument by which future wars might be avoided'.[22] That the League might be called upon to intervene in an already erupted conflict remained a possibility mentioned by no one within the party: Labour shared with the League's many supporters an unrealistic conception of the full range of its responsibilities.

Pacifism was the third major concern of the party which had been significantly influenced by the British war experience. At that time, pacifist influence made itself felt within the Labour Party through a liaison between the radical pacifist internationalists and the Independent Labour Party. A complex of reasons motivated the ILP war-resisters: some were Christian pacifists; others believed in the evil of all violence, and still others held the socialist belief that war was a product of imperialist rivalries which the working-classes had no cause to support.[23]

Disillusionment with the results of the war strengthened still further the strain of pacifism within the party, because war had proved to be – above all else – monstrously inefficacious. A foreign observer, Egon Wertheimer, asserted in 1929 that the ethical postulate of the repudiation of war provided the theoretical basis of Labour's foreign policy. However, because this advocacy of peace as an absolute good ' . . . takes account at the same time of political and economic considerations . . . [Labour's] pacifism is freed from Utopianism and brought back to earth'.[24] Wertheimer then regarded as realistic the desire of Labour pacifists to abandon the concept of League sanctions and to

8

rely instead upon the conciliatory aspects of the Covenant, transforming the League of Nations into a pacifist institution.

Wertheimer's assertion that British pacifism ran deeper than elsewhere in Europe is interesting and relevant:

> To the average Englishman the war was incomparably more upsetting and incomprehensible [than to the European]. And in England, therefore, the reactions of [sic!] the war were far more profound than in any other country ... The romance of war, for Great Britain, is dead. Although she signed the Pact of Paris [the Kellogg-Briand Pact] only subject to reservations, Great Britain is, as a nation, more instinctively pacifist than any other nation in Europe.[25]

Yet for most Englishmen this pacifism remained only instinctive: very few among them sought to build a political programme about their belief in pacific ways. Upon those who were members of the Labour Party the attraction towards political expression was stronger, for Labour's own pacifist tradition served to reinforce the instinct. That tradition of course sprang from socialist tenets: 'It was an expression of its [Socialism's] idealism, of its belief in human brotherhood and international socialism, its suspicions of imperialism and the economic and political exploitation of man by man. It represented much that was best and most inspiring in early socialism.'[26] No wonder then that pacifism was a strong force within the Labour Party.

That the sentiment found expression in Labour policy is clear in resolutions adopted in 1922 and 1926 at party Conferences. In the former year Conference adopted a resolution which committed the party to oppose any war; in its debate Conference refused to declare its support for a nation forced by some armed aggressor to defend its independence or democratic institutions.[27] Four years later, no one even bothered to oppose a resolution introduced by an ILP delegate, Fenner Brockway, calling for general resistance, ' ... including the refusal to bear arms, to produce armaments, or to render any material assistance' to meet any threat of war.[28] Logically, sanctions under the League of Nations were ruled out. So great was the pacifist loathing of war, so massive was the general disillusionment in its efficacy, that the pacifists displayed no concern for the problem of confronting aggression. The extreme pacifists were quite aware of the consequences of their position: they did not claim that war could be

9

averted, but rather they taught a way of meeting any war – refusal to fight, acceptance of the result as a lesser evil than war. But few were so absolute: ' . . . most pacifists did actually encourage the belief that by refusing at all costs to provide armaments and by counselling non-resistance they were helping to avoid war'.[29] Precisely such a belief was encouraged by the pacifist Arthur Ponsonby, speaking on behalf of the war-resistance resolution at the 1926 Conference; by so resolving, Labour ' . . . would withdraw the war card from diplomacy'.[30] Thus an instinctive but inconsistent pacifism prevailed within the councils of the party.

That an arms race had led to war provided yet a fourth concern with which the party engaged in the post-war years; in this matter – disarmament – all sections of the party were agreed. Party members differed as to whether disarmament should be accomplished by international agreement or pursued unilaterally, but all concurred that the arms race was a vicious spiral from which there was no escape save that of disarmament. Pacifist sentiments naturally provided much of the impetus, but official Labour, in the person of Arthur Henderson, was equally certain of the cause of the outbreak of war in 1914. Speaking in 1931, he argued that the concept of balance of power, so often faulted, was not intrinsically responsible: 'It was . . . competitive preparation for war which at last submerged what was good in the Balance of Power and transformed it into that hostile grouping of opposing forces so powerful and so dangerous, that, soon or late, they were bound to burst the bonds which held them.'[31] To Henderson the lesson was clear: if the arms race were again to go unchecked, the bursting point would in time be reached and another, far ghastlier, war would result. The League of Nations, he commented, was working well, but arbitration, however important in itself, could not ensure permanent peace unless disarmament were also established. This conviction that the piling-up of armaments could lead only to war was stated even more cogently by the man who has proved to be this century's most persistent advocate of disarmament, Bertrand Russell: 'Fear of war is used to justify armaments; armaments increase the fear of war; and the fear increases the likelihood of war.'[32]

Though the Labour Party only slowly yielded its hope for

general disarmament, it never went as far as the extreme pacifists desired, namely unilateral disarmament. In 1928 Ponsonby suggested that it was time for a new approach to the problem of disarmament:

My suggestion . . . is that we should not continually say, 'We will do it if you will do it ', but that we should go to the League of Nations and say, 'We find that war does not solve any problems. We find that . . . a war anywhere will in future be a war everywhere . . . We believe that so long as any armaments exist the probability of war remains, and we refuse to believe that the peace of the world can be secured by violence through modern armaments. Therefore, we renounce the war weapon . . . in all circumstances, and shall proceed to disarm on a basis regulated by economic consideration and the methods necessary for the gradual disestablishment of the fighting services.'[33]

Such relentlessly logical unilateralism was not adopted by the party, then or subsequently: a majority regarded it as utopian. A variety of reasons, however, led the entire party to oppose continuing expenditure on armaments: 'Large armaments were opposed because they were expensive, unnecessary, inexpedient, futile, un-Christian, inimical to social reform, productive of international rivalries and war, germinative of an anti-democratic and militarist spirit, and the result of capitalist greed.'[34] These factors operated to place disarmament, along with the hope of strengthening the League, at the heart of Henderson's approach to European problems.[35] In this connection disarmament became a higher aim than collective security, though Henderson, unlike the pacifists, never forgot about the possible need for sanctions.

This very order of priority in turn affected official Labour's interpretation of how best to strengthen the League: that body would be strengthened not by a backing of force but by tightening the obligations of the member states. Alan Bullock has incisively summarized the attitude of the Labour Party:

If an act of aggression occurred, it was assumed that, provided that the British Government stood by its obligations to the League, moral sanctions, the solemn naming of the aggressor, or at most economic sanctions, would be sufficient to halt it. Support for the League, therefore, and the campaign for disarmament, collective security *and* resistance to war went hand in hand.[36]

In such a manner, then, were Labour's concepts of international policy interlocked, in a seemingly paradoxical fashion; yet given the context of the post-war period, and the legacy of party beliefs, Labour's international policy is both comprehensive and comprehensible.

If the war influenced decisively the formulation of Labour's policy in these four major areas, taking the party in new directions in the 1920s, the deteriorating international situation in the following decade brought still further, and farther-reaching, changes in the party's international policy. Was Labour's adaptation of its policy to the shattering of the Versailles settlement rapid or slow, realistic or delusive?

Whatever the answer, Labour's adaptation can be studied primarily in terms of those concerns which the party had inherited from the Great War. Well into the second decade of the post-war period, Labour continued its quest for revision of certain of Versailles' provisions. The colonial settlement was long a target for criticism, because of Labour's opposition to imperialism.

Germany's colonial empire had been taken from her; critics argued that the victors had once again divided the spoils, this time under cover of the mandate system. A prominent member of the Labour left, G.D.H.Cole, argued as late as 1937 that Germany's claims for restoration of her colonies could best be countered by the abolition of all other colonial holdings: 'Colonial empire is a plain denial of democracy: it is a predatory institution which no real democracy can defend. It is, moreover, an insuperable barrier to the secure establishment of peace. Away with it!'[37] The radical voice in the formulation of Labour policy was not yet stilled.

The advent of Hitler to power had served to renew opposition within the Labour camp to yet another shortcoming of the Treaty. Leonard Woolf, an able Labour propagandist as well as publisher, argued in 1933 that the party must act quickly on the question of Article 231, which stipulated German war guilt; failure to act would imply a rejection of the German petition for revision of the Treaty.[38] At the very least, the German claim should be investigated. Thus the question of revision remained very much alive fifteen years after the Treaty of Versailles: the Paris peace conference continued to symbolize an unjust, rapacious, imperialist settlement. Aspects of that settlement were challenged until the threats posed by an obviously more unjust system, practised in Nazi Germany, caused Labour to deal with the German nation in terms other than meeting the just claims of the vanquished.

In the 1930s the Labour Party continued to champion the cause of the League of Nations, though an internal conflict over the place of sanctions raged through the better part of the decade; this controversy detracted from Labour's commitment to the League of Nations.

Labour's ingrained, instinctive pacifism also impaired that commitment. Pacifism was widespread in Labour ranks in the early thirties; indeed the party's leader for three years in that decade was himself a pacifist. Though the rational and systematic advocates of pacifism never prevailed within the councils of the party, the purgation of instinctive pacifism, rendered necessary by the events of the decade, was a slow and painful process.

The party's hopes for disarmament were also dashed in that troubled decade, which witnessed the challenge of fascism and the collapse of democratic régimes in central Europe. These related phenomena undercut the very structure of the League of Nations, upon which Labour had grounded its hopes, ultimately, for a new democratic international order. The preservation of peace in these circumstances became increasingly difficult; Labour's contribution is our chronicle.

Before beginning this chronicle, one must, in all fairness to the Labour Party, take account of the large measure of agreement among British political parties in several matters for which only the Labour viewpoint has been given. Initially the parties had divided sharply over the merits of the Versailles Treaty; however, Labour's decade-long amendment of its position had by 1930 narrowed the gap considerably. Certainly pacifism, politically speaking, found its home in Labour ranks; the conflict between pacifist ideals and collective security was waged largely within the confines of the Labour Party.

Yet the Conservatives, we shall see, interpreted the concept of collective security in an even more ambiguous fashion, though for reasons quite different from Labour's. In the 1930s the Conservatives, and the National Government which they

13

dominated, followed a course of action inimical to the collective security which they nominally supported.

On the issues of support for the League of Nations – though what that commitment might entail was rarely spelled out – and the need for disarmament there was near-unanimity among political parties well into the 1930s.[39] With either the League or disarmament in mind, we can justly speak of a British position, sharply differentiated from the French. This disagreement weakened Anglo-French relations for the better part of the inter-war years; the British point of view was shared by the Labour Party, Liberals and most Conservatives alike:

> The British inclined to the view that armaments provoked fear and suspicion, and so were themselves a cause of war. Nations should first disarm, and security would then ensue ... The French looked at the matter in a different way. The fear of war, they said, makes nations arm for their defence. Remove the fear of attack and armaments will wither away ... Let us, they urged, build up the apparatus of security; then nations will be able to disarm.[40]

What is of particular importance in this connection is that the lag in British military preparedness which became excruciatingly evident in the thirties is usually ascribed to pacifism, in the broadest sense of the term. Consequently a debit is attached to Labour's account, for fostering that pacifism. Yet pacifist sentiments were never dominant in the government, whether briefly under Labour, or for a far longer period under Conservative or National, direction. Thus pacifism is no complete explanation: pacifism ' ... could never have decided Britain's course if the party which was in control of the government most of the time and which was least affected by pacifist ideas had not, for very different reasons, favored the very same policy [disarmament] with almost equal fervor'.[41] Persistent advocacy of disarmament rather than pacifism is at the root of Britain's military decline between the wars; from 1924 to 1929 that cause was furthered at the Treasury, which presided over all military expenditures ultimately, by a no less redoubtable figure than Winston Churchill. Thus allegiance to the League of Nations and support for the goal of disarmament – agreed to in theory by all signatories to the Treaty of Versailles – cast their nets widely in post-war Britain: it is no exaggeration to contend that in these matters official Labour stood closer to its political rivals than it did to dissenters within the party on the related question of the type of disarmament to be pursued. British political parties generally agreed in placing hopes for disarmament above the means of implementing collective security, in sharp contrast to the French approach.

The roots of the international policy subscribed to by the Labour Party in the 1930s were thus firmly planted in the soil of the post-war decade. Ideals then associated almost exclusively with Labour were in the previous decade shared by the other political parties. Labour's international policy, evolved in the years following the World War and based upon the League of Nations and disarmament, was very much in the mainstream of British attitudes; revision of the Treaty and pacifism were, to be sure, branches which found easier passage in Labour soil, but even they were clearly tributaries of the mainstream, whose principal source was the war. In short, though Labour's policy was socialist-influenced, so too was it distinctively British.

With this legacy in mind, we may now turn our attention to those fateful days of August 1931 when Labour's international policy was condemned to an opposition role for the long and agonizing years which witnessed the decay and overthrow of the European order established at Versailles.

2 Politics and policies of the Opposition

I

The sudden collapse of MacDonald's second Labour government, on 24 August 1931, initiated a chain of events whose consequences were felt long after the immediate crisis had eased. In its traumatizing impact upon the Labour Party, as well as in its effect upon the British political scene, this crisis – and its unprecedented resolution – is quite without peer. The politics and policies of the party, doomed to a long period of ineffective opposition, were shaped by this event in manifold and subtle ways. To be sure, the parliamentary remnants of the Labour Party inherited an international policy evolved at an earlier time. In a time of intense domestic crisis, however, little attention was given to international developments or to the viability of the premises upon which Labour's policy had been based. The result was that hardened attitudes were applied to changing conditions, with devastating results. The crisis of 1931 thus had a lasting, albeit indirect, effect upon international affairs, which by the end of the decade overshadowed its domestic consequences.

Though the ultimate fall of MacDonald's government was not unexpected, his subsequent formation of a National Government, in concert with Conservative and Liberal leaders, was a political surprise of the first order.[1] Only after the event did party loyalists begin to discover, in past events, portents of what they regarded as the 'betrayal' of 1931. As a result, many in the party reacted against the 'gradualist' or reformist doctrines practised by the late government.

That government had clearly been hampered by their minority nature: only at Liberal urging had they agreed in early 1931 to the appointment of a special committee to review government expenditures and to recommend economies, in view of the world

16

financial crisis. Projecting a large budget deficit, the Committee on National Expenditure, presided over by Sir George May, advised (with its two Labour Party members dissenting) new taxation of £24 millions and economies of £96 millions, the major portion in unemployment compensation. With the super-imposition of such harsh measures[2] upon a country already burdened with unemployment (which the Labour government had failed conspicuously to alleviate) the financial crisis assumed major proportions.

After a sudden return from holiday on 11 August, MacDonald consulted prominent bankers and financial authorities, who entirely agreed with the spokesmen of the Bank of England regarding the nature of the problems facing the country. Neville Chamberlain summarized their interpretation of the situation:

(1) that we were on the edge of the precipice, and, unless the situation changed radically, we should be over it directly, (2) that the cause of the trouble was not financial but political, and lay in the complete want of confidence in H.M.G. [government] existing among foreigners . . .[3]

A Cabinet Committee implicitly accepted this view by agreeing to secure a reduction in expenditure of £100 millions, thus balancing the budget.

Powerful trade union elements within the party, however, regarded the crisis as financial rather than political in nature: it had been precipitated not by a lack of foreign confidence in the government but by a collapse of the currency system based on the gold standard, a breakdown with which unemployment benefits had nothing to do. Their leadership rejected from the first the Bank's interpretation and the advice which they had given the government.[4] The General Council of the Trades Union Congress told the Prime Minister that the proposed economies were unacceptable: they 'must oppose the whole thing'.[5]

On the following day, the Conservative and Liberal parliamentary leaderships, with whom MacDonald had been in contact, rejected the proposed economies as insufficient. The Labour government were caught between two grinding millstones. As the Cabinet was itself split nearly evenly on the question of further economies, its collective resignation followed in short order.

Even among those Cabinet members who had supported

17

MacDonald's economy proposals,[6] few followed the course he set once his aims had been frustrated in Cabinet, namely the formation of a 'Government of Co-operation'. That government, which MacDonald formed in conjunction with Conservative and some Liberal leaders on 24 August, disclaimed the status of coalition government in the 'usual sense of the term'; rather they had only one purpose in mind – to deal with the existing national emergency.[7]

MacDonald's former colleagues could not but wonder at the swiftness with which he had acted. Yet initially they concentrated not upon the possibility of pre-arrangement or betrayal; instead they denounced the National Government as ' . . . one of persons acting without authority from the people . . . [seeking] to enforce a complete change in national policy . . . primarily because financial interests have decided that this country is setting a bad example to other countries in taxing the rich to provide for the necessities of the poor'.[8] The three executives of the movement – the General Council of the TUC, along with the executives of the Parliamentary Labour Party and the parent party – demanded instead sacrifices so far unasked of the wealthier sections of the nation.

Thus at first the numbed party displayed no personal rancour against its late leader or those few who had followed him; in part this reflected a natural hesitancy on the part of those former Cabinet ministers who had supported MacDonald's financial proposals to criticize too recklessly those who were now effecting such measures. As late as 8 September, Arthur Henderson mourned the loss to the Labour Party of its leaders, whether their 'withdrawal' be long or short.[9] MacDonald's own remarks to the Commons at this time were less gracious; they served to strengthen a particular interpretation of his recent actions.

When MacDonald calmly told men with whom he had worked in many cases for a quarter of a century . . . that he now proposed to head a Government composed of their bitter and lifelong political opponents, there was, inevitably, a stunned sense of having somehow been tricked; this was what he had, throughout, been leading up to. Unjust this view may have been. But at the time, to minds naturally simple and straight-forward, it leapt as the one possible explanation of conduct they could not otherwise explain.[10]

Convictions of 'betrayal' were reinforced early in October when

18

the government decided to appeal to the country for an electoral mandate, ironically because of their failure to maintain the gold standard, which had been one of the few items on their co-operative agenda.[11] Thus came to pass an election for which the Prime Minister had not seen any justification only a fortnight earlier.

When the dissolution of Parliament which preceded that election was announced, the Labour Party was meeting in Conference, at Scarborough. Its attitude continued to be less than harsh: indeed the chairman of that gathering asked it to refrain from recrimination against its departed leaders.[12] Little criticism of the performance of the late Labour government was voiced. Stafford Cripps came as close as anyone to criticizing the government of which he had been a member: 'It is not now a question of the inevitability of gradualness. The one thing which is not inevitable now is gradualness.'[13]

Though *ad hominem* arguments had not yet been raised, the campaign soon evolved into one of the most savagely contested elections of the century. In the absence of the discussion of issues – MacDonald appealed for a 'doctor's mandate' to treat problems and advance remedies as changing circumstances rather than party policies dictated – the election of 1931 became ' . . . as much a verdict on the formation of the National Government as on whether or not it should continue to function'.[14] Once the former issue was raised, the campaign centred increasingly on the conflict between the ex-Labour leaders and the party. The resentment of one of MacDonald's supporters had been building since the late days of August: Philip Snowden, continuing to serve as Chancellor of the Exchequer, took umbrage with the joint manifesto issued at that time by the Labour executives. He regarded that document as ' . . . a shameful travesty of the facts which had led to the resignation of the Labour Government, and a gross misrepresentation of the purpose for which the National Government had been formed'.[15] When subsequently recriminations concerning the discussions of the late Cabinet were bandied about in the House of Commons, Snowden claimed to detect an increasing rancour in the conduct of a section of the Labour MPs.

Aggrieved though he may have been, Snowden himself supplied the major infusion of excessive partisanship into the campaign.

19

Surely his former colleagues could hardly believe Snowden's electoral broadcast of 17 October:

> The one thing on which you [the nation] should vote is . . . whether we should have a strong and stable government in this time of national crisis, or whether we shall hand over the destinies of the nation to men whose conduct in a grave emergency has shown them unfitted to be trusted with responsibility.[16]

Further, the Labour Party's 'most fantastic and impractical' programme was not socialist, but 'Bolshevism run mad'. MacDonald too criticized the party which had 'run away'. Thus were men who had stood for principles as they had conceived them stigmatized by their former colleagues.

The party was, however, in no position to return this barrage of invective: too many of its remaining leaders had implicated themselves in MacDonald's budgetary proposals for their efforts at dissociation to carry much weight.[17] Their arguments, centring about financial dictation to the late government, were hesitant and defensive. That their government had been sacrificed to the clamour of bankers and financiers seemed highly unlikely, given the presence of MacDonald and Snowden, historically men of principle, in the National Government. Entirely lost to them was the opposition's major advantage at election time, the opportunity to attack the record of an established government: the Labour Party had no choice but to praise the record of the late MacDonald administration. Arthur Henderson expressed the hope (possibly because little else was left to the party) that if Labour stood 'four square' for the high ideals of its socialism ' . . . some people will get a surprise at the next General Election that they never expected'.[18] With its former leaders in the enemies' camp, Labour could not give the appearance of standing four square for anything: the surprise came, not to the National Government, but to Henderson and his followers.

All political parties alike were shocked by the dimensions of Labour's electoral defeat. Only fifty-two Labour candidates survived the rout to return to Westminster, to constitute an opposition less than one-third the size of any such group since 1832.[19] So great was the deluge that the National Government, established with a majority of 497, returned more candidates unopposed

than the Labour Party was able to elect.[20] The Labour Front
Bench was decimated: among ex-Cabinet ministers only George
Lansbury survived, along with the more junior ministers, Clement
Attlee and Sir Stafford Cripps. Quality as well as volume of
opposition was impaired: thirty-four of the Labour MPs were
trade unionists (twenty-three of these tied to the Miners'
Federation), and their concerns were in the main industrial. Such
was the price exacted from the Labour Party for awarding its
safest seats to superannuated trade union officials.

In retrospect it is clear that the rout shattered the parliamentary
shield against the shortcomings of the men in office. The size of
the minority tempted the government to a neglect of criticism:
the gap across the floor of the House of Commons widened, and
the possibility of compromise (a main purpose of the parliamentary system) diminished.[21] The weakness of the opposition
also freed the government from the need to choose its best men
for office; loyal and uncritical supporters instead sat on the
Government benches.[22] A weak opposition serves no one well,
least of all the nation.

Such were the important consequences for governmental pro-
cesses of Labour's defeat; the rout shook the Labour Party deeply
as well, as its leaders realized. Herbert Morrison later wrote:

The spiritual and psychological effects upon the Labour Movement of
what became known as 'the Great Betrayal' were, I am inclined to think,
as serious as the thing in itself and its immediate electoral consequences.
It left in the Party a spirit of distrust of the idea of leadership, a determination that for the time being there should be no more great men, and
seeking to tie the leadership with conditions and checks of one sort and
another. This spirit of distrust and apprehension of other betrayals
went on for round about ten years.[23]

Clement Attlee, for years handicapped by that attitude, revealed yet another legacy of 1931. Six years later, he attacked
MacDonald's political philosophy, namely that as good men
could work together for a common end there was no need for
political parties: 'MacDonaldism is, in fact, in its philosophy
essentially Fascist. MacDonald himself uses the same phrases
that may be found in the mouths of Hitler and Mussolini.'[24] The
association of the National Government with fascism's cause
illustrated in this intemperate remark characterized the Labour

Party's bitter attitude towards its political foes, stemming from the events of 1931. Internally and in its relations with those political parties which comprised the National Government, the Labour Party needed the better part of a decade to recover.

An unprecedented course of events had encompassed the collapse of a government and the creation, amid the rubble, of an embittered and distrustful opposition. For a time the Labour Party was reduced to ineffectual opposition, to a degree which weakened the normal underpinnings of parliamentary government. The party had meanwhile to set its own house in order, before it could presume to speak with one voice in the councils of the nation. In an atmosphere of general distrust of leadership, the Labour Party had to deal with the threat of secession from its left.

2

From the time of the formation of the Labour Representation Committee in 1900 down to the present time, the Labour left has assumed a variety of political forms; no group on the left, however, has matched the size or the influence of the Independent Labour Party, which from 1900 to 1932 served as the main political expression of the Labour left.[25] In its liaison with the radical ex-Liberals accomplished after the World War, the dissent of the ILP was directed to foreign as well as domestic policy. Such dissent is evident within the four major areas of concern derived from the war experience, but the voices of criticism were scattered: no challenge to Labour's international policy was issued.

Indeed domestic affairs provided the decisive turning point in the fortunes of the ILP, in the years after 1926: the Labour Party swung to the right as a result of the 'lesson' of the failure of the General Strike, but the ILP read the signs in an opposite sense and moved instead to the left.[26] Consequently its relations with the Labour government of 1929–31 were strained; the measure of its loss of influence is the decline of its 'Parliamentary Group' from 142 in 1929 to eighteen two years later. These were annihilated with the Labour Party in the General Election; only five ILP candidates, the rump of the once-powerful Clydeside brigade, were returned.

Yet the rout did not serve to reconcile the two; the ILP remnant maintained that the Labour Party was still being led '. . . by men who had as great a responsibility for the [August] disaster as had the renegades'.[27] The ILP viewed the National government both as a confirmation of their forecasts and as an open declaration of a new phase in the continuing class struggle, which demanded on Labour's part the acceptance of revolutionary approaches.[28] To these voices now swelling in chorus, gradualism and reformism were anathema, though the ILP wished to remain within the fold of a Labour Party which had not repudiated either approach.

For its part, the party leadership was displeased with the antics of the ILP, which they held had hampered the work of the recent Labour government. The Scarborough Conference stipulated that all Labour parliamentary candidates agree to accept and act in harmony with the Standing Orders of the Parliamentary Labour Party. The five successful ILP members had refused, and so they had been denied Labour's endorsement. They held that much more than Standing Orders – namely, the very survival of socialism – was at stake. The ILP, meeting in conference, hoped that continued affiliation with the parent body could be salvaged, but as neither disputant was prepared to yield in the matter of the Standing Orders, a special conference of the ILP decided in July 1932 to disaffiliate.

Severed from the mass backing of the working classes, ILP fortunes quickly and irreversibly declined: whatever hopes its leaders may have held to build a viable political entity resolute upon a socialist policy were soon dashed.[29] The Labour Party, for better or worse, was rid of an organized body of leftist dissent which had long been critical of the ideas and methods of the party leadership.

Just at this time, however, there arose a grouping of malcontents within the party determined upon socialist reform from within, by methods short of an outright break with the party leadership. These forces were bolstered by a sizeable minority of ILP members who had voted against disaffiliation and who subsequently declined to accompany their leaders into the political wilderness in search of socialism.[30] Instead they chose to regroup the forces of the left within the Labour Party.

This informal grouping took concrete form in the Socialist

League, founded in 1932 immediately prior to the annual party Conference, meeting at Leicester. The League traced its lineage to a body which had been formed within the party even before the fall of the Labour government, to serve as a propagandist organ for the adoption of a 'well-considered socialist policy'.[31] That Society for Socialist Inquiry and Propaganda (SSIP) had undertaken to disseminate the results of research into the development of a socialist policy, sponsored by the New Fabian Research Bureau (NFRB). SSIP won a wide measure of support from those who were disillusioned both with the general intellectual inertia of the Labour Cabinet and the all but moribund Fabian Society. These professed 'loyal grousers' were for eighteen months buoyed by the range of SSIP activities.[32] Substantial gains had been made under the capable leadership of Ernest Bevin, a powerful trade union official, and G.D.H. Cole, an academic and able propagandist.

In 1932 the ILP secession presented a major problem: those who remained behind in the Labour Party now called upon the SSIP and the NFRB, who had so far resisted amalgamation, to join with them to form a new socialist society, affiliated with the Labour Party, to replace the ILP. SSIP had to choose either to come to terms with this new left grouping or to compete with them in a field where there was not room for both to work effectively.[33] Conversations nearly collapsed when the ex-ILP group refused to accept Bevin as the chairman of the combined group; they insisted upon Frank Wise, who had led their revolt. Cole regarded this as an unfortunate condition, for Bevin was capable of rallying support for a socialist policy among the trade unionists. Nonetheless Cole accepted the majority decision, though he soon came to regret it: within a year he judged that the Socialist League was courting the same fate that had overtaken the ILP, by putting forth its own programme in opposition to that of the Labour Party.

Harmful though Cole's resignation from its executive may have been to the League's cause, the earlier alienation of Ernest Bevin was a far graver error. Bevin's attempt to work closely with Cole to bridge the gap between trade unionists and intellectuals had ended in his loss of the chairmanship: the incident served to deepen his distrust of the left-leaning intellectuals.[34] Embittered as well as frustrated in this effort, Bevin had meanwhile succeeded in his reorganization of a body in which the trade unions were able to influence the party's foreign policy. To this National Joint Council, later known as the National Council of Labour, the Labour Party Executive and the PLP Executive each delegated its chairman and two members to meet with the chairman and six members of the TUC General Council. Though advisory in nature, the Council became an authoritative body. Bevin regarded it as the main forum in which the trade unions could regularly develop views on foreign policy for the benefit of the political wing. Its monthly meetings on the fourth Tuesday were timed to exert maximum pressure on the deliberations of the Labour Party Executive, which met on the fourth Wednesday.[35]

Initially the Socialist League concerned itself primarily with domestic policy. Its first General Secretary, J. T. Murphy, viewed the Labour Party as ' . . . never a homogeneous party fighting for power, but a combination of trade union organizations fighting a defensive struggle against any encroachments on their interests and aiming at immediate social reforms, although it gave itself the distant aim of Socialism'.[36] Thus the gap between trade unionists and intellectuals which the SSIP had been designed to bridge was likely to be widened by the Socialist League doctrinaires. Nor could this intraparty struggle between the forces of social reform and socialism be confined to the domestic sphere: such strife will necessarily affect considerations of foreign policy.[37] For the moment the League's criticisms were, however, directed toward the 'gradualist' leadership of the Labour Party and the reactionary policies of the National Government.

Even setting aside the potential threat posed on its left, the Labour Party was far from unified in 1932. Amid the shock and confusion resulting from the 'betrayal' of 1931 and the electoral rout, the Labour leadership was hardly pulling together, as Hugh Dalton recognized at the time. On the eve of the 1932 Conference he recorded in his diary:

The whole problem of personal relationships is increasingly difficult. The Parliamentary Party is a poor little affair, isolated from the National Executive, whose only MP is George Lansbury. Attlee . . . and Cripps, who are in close touch with Cole, sit in Lansbury's room at the House all day and all night, and continually influence the old man. With none of these are Henderson's relations close or cordial. Cripps has many good points, including political courage and some personal charm, but he breaks down unexpectedly. Though a first-class lawyer, he doesn't . . . 'know a good point from a bad one' . . . Morrison is important on the National Executive, intellectually able but aggressive and a pedantic stickler for procedural precision and Party discipline. He is often against Henderson on particular points. Greenwood got the first by-election at Wakefield, but, having returned to the House, is rather out of tune with Lansbury, Attlee and Cripps . . . Alexander has retired into his Co-operative shell . . . and Trevelyan [seems] to have given [politics] up altogether, fascinated by the administration of his Northumbrian estate . . . And where are the coming Trade Union leaders on the political side? We are in a vacuum![38]

The rush to fill that vacuum was the keynote of the 1932 Conference, which met in early October; that gathering provided trying days for the Labour leadership. Time and again Conference rode roughshod over such executive-sponsored domestic proposals as those dealing with currency and banking, and transport and electricity: in both cases the delegates demanded more resolutely socialist programmes from their leadership. Illustrative of the anti-gradualist mood was Conference's approval, despite the objections of the party's leader, Henderson, of a resolution demanding that any future Labour government immediately apply socialist principles to legislation. Sir Charles Trevelyan had at least temporarily abandoned his Northumbrian estate to demand ' . . . that the Party shall stand or fall in the House of Commons on the principles in which it has faith'.[39] Probably with the second Labour government in mind, Trevelyan added, ' . . . we must have Socialism in deed as well as in words'.

Henderson objected to tying the hands of the party in this manner, but the delegates were hardly prepared even to hear him out, interrupting him on several occasions. Dalton recorded Henderson's immediate response to this reception: 'He was so disgruntled at the general atmosphere of the Conference that he told me on the last morning that he had decided to resign the Leadership . . . I thought that this was right, for he was carrying much too heavy and varied a responsibility.'[40] Subsequently George Lansbury, the sole Cabinet minister to survive the rout of 1931 but an avowed pacifist, was elected leader by the PLP, precisely at a time when the anti-gradualist tide had eroded the authority of the party's National Executive.

The forces of the left exulted in what one of them described as the Conference's 'warm red tone'.[41] *The Times* sombrely detected the same tinge but warned that Conference had got out of hand, with possibly disastrous consequences: 'Gradualism is dead ... The next Labour Government will be all red, and pledged to ride for an ignominious fall if it takes office a day before the country is as Socialist as the Labour Party Conference.'[42] The policy decisions favoured the left, but few noted that the annual elections to the executive made at Conference failed to reflect this trend. The moderates Dalton and Herbert Morrison were returned easily by the Constituency Party Section,[43] while the chairman of the Socialist League, Frank Wise, and a member of its executive, Clement Attlee, trailed far behind. The party's executive, with its predominant trade union composition, remained reformist; the Leicester Conference had however increased the executive's awareness of the rank and file's desire for a bolder domestic course.

Against this backdrop of crisis passing into a leftward reaction, of a divided party shedding one rebellious minority only to see another develop, of a mass membership distrustful of a leadership divided and unsure of itself – in short, of a party seeking an identity – Labour's efforts to cope with a deteriorating international situation can be depicted.

3

The Sino-Japanese dispute which erupted in 1931 was the first international crisis to reveal differences between the National Government and the Labour opposition in matters of foreign policy. Retrospectively, Labour spokesmen correlated the turn for the worse in the international situation with the demise of the Labour government. In 1935 Attlee reminded the House of Commons that his party had urged the imposition of economic sanctions against the Japanese aggressors, quite in vain; instead they were told that they were clamouring for war.[44] Much later Hugh Dalton argued that the Far Eastern crisis had presented a favourable opportunity to fulfil the Covenant of the League of Nations. Sir John Simon, the Foreign Secretary, and the National

27

Government had, however, shied from the slight risk of war: 'From this turning point the League now went rapidly downhill.'[45] That no Labour régime would have traversed that path is the clear implication.

Not all historians have deferred to the Labour interpretation of its actions in the Sino-Japanese dispute: the claim has been advanced that the party's spokesmen fell victim to their own propaganda. The Labour Party, we are told, '. . . never presented anything like a clear demand that this country should apply, or should propose to the League of Nations the application of economic sanctions against Japan'.[46] What then was the nature of Labour's response to this initial assault upon the Covenant of the League of Nations?

Provocation in the Far East lay not exclusively with one side – the Japanese had suffered numerous acts of harassment. Thus the contemporary could not know that the Japanese premise for the seizure of the Chinese town of Mukden in September 1931 was 'a complete fabrication . . . of certain members of the [Japanese] army'.[47] He could, however, quickly sense that the alleged sabotage of some thirty-one inches of the Japanese-controlled railway, which precipitated the Far Eastern crisis, was hardly sufficient excuse for the Japanese seizure of a large, rich Chinese province, accomplished by the military in several months' time, in a systematic fashion which belied the spontaneity of their 'response' to Chinese provocation. By February 1932 the Japanese authorities had established the puppet régime of Manchukuo; meanwhile her armed forces had resorted to naked aggression in bombarding the Chinese district of Chapei, an action which impinged upon the various international settlements in Shanghai.[48] Well before this act, the British Ambassador to China had warned his government of the dangers:

> Seen from this end the whole structure of our post-war peace organisation seems at stake . . . If the League machinery and the Kellogg Pact now fail, I submit that they and all their sponsors will suffer a set-back, extent of which it is hard to estimate. I am most anxious not to exaggerate but Japan's action has set currents stirring of more far-reaching import than she or any of us can have anticipated.[49]

In December 1931 the League of Nations, which had earlier

played a successful part in the settlement of international disputes, dispatched a commission of inquiry presided over by Lord Lytton.

While that commission worked on the scene, the British government made no effort to concert international pressures: on the contrary, Simon in effect negated the doctrine of non-recognition proposed by Stimson, the American Secretary of State.[50] Simon and the British government shied from any course which would involve the use of sanctions: 'I am strongly opposed to any treatment of the [Manchurian] question which will bring up the question of sanctions,' the Foreign Secretary noted on 14 November. 'We ought to co-operate in any course that will preserve the moral authority of the League and a futile reference to Art. 16 [sanctions] would surely have the opposite effect.'[51] One would think that in the absence of sanctions, the British government would be all the more concerned to secure a measure of co-operation with the United States as a passive restraint upon the Japanese; in fact, however, they rebuffed the American lead and undercut (contrary to the advice of their Ambassador) the post-war peace organization.

In this initial period, the Labour Party's policy towards China was not significantly different from Simon's, though they of course were not privy to his sources of information. All shared acceptance of certain principles of that policy, enunciated in a Foreign Office memorandum prepared two years before, under the Labour government:

Our first concern is to maintain our position in the trade of China, which is largely bound up with the prosperity of Hong Kong and the fortunes of the Maritime Customs Administration, and to secure adequate protection for British lives, property and business enterprises. Our second concern is to maintain the principle of the 'open door' and equal opportunity for all and to see that China does not fall under the tutelage of any single Power.[52]

Since these aims were not immediately threatened by the Mukden incident, the lack of reaction on the part of government and opposition alike is explicable. When in the following weeks the nature of the Japanese aggression became clearer, British attentions were directed to the electoral campaign.

The Labour leadership did not take up the Sino-Japanese

dispute until 25 November, two weeks after Parliament had convened. On that occasion George Lansbury spoke in an ambivalent manner. Prophetically he foresaw that ' . . . the League, in its handling of this very big Manchurian question, will either prove itself of value in preventing war, or will have to confess its inability to restrain a powerful Power when that Power makes up its mind to go its own way'; he drew the logical conclusion that if the League were to accomplish the former, it would have to uphold its principles against ' . . . all the opposition which Japan can put against it'.[53] Despite this recognition, Lansbury specifically disclaimed any argument that the moment had come for the application of League sanctions; at this point Labour's leader did not envisage settlement of the dispute by means other than peaceful.

In replying for the government, Simon commented that they did not wish to judge the dispute before the League itself had acted. While the Lytton commission investigated and the British government waited upon the results (though the threat to the international settlements in Shanghai provoked considerably more interest in the matter[54]) the Labour Party protested against the Japanese aggression in a manifesto issued by the National Joint Council on 23 February:

> Political disorder in China is no justification for the invasion of its territory by any Foreign Power . . . Japan has chosen the policy of force . . . If the nations of the world take no action to uphold the Covenant of the League of Nations they will thereby destroy the collective system of world law; they will be unable to appeal for its aid in one part of the world if they allow it to be defiled in another . . . Other wars will then become inevitable.[55]

Consequently, the council urged the government to call upon members of the League and signatories of the Kellogg-Briand Pact to withdraw their ambassadors from Tokyo; were Japan to continue the war, Labour would consider the British government obligated ' . . . to propose to the Special Assembly of the League whatever co-operative and graduated measures of financial and economic constraint may be necessary – in association and agreement with the United States and the Members of the League – to restore peace . . .'[56]

In spite of this strongly worded warning on the part of the

council, the Labour Party both in and out of Parliament took no further action. Labour apparently chose to await the issuance of the Lytton report, in the hope that it would provide an indisputable basis for League action. Six months passed with the Labour Party quiescent; the Leicester Conference, held only a few days after the publication of the Lytton report, almost totally neglected the Far Eastern crisis.[57]

That report, published on 2 October, criticized Japan's recent actions, although its authors deprecated any attempt to restore the tenuous *status quo ante*; rather they hoped that while Japanese rights and interests would be recognized, Manchuria should secure a large measure of autonomy under Chinese sovereignty. The League of Nations attempted conciliation along these lines; the Japanese army replied with an offensive on New Year's Day 1933. Subsequently a League report recommended the withdrawal of Japanese troops from areas of conquest, but the only withdrawal Japan effected was from the League; meanwhile her army advanced and by the middle of March controlled all passes in the Great Wall. With Peiping now threatened, the Chinese treated for an armistice, signed at Tangku on 3 May, which provided for the demilitarization of an area of five thousand square miles on the Chinese side of the wall. There followed no serious fighting until 1935.

Shortly after the publication of the Lytton report, the Parliamentary leadership followed the lead given sometime earlier by the Joint Council. In a major debate on the international situation, on 10 November 1932, Attlee warned the government: 'I believe that the Manchurian question is a vital one, and that unless it is settled satisfactorily through the League of Nations, we shall find that the League will lose its moral authority . . .'[58] With so much at stake, Simon's inaction was lamentable; in a criticism of the Foreign Secretary's legalistic delay which one might apply to Labour's own conduct in previous months, Attlee continued: 'While my house was being overrun and my family were being ill-treated, an inquiry about title deeds should have been rather cold comfort to me.' Simon, however, persisted in his set course; shortly thereafter, in a reply to the Japanese refusal to accept the findings of the Lytton report, he supposedly won the approbation of the Japanese minister for saying in a half-hour what the minister had been arguing for two days.[59] Whether or not the story is apocryphal, one can argue that ' . . . in light of the actual findings of the Lytton Commission, Sir John's speech was definitely pro-Japanese'.[60]

The Labour Party adopted a markedly different policy by endorsing the attempt of the League of Nations to settle the dispute. A joint meeting of the TUC General Council and the Labour Party Executive on 22 February 1933 adopted a resolution asking for the application of an economic boycott under Article 16, if Japan rejected League proposals; it also proposed an embargo upon the shipment of arms to either disputant.[61] Though Labour, in endorsing sanctions, had now moved considerably beyond Lansbury's position of November 1931, the party had not yet apparently considered military sanctions. Lansbury may well have had in mind that ultimate sanction when he commented in the Commons on 27 February 1933 that ' . . . all the sanctions, all the obligations of the Covenant ought, in our judgment, to be carried through'.[62] Yet his speech was sufficiently ambivalent as to weaken the effect of this demand for sanctions; the reason may well have been that his own pacifist beliefs were already at variance with the party's.[63] The Foreign Secretary, on the other hand, was anything but ambivalent: ' . . . in no circumstances will this Government authorise this country to be a party to the struggle'.[64] In the face of Japanese aggression, sanctions were ruled out.

Though government and opposition policies had diverged, the latter's criticism was spasmodic: in April Attlee merely reiterated the demand for an arms embargo; in July Arthur Henderson wrote that Labour demanded ' . . . with all the emphasis at its command that the Covenant should be upheld against the aggression of Japan'.[65] In December Attlee inquired whether the government were acquiescing to a *fait accompli* in Manchuria; a Conservative MP thought it worth while to remind those members who ' . . . advocate automatic sanctions for the preservation of what they call the collective peace system' that such sanctions became more dangerous as Britain's armed forces were reduced.[66]

The inference that Labour MPs had earlier desired sanctions is an important one. Labour might well have been more persistent and outspoken in advocating sanctions, but this is not to say that their opposition to government policies was of the token sort, a part of the normal course of parliamentary affairs.[67]

The Labour Party had only slowly come to advocate sanctions: they had waited upon the Lytton report nearly as patiently as the British government, but once the League took the initiative against Japan, Labour supported the imposition of economic sanctions consistently, if infrequently. Government supporters testified to the belief that Labour would have imposed sanctions in 1933: when two years later a Labour MP stated this in the Commons, no one disputed the assertion; rather the government benches laughed at his assertion that war might not have ensued.[68] Sir John Simon himself retrospectively wrote of the League of Nations using every step short of coercion to settle the dispute, while 'the Labour Opposition of the day clamoured for more', a course which he resisted.[69] Labour spokesmen did not then fall victim to their own propaganda: they had no need to.

It is quite true that Labour had nothing to say about military sanctions, but neither did the party declare with Simon in February 1933 that Britain would not be a party to the dispute. No one can say with certainty where Labour's slowly developing Far Eastern policy might have led, but it is unlikely that Labour policy would have encouraged the Japanese militarists, as Simon's failure to remonstrate probably did. It is certain that, following the publication of the Lytton report, the Labour Party enunciated a policy for the Far Eastern dispute distinctive from, and critical of, the course followed by the British government.

4

The course of the Far Eastern crisis had a pronounced effect upon Labour's attitude towards disarmament. The party saw that the Sino-Japanese conflict undercut the prospects for general security, which could only be brought about by general disarmament. A joint statement of the General Council of the TUC and the National Executive specified this interdependence: 'It will be impossible to give the nation a feeling of security, which is a condition for International Disarmament, unless determined steps are taken against the war-like policy of Japan.'[70] While this

B*

statement was a curious endorsement of the decade-old French position,[71] it sprang from a pragmatic concern for the effect upon disarmament of successful Japanese aggression, reiterated by Attlee in November 1932:

... we link disarmament and the Manchurian question together, for the reason that security and disarmament must go together ... You cannot expect States to rest on the security of the League, if in a leading case they find that a Member-State has been denied security.[72]

Eighteen months later, when the prospects for disarmament were rather dimmer, Stafford Cripps was not hard pressed to explain why: 'With this example of the callous desertion of China as an object lesson of what may happen to any other country which is protected by covenants and treaties it is not surprising to find that people are very insistent upon something more than nominal security.'[73] Thus Labour argued, throughout nearly the entire Disarmament Conference, that the government's mishandling of the Sino-Japanese dispute undercut any hope of agreement at Geneva.

Though one can say with certainty that the Disarmament Conference was ineffectual, one cannot hold that its participants were ill-prepared. The items on the agenda were familiar. At Versailles, the victorious powers had assumed certain responsibilities for disarmament in the treaty proper; upon these the Germans based their case for equality of status in armaments. Moreover, these responsibilities, regarded as binding by a leading authority,[74] had been confirmed as late as 1930, in the draft convention drawn up for the conference's discussion. In a sense then, twelve years of preparation preceded the gathering; yet conditions had only lately altered radically: the general European economic and financial crisis had so occupied statesmen that they had given only scant attention to disarmament in recent months.[75] Yet Europe had survived the worst of these crises by February 1932, and disarmament did not seem to be a lost cause, if only the Franco-German problem could be solved.

Twice victim of German aggression, France had at last gained security in the relative disarmament of Weimar Germany. She was unwilling to abandon her own preponderance of military power; the confidence in German intentions which alone could justify some measure of disarmament was still lacking.[76] Germany, however, felt that her claim to equality of status was long past redemption on the part of the Allies; this her government regarded as the roadblock to general disarmament.[77] The British government had, in the past, quarrelled with the French position; in 1932 however the National Government conceived its role to be that of mediator between the divergent points of view.[78] Though conscious of basic disagreements, Arthur Henderson, who in May 1931 had been invited by the League of Nations Council to become conference chairman, assumed the chair with great hopes, refusing even to contemplate the possibility of failure.[79] Yet even Henderson must have been discouraged by the setting of the first session, on 2 February 1932, because its opening had been delayed an hour while the League Council met to discuss the Sino-Japanese dispute, then at the point of maximum eruption: the conference convened as the Japanese fleet bombarded Shanghai, in ' . . . the fiercest artillery operation which had been conducted at any time since the Armistice of November 1918'.[80] Sir Samuel Hoare, who attended that session for the National Government, showed little enthusiasm for the cause of disarmament, though he thought it possible that ' . . . this curious body, half Congress, half mass meeting, might rumble into some important action. In any case, if we cannot get on with it, we cannot get on without it.'[81] At least one independent Conservative doubted the British government's depth of conviction for disarmament: Viscount Cecil declined to sit in the British delegation because he did not feel that the government would play a resolute part in working for limitation of armaments.[82]

The conference quickly settled down to a few unhappy months. No participants save the German representatives proposed limitations upon the armaments of any country except Germany; and the German delegates closed the circle of futility by rejecting such discriminatory treatment. Frustrated at this upper level, the conference instead set up committee after committee, which proceeded to choke themselves with minutely detailed discussions of the size of airplanes or the tonnage of ships. Meanwhile Franco-German relations worsened, and the conference seemed headed for breakdown. Official Labour reacted with contempt to one of the British government's few proposals during this period, that of 'qualitative disarmament', i.e. the classification of weapons as

35

offensive or defensive and the prohibition of the former. The editors of *Labour Magazine* passed a sad commentary upon the initial proceedings: 'When are weapons of war mainly defensive in character? This insoluble crossword puzzle . . . befuddled the experts of three commissions at Geneva . . . The experts [military officers] only kept their sanity by holding grimly to the goal of no disarmament, qualitative or quantitative.[83]

In June 1932 President Hoover proposed a new plan for disarmament, but in British eyes this raised as many questions as it proposed to settle.[84] There remained at the heart of the problem of disarmament the attitude pithily described by the French statesman Herriot in terms of the grammatical irregularity of the verb 'to disarm': 'It is conjugated only in the future tense, and it has only the form of the second person.'[85] As the conference seemed unable to supply either the present tense or the first person, the German delegation grew more outspoken in asserting their claim to equality of status with other nations in disarmament; at the same time they were prepared to make concessions on specific matters, in return for the grant of equality of status in principle.[86] On the eve of the adjournment of the conference in July Nadolny warned that failure loomed unless that principle were admitted.[87]

In this central issue, German equality of status, the Labour Party's position was consistent and unequivocal. Criticism of the Allied treatment of Germany had already won the party the label of 'pro-German', quite unjustly. In 1931 the TUC meeting had specifically declared for general equality of rights and duties, including equality of disarmament in all forms. Congress called for a twenty-five per cent reduction in arms expenditure as the minimum test of success for the forthcoming disarmament conference.[88] The subsequent Labour Party Conference, with its attention fixed on the domestic scene, held only a perfunctory debate on disarmament, but it agreed to an executive resolution stipulating 'drastic and far-reaching reductions, by international agreement, in the numbers and equipment of all armed forces and in military, naval and air expenditure'.[89] At the same time the Scarborough Conference rejected an ILP amendment calling for 'disarmament by example', i.e. unilateral disarmament.

When the Geneva talks began the next spring, the party followed their course closely, trusting in the ability of Arthur

Henderson to negotiate a solution. The implicit British rejection of the Hoover Plan disturbed the advocates of disarmament; one of the foremost has since commented:

It made nonsense of Simon's defence of Qualitative Disarmament ... In effect, the British Government were saying now that Qualitative Disarmament did not mean the abolition of any of the main weapons which had been forbidden to Germany by the Treaty of Versailles; except for poison gas and bacteria, it meant the retention of them all.[90]

Though Lansbury had on 8 March in the Commons commented that ' ... we are going to accept the statement that to the fullest extent the Government intended to pursue the policy of Disarmament with the rest of the nations of the world',[91] developments at Geneva impaired that confidence.

During the summer recess of the Disarmament Conference, the German government attempted to negotiate the claim to equality of status directly with France;[92] that discussion led nowhere, and consequently the German Foreign Minister informed Arthur Henderson on 14 September that his country refused to attend the reconvened conference.[93]

The British government deprecated this rupture: they attempted to bridge the Franco-German gap, by refusing on the one hand to accept the legal base of Germany's claim, namely the reference to general disarmament in the Treaty of Versailles, while on the other maintaining that there should be no distinction of status in multilateral disarmament.[94]

The Labour Party objected to the British attempt as a concession to the French position, which held that Part V of the Treaty (containing the military, naval, and air clauses directed against Germany) would cease to be binding only by agreement. The party spurned such a narrowly legalistic course; justice was to be sought within a broader international context. Thus the Leicester Conference, which met only two weeks after the German withdrawal, declared that ' ... the victors in the last war cannot evade their solemn responsibility and obligations towards the former Central Powers and the world. If Great Britain and France continue to reject any substantial measure of disarmament, their responsibility for a situation which may have the most

37

serious consequences will be grave.' The Conference recorded support for ' . . . immediate, universal, substantial and controlled disarmament, with equality of rights and duties for all States'.[95] An official spokesman, J. R. Clynes, captured Labour's attitude in ringing words: 'We have failed to keep faith with the world, and not merely faith with Germany in what we professed in the Peace Treaty. We imposed disarmament upon Germany, and we pledged ourselves in due course to follow the example. We have failed to do so . . .'

Though this attitude was endorsed unanimously by the delegates, the National Executive's Advisory Committee on International Questions[96] undertook the re-examination of Germany's claim to equality. Late in 1932 the ACIQ reported that the problem had grown more pressing with the advent to power in Germany of General von Schleicher's openly militarist government. Further delay in the recognition of the justness of the German claim would be a dangerous act: in the long run 'the deadliest weapon we could give the German militarists is a just grievance'.[97]

In the House of Commons, Lansbury argued that recent developments in Germany had reinforced the Labour position. Because Britain had not honoured the peace treaty, Germany had grown sick with hope deferred. ' . . . The German people had been forced to come right out into the open and say: "You are not carrying out your word. Your Disarmament Conference goes on month after month and nothing is done. Now we are going to take the matter into our own hands, and re-arm." '[98] Certain that the British government could not possibly favour such a step, Lansbury argued that they must then recognize the need for, and implement measures of, disarmament based upon equality of status for all powers.

At this time, Simon replied that the British government were prepared to supersede Part V of the Treaty of Versailles, in order that the limitations on German armaments ' . . . would be arrived at by the same process and expressed in the same document as those of other countries'.[99] The German government viewed this proposal with favour.[100] After joining in a five-power conference early in December 1932, the German government agreed to return to the Disarmament Conference.

In essence the compromise which had been reached

incorporated the slogans both of France and Germany, as both countries agreed to seek ' . . . equality of rights in a system which would provide security for all nations'.[101] The device was ingenious, but verbal facility did not touch the substance of the problem. As a further complication, by the time the Conference actually resumed on 2 February 1933, Adolf Hitler had become Chancellor of Germany. His accession to power, and his techniques used to ensure the perpetuation of his régime, were to link together questions of disarmament, collective security and Anglo-German relations in a novel and trying fashion. The Labour Party, faced with developments in Nazi Germany, was forced to re-examine its attitudes in these matters. That continuing re-evaluation of the content of a socialist foreign policy and the means of its implementation proved the dominant theme in the party's policy discussions throughout the thirties.

After Hitler's rise to power, the Disarmament Conference came to a melancholy end. Its demise can be briefly told. The British government decided a new approach was required. As Simon explained to the French government: 'Our idea was that questions dealt with by the Conference had been too much subdivided, and we thought it would be practicable and useful to present some more comprehensive proposal containing suggestions for all the matters which had previously been treated apart.'[102] The result was the MacDonald Plan of 16 March, which proposed definite, though provisional, figures for military manpower.[103] Material was to be considered qualitatively, with weight and calibre of certain weapons restricted. The German negotiator at Geneva recognized that 'the draft represents an attempt to find a middle way for the most important conflicts of interest that have come up during the Conference, particularly between Germany and France'; Hitler himself, though he thought solution at the conference table unlikely, agreed to accept the MacDonald Plan as a basis for discussion.[104] On 7 June the General Commission decided to follow such a procedure when the Disarmament Conference resumed in the fall.

Meanwhile the Commission asked Arthur Henderson to conduct private negotiations with the several key governments. Though some observers regarded this gesture as 'buck-passing',[105] the dedicated advocate of disarmament set out upon his mission, hoping to use the World Economic Conference then assembled in London as an unofficial forum. His reception was disappointing:

... there have been few more pathetic pictures than that of Mr Henderson sitting alone in one of the lounges in the delegates' *foyer* and gazing enviously at milling groups of representatives who surged up and down the floor and cast not a glance at the lonely, rubicund, kindly figure in the corner ... This state of things continued for upwards of a week, and by the middle of July Mr Henderson realized that the delegates were 'too busy' to discuss disarmament.[106]

Henderson next visited the various European capitals, where he was received with courtesy, but to little effect. The familiar barrier to progress, Franco-German relations, remained intact; the one refused to disarm because she believed the other to be rearming, the other rearmed because of the refusal of the other to disarm. On 1 August, Vansittart, at the Foreign Office, noted that German rearmament was in fact undercutting any remaining hope for success at Geneva; he wondered if this should not be made clear to Henderson.[107] Whether he was so informed we do not know, but his efforts continued. The embodiment of Labour's hopes for disarmament, Henderson's great efforts should not go unrecorded.

That those efforts had, however, been in vain was made clear with crushing impact upon the reassembly of the Disarmament Conference on 14 October 1933, when Germany unexpectedly[108] announced her withdrawal from that body and the League of Nations. Germany's premise in so acting was the continued denial of her claim to equality of status implicit in the Anglo-French insistence upon disarmament in two stages, with their own coming only in the latter phase.[109] The British government had arrived at this two-stage approach because both of the fact of German rearmament and the demands made by the German delegates for certain new model weapons; Simon considered the latter to be ' ... nothing less in practice than a demand for an immediate and authorised rearmament ... It would belie all our hopes of progress in a world built up on a basis of secured peace'.[110] Developments in Nazi Germany thus pushed the British government close to the traditional French position; in stipulating a two-phase disarmament, they relied on the first to establish the sense of security which had to precede general disarmament.[111]

The decade-old vicious circle was closed more tightly than ever.

The date 14 October 1933 can justly be seen as marking the end of the Locarno period.[112] After this climacteric, hopes for any measure of disarmament faded away: the proceedings at Geneva were wearisome, the attempts of the British government to bring Germany once again back to the table were quite without success. Neither is of great concern, for the lines drawn in October 1933 remained intact thereafter. Henderson was to persist in his once noble efforts for several years longer; in time those efforts became delusive, even divisive.[113] Naturally the Labour Party remained associated with Henderson's attempts; the practicality of their approach is open to question.

On 21 November, the Disarmament Conference adjourned, in favour of parallel and supplementary efforts by the governments. The British government too refused to give up all hopes of securing a convention, which while granting some rearmament to Germany, would result generally in a limitation and reduction of armaments.[114] The German government, however, viewed the British attempt in January 1934 to break the stalemate as far too pro-French.[115] Even when progress was made in Berlin, largely through the efforts of Anthony Eden, the French government refused to go along, as in April of that year. As a result, the Disarmament Conference survived in 'a state of suspended animation'.[116] Meanwhile Germany was rearming, in defiance of the provisions of Part V of the Treaty of Versailles; though that rearmament was as yet covert, the British Ambassador in Berlin had warned that Hitler ' . . . will in all probability continue the rearmament of Germany until his security is such that he can afford to display openly what now he still condescends to conceal'.[117] Europe's turn away from disarmament was a denial of the assumption upon which the concept of collective security had been based. Labour's endorsement of disarmament had been called into question by the events of 1933, just as the British government's attempts to mediate between France and Germany in this matter had met with no success. Similarly the Labour Party and the National Government had endorsed the concept of collective security. How had that method of keeping the peace fared?

5

Confronted by the rude shock of German withdrawal from a conference in which his party had invested great hopes, Clement Attlee on 14 March 1934 expounded Labour's international policy:

We believe that no nation should enter into international obligations which it is not prepared to honour; we believe in a system of pooled security under the League of Nations; we believed that such a system had been built up; we hold that there has been a failure to honour the obligations of the League of Nations to China ... and we therefore stated that it was not possible to get the kind of security that we have been trying to build unless the members of the League felt that those obligations would be honoured to the full.[118]

Thus Labour held that the Far Eastern crisis, in addition to undercutting hopes for disarmament, had vitiated the system of pooled security to which Labour gave allegiance. That Labour had long supported such a concept is clear; such Labour leaders as Henderson and Dalton had even specified sanctions as the ultimate means of implementing collective security. The party viewed the League of Nations as a system of mutual guarantee.

Yet for the purpose of preserving the peace this was not the League's sole function: it was also to serve as a commission of conciliation, which could exercise quasi-arbitral functions.[119] The concept of collective security was in itself ambiguous, because the manner of the drafting of Article 11 made it unclear whether it only asserted a principle without creating a definite obligation. Though Labour placed an obligatory construction upon Article 11, the ambiguity bolstered those forces in Great Britain and the dominions which held that the sanctions associated with collective security were a dangerous matter. This view triumphed when Great Britain, under the aegis of a Conservative government, rejected the Geneva Protocol in 1925. On the other hand, Arthur Henderson had played an important role in the drafting of the protocol, which impressed many as the best attempt to put 'teeth' in the League provisions.[120] The debate over the provisions of the protocol illustrates the continuing conflict in post-war Britain between collectivists and traditionalists.[121]

The latter were in the main Conservatives, but the collectivist desire to bring British policies into conformance with general rules and high moral principles cut across party lines. The traditionalists generally looked to national interests and were concerned with definite geographical areas (e.g. the Locarno arrangements); the collectivists worked with general and abstract terms, conceiving of security and arbitration without reference to specific countries. Collectivists thus conceived of the international community in the broadest sense, a concept of foreign policy well attuned to Labour's dominant sense of internationalism, typified by Henderson's assertion: ' . . . in international policy we shall strive for world planning, world action, and world control in economic and financial matters . . . and every other matter of common international concern'.[122]

Dangers can lurk in such abstract thought: one may inadvertently lose sight of realities or use abstractions as a barrier against considerations of a more practical nature. Collectivists of course need not lose contact with reality, for as we have seen certain Labour leaders were concerned with the practical implementation of the collective system. Such a consideration no doubt explains Dalton's 1928 dictum that ' . . . sanctions in support of any legal rule can only operate if the supporters of the rule are stronger than those who seek to break it'.[123] Yet collective security, as an abstraction, was espoused by those with pacifist sentiments as well; these were prepared to accept collective security as part of Labour's peace policy, though their emphasis was placed upon revision of Versailles.[124] Implementation of collective security was not a concern, for war had become unthinkable. As late as 1934 collective security was all things to all people within the Labour Party: only the events of the 1930s forced the fissure in the party's view of collective security to the surface.

Before the fissure became apparent, the pacifist advocates of war resistance sought to transform that ethical postulate into a method of procedure binding upon the General Council of the TUC, the industrial wing of the Labour movement. Had they succeeded, Labour's commitment to collective security would have been badly compromised. Ernest Bevin saw the danger, and the practical difficulties as well, in responding at the 1932 Congress to those who sought a trade union strike against participation in, or support of, war:

Why lead the great British public – who have within their means the power to end this business together with the democracies of other parts of the world – to believe that we are ready to accept the responsibility for their apathy, their indifference, their toryism, and their opposition to us, when we are advocating disarmament and peace? . . . I hate war, and all that it represents. I will do everything I can to end it, but I am not going to be a party to accepting a responsibility that I cannot carry out.[125]

To his practical argument Bevin might have added the theoretical objection that the war resisters either did not see or care that ' . . . the refusal to endow law with power did not diminish the total amount of force in the world, but left it in the hands of the lawless, the most violent . . .'[126] Practical considerations however prevailed in the TUC after 1926, so that the latter argument was not used. In 1932, Labour could afford the luxury of numbering war resisters among the supporters of collective security, for it still seemed inconceivable that any European power – Japan's example notwithstanding – would dare defy the writ of the League. The threat of sanctions would deter aggression; armaments were not even a consideration. Such a belief was convenient to a party strenuously advocating disarmament, since pooled security made possible the reduction of national armaments.

In late 1932, Labour began to question systematically the unwillingness of the British government to apply sanctions against Japan, inaction which boded ill for collective security. The widespread acceptance of the collective system within the party, sapped by the negating forces of pacifism and war resistance, was in turn openly questioned by the Labour left, whose faith in the efficacy of the League was shattered by the League's failure to act effectively in the Far East. Thus collective security was called into question within the Labour Party precisely when that 'system' might have served as a barrier against the disintegration of Europe.

This developing scepticism was brought to the attention of the Labour Executive in March 1933 by the Advisory Committee on International Questions.[127] That committee directly assessed the viability of the League system: concluding that the alternatives to a League-based policy were considerably worse than at an earlier time, the ACIQ declared that a genuine pro-League policy was more than ever necessary.[128] Yet they also warned that such a policy must be used as an instrument of peace and not as camouflage for imperialist purposes. Ironically they had anticipated an argument which the Labour left was subsequently to use in criticizing the policies of the executive.

A factionalized, uncertain leadership and a distrustful membership together constituted a party of divided domestic counsel in the period immediately following the political rout of 1931. Despite that growing debate in matters of domestic import, the Labour Party generally agreed upon an international policy shaped in the 1920s; few denied its validity and viability in the preservation of peace. Indeed that policy had been applied to the Far Eastern crisis by the Labour Party, though its concurrent criticism of the British government's policy had developed slowly. Japan, however, had prevailed against the League, and the League's failure triggered internal criticism of Labour's agreed international policy.

Ambiguities long implicit in Labour's concept of collective security came to the fore. At the same time that major element of international policy still subscribed to by all sections of the party, disarmament, was by the end of 1933 an all but lost cause. Europe's failure to attain that goal symbolized its political disintegration, which Labour's international policy had increasingly to take into account.

3 The menace of fascism

Hitler assumed the Reich chancellorship in a legitimate and legal manner, helped in his climb to power by the Catholic leaders of the Centre Party, ' . . . their calculation being that, if he were given enough rope, he would hang himself'.[1] With that rope he fashioned a noose for all opposition in the form of the Enabling Act of 23 March 1933; the Nazi revolution followed. Hitler aimed to bring the whole of organized life under the control of the NSDAP; *Gleichschaltung* first affected the state governments, but on 2 May came the turn of the trade unions. Throughout Germany SA and SS units occupied union offices, arresting and imprisoning many officials. Later the unions were merged into a Nazi-controlled German Labour Front; collective bargaining was abolished. In June the Social Democratic Party went the way of the trade unions, shortly to be followed into oblivion by the other political parties; on 14 July Germany became a one-party state. A great labour movement lay crushed at the feet of the Nazi dictatorship.

Labour movements in other countries saw with trepidation the events in Germany. The German trade union officials and the SPD leaders had been colleagues and comrades. Was their fate likely to be suffered elsewhere? This was the central question which the leaders of the British labour movement had to consider, when they tried to confront the fascist threat. Another question which faced the leaders of the political wing in particular, was the effect which Hitler's consolidation of power would have upon Anglo-German relations. After all, Labour had long inveighed against the iniquities of Versailles, a German grievance which Hitler had ridden to power. What role would the new Germany play in discussions of disarmament and collective security?

Since time was required to ascertain Hitler's intentions for Anglo-German relations, Labour's first reactions to Nazism were fears for the rise of a comparable dictatorship in Britain. Trade union officials understandably led the way in denouncing the Nazi destruction of democracy. On 24 March the National Joint Council, a trade union-dominated body, issued a 'call to the People' renouncing all dictatorships, whether of right or left.[2] Since British Labour stood firm for the democratic rights of the people which could ' . . . stem and reverse the streams of reaction in our midst', the strengthening of the trade unions and the party was the best safeguard against dictatorship.

Labour's continuing concern with the internal danger of fascism is evident in a pamphlet, *Hitlerism*, issued by the NJC in May 1933. Here, the chairman of the Labour Executive, Joseph Compton, outlined fascist repression of public opinion, education, trade unionism and socialism.[3] In the same pamphlet, however, Walter Citrine, Secretary of the TUC, indicated that fascism was not the only threat to democracy: 'Far too many people in the Labour Movement are not only critical but scornful of Parliamentary Government. It is about time we cleared the decks for the settlement of the issue of democracy or dictatorship.'[4] Citrine clearly desired no part of anti-democratic practices of the left, which might well arise in reaction to fascism; in warning against such over-reaction, Citrine initiated discussion of an issue which was to trouble the Labour Party for the remaining years of peace. Subsequently, this prominent trade unionist strove to give wide circulation to the bitter truths about Nazi Germany, chronicling Hitler's rise and Germany's tragedy in a three part series in *Labour Magazine*.[5]

The National Joint Council, meanwhile, by way of popular protest, held a mass meeting in the Albert Hall on 12 April 1933 which denounced developments in Germany. Three months later the Council resolved upon a boycott of German commodities and services, which they asked the public to support.[6]

The trade union leaders thus should be numbered among the first Britons to grasp and speak out against the very nature of the Nazi régime. Such a decisive reaction on their part is of course readily explicable:

The suppression of the German trade-union movement and the

confiscation of its property and funds brought it home to them in a way that diplomatic moves or changes in the balance of power could never have done ... No trade union, [Ernest] Bevin wrote in an article for his own [TGWU] members, could ask for a clearer illustration of what dictatorship meant and how it would affect him in his everyday life.[7]

Though Citrine had in his article in *Hitlerism* mentioned a 'war spirit' abroad in Germany, the trade union response was directed strictly to the internal menace of fascism, represented by the British Fascists and Mosley's British Union of Fascists.[8] Such a response was natural enough; it is no denigration of the trade unionists' concern that they did not see the external threat posed to Britain by Nazi Germany in 1933. In calling attention to the brutalities of the Nazi régime, in convincing public opinion that things which were daily events in Germany could happen in any civilized country, the union leaders served their party – and their country – well.

The political wing of the movement, represented by the Parliamentary Labour Party, did not move with such certainty; this may have stemmed in part from the fact that the politicians were not so personally allied to the SPD leaders as were the industrial leaders to their German counterparts. Also important is the incomplete information conveyed to the parliamentary opposition, through official channels, of developments abroad: although the British Ambassador in Berlin, Rumbold, reported on the unsettling theses of *Mein Kampf* to his government on 26 April 1933,[9] it is unlikely that his perspicacious reportage was communicated to the opposition.

Most important of all in hampering an unequivocal response was Labour's dilemma in reconciling opposition to Nazi Germany with its declared policy of redress of German grievances. Two months after Hitler had come to power, Stafford Cripps expressed Labour's conviction that ' ... if you are ever going to remove the unrest from Europe you will do it only upon the basis of justice, and in order to do that, you must remove first of all some of the iniquitous provisions of the post-war Treaties'.[10] Only three weeks later, however, the other Deputy Leader of the Labour Party, Attlee, qualified Labour's revisionism: 'What is feared is that revision may take place in the interests of great Powers at the expense of smaller nations ... I think that this

House and this country ought to say that we will not countenance for a moment the yielding to Hitler and force what was denied to Stresemann and reason.'[11] What was at issue was not the justice of the German claims, but rather Hitler's right to press them.[12]

At this time revision was even more strongly questioned by Austen Chamberlain, a supporter of the National Government who had striven to conciliate the Germans: 'We have revised and revised and what have we got for it? What concession once made has any longer kept the value it had before it was revised?' His half-brother Neville, who was to bring to pass the fear voiced by Attlee, might well have heeded these words, but this is to anticipate. What is immediately relevant is the judgment offered by an MP near the close of this debate: 'The revision of the treaties is dead . . . all here today realize that all they have said and done during the last thirteen years has to be scrapped.'[13] For the Labour Party, and indeed for the British nation, such realization was dawning, but attitudes developed through a decade do not pass away overnight and rarely without a struggle.

The changing climate of opinion was both clear and unwelcome to the German government, which directed the German Embassy on the day following the Commons debate to protest formally that ' . . . Sir John Simon did not object energetically to the insults directed at Germany in the course of the debate . . . '[14] A month later, the German Ambassador in London specified a leading source of that criticism: 'The Labour party and the entire working class, which had formerly shown most understanding for Germany's sufferings, regard the new Germany with implacable enmity.'[15] No doubt he had the declaration of the National Joint Council in mind; possibly the pamphlet on *Hitlerism* was also in his hands. Though 'enmity' is an accurate description, the depth of that feeling had not yet outstripped the PLP's hopes for disarmament and revision, as George Lansbury indicated early in July:

> We who sit on this side want Germany to have fair play in regard both to aviation and armaments but we are not, without protest, going to see Germany rearm . . . We believe that the best method of dealing with that position is for this country to carry out in the letter and the spirit all the implications of the treaty of peace and to challenge the German Government to adopt the same policy . . . We on this side view with

great apprehension this re-arming under the control of such people as are in power to-day as a great menace to the peace not only of Europe, but of the world.[16]

In Lansbury's remarks we find a recognition of the potential external threat of fascism posed by Nazi Germany, but the party leadership was hopeful that the situation could be peacefully contained. Official Labour, while hostile to Nazism, was as yet reluctant to abandon the basic tenets of its international policy.

Meanwhile the Labour left had proposed an alternate interpretation of the phenomenon of Nazism and offered a policy with which to confront it. Where the leadership had viewed Nazism in the larger context of the struggle between democracy and dictatorship, the left, grounded to the concept of the class struggle, associated Nazism with capitalism. The thesis that capitalism would submerge the working classes unless they moved to break its stifling hold was best presented in a widely-praised book by John Strachey:

> The truth, which, as the crisis in capitalism deepens will become inescapably apparent to everyone . . . is that it is capitalist imperialism which outrages, ravages and despoils the motherland of every race of men in turn; and it is communism alone which can bring national liberation to the peoples of the earth.[17]

In such a view, the National Government could be seen as an agent of the impending fascist take-over. Even such a moderate as the then President of the TUC told the 1933 assembly that although democracy might not be tested in Britain as it had been in Germany, where capitalist interests had supported Hitler's attack on the trade unions, they dare not forget that 'capitalism in this country has as much to lose by the triumph of democracy as it has elsewhere . . . they are fighting in the last ditch'.[18] The Secretary of the TUC, however, disagreed throughout the decade with a cynical interpretation of the intentions of the National Government.[19]

The Labour left, however, contained a number of those who agreed with Strachey, for despite such an abstract endorsement of Communism, they remained within the Labour Party, thereby adding to the internal conflict already evident in 1932. The Nazi triumph in Germany only served to increase the doubts of the

Labour left ' . . . as to the viability of capitalist democracy in an age of crisis, and . . . the possibility of a peaceful and parliamentary transition to Socialism, in Britain as anywhere else'.[20] Such doubts assumed concrete political form in the left's advocacy of a united working-class front against fascism, which was to bring them into constant conflict with the Labour leadership for the balance of the decade. Since the 1933 campaign was the first in a long series backed by the left, we would do well to survey the intentions of its supporters.

2

International Labour reacted quickly to Hitler's take-over; even before the German trade unionists succumbed to *Gleichschaltung*, the Executive of the Labour and Socialist International called upon the German workers and workers of all countries ' . . . to cease their attacks upon each other and join together in the fight against Fascism'. To expedite that process, the LSI reiterated its willingness to negotiate directly with the Communist International. That Moscow-based body chose another course, however, instructing the national Communist parties to seek 'United Front' pacts within their respective countries along lines laid down by the International. The LSI retorted that experience had shown that such negotiations were too easily turned into manœuvres by the Communists, which increased mistrust and poisoned the situation.[21] Consequently the LSI's Administrative Committee asked affiliated parties to stay their hand on such negotiation until the full Executive could examine the proposal more closely.

The British Labour Party was favourably disposed to such a suggestion, because relations with the Communist Party of Great Britain had never been cordial; the trade union leaders in particular were cool to Communist proposals. Ernest Bevin, for example, could recall Communist machinations at the time of 'Black Friday' in 1921.[22] As if to supply a reminder, a London busmen's Rank and File Committee which Bevin considered was following the Communist line had recently criticized his leadership of the TGWU severely.[23] The CPGB nonetheless solicited support for a United Front from the Labour Party, the Co-operative Party[24] and the TUC. The ILP was the first to indicate

51

interest; negotiations ensued, and agreement was reached on 17 March 1933. Its General Secretary was anxious to limit co-operation to this one point, but the CPGB's Harry Pollitt constantly worked to widen the association. A troubled partnership ensued. [25]

Within the Labour Party, the Socialist League advocated support for the front; its members shared the belief of the Communists and the ILP that events in Germany showed the consequence of accommodation of the capitalists. The Labour leadership, however, placed the blame for Social Democracy's defeat upon the Communists, who by weakening and dividing the German working-class through their tactics had cleared Hitler's way to power. [26] Curiously then proponents and opponents of the United Front cited the very existence of Nazi Germany as a proof of the correctness of their position. In its strongly worded de-nunciation of all dictatorships, issued in March, the National Joint Council did not refer specifically to the front proposal; none-theless its treatment of Communism in the same fashion as Nazism must have galled the Labour left.

Official Labour subsequently exposed the Communist use of the concept of a united front as a tactic, in a pamphlet entitled *The Communist Solar System*. Its goal they found stated by the Soviet official Kuusinen: 'We must create a whole solar system of organizations and smaller committees around the Communist Party, so as to speak, smaller organizations working actually under the influence of our own Party.' [27] Since Communists were barred from Labour Party membership, the pamphlet argued, their agents within the party proposed support for nominally independent organizations which were in fact Communist satellites; the United Front was added to Labour's listing of such groups in 1933. Penetration may well have been a major aim of the CPGB's proposal of the front; the historian aware of the frantic somer-saults of that party in 1939–41 in reacting to the Nazi-Soviet pact, the outbreak of the war and the subsequent Russian involve-ment would be hard pressed to ascribe altruistic motives to its front campaigns.

Yet to treat the United Front as nothing more than a Com-munist tactic is to exaggerate the influence of the CPGB. The non-Communists who supported the fronts were simply not accomplices to the penetration; rather they held that the Labour

Party leadership was not waging a sufficiently vigorous domestic opposition to the policies of their class enemies in the National Government. Drastic slashes in unemployment benefits had been instituted, while the length of the lines awaiting such aid had not seemed to shorten. The National Unemployed Workers' Movement, which staged a number of hunger marches, was far more successful in publicizing the plight of those unfortunates than the Labour leadership.[28] The Labour left sought an activist leadership for causes held dear, whether the lead came from their own party or, as in the case of the NUWM, from the Communists.

The novelist Storm Jameson tellingly explained the sense of frustration felt by the left in Britain:

> What matters in all this is that past experience, as well as all we know about human nature, warns us that socialism, like any other faith, loses its power with us in measure as it ceases to be a faith and becomes an establishment. Communism, like Fascism, lives because it gives the people something hard to do . . . The command 'Go' is a force releasing and recreating energy. The prohibition 'Don't go' creates nothing but apathy and the feeling of discouragement and emptiness.[29]

Such a prohibition, applied to the United Front as to domestic matters, reinforced the left's distrust of the Labour leadership. They viewed Labour's manifesto 'Democracy v. Dictatorship' unfavourably, because, in the words of the left-leaning *New Statesman*, it ' . . . betrayed no realization that the issue is the destruction of the working-class movement throughout Europe'.[30] In such circumstances the rejection of the United Front was one matter, but the failure to offer an alternative was quite another, the journal contended. Another illustration of the leadership's inaction in face of the fascist assault upon the working classes was provided by their refusal to join in a protest meeting against the Reichstag trials because of the presence of Pollitt, the CPGB leader, on the platform. The *New Statesman*'s editor, Kingsley Martin, understood such a reluctance but argued:

> . . . if they will not work with Communists, even where their interests coincide, they should not leave it to the Communists to get on with the job. As it is, the Labour Party is too slow and cumbrous to begin, the Communists step in, and then the Labour Party, even when it would like to, as in this case, will not come in because the Communists have begun. The only way out is for the Labour Party to take the initiative.[31]

53

The taking of such an initiative on behalf of socialism and the working classes, at home and abroad, was what the Labour left demanded of the leadership; such a demand underlay every front agitation of the decade. To them the rise of fascism was the central issue of the time: seeing its consequences abroad and suspecting the National Government of a similar hatred of the Labour movement, the left demanded a pooling of resources to resist the latent fascist threat in Great Britain.

Labour's initial response – the NJC's declamation on the virtues of parliamentary democracy – was for the left no answer at all. It proved, however, to be an answer to which the leadership had recourse time and again, since they adamantly resisted such front movements. In the General Council's report to the TUC meeting in September, the union leaders argued that the front supporters ' . . . cannot understand that Communism stands for a dictatorship just as ruthless to minority opinion as Fascism. Such a demand, in effect, is asking those who believe in democracy to unite with those who believe in dictatorship to combat dictatorship.' Walter Citrine interpolated this point to Congress: 'Every support given to the institution of a dictatorship of whatever kind, weakened the fibre of their own people, and their belief in institutions to which they had subscribed.'[32]

The outraged reaction of the young leftist Aneurin Bevan to Citrine's speech, which he regarded as the most dangerous he had ever heard, typified the breach which had opened between the leadership and the left in regard to the United Front. What Bevan characterized as Citrine's academic description of democracy's virtues would mean very little to the cynical, disillusioned, unemployed young men of Britain. He urged Congress to send out a message to the working classes that democracy would be defended in the island through the very use of democracy; the gospel of quiescence should be overthrown so that the weapons of democracy could be used to secure economic gains. Bevan responded: 'If they [Congress] gave that call there was no need to fear Fascism, because democracy would have won an affectionate place in the hearts of the people. If they allowed the weapons of democracy to rot the workers would condemn them . . .'[33]

Though Bevan's appeal was overwhelmed by Congress, the left

raised the matter of such a united front approach repeatedly in the decade; despite defeat after defeat, they refused to abandon the concept and, consequently, the internal conflict. Not until 1939 did the party leadership proscribe further continuation of the debate, six years after the party had first rejected the proposal. That initial refusal came at the 1933 Labour Party Conference, which dealt with other problems as well, some inherited, others recently arisen.

3

Debate on the United Front proposal at that Conference, which met in Hastings from 2 to 6 October 1933, was, for all its importance, quite perfunctory. That body had shown its inclination by supporting overwhelmingly the Executive's action in issuing 'Democracy v. Dictatorship'. Nonetheless the left pressed for an endorsement of the United Front; the temper of its thought was captured in Ellen Wilkinson's criticism of the party's pamphlet, *The Communist Solar System*: 'The pamphlet . . . is a magnificent advertisement of the energy and drive of the Communist Party in this country. Why have these organizations flourished like this? Because our own Executive has not acted quickly enough, and has not acted in such a way as to appeal to the imagination.' The Executive, however, maintained its position; Herbert Morrison, powerful in London Labour affairs, protested against the misapplication of energies into divisive front movements, which he held were created and maintained by the Comintern for its own purposes. In referring to the Labour Party he argued: 'We are a united front, and I ask you to stand by the Executive in maintaining the united front which we have got.'[34] Without the need for a card vote, Conference gave the Executive that support.

The Executive begrudged the attention which they had given the United Front issue, for this had taken away from the time they could devote to their major activity of 1933, the continued development of Labour's new programme. Even those efforts failed to please the left, which voiced its disapproval, at Hastings, of the tempo of socialization recommended by the Executive. Speaking in effect for the Socialist League, Sir Stafford Cripps asked Conference to instruct the Executive ' . . . to specify the means to be adopted by the next Labour Government for a rapid and complete conversion of the Capitalist into the Socialist system . . .'[36] Cripps proposed measures which would expedite that crucial transformation, yet after arguing for a decided increase in tempo, he announced the left's willingness to grant the Executive a year for consideration of the problem. In so doing he fulfilled a pre-Conference prediction of the *Manchester Guardian*, that ' . . . the tacticians on the side of the Socialist League will go a long way to avoid a crushing defeat and that the Labour Party Executive will help to spare them'. Such a dilatory compromise in the midst of what the left regarded as the critical pass opened by Hitler's *Gleichschaltung* would be difficult to explain were it not for a direct consequence of that development, noted by the *Guardian*. Hitherto the Socialist League had preached a 'rapid and complete conversion' from one state of society to another, but Hitler had shown what emergency powers could mean in practice: 'Hitler and the British trade union revolt against Fascism have badly shaken the League, and it has been running away steadily from the implications of the dictatorial assumptions from which it started.'[37] The Labour Executive were willing to accept the compromise proposed by Cripps, whose proposals were taken into consideration in the next year. For the moment, direct confrontation was avoided.

The brief debate initiated by Cripps had, however, produced a personal confrontation of lasting impact upon the party. Ernest Bevin,[38] because of his role as a trade union leader, pronounced himself less tolerant of the left's position: 'Our work is eminently practical, and it is to deliver the goods to our members, and we know, as leaders, the absolute folly of putting up programmes that are not likely to be realised . . .'[39] Bevin here delineated the dichotomy between the pragmatic trade unionists and the resolute socialists who would settle for nothing less than the socialist commonwealth. It was inevitable that Cripps and Bevin should clash on this point; indeed, this disputation was the first of several between the two men. Their divergent approaches exemplify two conflicting forces within the Labour Party. Bevin's biographer has characterized the rationale of his dislike for Cripps and 'intellectuals', a term of opprobrium:

It had little to do with Left or Right or even with a university education ... All [intellectuals] ... had one thing in common: they displayed those characteristics which in Bevin's mind were the hallmark of the intellectual: unreliability and irresponsibility ... because they went haring off after new ideas and new enthusiasms. They were too likely to be swept along by some new intellectual fashion and forget what they had said six months before.[40]

Bullock depicts an earthy Bevin, with a critical power of judgment strengthened by years of experience in dealing with men, in conflict with the ascetic Cripps, '... the passionate doctrinaire to whom ideas were more real than human beings'. Yet one can grant Bevin strength of character and still argue a brief for Cripps and his commitments:

The concept that divided him from Bevin was that of loyalty. To Bevin, as to many other men grown old in the service of the Labour Party, the paramount meaning of loyalty was to the Party as an entity ... To Sir Stafford Cripps loyalty had another meaning; above all, one must be loyal to one's own beliefs ... To conform to the official party line was, to him, an act of mere political expediency.[41]

Clearly Bevin, the unionist, and Cripps, unacknowledged but undisputed leader of the Labour left,[42] brought divergent beliefs to the councils of the Labour Party. The one transferred the industrial concept of loyalty and responsibility to the political sphere, the other held that individual conscience had to prevail. Perhaps the major importance of this inconclusive debate about socialist legislation was its prefiguring of the clash of loyalties which, along with different interpretations of European events, produced continuing internal controversy.

The Hastings Conference also resumed the party-wide discussion of foreign policy, a topic that had not often been discussed since the fall of the Labour government. In 1932, for instance, only one pamphlet on foreign policy had been published by the party. Even that was not much use, for it was predicated on the existence of a socialist government; it did not consider the more pressing question of what should be the foreign policy of a socialist opposition.[43] The pamphlet reiterated the old positions – support of the League of Nations and of disarmament policies, in general terms. Unilateral disarmament was rejected.

C

In the spring of 1933, the quality of discussion improved. A pamphlet written by Arthur Henderson in response to the events of the winter of 1932–3 did re-examine more specifically the tenets of Labour foreign policy. Although Henderson emphasized the policies of a Labour government, he did develop the outlines of a policy for Labour in opposition. In agreement with the party's Advisory Committee on International Questions,[44] Henderson held that the set-back to the League in the Sino-Japanese dispute did not come from the failure of the League itself. Consequently the remedy lay not in scrapping the Covenant but in resolving that it should be applied and upheld against the aggression of Japan. He reiterated Labour's support for pooled security and its renunciation of war as an instrument of national policy. To make this latter pledge even clearer, he specified Labour's proposal of the parliamentary enactment of a 'Peace Act', spelling out the procedure binding upon any British government in the settlement of disputes.[45] Henderson was looking to a better future in 1933, while hoping that the present would not get out of hand.

At Hastings the Socialist League showed its concern with that present, for it had adopted a more catastrophic interpretation of recent events. Their attitude towards the League had altered:

. . . from the League of Nations there is no final safety now. The League . . . is worked by feeble and sceptical Governments like our own, or by Governments that openly deride world peace, like Italy and Germany. If our Government would not use the League of Nations to try to check Japan, have we any belief at all that it would itself be checked if it embroiled itself with other nations?

Distrust of that government only served to strengthen the left's case for war resistance, argued, appropriately enough, by one of the UDC converts, Sir Charles Trevelyan. He asked that Labour

. . . pledge itself to take no part in war and to resist it with the whole force of the Labour Movement and to seek consultation forthwith with the Trade Union and Co-operative Movements with a view to deciding and announcing to the country what steps, including a general strike, are to be taken to organise the opposition of the organised working-class movement in the event of war or threat of war . . .[46]

This very first recommendation of the recently reorganized Labour left in the area of foreign policy dealt with a matter in which working-class sentiments were crucial; conflict with trade union leaders was likely to ensue, for the TUC leadership had resisted such a policy in 1932 and had in effect shelved a similar suggestion at the 1933 Congress.[47] Though the Socialist League's support for war resistance was not surprising, certainly the decision of Executive to accept the resolution in its entirety, including the pledge to 'take no part in war', was quite unexpected.

Speaking for the supreme body of a party pledged to collective security, Hugh Dalton welcomed the proposals and the speeches offered on its behalf, rejoicing to see ' . . . the rising flame of the hatred of war'.[48] His sole reservation was the failure of the resolution to commit Labour ' . . . to the economic and financial boycott of any war-mongering State'. Labour's Executive had seemingly squared the circle, in reconciling a sanctionist policy with war resistance: they desired the use of economic sanctions, but in no case, including a war resulting from those sanctions, would Labour take up arms. The resolution had made no exception for a war on behalf of the enforcement of League sanctions, nor had Dalton. The concept of sanctions for the enforcement of peace became a meaningless one.

Only recently has Dalton explained how the NEC had become involved in such a 'wildly unreal' policy. Since the resolution was a composite, floor-initiated one, the Executive had no power under the Standing Orders to amend it. The only choices then were passage, rejection or withdrawal. They judged that Conference was in no mood for the latter alternatives; only an all-out attack on their part might defeat the resolution, which was scheduled to be followed by an important foreign policy address delivered by Henderson. The Executive was cornered: 'We did not want a wrangle and an excited vote immediately before this speech by the President of the Disarmament Conference.'[49] Wishing to maintain a façade of unity, the Executive blithely agreed to pledge the party to a policy of unconditional war resistance for at least a year. The attitude thereby encouraged is evident in the title given to a pamphlet stemming from Henderson's speech, *Labour Outlaws War*. Volition alone would suffice to overcome war, Labour's stand seemed to argue, regardless of the existence of Japanese militarists, or Adolf Hitler.

Yet this contradiction between Labour's espousal of collective security and war resistance was but an extension of the ambiguity of policies which had made possible the conciliation of divergent elements within the party. The contradiction, perfectly apparent at the time, was either quickly explained away or sharply criticized. The *Guardian* resorted to the latter course, while the *New Statesman* attempted the former:

The meaning of the Hastings resolution may be best summarized by saying that, while the Labour Party as a whole supports Mr. Henderson's efforts to transform Geneva into a centre of security, it is prepared, if the League fails again, to undertake a revolutionary strike rather than to support what would then be a nationalist war.[50]

The *Guardian* was rather more concerned, as it commented validly: 'Read literally, the Hastings resolution is . . . an extreme pacifist declaration which is, as its Tory critics point out, equivalent to support of unilateral disarmament.'[51] The *Guardian*, however, reasoned that Labour's critics had misconstrued the resolution's meaning. Their criticism, the paper continued, was accurate only if Henderson had repudiated his long-held justification of two kinds of war – repulsion of actual aggression, and concerted measures of League members against a state resorting to the crime of war. The *Guardian* trusted that the Hastings resolution was limited to the case of unjustifiable war. Such trust, pure and simple, in the consistency of Henderson's belief was required, for he himself had not clarified his position at Hastings. Time was to prove the *Guardian*'s surmise correct, but the Labour Party had in the meanwhile adopted a resolution which taken word by word undercut the structure of the party's foreign policy.

For some months the Hastings resolution engendered considerable confusion. Though Labour within the year repudiated this ill-worded resolution, Conservatives long remembered the 1933 Labour Party Conference. Sir Samuel Hoare viewed it as an important step in the 'landslide towards unconditional pacifism' characterizing that year's events.[52] Such a literal reading of the resolution is misleading, but Labour's action exposed their policy to telling criticism. As for the 'landslide', those pacifist phenomena which attracted Hoare's attention will directly occupy ours.

In characterizing the Hastings Conference generally, one would be hard pressed to dispute G. D. H. Cole's conclusion that it was ' . . . marking time in respect of the controversy between

the left and right wings'.[53] Compromise was the principal theme
of the 1933 party gathering. Domestically this caution resulted
from the incomplete nature of Labour's programme; only with
the presentation of additional reports in 1934, and the resolution
of the debate on the pace of socialist legislation, would the platform of Labour emerge in its totality. In matters of foreign policy
Labour's hopes would have to meet the test of developments
on the continent of Europe – in Berlin no less than in Geneva.
The nature and scope of the already ominous fascist threat could
not but shape the dimensions of Labour's response.

4

Three events of 1933–5 are generally taken to illustrate the
pacifist 'landslide' for which the Labour Party is often held
responsible.[54] To be sure, the party played no direct part in the
first; in the second, the party must accept full responsibility; and
in the last Labour shared the responsibility with other interested
groups. The role of the Labour Party within the general context
of these manifestations of pacifism has been greatly misunderstood.

The Oxford University Union on 9 February 1933 heard a debate,
resolved, that ' . . . this House will in no circumstance fight for
King and Country'. In what Churchill regards as an 'ever-
shameful'[55] act the resolution was carried 275–173. Though he
notes that such an incident could be laughed off in Britain,
Churchill sketches dire consequences abroad: ' . . . in Germany,
in Russia, in Italy, in Japan, the idea of a decadent, degenerate
Britain took deep root and swayed many calculations.' He provides no documentation for the latter assertion, and he errs in
suggesting that the debate was taken humorously at home.
R. B. McCallum has shown that the incident provoked shock and
dismay.

Yet that reaction was certainly uncalled-for. In the first place,
informed people should not have made so much of a vote which
need not reflect the personal convictions of the members of the
Union but rather their decision as to which case was better
argued. Second, people misconstrued the meaning of the
resolution. As McCallum argues:

... the important thing to notice is that the resolution does not say we will never fight, but rather that we will never fight for King and Country. After all, these young men were citizens of a State that had set itself upon a policy of outlawing war. By the Kellogg Pact it had renounced war as a means of national policy. Indeed, it would appear that we could not then fight for King and Country ... without violating international law which we ourselves had helped to make. It by no means follows that everyone who voted for the resolution was a pacifist in the sense of a non-resister.[56]

The 'yeas', he maintains, were better acquainted than their elders with Article 16 of the Covenant – sanctions – which shaped decisively their beliefs: 'They knew that our conduct in international affairs was now supposed to be regulated by a system of diplomatic action that was new in European history, and that defence against aggression was not the task or duty of any single nation.' Could not the same be said of the policy of the Labour Party, whose 'pacifism' was directed against the type of nationalist or imperialist war proscribed by the Covenant, the equivocation of the Hastings resolution notwithstanding? If Labour had cause to cast a ballot on the terms of the Oxford resolution, the party conceivably would have supported it, for the pacifist content ascribed to that statement has been consistently exaggerated and misunderstood.

Direct involvement of the Labour Party in the 'pacifist landslide' took place in the East Fulham parliamentary by-election of October 1933, in which the Labour candidate, John Wilmot, overcame a 1931 Conservative majority of 14,521 to win by 4,840 votes – a stunning electoral reversal. Since Wilmot professed pacifist tenets, there followed a good deal of controversy over the importance of his pacifism in winning the election, and over the significance of a pacifist victory for the future of British politics.

That controversy was fed by Wilmot's platform, which was no model of clarity – or so it would seem from reports in the *New Statesman*. On 28 October, that journal noted that Wilmot had raised '... issues ... both international and domestic – disarmament and poverty'. Three weeks later, however, the editor of that journal asserted that 'Mr. Wilmot's campaign was very largely fought on the peace issue'.[57] Yet 'the peace issue' is too simplistic a term, for Wilmot himself informed the House of Commons that his victory had stemmed from ' . . . a passionate and insistent desire for peace, not merely a purely nebulous desire for peace, but a demand that that desire should be translated into some practical disarmament accomplishment'.[58] In this he was only asking what Labour, at Hastings, had demanded of the British government, namely, 'to abandon its retrograde attitude on the question of air bombing, and to submit proposals for a large and immediate reduction in the expenditure of all nations on armed forces . . .'[59]

It seems clear now that Wilmot's campaign was not purely a pacifist one. Contemporary accounts in *The Times* recorded Wilmot's raising of domestic issues, though his success ' . . . in identifying his opponent with at least some tolerance of the idea of war', through gross misrepresentations of the actions and intentions of the British government (according to the paper) too was noted. Wilmot's propagandist division of the political parties into 'peace men' and 'war mongers' was regrettable, said *The Times*, but the paper admitted that in other regards he had conducted an expert campaign: 'Indeed Mr. Wilmot's victory is in every sense one of those personal triumphs which are occasionally secured at by-elections by strong candidates faced by feeble opposition.' Nor should readers of that respected journal have been unduly shocked by the poll, for they had been twice warned that Wilmot might achieve the 'apparently impossible'.[60] Its correspondents had stressed the inflated nature of the Conservative majority in 1931 and had regarded that party's 1929 majority of 1,700 votes a more accurate guide to the constituency. Further, Hugh Dalton, who had spoken and canvassed on Wilmot's behalf, attributed his victory to his effective exposure of bad local housing conditions, superior electoral organization, personality and outstanding political ability, as well as his advocacy ' . . . not of "pacifism", but of collective defence through a strong League of Nations, and of a General Disarmament Treaty . . . '[61]

Why then the constant citation, both then and since, of East Fulham as a pacifist manifestation? The answer lies in the person and opinions of Stanley Baldwin, who a little more than three years after that by-election recalled to the House of Commons:

You will remember . . . that . . . the Disarmament Conference was sitting in Geneva. You will remember at that time there was probably a stronger pacifist feeling running through the country than at any time since the War. You will remember the election at Fulham in the autumn of 1933, when a seat which the National Government held was lost by about 7,000 [*sic!*] votes on no issue but the pacifist.[62]

The conclusions which Baldwin drew will be treated below, but here the argument that pacifism alone explains Wilmot's triumph cannot go unchallenged. No doubt Baldwin's belief was sincere – if perhaps self-induced – for his 'official' if unsympathetic biographer, G. M. Young, writes: ' . . . East Fulham . . . always East Fulham. He clung to it as the justification of all he had done, or failed to do.' Possibly East Fulham even broke Baldwin's nerve;[63] certainly it did pose practical problems bearing on the question of British armaments and the disarmament conference. Yet to hold John Wilmot or the Labour philosophy he espoused responsible for the Government's failure to rearm in 1933–4, as that government's defenders are apt to do, strains credulity. In October 1933 Hitler had just withdrawn from the disarmament negotiations; the British government's attempts to get him back to the conference table were still in the future. These efforts persisted into the summer of 1934, for, in the words of Baldwin's own son, ' . . . so long as the smallest chance of an agreed limitation of weapons remained, all the powers of the Government were bent towards averting what the post-1918 generation held was the great penultimate calamity: a new race in armaments'.[64] Perhaps only when that hope faded did Baldwin find the psychological need to cast about for an explanation of Britain's failure to rearm earlier; East Fulham may well have supplied the answer.

Baldwin's motivations aside, it seems certain that the deterrent effect which the 1933 by-election played in the question of British armaments has been exaggerated along with the supposed 'pacifism' of the Labour candidate. Further, it served neither as a turning point in Labour's electoral fortunes nor as the precipitating agent of any 'pacifist landslide'. Government supporters were discomfited by the electoral trend culminating in Fulham. A correspondent writing to *The Times*, in what one might surmise as a shaking hand, found that in the sixteen by-elections of the last two years where comparisons to the 1931 results were possible, ' . . . the Government vote . . . fell by over 150,000 or nearly 10,000 a contest. There has been no increase in the [total] Labour vote, only 20,000 or so.'[65] When one applies the same method to the nineteen comparable by-elections held after East

Fulham, to 27 July 1934 (the 1933–4 season, so to speak) one finds that the government vote continued to fall short of the 1931 poll at the rate of about 10,000 per contest, while Labour increased its average poll by some 2,000.[66] Thus the Conservative loss of some 10,000 supporters at Fulham was quite in keeping with a three-year trend; only Labour's gain of some 9,000 was not. Probably this increase was due, as Dalton's account suggests, to a superior canvassing organization's getting out the vote, for few constituencies holding by-elections in 1933–4 so closely approached the total 1931 poll as did East Fulham. A turning point it was not; Stanley Baldwin, it seems, had deceived himself and posterity into ascribing great importance to this one by-election. Though Labour's campaign there may have been a futile exercise on behalf of disarmament, surely the pacifist myth of East Fulham has outstripped the reality.

Although the results of the third 'pacifist' manifestation of the period, the Peace Ballot, were not announced until 27 June 1935, the genesis of that campaign lay not far removed, temporally or geographically, from Fulham. The place was Ilford, the time January 1934, when the editor of the *Ilford Record*, himself a leading member of the local branch of the League of Nations Union, conducted a survey on matters concerning the League.[67] The Independent Conservative statesman, Lord Cecil, was impressed by the four or five to one sentiment (in a poll of some 25,000) in favour of Britain's continued membership in the League, the continuance of the disarmament negotiations and the abolition of the private manufacture of armaments. He established a National Committee to conduct 'The National Declaration on the League of Nations and Armaments', a better title than the short form 'Peace Ballot', which implied that an affirmative response was in all cases one for peace.[68]

Cecil's energetic committee decided to make an attempt to ascertain truly national feelings, establishing machinery to collect millions of ballots. The five questions they framed to be sure betrayed their own sentiments, but perhaps more damaging to the authority of the Peace Ballot was the fact that the questions assumed the existence of international co-operation.[69] Thus Question 5 asked, 'Do you consider that, if a nation insists on attacking another, the other nations should combine to compel it to stop by (*a*) Economic and non-military measures? (*b*) If necessary, military measures?' Government supporters argued that precisely such co-operation had been lacking in the Far Eastern crisis, so that the ballot was based upon an idealized and flawed model. Leo Amery found the Peace Ballot's direction erroneous: ' . . . the whole business is futile, for it is not our Government, but the governments of other countries that need persuading on these issues.'[70] Cecil himself was less sure of the intentions of the British government; at the same time he maintained that he had in mind no pacifist purpose but felt that ' . . . with the Disarmament Conference evidently moribund and the power of the League diminishing, we ought to exert ourselves to convince the Government that if they would pursue a really vigorous League policy they would be supported by British opinion'.[71]

The question of the pacifism expressed by the British citizenry in replying to the Peace Ballot, conducted between November 1934 and June 1935, centres about their response to Question 5. Following affirmative responses to the first four questions ranging from 9·5 million to 11·1 million (out of 11·6 million ballots, a poll beyond all expectations) ten million supported economic and non-military sanctions and 6·8 million military measures. Thus some 4·3 million supporters of continued British membership in the League of Nations (from Question 1) refused to accept the full obligations of the collective security system – i.e. answered 5 (*b*) negatively – while 3·2 million of those drew a line between types of sanctions, agreeing to support non-military sanctions. This distinction reflected the dubious proposition that economic sanctions could be applied without the ultimate willingness to enforce them if need be. Yet despite such ambivalence, 74·2 per cent of those voting – if abstentions be disregarded – supported military sanctions; even regarding such abstentions as in effect negative votes, a clear majority of 58·6 per cent remained in favour of meeting aggression with force.[72]

'Pacifism' was by no means in the ascendancy. Winston Churchill, himself critical of the Ballot's combination of 'the contradictory proposition of reduction of armaments and forcible resistance to aggression', found solace in the results:

It was regarded in many quarters as part of the pacifist campaign. On the contrary, clause 5 affirmed a positive and courageous policy which could, at this time, have been followed by an overwhelming measure of national support. Lord Cecil and other members of the League of Nations Union were, as this clause declared, and as events soon showed, willing, and indeed resolved, to go to war in a righteous cause, provided that all necessary action was taken under the auspices of the League of Nations.[73]

Another observer saw the freedom of action of the British government limited by the results of the Ballot, though hardly in a pacifist direction. The German Ambassador in London reported to his government on 2 July 1935 that 'British public opinion . . . in the so-called "Peace Ballot" has only just recently proclaimed itself to be overwhelmingly in favour of the maintenance of peace by the extension of the system of collective security . . . '[74] Certainly he was under no delusion that the Ballot was yet another 'pacifist' manifestation which made impossible resolute action toward the maintenance of peace by the British government. Once again the myth of pacifism has obscured the actuality.

The Labour Party enthusiastically supported the Peace Ballot in the sense it had been intended by its organizers and accepted by a majority of those answering – a declaration on behalf of the League of Nations and its principles. Hugh Dalton judged at the time that ' . . . no piece of political work that we have done in this Parliament was more worthwhile than the work we did for the Peace Ballot'.[75] The reason was simple: 'I say that great popular mandate on behalf of the Labour Party's foreign policy given through the Peace Ballot – I say that this is one reason why the British Government has changed its tune.' Here was no pacifist exultation in the results of the Peace Ballot, but rather the satisfaction of a man committed to genuine collective security.

In the case of the Peace Ballot as in the two earlier events the myth of pacifism has outstripped the reality. While we have not examined pacifism in Great Britain in the years 1933–5 in a comprehensive fashion, these three cases serve to establish that 'pacifism' is a much-abused term, inadequate – even misleading – when applied to actual events and attitudes. Viewed within its proper context, the role of the Labour Party in these events can no longer be characterized as pacifistic.

5

The new tune of the British government, brought about by the pressure of the Peace Ballot, will concern us below, but first we must consider that Labour foreign policy which Dalton associated with the Ballot, for we have last seen it in some disarray at the Hastings Conference. Had Labour resolved its ambiguities so as to stand unequivocally for collective security and sanctions? And meanwhile what had happened to the party's advocacy of disarmament? It is important to remember that although disarmament was an integral part of Labour's defence policy, other political parties too had served the cause. In the post-Locarno period, Great Britain alone among the major powers had reduced defence expenditures, beginning in 1928 under the Conservative government, with Winston Churchill at the Exchequer, continuing under the second Labour Government and culminating in the economies imposed by the National Government. In sum, expenditures had fallen from £117·3 millions to £102·7 millions in 1932–3.[76]

Defence expenditures were still falling when Attlee had criticized the first Service Estimates brought in by the National Government, on 8 March 1932, on the grounds that ' . . . we get no reference at all . . . to the fact that we are living in a time when the leading nations are supposed to have renounced war'. Labour asked for a defence policy specifically grounded upon Britain's League commitment, for the failure to do so meant ' . . . a maximum of expenditure for a minimum of security'. Any other basis for a defence policy he considered self-defeating, because armaments justified by one nation as the irreducible minimum for its security constituted a potential menace to other nations. The Labour Party claimed to have learned the lesson of the outbreak of the First World War that, as challenge provokes response, national arming begets an arms race bound to lead to war.[77] At the same time, Attlee pressed for a greater reduction in armaments expenditure, which would serve to ease the military strains upon the Exchequer as well as to lessen the tensions engendered by arms competition. Labour of course did not ask for unilateral disarmament; Attlee admitted the need for certain national armaments, though he felt these should be under the control of but one responsible minister, who also would formulate defence policy.[78]

The parliamentary leadership raised essentially the same criticisms a year later, when the Service Estimates were again taken up. Government and Opposition benches alike continued to entertain hopes for disarmament; as yet they were untroubled by the threat of Nazi aggression. Attlee reiterated the need for a better organization of defence, which would yield substantial benefits.[79] Labour's leader, George Lansbury, agreed that the party desired efficient military forces, but he confused matters by grafting on to this declaration his own personal pacifism, in adding 'either you go to war and prepare for war in the most thorough manner possible, or you must take the view, as I do, that it is wrong to go to war at all'.[80] Here Lansbury clearly was speaking for himself: nonetheless he managed to obscure the position of the Labour Party, which in practice fell considerably short of pacifism. However, as the party was concurrently pressing the British government to act on the basis of the Lytton Commission's findings against Japan, its parliamentary pressures for measures of disarmament struck some of its critics as a 'fatal contradiction'. Lansbury's personal interjection exposed the party all the more to the charge of 'bloodthirsty pacifists'.[81]

Unfair the latter allegation is, but the former also misses the mark, for Labour's position must be understood within the larger context of its quest for disarmament by international agreement. The need now was to bring Germany back to Geneva; Lansbury consequently pressed the British government to submit proposals calling for

a large and important reduction in the expenditure of all nations on armed forces, for the general abolition of all weapons forbidden to Germany ... for the abolition of military aircraft ... and the suppression of all private manufacture of and trade in arms, and for strict international inspection and control of the execution of the Disarmament Treaty.

With solemn understatement, Lansbury assured the Commons, 'This means disarmament.' Government proposals, he continued, meant in fact German rearmament, a course which could lead to war: 'Nations do not arm merely for the fun of it, and we believe that the only way out, and the only proper line to take, is to bring the whole of the armaments of Europe down, and not to allow Germany to re-arm in any way whatsoever.'[82] The government regarded Labour's proposal as utopian; Sir John Simon argued that a more sensible line had to be taken – it was no good, he insisted, to try to perform the impossible to comfort one's own moral sense.[83] What success a Labour delegation might have had at Geneva is of course speculative, but it is difficult to imagine that their proposals might have lured Hitler back, when the National Government's more lenient terms failed.

Those terms were criticized from the government's right as well as from the opposition: certain private members deprecated inadequate provisions for air defence and urged the government to fulfil even those requirements established as the minimum necessary for national security in 1923. Stanley Baldwin indicated that the National Government might have to yield to this pressure if an agreement on disarmament were not soon forthcoming: lacking such an agreement, Great Britain's defences could not remain indefinitely as they were. Lansbury interpreted this statement as a conditional determination to increase air armaments,[84] though Baldwin refused to accept such a construction. Nonetheless Baldwin's remarks represent the British government's first step towards air rearmament.

One facet of Labour's opposition to rearmament was its belief that the private manufacture of, and trade in, armaments was an inducement to the stirring-up of strife and to the creation of an artificial but dangerous demand for armaments. Labour periodically raised this matter in the Commons, typically on 14 February 1934. David Grenfell, angered that because of the armaments manufacturers' pursuit of profits British ' . . . war implements, armaments, shells, projectors [sic !] of all kinds were used against our own people in almost all the theatres of war', drew what Labour held a historical lesson: 'If there were no profits, there would be no dangers; it is in the profits that the danger lies, and we say that the private profit should be eliminated.'[85] The argument never, however, swayed the Conservative-dominated Commons.

In March 1934 Attlee[86] returned to Labour's traditional criticism of the National Government's defence policies. He argued that defence estimates had to be considered as a function of foreign policy. Since Labour based its foreign policy on collective security, the party opposed national rearmament,

' . . . the utmost possible danger both to this country and civilisation', for the reason that rearmament undermined that security. Genuine security could come only with multilateral disarmament.[87] Thus for the Labour Party disarmament continued to be a necessary, logical part of the collective system. On the other hand, Winston Churchill was already arguing that danger lay elsewhere, specifically in permitting the means of threatening the British Isles to pass into the hands of Nazi Germany's leaders; to counter this not-distant threat, he asked the government to take measures to raise the RAF from fifth to parity in air strength.[88] Churchill saw salvation in national rearmament, and disaster in anything less; the Labour Party reversed the combinations, seeing security in general disarmament, and the spectre of war in rearmament. The National Government chose neither pole: Baldwin announced that they would continue to work for an armaments agreement, but if their efforts failed he promised that ' . . . in air strength and air power, this country shall no longer be in a position inferior to any country within striking distance of its shores'.[89]

In contrast to the policies of the British government, Labour's foreign and defence policies, in the view of the party's leaders, went hand-in-hand. Attlee stated this conviction later in March 1934:

. . . it is perfectly clear, I think, to everyone that you cannot build up a system of pooled security unless you are prepared to take certain risks. I am asked, 'If you say that, why, then, did you oppose the Estimates?' . . . I said that we on these benches did not believe in national armaments; that we could only agree to armaments if those armaments were part of a system of pooled security to be used on behalf of the League for keeping the peace of the world; and inasmuch as, owing to past events, we do not believe that there is that system of pooled security to-day, because when the test came the League failed, therefore we are not prepared to vote for the Estimates.[90]

This parliamentary tactic of opposing the Service Estimates to register disapproval of government foreign policy rather than as outright opposition to the existence of armaments was utilized for another three years. In no other parliamentary fashion could the party so forcefully indicate its belief that the British government were not fulfilling their obligations to the collective system.

The charge of 'bloodthirsty pacifists' laid against the party for this opposition is disproved on two counts: Labour was neither eager for war because of its advocacy of sanctions, nor pacifist because of its hopes for disarmament. Such hopes for Geneva may have been misplaced in 1934, but British national security was not yet endangered, for collective security remained a viable policy if the major governments were willing to apply it. Labour's international policy is thus comprehensible; only a term of power could have proved it right or wrong.

Labour's outspoken criticism of the first actual measure of British rearmament is quite understandable. On 30 July 1934, in a move characterized by Churchill as 'tiny, timid, tentative and tardy', the government proposed to strengthen the RAF by 41 squadrons (820 planes) within five years. Labour, however, stigmatized the government's entry upon '. . . a policy of rearmament neither necessitated by any new commitment nor calculated to add to the security of the nation, but certain to jeopardize the prospects of international disarmament and to encourage a revival of a dangerous and wasteful competition in preparation for war'.[91] The party refused to accept Baldwin's contention that British rearmament could serve the interests of the League. Attlee retorted that the League's purpose, on the contrary, was the reduction of armaments. Churchill, normally a persistent critic of the government, turned now upon Labour's criticism; if implemented, Labour's recommendations would cause Britain to disarm her friends, forgo her allies, affront powerful nations, and neglect her own defences. He failed to shake the party's convictions, for in the words of Sir Stafford Cripps, 'We deny, as we have always denied, that the strong man armed is most likely to create peace in the world . . . '[92] That Labour in 1934 should reject the concept of the 'strong man armed' was inevitable in view of the complex of events which had shaped and formed the party.

Labour's advocacy of collective security had been called into question at the Hastings Conference by a resolution pledging Labour to resist war. Had the leadership since worked to clear up this ambiguity? The trade union leaders had opposed such a pledge in 1932 but had shelved the matter in 1933 by agreeing to take it under advisement. Ernest Bevin personally had no illusions about the possibilities of an international general strike against war:

Who and what is there to strike? Trade unionism has been destroyed in Italy and Germany; practically speaking, it does not exist in France; it is extremely weak in the USA ... while there is no possibility of a general strike against the Russian government in the event of war. What is left? Great Britain, Sweden, Denmark and Holland; virtually, these are the only countries in which any strong trade union organisations exist. Ought we, in the light of these facts, to go on talking glibly, misleading the people and ourselves as to what we could do with the general strike weapon in the event of a world war?[93]

Bevin thus calculated that Labour's alleged supreme weapon had little if any cutting edge. Hugh Dalton had had second thoughts about the brashness of that resolution as well.[94] The three executives of the Labour movement nonetheless agreed on 28 February to appoint a joint committee to consider the means so far proposed to stop the outbreak of war and to canvass the possibility of organizing mass resistance.

The draft report of that committee was almost certainly influenced by the collapse of yet another European workers' movement. In February 1934 the Austrian Government of Dollfuss, which had the previous year proscribed both Communists and Nazis, dissolved all other political parties save Dollfuss' own. When the Socialists replied with a general strike proclamation, Dollfuss promptly arrested their leaders; full scale civil war soon broke out. The Socialists, who were well armed, barricaded themselves in some of the great municipal housing projects which were the pride of socialist Vienna; Dollfuss decided upon howitzer bombardment in preference to the use of infantry, in order to spare lives, we are told.[95] Loss of life was, however, considerable, and the uneven struggle quickly ended with the flight of those Socialists who had escaped arrest. The failure of the Viennese resistance confronted Labour's leaders with the realities of working-class opposition to forceful governmental actions.

February 1934 made an even deeper impression on Bevin than Hitler's rise to power the year before. The Austrian working-class organisations had long held a leading position in the international Socialist and trade-union movement; moreover, the Austrian workers had fought, the Germans had not. But it was the cumulative effect that counted. This was the second working class movement to be suppressed by a dictatorship within a year.[96]

Though one wonders whether the importance of the Austrian movement was exaggerated after their rout, or whether Bevin had simply neglected to mention them in his remarks of the previous autumn on strong trade union movements, their resistance assumed symbolic importance in Labour's eyes. The usually taciturn editors of *Labour Magazine* were moved to comment: 'The Austrian workers have shown that the Socialist faith is worth dying for. If they can die for it, we can live for it and if need be, and the hour comes, follow their supreme example.'[97]

Bravery, however, had not prevailed in the Austrian case; the joint committee asked to draft Labour's report on 'War and Peace' had accepted an awesome responsibility. This document, running to more than three thousand words, was meant in their view to close a gap left by the Hastings resolution, which the Labour leadership contended had been exclusively concerned with propaganda against, and resistance to, war. What was now needed, the three Executives maintained, was the incorporation of that aspect of policy into Labour's positive proposals for preventing war by organizing peace. Consequently the drafting committee left no doubt that Labour's international policy remained grounded securely upon the collective peace system found in the League of Nations. The League system could, however, be improved; for instance, its effectiveness could be improved by abolishing national armed forces and substituting in their place an international police force. In these matters the committee's proposals were not innovatory.

What was original with 'War and Peace' was the formal reconciliation of war resistance with the collective system, which the committee accomplished by limiting the application of such resistance. They recommended this 'Peace Act' to all countries, in order to create a 'World Peace Loyalty', with three duties devolving upon all peoples:

(a) *Arbitration-Insistence* – the duty to insist that our Government settle all its disputes by peaceful means and eschew force.

(b) *Sanctions-Assistance* – the duty unflinchingly to support our Government in all the risks and consequences of fulfilling its duty to take part in collective action against a peace-breaker.

74

(c) *War-Resistance* – the refusal to accept our Government's unsupported claim to be using force in self-defence; insistence on submitting their claim to the test of international judgment, or of willingness to arbitrate; refusal to support or serve our Government if it were condemned as an aggressor by the League or designated itself as an aggressor by becoming involved in War after refusing arbitration.[98]

War resistance thus became operative only under certain conditions. A pacifist loose-end from Hastings was tied into Labour's concept of collective security; indeed it was now meant to ensure that collective security would operate. The authors of 'War and Peace' deflated the importance of war resistance in recognizing that ' . . . there might be circumstances under which the Government of Great Britain might have to use its military and naval forces in support of the League in restraining an aggressor nation which declined to submit to the authority of the League and which flagrantly used military measures in defiance of its pledged word'. The Hastings equivocation was at an end.

Along with Labour's reduction of the importance of war resistance went the recognition of the weakness of the international general strike weapon. Probably the abject failure of the Austrian masses to rally to the signal given by the Socialist leaders for the general strike against Dollfuss' Government[99] was not lost upon the drafting committee, for, in language reminiscent of Bevin's remarks, 'War and Peace' maintained that a general strike could not possibly prove efficacious in those countries from which aggression might come. Even the idea of a British general strike was considered unfair: 'The responsibility for stopping war ought not to be placed upon the Trade Union Movement alone. Every citizen who wants peace and every other section of the Labour Movement must share the responsibility of any organised action that might be taken to prevent War.'

At this time, Labour's commitment to a League-based policy was strengthened by the admission of the Soviet Union in September 1934; the party had long held that Russian presence in the League would increase the likelihood of the League's success. The National Council of Labour, as Labour's advisory body was now known, had urged the British government in May 1934 to facilitate Russia's entry; in reply the government commented that Russia only need apply to the League, for they would welcome such an application.[100] The Soviet Union, recently faced with the threat of war from an expansionist Japan and from the rise of Hitler in Germany, now undertook to make that application. Communist Russia was taken into the comity of nations.

6

Labour's annual Conference met at Southport on 1 October 1934; the major document considered was the result of nearly three years' labour by the Policy Committee of the NEC. This report co-ordinated various reports made to Conference since 1932 with newer policy statements; taken together, they surveyed the full range of Labour's policy, foreign and domestic. Those sections dealing with the former had much in common with the 'War and Peace' report. *For Socialism and Peace* reflected the traditional socialist belief that 'to have peace we must build a new type of civilisation'.[101] This reference was clearly to peace in the long-range sense, which would always be threatened so long as un-bridled economic competition existed. In the short run, before that new society was forged, the authors of *For Socialism and Peace* recognized that the system of collective security was essential to the preservation of the peace.

At the Weymouth TUC, held a month earlier, a delegate had challenged the validity of this reliance upon collective security in the transition stage to socialism:

As long as the economic well-being of nations is held to depend on finding suitable markets, manufacturers will have access to those markets, and, as the habits of Japan have made manifest, if they cannot obtain them by peace, they will obtain them by war. In international finance, capitalists know no sentiment. Rent, interest, and profit are the only things that matter.[102]

The Labour left's ideological challenge to the peace-keeping apparatus supported by the leadership is here evident; the union leaders in response raised considerations of reality, as phrased by Clynes: 'I suggest to you as sensible, common-sense business men that we have to deal with the world as it is. We cannot wait for the remodelling of the whole social structure. We must envisage the probabilities of action in such a world as we have got.' With the pragmatism of Labour's policy established, Walter Citrine delineated its implication:

Do you think Japan is going to be restrained by a resolution of the League of Nations? Do you think that economic sanctions would be sufficient to restrain Japan? . . . You come, by the sheer logic of the case, to the only way in which you can resist an aggressor determined to take no notice of your resolution and moral influence. You can only restrain him by force.[103]

Though Citrine recognized that the left generally ' . . . were irritated at the reluctance of the trade union leaders to respond to their flights of idealism in a world of stern realities',[104] he nonetheless spoke out clearly, in language stronger than anything Labour had hitherto used, about the real possibility of a League war within the existing capitalist system. The events of recent years – surely Citrine had more than Japan on his mind – had forced the union leaders to advocate a policy which was anathema to the Labour left.

At Southport, Arthur Henderson presented 'War and Peace' to the Conference, in an explanatory rather than argumentative fashion. From the first he insisted that 'the Executive is not putting forward a new policy . . . We are restating Labour's aims and Labour's policies, and indicating the method by which we hope that policy may be applied.' In such a vein he maintained ' . . . we have not abandoned the idea of the general strike, nor have we in any way repudiated the Hastings resolution. We have a war resistance policy that is consistent with the whole of our foreign policy.' Yet left criticism was not damped, for a delegate cited the wording of the Hastings resolution, 'Conference instructs the National Executive to pledge itself to take part in no war . . .'[105] Since 'War and Peace' contained no such pledge, the party leadership had compromised Conference's renunciation of war. Henderson's attempt to obviate conflict was misleading, as More's criticism had made clear: he could not disguise the fact that war resistance was no longer an absolute tenet, not even in theory. Labour's leaders were rather more comfortable. Hugh Dalton reflected subsequently upon the healthy change: 'We had moved a long way in twelve months, partly because we had another twelve months in which to observe Nazi Germany; still more, I think, because Soviet Russia had joined the League of Nations and so made this body respectable to many of its previous critics.'[106]

Those critics were not, however, as quiescent as Dalton's account suggests, as Arthur Henderson learned in attempting to use Russia's entry to gain Conference-wide support for a League-based policy:

> The next Labour Government will not only need to survive, but to succeed and to work for peace – as the Soviet Government has decided to do – in a world inhabited mostly by capitalist and partly by violently nationalist governments . . . The only hope for world peace lies not in paying lip service to the League of Nations, but in making it stronger and truly world-wide.[107]

Despite Henderson's reference to Russia's action, the Socialist League took a diametrically opposed position, arguing that that body, which reflected the economic conflicts of the capitalist system, ' . . . cannot end war. To rely blindly upon it is to endanger peace.'[108] Though the Socialist League did not seek British withdrawal from the League – Geneva remained a convenient meeting place and platform for socialist views – they advocated a collective system only among peace-loving nations. A socialist Britain could then use force to defend the new international social order, but for no other purpose. Collective security under the present League was specifically ruled out, ' . . . for under the Capitalist system it is impossible to allocate the blame for war . . .' The *Manchester Guardian* properly pointed out the extreme position taken by the Socialist League: 'It is prepared . . . to turn the Labour movement into a party of dogma, which must be fulfilled down to the last detail or not at all. It sets up its own variety of Socialism as an exclusive faith.'[109] While their extreme position was an outgrowth of the League of Nations' failure in the Far East, so too was the Executive's relegation of the left-backed idea of war resistance to a secondary role a reaction to external developments. The pressure of world events was forcing apart left and right in the Labour Party.

The leadership was, however, not spoiling for a fight over foreign policy in 1934; they did not respond in a hostile fashion to the left's criticism.[110] Perhaps because of this leniency, 673,000 votes were cast in opposition to the 'War and Peace' resolution;

1,519,000 accepted the Executive's policy. Dalton regarded this as a great triumph for Henderson but recorded ominously:

... Lansbury, though Leader of the Parliamentary Party, didn't speak at all at the Conference[111] and was sore at not being asked. He was asked to speak on Peace, but refused. He is always slipping back into his old non-resistance attitude. If we won a majority at the next election, we should be in an awful mess![112]

Though now in the ascendancy at Conference, the Executive had yet to confront the challenge of the Leader of the party with regard to foreign policy. Events were to force open that breach by the next gathering in Conference.

'War and Peace', as approved by the delegates, marks a significant change in Labour's approach to the methods by which a socialist foreign policy might be implemented. A young socialist, R. H. S. Crossman, wrote that the party had at last admitted that the world was a jungle and that ' . . . while the world remained of this sort, a Socialist Government would be constrained to react as beseems any rational creature who finds himself alone in the jungle. His first job is to defend himself.' Disarmament to him was no longer a serious proposal; if a British socialist government were to play a part in the reconstruction of Europe or the world, they would have to possess the military and moral force which Crossman considered the only weapon of foreign policy. How then could socialist conduct of foreign policy differ from the much-criticized Tory policy? 'What marks it off from the other party programmes is its notion of *what* the nation's interests are, not of *how* we are to achieve them. It is by its ends, not by its means, that Socialism is to be known.'[113] Though the adoption of 'War and Peace' took Labour some distance towards recognition of military force as the agent of foreign policy, the Parliamentary Labour Party continued to protest against rearmament as dangerous and unnecessary; means as well as ends were questioned at Westminster. Labour had come a 'long way' since 1933; it had yet some distance to go.

The Socialist League challenged the domestic policy laid down by the Executive in *For Socialism and Peace* as well; they doubted that the transition to socialism could be brought to pass by traditional practices of parliamentary government. The

79

Executive had maintained to the contrary that they did not expect that emergency powers would be required: 'It [the Labour Party] sees no reason why a people who, first in the world, achieved through Parliamentary institutions their political and religious freedoms should not, by the same means, achieve their economic emancipation.'[114] Cripps and the Socialist League found in such reasoning the likelihood that Labour's leaders were prepared to modify the party's programme in the direction of gradualism in order to win support from non-socialist progressives and radicals. The left wing consequently insisted on specifying certain basic steps which any Labour government would take to accomplish economic change.[115] The embers of the 'great betrayal' of 1931 were stirred in this clash between the Socialist League and the Executive. Despite their efforts, the left's domestic proposals were rejected, in a far more overwhelming fashion than its foreign policy had been received: only 206,000 supported their idea of 'Labour's Aims', while 2,146,000 opposed. The only triumph which the Socialist League could claim was the election of Stafford Cripps to the National Executive. Yet the voting for the division which returned Cripps was subject to trade union predominance; we may safely assume that his 'victory' represented an attempt to saddle Cripps with responsibility.[116] The Labour Party had, however, tried such a manœuvre at least once before, and failed – with an outspoken critic named Oswald Mosley.

Labour's domestic course for the balance of the decade was largely set by *For Socialism and Peace*; after 1934 we need pay less attention to such matters. This attention has, however, so far been justified by the light shed upon the nature of the breach between the majority of the Labour Party and their persistent critics to the left. That breach, stemming from the events of 1931 and rooted deeply in the more distant past, and exacerbated by the various front appeals, was to divide the party throughout the decade. The issue of the united front, solicited again in February 1934 by the ILP and the CPGB, was raised at Southport, but the NEC had not even to intervene to secure a huge majority in favour of their refusal to join. More heatedly disputed was the Executive's decision to place an organization known as 'The Relief Committee for the Victims of German and Austrian Fascism' on Labour's proscribed list of Communist auxiliaries. This action was galling to the left wing, a number of whom supported its work; indeed, its chairman, Lord Marley, at the same time was Labour Whip in the House of Lords. Marley, ably supported by Harold Laski, maintained that the Committee was pursuing the non-political objective of aiding the distressed, under the direction of a majority who were members of the Labour Party. Herbert Morrison, speaking for the NEC, insisted that any such co-operation with the Communists, for whatever purpose, harmed the Labour Party: ' . . . we cannot choose between loyalty to the decisions of Conference . . . and flirtations with people who are enemies of our Party, who wish to do our Party the maximum amount of damage, and who are not friends, and who cause us a great deal of trouble.'[117]

The conflict here raised by divergent views of loyalty and conscience was not a new one. Nor was the left's dissatisfaction with the Executive's efforts; Aneurin Bevan argued at Southport that much of the work undertaken by proscribed organizations ' . . . would never have been necessary were it not for the inertia, lack of enterprise, and insipidity of the Executive between Conferences . . . ' Ernest Bevin strongly countered, criticizing those politicians and intelligentsia who derided the concept of loyalty to party decisions, despite the fact that recent German history demonstrated the need for such loyalty. 'A previous speaker', he acidly noted, 'said that the Communist Party was an insignificant Party. It would not have been if you gentlemen [the left] had had your way; we would have been split like Germany was split; we would have been rent if we had not kept down this intrigue. And if you do not keep down the Communists, you cannot keep down the Fascists.'[118] Bevin and the Labour leadership evidently feared a pro-fascist reaction to any extension of the power or influence of the Communist Party, which of course was another reason for opposing the front proposals.

How real, in Labour's view, was the threat of fascism in Great Britain? That the Labour Executive was deeply concerned is evident in the amount of material on fascism which the Labour Party published in 1934 – a report, two pamphlets and four leaflets. Most important was the report, 'Fascism at Home and Abroad', which first surveyed the German and Italian models, which had lowered standards of living and committed base brutalities. It then assessed the only attempt to import fascism to

Great Britain which had met with any measure of success – Mosley's British Union of Fascists.

> The main object of the BUF is to transform Britain into a so-called corporate State . . . It is quite clearly the BUF's intention to establish a dictatorship. . . . If the Fascists had their way there would be in Great Britain the same brutality and violence, the same suppressions of Trade Unionism and the Socialist Movement, the same denial of free speech and free religion, the same resort to the bullying methods of dictatorship, that have signalised the triumph of Fascism abroad.

Though this report placed BUF membership at no more than 20,000, its authors were disconcerted with Lord Rothermere's announcement early in 1934 that he supported Mosley's activities and was opening his newspaper chain to fascist propaganda. The Labour leadership decided at that time to embark upon a nation-wide campaign, involving meetings and demonstrations as well as the distribution of literature '. . . exposing the hollowness of the Fascist claims and opening the eyes of the electors to the disastrous results to the working class of Fascism in other countries'.[119]

The leadership was subsequently much troubled by what they considered police indifference to the brutality associated with Fascist meetings. The climax had come at a Fascist mass meeting held at Olympia on 7 June 1934, which the Communists had threatened to break up. Fascist stewards resorted to strong-arm tactics to counter any heckling within the hall, while the police busied themselves only with arresting Communist and other anti-Fascist demonstrators outside Olympia.[120] The House of Commons discussed, at times rancorously, the Olympia violence and British Fascism for seven hours on 14 June. The National Council of Labour remained dissatisfied with the government's attitude; a Labour deputation was later sent to the Home Secretary '. . . to impress upon the Government the extreme danger of allowing the militarisation of politics to become an accomplished fact'.[121] In time the National Government responded with an 'Incitement to Disaffection Bill' which strengthened provisions against the possession and propagation of seditious materials. Since the party was still disturbed by police behaviour, the PLP protested against that Bill's extension of police powers of search and confiscation and secured some limitations.[122] Probably the most important result of the Olympia incident was the general revulsion, typified by Rothermere's withdrawal of support, felt with the methods employed by the Fascists. This revulsion was certainly strengthened by Hitler's famed 'Blood Purge' which came at the end of the month.

The Labour leadership strove to keep the British Fascist threat in proper perspective. Citrine told the Weymouth TUC in September of the need for circumspection: 'On the one side, if we give too much publicity, we shall exaggerate its importance and perhaps help the movement in some measure. On the other, if we underestimate or ignore it, we are running a very considerable risk.' He also sagely reminded Congress that the Labour movement must recognize the need to combat fascism on two fronts, international as well as domestic; in the modern age, the outposts too must be watched.[123] Both that TUC and the Southport Conference supported the leadership in condemning the spread of fascism abroad and in deploring the insidious moves to further its growth at home. The left was in complete agreement on this issue; Cripps took the events of 1934 to show that Britain could slide into its own form of tryanny, a 'county gentleman's Fascism',[124] if great vigilance were not exercised.

The Southport Conference of the Labour Party has served to focus the various reactions to a deteriorating international situation. The Executive there gained approval for a peace policy which they considered a realistic response to the spread of fascism; the leadership had in the process established an ascendancy, lacking at Hastings and Leicester, over the rank and file. Left dissent was plain, though the pacifist dissenters had remained silent. Labour's peace policy, based on the League of Nations, had been formulated only on paper; collective security in Europe was as yet untested. The year 1935 would see posed the acid test, both of that system and of the determination of the Labour Party to support collective security in practice as well as theory.

4 Challenges external and internal

The foreign policy of an opposition party is necessarily influenced by actual international developments, as well as by that party's own precepts. Those external forces which helped to shape Labour's policy from 1931 to 1934 can be treated separately, but as the calendar turns to 1935 such a separation proves less meaningful: a complex of interrelated events replaces the Far Eastern crisis, or the rise of Hitler, or the destruction of Austrian socialism in the determination of Labour's policy. Thus to assess the nature of the party's policy in 1935 we must survey the decisive events of that year. Only in the light of the course of international developments and of the actions of the British government can one realistically appraise Labour's international policy.

In July 1934 Mussolini had been angered and mortified by the attempted *putsch* of the Austrian Nazis, in which Chancellor Dollfuss was murdered. Despite immediate official disclaimers, there is no doubt that the *putsch* had been prepared with Hitler's foreknowledge and consent, though it is likely that he had been misled as to the extent of support by the Austrian conspirators.[1] Hitler had not yet mastered the art of internal subversion, for he had permitted the Nazis to act when Madame Dollfuss and her family were visiting Mussolini, who had recently strengthened the ties between the two countries. Indeed the Italian dictator conveyed the news of the assassination to Dollfuss' wife; at the same time, he ordered Italian divisions to the Brenner and sent the Austrian government a pledge of support in the defence of Austrian frontiers against 'those involved from afar'.[2] The immediate effect of these events, aside from Hitler's speedy disengagement, was a measure of reconciliation between France and

Italy, for the latter now seemed committed to the anti-German camp; under Mussolini's direction the Italian press unleashed a strong attack upon the German role. During 1934 the French Foreign Minister, Barthou, attempted to strengthen French ties with eastern European countries; he was an advocate of an 'Eastern Locarno', including Russia, to restrict German ambitions there as well as in the west. His successor, Pierre Laval, was however less concerned with eastern Europe and system building in general; rather he preferred a series of straight bargains between one nation and another for mutual assistance, in order that one defection would not collapse the whole. He conceived of Italy as the pivot and so undertook to shore up Franco-Italian relations at a time when Mussolini had just taken the initial military stages of his aggression in Abyssinia.[3]

By his own subsequent admission, Mussolini had interested himself in the Abyssinian 'problem' since 1925, though he did not begin to pave the way for military operations until 1932. The immediate circumstances of the first important clash, at Wal Wal on 5 December 1934, are not nearly so important as Mussolini's intentions to use that incident as a justification of his military build-up in Italian Eritrea: '. . . during the first five months of 1935 it became clear to the world that Mussolini was making preparations for an important military enterprise in Abyssinia.'[4] He rebuffed Abyssinian offers of mediation of the Wal Wal dispute, which Haile Selassie's government took to the League of Nations in January 1935. Just at this time M. Laval paid a call on Mussolini in the interests of Franco-Italian rapprochement. Three days of negotiation culminated in an agreement on a number of outstanding questions, apparently rather more favourable to France. Yet Mussolini had secured a secret verbal agreement from Laval that gave Italy a free hand in Ethiopia, despite Laval's subsequent assurance to the French Senate that 'nothing in the Rome Agreements tampers with the sovereignty, independence, and territorial integrity of Ethiopia'.[5] That Laval went so far as to commit France to support of an Italian war is doubtful; probably that support related only to economic questions.[6] Eden's judgment indicates what Laval could offer Mussolini: 'The truth of what was said will never be known. My own opinion, having heard and read their explanations, is that Laval was sufficiently equivocal to give Mussolini the chance to exploit

85

his attitude. Certainly the Duce got the worst of the bargain, on paper, and the best in license.'[7]

For the public record, Mussolini agreed to arbitrate the Abyssinian dispute, but Italy deadlocked those negotiations almost immediately. The League of Nations, hopeful of settlement between the two parties, did not take up the matter again until 31 July. Meanwhile, Laval had followed up his trip to Rome with one to London, early in February. From this consultation emerged an offer to Germany to couple her adherence to an 'Eastern Locarno' with an 'air Locarno' in which the signatories would pledge their air forces to the support of any signatory who had been the victim of unprovoked aggression. Implicit in the latter proposal was the official acknowledgment of the air force prohibited to Germany by the Treaty of Versailles; at this time the French also agreed that that document's armaments clauses should eventually disappear. Eden considered this a significant diplomatic step forward: 'All this would have been unexceptionable as policy, if it had been accompanied by the vigorous expansion of the one argument Hitler understood, military preparedness.'[8] Eden was distressed that the French effort was insufficient and that the British was only '. . . getting under way in a laboured fashion and under shrill opposition criticism'. Consequently he welcomed the issuance of the British government's White Paper on Defence on 4 March, a nine-page document of great import.[9]

Over the initials of Prime Minister MacDonald, the pacifist foe of World War I, the White Paper explicitly drew attention to German rearmament, which could lead to a situation '. . . where peace will be in peril'. The British government concluded that 'an additional expenditure on the armaments of the three Defence Services can, therefore, no longer be safely postponed'. The White Paper had immediate diplomatic repercussions: German Foreign Minister Neurath cited the '. . . resentment caused by the tactless British White Paper . . .' as the reason for the postponement of the visit which Simon and Eden were to make to Berlin to discuss the Anglo-French proposals.[10] The British government were informed that the postponement stemmed from Hitler's indisposition, but they soon saw that he was well enough to repudiate openly, for the first time, a provision of the Treaty of Versailles. Seeing that the British and French governments were evidently prepared to admit technically illegal measures of German rearmament (e.g. the 'air Locarno' proposal), Hitler announced, on 9 March, that a German Air Force indeed existed. He subsequently announced that Germany intended to reintroduce conscription and to build an army of thirty-six divisions (550,000 men), using as a pretext recent French military decisions. The British government protested this breach of Versailles but undercut the effect of that protest by agreeing to discuss the Anglo-French proposals later in the month, as had been arranged when Hitler's 'cold' had improved.[11] Eden and Simon undertook that trip to Berlin, though the former considered that Britain ought to have expressed its disapproval by postponing their visit.[12]

The British government chose a positive means of protest by participating in a display of unity at the Stresa Conference, where on 11 April they joined with the French and Italian governments in condemning Germany's recent actions, reaffirming Locarno and declaring the necessity for maintaining Austrian independence. The German Chargé d'Affaires in Great Britain warned that '. . . the achievement of a surprisingly close understanding between the three Powers . . .' posed danger signals for Germany, since a system which appeared, at least in spirit, like the pre-war Entente could well be evolving.[13] Since the sole concern of the Stresa powers was Germany,[14] Mussolini's actions on the borders of Abyssinia went unmentioned: Vansittart had urged MacDonald and Simon to warn the Duce that he would hardly strengthen peace by thirsting after sand and fame in Africa, but they chose not to broach the topic.[15] Perhaps they reasoned that if the Abyssinian problem were not raised, the passage of time would resolve the conflict, without breaching the unity of the Stresa powers. Mussolini, who was prepared to discuss his African designs, was surprised by the Anglo-French failure to raise the matter. The consequence was disastrous: '. . . Mussolini left Stresa with the clear conviction that Britain, who was fully aware of his military preparations, attached little importance to Abyssinia. Now that Laval had signified the acquiescence of France, the way was clear.'[16]

Yet curiously enough, it was not Mussolini's lust which first undercut the solidarity of the Stresa front, but rather the calculated British decision to conclude a bilateral naval pact with

87

Germany, in contravention of a provision of the Treaty of Versailles. That agreement had been discussed as early as 25–26 March, when Simon and Hitler assented to holding discussions concerning a possible naval pact in London; even at that time, the idea of a 100:35 ratio was advanced by the German Chancellor.[17] Hitler strengthened his commitment to that figure in one of his periodically temperate – and tempting – speeches, on 21 May, in which he promised to fulfil all obligations arising from the Locarno Treaty and to limit German rearmament, though he did claim air parity. Anglo-German negotiations were opened on 4 June, and two weeks later the agreement was signed. The terms stipulated a ratio between British and German naval tonnage of 100:35, except in the case of submarines, where German tonnage could equal that possessed by the entire British Commonwealth.[18] Germany had already announced to the British government the construction of a number of submarines in violation of the Versailles Treaty; Britain preferred to maintain her naval supremacy by agreed limitations on the size and number of ships constructed rather than by costly rearmament.[19] Given the fact of German naval rearmament, the British government's rationale was expressed incisively by Anthony Eden as circumscribing a unilateral decision.[20] The positive decision of the Cabinet was conveyed to the German delegation on 6 June, though the British intended to solicit the 'observations' of the other maritime powers before signing a formal agreement. When questioned by Ribbentrop whether other powers '. . . were still to have a say in the matter', Simon replied that '. . . the British government's decision was final and they merely wished to inform the other Powers that the British government "had decided" to accept the German Reich Chancellor's proposal'.[21] Though the British documents containing those 'observations' are not yet available, the American government left the decision entirely to Britain, the Japanese had no objections, the Italians avoided a direct answer, and the French failed to reply officially, though they were known to dislike any such bilateral agreement with Germany.[22]

Though these answers were considered academic by the British, the fact that they were at least solicited makes implausible Eden's memoir account of the effect of the signature of the agreement: 'Paris and Rome were inevitably offended and indignant when it was known that the Agreement had been

signed without any consultation with them.'[23] Rather, the grava-
men of the criticism of the action of the British government is
contained in a German Navy critique of the political meaning
of the treaty:

> As a result of the Agreement the most powerful of our former enemies
> and of the signatories of the Versailles Treaty has formally invalidated
> an important part of this Treaty and formally recognized Germany's
> equality of rights. The danger of Germany's being isolated, which defi-
> nitely threatened in March and April of this year, has been eliminated
> . . . The front recently formed against us by the Stresa Powers has been
> considerably weakened by the Agreement.[24]

Mussolini had joined that front because of the threat to Austria;
in so doing he ran a risk acceptable only if the western powers
hung together. 'Now it seemed that Britain had left the Western
bloc in order to make a selfish deal to her own advantage.'[25] His
vacillating policy veered back toward the German pole. Eden,
who defended the pact at the time, now argues that it was not so
much the terms which roused French opinion as the manner in
which the treaty was made, with Britain acting in isolation.[26] Not
only had a provision of Versailles been infringed, but the Anglo-
French understanding of 3 February 1935 that the various parts
of the security and armaments problem were to be treated as an
indivisible whole had been ignored. British ineptness culminated
in the signature of the Naval Treaty in London on 18 June,
anniversary of Waterloo.

Military arguments favouring such a limitation of German
naval rearmament were advanced, but Churchill has swept these
aside in one sentence: 'What had in fact been done was to
authorise Germany to build to her utmost capacity for five or six
years to come.'[27] Though that contention is borne out by the
German Navy belief that 'any substantially larger figure than
that permitted by the Agreement could hardly be reached in the
next decade',[28] more important to our purpose is Churchill's
assertion that the pact dealt another severe blow to the League of
Nations, that body upon which Labour had based its foreign
policy. Weakened or not, the League finally began to pay serious
attention to the Abyssinian crisis in August; Mussolini's hostile
intentions were then quite evident, as in his summary rejection of
Anglo-French compromise proposals. Faced with this threat to

D

peace, Sir Samuel Hoare, Simon's successor, informed the League of Nations on 11 September of Britain's intentions. With the sole proviso that risks for peace were to be run by all, he declared:

In conformity with its precise and explicit obligations the League stands, and my country stands with it, for the collective maintenance of the Covenant in its entirety, and particularly for steady and collective resistance to all acts of unprovoked aggression. The attitude of the British nation in the last few weeks has clearly demonstrated the fact that this is no variable and unreliable sentiment, but a principle of international conduct to which they and their Government hold with firm, enduring and universal persistence.[29]

Hoare's reference is of course to the Peace Ballot, which he then evidently regarded not as a pacifist credo but as an indication of vast popular support for collective security. In retrospect he regards his speech as an attempt to instil life into the moribund League. 'At best,' he comments, 'it might start a new chapter of League recovery, at worst, it might deter Mussolini by a display of League fervour.'

His speech elicited a fervid response, both in Britain and abroad, though only Simon among his colleagues congratulated him.[30] The response of the *Spectator* pointed out the alternatives posed by Hoare's speech: if Mussolini persisted in his Abyssinian adventure, the choice was one of war or the abandonment of the collective system 'whose vindication even by the ordeal of war would substitute the rule of law for the rule of force in the world'.[31] Thus the League of Nations had in effect called Mussolini to order when the Labour Party gathered at Brighton in early October, there to settle some internal difficulties posed by Britain's pro-League stand. Before we turn to that assembly, we must take careful note of Labour's reaction to these events. What had the party offered by way of criticism of the British government's foreign policy, or on behalf of its own?

2

In a report prepared for the party Conference, Labour's National Executive criticized governmental policies which had '... allowed Hitler and Mussolini to assume the initiative in European politics and to compel Great Britain to treat with them not on the basis of collective security, but on the basis of unlimited national sovereignty'.[32] The NEC regarded the Anglo-French proposals of February 1935 as an unfortunate step in that direction, because of the emphasis on regional pacts, which Labour generally opposed unless they were definitely part of the League system. Subsequent events had however rendered useless all aspects of those proposals save that of an air pact, which the Executive regarded as a costly method to achieve pooled insecurity. Agreeing with a memorandum prepared by the ACIQ,[33] they recommended a solution of the air threat through disarmament of the national air forces, the internationalization of civil aviation and the establishment of an international air police force; thus the arms race might be checked.

After this excursion into the clouds, the NEC returned to hard, if barren, earth in the form of the Abyssinian question. They deprecated what they considered British government pressure upon Abyssinia to negotiate with Italy, while noting that apparently neither the British nor the French government had informed Mussolini that his military expedition was a 'strange commentary' upon the Stresa resolutions. The complaint was just, but had Labour throughout urged a resolute course upon the government? As early as March 1935 the ACIQ had stated flatly: 'There has never been any dispute between two Powers in which the fundamental principles of the Covenant were so clearly at stake: and there has never been any case in which those principles have been so plainly and deliberately set aside.'[34] They saw clearly that Italy was aiming at the annexation of a strip of Abyssinian territory at the least, and possibly at a war for total conquest. If in face of this threat the Manchurian mistake were repeated, the League of Nations would be dealt a severe blow: 'It will be impossible to maintain the thesis that there is any longer an International Law against aggressive war; and without such International Law we can have small hope of creating a stable League . . .' The ACIQ recommended strong British support of Abyssinia's case at Geneva, but no discernible action by the Executive followed the forwarding of the Advisory Committee's views.

As Sir John Simon has indicated in defence of the government's policy, no one in the Commons raised the question of Abyssinia in the course of a major debate on foreign policy in

early May;[35] the problem had not yet assumed major proportions. Shortly thereafter questions bearing on the dispute were
raised,[36] and on 7 June Attlee provoked the first substantial
discussion. He expressed Labour's concern that Italy had not
yet renounced any use of force in the quarrel, the handling of
which he considered a test of the League and the sanctity of its
Covenant. Britain had every opportunity of acting effectively at
Suez, and he warned against the dangers of failing to act. In
reply, Eden reminded Attlee that under British law a man was
innocent until proved guilty; no such verdict had yet been
returned against Mussolini.[37] To those who remembered
Simon's legalistic defence of Japan such an argument must have
provided cold comfort. In July the PLP returned to the Abyssinian
dispute. Attlee argued:

> We are out to make the League of Nations a reality. This Government
> has reduced it to a farce . . . what has disturbed me during recent years
> is that in all these discussions about the position of Abyssinia and so
> forth what has appeared to concern us most has been, not so much what
> is right, as what will be the effect on something else in connection with
> foreign affairs. Can we afford to break with this Imperialist Power
> [Italy]?[38]

Attlee here put his finger upon the dilemma which the Government faced, the problem of restraining Mussolini without driving
him into league with Hitler. Labour's solution was to look first
to restraining Mussolini, thereby re-establishing the rule of law,
which in turn could check Hitler. Attlee took care to stress that
Labour's restraint would be exercised through the League, not
unilaterally. The Labour Party here advocated virtually the same
approach which Hoare took in his speech to the League two
months later.

In the interim, Labour held firm to that course, though the
ACIQ recognized that such a policy was open to misrepresentation: 'the die-hards in all countries are certain to denounce with
great vigour the bloody-minded pacifists who desire to make war
to stop war.'[39] They were however prepared to pay this 'small
price' for the re-establishment of world law. The National
Council of Labour next spoke out on the dispute late in July,
asking the British government to declare that they would discharge their duties and obligations as a member of the League

without fear or favour. Fascist Italy would thus be made to realize that it stood in danger of confronting the obloquy and resistance of the world.[40]

Yet the British Labour Party could not long speak with but one voice in forcing this realization upon Mussolini. Its leader was out of sympathy with the policy of the party, though he had striven in his parliamentary duties to mask his personal feelings, for the most part successfully. However, just before Parliament adjourned for the summer, Lansbury asserted that Labour stood by the League of Nations in the Abyssinian dispute, though he added that he would not himself send the British Fleet to inter- vene. Such a reservation on the part of the 'shadow Prime Minister' made rather a shambles of collective security. Lansbury chose instead to emphasize another Labour concept:

Why cannot the British Government, taking the British people into their confidence, go to a disarmament conference and put our whole on the altar of international service, and go to a world economic conference and say, 'We are the greatest Imperial nation in the world, we built up the biggest Empire in the world; we are willing, for the sake of peace and security, to put it all at the service of mankind.'[41]

Though this may have represented an ideal Labour solution to the world's problems, provided other nations acted in a like manner, it was hardly a policy appropriate in the context of the Abyssinian dispute.

Shortly thereafter, the Labour Executive fractured: Stafford Cripps broke with the majority and resigned in September, the experiment of burdening him with responsibility a failure. Cripps did not follow Lansbury into a profession of absolute pacifism; instead, his dissent was rooted in the philosophy of the Socialist League, which had grown increasingly suspicious of the League of Nations. As Cripps explained his resignation to his father, Lord Parmoor: '. . . it has become more and more obvious every year that the League is being run by France and England for purely imperialist purposes, and I think the people must be made to face up to this or else we shall be led under the banner of the League to another imperialist war.' Unless the workers held power war could serve only imperialist purposes; therefore, he wrote in the *Sunday Referee* of 15 September, 'we cannot support wars – whatever excuses may be made for them – the objective of which is to perpetuate the system we not only dislike but which we believe to be the fundamental cause of war'.[42] This theoretical argument was bolstered by the Labour left's belief that no capitalist government of Baldwin and Chamberlain could be entrusted with the workers' allegiance in making or threatening war.[43] Also the frequently-heard taunt that Labour's foreign and defence policies were contradictory may have caused the left to fear that if collective security were now enforced, the government's rearmament programme could not then be denied. In any event, their fear of capitalism and imperialism caused the left to reject collective security under the League; they refused, in effect, to distinguish among various forms of capitalist governments, even between those who claimed to uphold the rule of law and those who openly resorted to the use of force. The pity is that in December 1935 they were proved prophets in their own time.

For their part, the trade union leaders had no great illusions about the League of Nations; generally their support for that body ran along pragmatic lines, namely that the League with all its imperfections remained a preferable alternative to balance of power diplomacy.[44] As for Britain's obligation to support the Covenant, Bevin held a domestic parallel binding: 'It is like a man entering a Union. You cannot enter with reservations. You have got to be straight. I cannot help what the National Government is doing.' The resolute temper of the trade unions was reflected in Congress's overwhelming approval of a declaration that 'all the necessary measures provided by the Covenant should be used to prevent Italy's unjust and rapacious attack upon the territory of a fellow member of the League'. Citrine, as usual, carefully spelled out the meaning of the resolution; since Italy was preparing for war, there was but one way to deal with such a bully, through the use of force. The situation was indeed serious, but in such peril Labour dared not flinch:

I overheard a delegate say at the commencement of my speech, 'It means war.' It may mean war, but that is the thing we have to face . . . But I say this. If we fail now, if we go back, war is absolutely certain. I ask you what will happen to Germany if Italy can break through her treaties, if Italy can treat with contempt the nations of the world who have plighted their word to preserve peace?[45]

Just as the Labour left's suspicions were confirmed in December 1935, so did Hitler answer Citrine's question in March 1936 –

and for three agonizing years after – and all because the British Government refused to be as resolute on behalf of the League and collective security as Labour demanded. The nation may well have been at one with Labour in this policy; Alan Bullock has suggested that the vast trade union majority for such a course was '. . . the reflection of a much larger body of opinion in the country as a whole which was more strongly in favour of resisting aggression than at any time again until after the occupation of Prague'.[46] Sir Samuel Hoare was not unaware of this body of opinion when, a week after the Margate TUC, he declared for that very policy which Labour had advocated.

Though government and opposition consequently stood in agreement after 11 September in this major matter, they disagreed on the defence policy necessary to effect collective security. The Labour Party was consistently attacked for its linkage of collective security to disarmament; Winston Churchill exposed this flaw in Labour's approach, while crediting the party with effective criticism of Nazi Germany:

> We read almost every day – certainly every week – in their [Labour] great popular newspapers the most searching and severe criticism of the existing German régime . . . Things are said that are capable of raising the deepest antagonism . . . in the breasts of those powerful men who control the people. How can honourable members opposite reconcile that with the other parts of their policy, which is to cover with contumely and mockery and odium every attempt to secure a modest and reasonable defence to maintain the safety of the country?[47]

The reply of the Labour spokesman, Morgan Jones, was couched in traditional terms: the party conceived of armaments in the collective sense; simply to compare national armaments was no contribution to peace. The path to peace lay in '. . . push[ing] ahead as vigorously as we can with the policy of disarmament in the world'.[48] Prior to the posing of the Italian threat, Labour viewed national arms as a one-way avenue to war. Predictably the PLP bitterly assailed the White Paper on Defence, which ironically found their old leader now advocating rearmament across the floor of the House. Labour argued that such rearmament '. . . gravely jeopardises the prospect of any Disarmament Convention, and, so far from ensuring national safety, will lead to international competition and the insecurity thereby engendered,

95

and will ultimately lead to war'.[49] Attlee castigated the attempt to prevent war by rearmament as not unlike casting out Satan by Beelzebub. Labour, he commented, refused to revert to the 'pre-war atmosphere' of the White Paper. The elder Conservative statesman Austen Chamberlain, however, warned Labour of one of the possible consequences of the failure to maintain a national strength comparable to possible dangers: '. . . if . . . [Attlee] and his friends be sitting on the Government bench when London is bombed, do you think he will hold the language he held to-day? . . . If he does, he will be one of the first victims of the war, for he will be strung up by an angry, and justifiably angry, populace to the nearest lamp-post.'[50]

In following weeks, Labour tenaciously opposed what they considered the excessive sums asked for the fighting services. The party which shortly was to speak of blockading the Suez Canal proclaimed, with reference to the naval estimates, that 'arms have never yet saved a nation from war nor have they given security to either strong or weak nations against attack'.[51] Frustration no less than partisan politics may well have been responsible for the epithet used against the Labour Party, 'mouth fighters' or 'tongue heroes'.[52] Despite such taunts, Labour remained so deeply committed to disarmament that a majority of the PLP, upon the publication of the White Paper, had urged Arthur Henderson to resign in protest as President of the Disarmament Conference. Henderson was angered at this attempt to dictate to him, and he refused to resign on such political grounds.[53] The announcement of German rearmament served only to convince Labour of the correctness of its belief that Britain would have to work harder to cast out war by way of peace.[54] No protest was lodged against the Simon–Eden visit to Berlin. The Stresa front provoked only Labour's warning that the government should not revert to the path of power politics, for at its end lay only war.[55] Baldwin's confession to the Commons that he had been wrong – and Churchill correct – in his projection of the strength of the German *Luftwaffe* failed to shake the PLP. Attlee was more concerned with Hitler's recent moderate speeches, which might mean a chance to halt the armaments race; Britain's answer should not be rearmament.[56]

Nonetheless the open rearmament of Germany provoked some in

the Labour Party to reconsider their defence policy. Bevin recognized the force of the left's argument that to vote for increased expenditures meant trusting the National Government to use those forces to uphold the authority of the League; but hc was concerned, as they were not, that opposition entailed also the risk of reducing the League of Nations to impotence, for lack of sufficient force to make its authority effective.[57] Citrine too saw that 'the league had no forces of its own and it was patent . . . that it must rely on those of its member states who were ready and capable of shouldering the major responsibility of defending the collective security we talked so much about'.[58] The first substantial questioning of Labour's defence policy took place in trade union circles: the *Morning Post*, admittedly no friend to Labour, reported that in a meeting of the movement's three executives (the NEC, the General Council of the TUC and the PLP Executive) scheduled for 21 May 'a determined attempt will be made by the Trades Union Congress to secure the acquiescence of the Socialist Party in the programme of Royal Air Force expansion'. That paper reported on the next day that the meeting had been adjourned, though a final decision was expected that day: 'It is thought to be likely that the views of those who desire to support the Government . . . will prevail. Indeed, it is already evident that the Pacifists, if any remain, will not dare to register a vote against the Government on this subject; it will be a case either of abstaining or of voting with the Government.'[59] The *Morning Post* was as outraged as *The Times* to learn of Labour's decision to divide against the expansion; the parliamentary correspondent of the latter reported that Hitler's conciliatory speech of 21 May had made the difference. 'It was argued', he wrote, 'that the speech ought to be accepted by the British Government as a starting point for resumed negotiations and for a fresh effort by the Disarmament Conference.'[60] The validity of that argument was accepted by the British government as well; the Anglo-German Naval Pact followed in short order.

Possibly then Hitler's skilled intervention – though its purpose lay elsewhere – kept Labour from accepting a measure of rearmament in 1935. Instead the party denounced the results of the British government's negotiations with Hitler: Labour regarded the naval agreement as yet another retrograde step towards the pre-war foreign policy of alliances and armaments. Attlee,

D*

ignoring the fact that Germany had at long last gained equality of status, for which Labour had long campaigned, commented ironically that Hoare '. . . welcomed it as a great step towards disarmament – the re-armament of Germany as a great step towards disarmament'.[61] In May 1935 Labour had come very near supporting the government's defence policy; in September the government, after tortuous sorties into alliance, actually enunciated the League of Nations-based foreign policy advocated by Labour. Mussolini might then have confronted a Britain united in support of the theory and practice of collective security; the British government might not then have faltered in December. Yet such speculation is idle, for Labour in fact resisted rearmament and the government did not long back the League. The party's decision maintained the consistency of its attitude towards the components of collective security.

3

Despite superficial consistency, dissent from Labour's policy of collective security was present among the Labour leadership well into September 1935. When the TUC met at Margate on 2–6 September, Cripps and Lansbury yet remained in positions of responsibility. Indeed Citrine took care to associate Lansbury with Labour's foreign policy by stating that to vote against that policy '. . . will mean turning down our leader, George Lansbury'.[62] Dalton's account corroborates Citrine's association of Lansbury with the collectivists. Immediately prior to Congress, the three executives of the Labour movement had met to formulate an official statement of support for collective security. Cripps made clear his opposition to sanctions, in what Dalton regarded as an effort '. . . not to persuade but only for the record'. In addition the three Labour Lords present – Ponsonby, Marley and Sanderson – made known their opposition, but that was all; implicitly then, Lansbury agreed.[63] Citrine's forceful remarks at Margate signalled an end to Labour's vague conception of the meaning of collective security, which had so far encompassed pacifist elements as well as sanctionists.

Mussolini had not meanwhile been deterred from his designs on Abyssinia; on 18 September he rejected another suggested compromise. Increasingly confronted with the prospects of enforcement of collective security, the pacifists at this time openly indicated their refusal to go along. In mid-September both the Leader of the Labour Party and the Chairman of the Labour Lords (thus the parliamentary leaders in both houses) criticized that policy so recently agreed upon and so soon to be presented to the party Conference. Ponsonby shortly resigned his leadership, and Cripps his membership in the National Executive. Recognizing an internal crisis, Dalton returned from holiday and went immediately to Transport House, where Lansbury's position was being discussed:

He wouldn't resign on his own initiative, and was asking us to settle the question for him. But every day he was rushing about the country speaking against the Party's international policy. We decided, however, to leave it to him and to the Parliamentary Labour Party. We did not, as a National Executive, think it was any part of our duty to push him out of the Parliamentary Leadership at this stage.[64]

What had provoked Lansbury into this apparent reversal of position? Possibly Ponsonby's decision to resign, rather than subordinate his opinion to a policy with which he basically disagreed, had been decisive. 'I have increasingly maintained', Ponsonby wrote in informing Lansbury of his decision, 'that peace can never be secured by force of arms, and no single event during the last 30 years has contributed to make me alter this conviction by a hair's breadth. On the contrary, I have been strongly confirmed in this view.'[65] Lansbury, he knew, held the same views, but Ponsonby maintained that his decision should not reflect upon Lansbury's continued leadership: rather lamely he argued that Lansbury did not often speak on foreign affairs in the Commons, whereas he spoke regularly in the other House. Ponsonby may well have hoped to bring about Lansbury's resignation by his own example.[66] Cripps' concurrent resignation did not much matter, for his cause was not Lansbury's own. Cripps stressed that he was quitting the Executive rather than embarrass his colleagues.[67] Whether or not he resigned, Cripps' socialist pacifist views were bound to embarrass a party anxious to maintain a united position, in face of war – and, one should add, in face of an impending general election. Also that resignation, superimposed on Ponsonby's, made Lansbury's position

99

more difficult, since he had recently made clear his own opposition to sanctions.[68]

Lansbury compounded that difficulty with his comments upon these resignations: admitting that he could not accept the doctrine of war in any form, he commented that 'if his colleagues thought later on that he ought not to be the leader, he did not believe they would think him unworthy to remain a member of the Labour Party'.[69] He missed the point that his membership was not at issue; what mattered was his leadership in a moment of crisis, and therein he was at odds with his party. His opposition to sanctions exposed him, unlike those who had resigned, to angry charges of inconsistency, for he had accepted that policy just three weeks earlier, according to Dalton's account.

Lansbury's son-in-law and biographer, Raymond Postgate, maintains on the contrary that the leader had been consistent throughout September; he was in fact a victim of misrepresentations by trade union leaders, particularly Citrine. In the first place, Lansbury resisted going to Margate as the Labour Party's fraternal delegate, but he was urged to attend, as, in view of the rumours of disunity in the party, his absence might seem intentional. Consequently he attended, to hear Citrine urge the delegates not to let George Lansbury down by voting against the Executive's declaration:

> This he thought was intolerable; the Congress leaders knew what his views were, and his name should not have been used; when he had to make his delegate's speech he would have to say he would not have supported the resolution. Sir Walter, hearing this, was alarmed; he discussed the problem with his colleagues, and brought back the reply that Lansbury's only right to speak rose from his being the Labour Party's fraternal delegate, he must only deliver the Party's message.[70]

Citrine's recently published account agrees that such a message was indeed given Lansbury, though he alters the details considerably: Lansbury sought him out on the morning when the declaration was to be debated and confessed that he could not reconcile his personal position with his duties as a representative of the Labour Party; Citrine first reasoned with him, and then applied the pressure described above.[71] If Citrine's first-hand account is accurate, his subsequent use of Lansbury's name was bound to be considered a misrepresentation by Lansbury; further, the trade union leaders refused him the right to correct that statement. No wonder then that he took to the countryside to state his deep convictions: the floor of the Congress was denied him and Parliament was in recess. His resignation could of course have clarified the matter, and Lansbury canvassed that possibility at the time of the Congress; all but three of the colleagues whom he consulted advised against it. In his fraternal address he managed to denounce war without repudiating Citrine, but he made his own views clear to a joint meeting of the Labour executives: '. . . he told both them and the Labour (parliamentary) candidates what his real views were, and how deeply he felt them in his conscience. He was assured again that his position was understood, and that his work as leader was indispensable.'[72]

Ernest Bevin's angered reaction[73] to the news that Lansbury had made public his disagreement with the party's policy in the Sunday press of 22 September thus cannot be explained in terms of his surprise; it stemmed from his belief in absolute loyalty to majority decisions. The resignations of Ponsonby and Cripps were vitiating enough, but the public criticisms of the leader, who had voted for sanctions at the meeting of 3 September – a vote which Bevin swore to[74] – were even more damaging. Bevin thought that Lansbury's action could only give the impression of a divided leadership unfit to bear the responsibility of government. Further, he regarded it as a betrayal of the party:

> To accept a decision and then, when the moment to implement it came, to back down and claim conscientious scruples as Lansbury had done really was to Bevin as much a betrayal as that of a man who having accepted a strike decision blacklegs on his comrades when the moment for action comes. By the standards of his tough logic, which left him little sympathy for the moral dilemmas which beset men more complicated than he, Lansbury and Cripps should have resigned a year earlier or not at all.[75]

The application of such loyalties can indeed be dangerous, but so too can loyalty to humanitarian aspirations prove disastrous in an imperfect world. Lansbury and his fellow pacifists either did not recognize or care that the New Jerusalem would not be built in England if Mussolini or Hitler were permitted to turn other parts of the world into fascist infernos. Such conflagrations are no less contagious than arms races.

The lines were drawn as the party assembled at Brighton;

indeed the decision was not in doubt, for the massive trade union vote had already been recorded. The resolute position of the industrial wing was welcomed by some members of the political wing as well, such as Dalton, who held that 'to argue that, in the sorry pass to which we had now come, because we had a damned bad British Government therefore the British nation should not be better armed, was piffle – the arms, one hoped, would outlast the Government. And it was damned bad politics as well.'[76] Though the Parliamentary Labour Party had opted for 'piffle' they were deeply committed to sanctions – and to politics as well. If the impression of a party too divided to govern were to be eradicated before the General Election, a strong majority for the collective system and sanctions must emerge at Brighton. In addition, pacifism would have to be utterly discredited. There were those within the party who were willing to do no less.

4

The Labour Party gathered at Brighton on 30 September 1935, with its attention fixed upon the Italo-Abyssinian dispute and on the division within its leadership brought about by the prospect of war. Regrettably absent from those counsels was the major architect of Labour's policy of collective security, Arthur Henderson; ill and exhausted, he had journeyed down to Brighton, only to suffer a relapse which forced his return to a London nursing home, where he died on 20 October. After the crushing defeat of 1931, Henderson concentrated his attentions upon disarmament – the British Ambassador to Washington, Lindsay, had remarked not unjustly that Henderson had 'a simple mind but when he took hold of an idea he hung to it with great determination'[77] – gradually relinquishing his influential positions within the party. Despite his return to Parliament at the Clay Cross by-election of 1 September 1933, Henderson there played no significant role; the work of his last years must be judged in connection with his efforts at Geneva and on the basis of the international policy of the Labour Party, which he had played such a major role in forging. At Brighton the party passed judgment upon that system's viability in the moment of crisis; Henderson's efforts in this cause were not lost.

On 1 October, Dalton initiated what the Conference's Chairman considered '. . . possibly the biggest discussion, and one of the vastest importance, that the Conference had ever to deal with'. He moved a resolution which condemned Mussolini's defiant attitude towards the League and proclaimed Labour's readiness, in co-operation with other nations, to use all measures provided under the Covenant to restrain Italy and uphold the League's authority. Dalton expressed the hope that the threat of sanctions might suffice to prevent war or, lacking that, that the use of economic and financial sanctions might re-establish peace. If Mussolini were however to resist the League with force, Labour would proceed to war; Dalton indicated no great concern in the outcome of such a contest, because of British control of the Suez Canal, which he characterized as 'a narrow ditch in the Egyptian sands, which it used to be said any two men unseen could block in more ways than one with the greatest ease . . .' The question thus was simple and straightforward: 'Do we stand firm, or shall we run away? . . . Who is for running away? We shall count them at the end of this Debate.' He made clear that the Labour Executive was not contemplating a truce with the British government because of the latter's 'death-bed repentance'. Labour's choice had nothing to do with that government; rather it concerned the League and the collective system. In such a vein he concluded with a question – and all too near a prophecy:

Are we going to play the part of a great comrade among nations, or are we going to slink impotently into the shadows; impotent by our own choice; unfaithful to our solemn pledges; not a comrade but a Judas among the nations; deservedly left, as we should be, without a friend in the world; preparing, through our own dishonour, our own sure downfall at no distant date?[78]

The left however refused to accept Dalton's interpretation of Labour's 'choice'; Cripps considered that the central factor was not so much what Britain as a country should, or should not, do, but rather who was in control of those actions. Consequently, he refused to entrust the present government with the lives of British workers; he would, however, support sanctions if foreign policy were controlled by those workers, as then there would be no risk of the pursuit of capitalist and imperialist aims, nor use of the League of Nations as a cloak for imperialist bargaining and wrangling. Recalling his own advocacy of League sanctions in the Far Eastern dispute, Cripps admitted his personal inconsistency but shrewdly based this upon the League's own degeneration into 'the tool of the satiated imperialist powers'. Indeed it was the actions of the capitalists in the Sino-Japanese dispute which proved 'the hollowness of their present profession'.[79]

What then could Labour do? Did Cripps develop any practical solution to the immediate problem facing the party? He did propose a two-part solution: the first precept, working-class war resistance, had already been relegated by the 1934 Conference to a minor role in policy; the second part, overthrow of the National Government, was Labour's aim in the forthcoming election. Neither offered an immediately practical solution to the problem of Italian aggression; the left recommended a policy of impotence. Cripps' reversal cannot however be regarded simply as ' . . . a classic example of believing that a policy must be wrong when supported by one's normal opponents',[80] because he objected not to Conservative support for collective security *per se* but to the Conservative use of collective security as 'a way of defending the old imperialists against the dangers of their newer rivals'.[81] Such an argument recalls the warning of the ACIQ in 1933 that Labour support of the League should not be unconditional: the party, they had written, must not support the League ' . . . if it is used by our Government as an instrument of imperialist, anti-democratic, or anti-socialist policy . . . It is not beyond the bounds of possibility that when the time comes, the League itself may be used as a camouflage and the people of this country be deluded once more to fight a war which is going to end war'.[82] Cripps and his colleagues saw just this coming to pass in 1935.

William Mellor of the Socialist League sought consequently to divert Conference's attention from Abyssinia to the realities of the struggle in Britain: 'There are times when negative action is positive action. There are times when it is well to remember that the positive action of fighting your enemy at home is greater in value than the negative disaster of defending your home enemy abroad. Our enemy is here.'[83] Mellor failed to consider the consequence of such a position, the abandonment of the other, weaker, nations of the world to fascist aggression, until such time as the British working-class had turned out its masters. The Socialist

League's foreign policy may have evolved consistently since 1932, but theirs was a consistency at the price of an abject isolationism, a denial of the international struggle of the socialist movement. Their policy too might have made a prophet of Dalton.

The pacifist case, in its several aspects, was put by the two parliamentary leaders whose convictions had undermined the party's unity. Lord Ponsonby, long an advocate of disarmament by example, based his pacifism not on religious tenets or morality, but rather on what he held a 'common sense' approach to the efficacy of sanctions:

By our action to-day we are going to urge the Government... to undertake sanctions which, through not being watertight, through having a bad leakage in several countries, will aggravate the situation and make it worse than it is at present. No one detests Fascism and Nazi-ism more than I do, but I do not want, with the lessons of the past, to forget that by force you strengthen these movements, and you do not crush them.[84]

Even granting to Ponsonby the point that League sanctions could divide Europe into two hostile camps, one must set against this danger that resulting from the failure of the League to deal with aggression against a member. The British government's action was to expose Europe to both dangers, we might add, but that development lay hidden in the future when Ponsonby addressed the conference; for their purposes his speech offered no real solution to the problem of aggression either.

Later that day George Lansbury developed yet another facet of dissent from the Executive's policy; his approach did offer a real alternative, relentless in its pacifist logic, overwhelming in its potential consequences. The revered leader received a tumultuous reception; the entire Conference, with the exception of two 'glowering' trade union delegations, rose and sang 'For he's a jolly good fellow'.[85] Though appreciative, Lansbury quickly noted his trying position, for he found it very difficult to repudiate a fundamental piece of Labour policy; he would certainly not do so if he were in any doubt, but never had he been more convinced that he was right, and the movement wrong. Lansbury too admitted to inconsistency, which however had been forced upon him, as he had believed one thing while stating quite another for the party; his paralleling of that dual role to Dr Jekyll and Mr Hyde was somewhat unflattering to the Labour

Party, whether or not intended by Lansbury. Throughout his philosophy had not changed a whit: 'I believe that force never has and never will bring permanent peace and permanent good-will in the world . . . I have no right to preach pacifism to starving people in this country and preach something else in relation to people elsewhere.' All mankind was one to this Christian pacifist who relied on the Bible for his course: 'I cannot believe that the Christ whom you worship, or the saints whose memory you all adore, that for any reason or cause, they would be pouring bombs and poison gas on women and children for any reason whatsoever. Not even in retaliation, because also it is written, "Vengeance is mine, I will repay".' Lansbury recognized that such an attitude made his position as leader untenable, but cries of 'No' welled up from the floor; he reiterated that he would gladly go for his beliefs and movingly concluded: 'If mine was the only voice in this Conference, I would say in the name of the faith I hold, the belief I have that God intended us to live peaceably and quietly with one another, if some people do not allow us to do so, I am ready to stand as the early Christians did, and say, "This is our faith, this is where we stand, and, if necessary, this is where we will die".'[86] The faith which Lansbury had accepted seven decades earlier sustained a genuine alternative to the confronta-tion of aggression: passive resistance to force, moral behaviour in the face of immoral. Who knows how many lives might have been spared by this solution? Saved, yes, but for what? For the concentration camps and crematoria of the Third Reich? For the greater glory of Fuehrer and Duce? For the propagation of evil in the world? Lansbury indeed gave Labour an alternative, and Conference fortunately rejected it.

Yet the strength of Lansbury's appeal must be recognized, for his audience was deeply stirred with emotion – emotion which endangered the Executive's rational position. Where Cripps' arguments rested on interpretation, Lansbury's appeal to idealism was much more difficult to combat. Ernest Bevin, long troubled by Lansbury's 'idealism', accepted the challenge. As he slowly made his way to the platform, amid what the *New Statesman* described as 'a singularly apposite hailstorm which beat a tattoo on the Dome',[87] the delegates resumed their seats, after a stand-ing tribute to their leader, departing with courage and honour.[88] Courage also was needed to resist the sentiment to which

Lansbury had appealed; 'the obvious course was to pay a personal tribute to Lansbury and then, leaving his declaration on one side, to turn the debate back to the argument in favour of sanctions',[89] but Bevin was in no mood to be diplomatic or to conceal his feelings. He went straight to what he considered the main issue:

Let me remind the delegates that, when George Lansbury says what he has said to-day in the Conference, it is rather late to say it, and I hope this Conference will not be influenced either by sentiment or personal attachment. I hope that you will carry no resolution of any emergency character telling a man with a conscience like Lansbury what he ought to do. If he finds that he ought to take a certain course, then his conscience should direct him as to the course he ought to take. It is placing the Executive and the Movement in an absolutely wrong position to be taking[90] your conscience round from body to body asking to be told what you ought to do with it . . . I have had to sit in Conference with the Leader and come to decisions, and I feel we have been betrayed.[91]

These blunt remarks brought shouts of protest from the floor, but Bevin was not to be deflected. Instead of withdrawing his assertion, as demanded by some, Bevin proved how Lansbury had time and again been a party to Labour's policy, including the declaration issued at Margate. The leader should have stuck by that decision, because if Labour were to win the country, Bevin argued, '. . . when it is faced with a crisis it has got to give confidence that it is capable of coming to a decision'. Cripps too undermined such confidence, and Bevin was in no mood to spare him or his middle-class friends. 'The middle classes are not doing too badly as a whole under capitalism and fascism. Lawyers and members of other professions have not done too badly. The thing that is being wiped out is the Trade Union Movement.' Such a generalization was unfair to Stafford Cripps, who gave to charity a major portion of his retainers and earnings and whose family lived a rather simple life;[92] it serves best to indicate the depth of Bevin's anger. He was, though, on firmer grounds in arguing that those who now opposed Labour's policy were a year late in coming forward, for they should have asked for Britain's withdrawal from the League of Nations in 1934 in order to make clear their opposition to sanctions.

After a brief rebuttal of Ponsonby's case as well, Bevin had discredited the three specific dissents individually; in concluding he treated Lansbury, Ponsonby and Cripps together, conjuring up the spectre of 1931 for good measure: 'I feel that we have been let down . . . The great crime of Ramsay MacDonald was that he never called in his Party, and the crime of these people is that they have gone out, they have sown discord at the very moment when candidates want unity to face an election.' Bevin's speech was regarded as brutally strong; the sympathetic correspondent of the *News Chronicle* referred to a ' . . . virulence distasteful to many of the delegates'.[93] The epitome of Bevin's rancour came in a remark, when told by friends that he had been unduly harsh toward the idealistic Lansbury: 'Lansbury has been going around dressed in saint's clothes for years waiting for martyrdom. I set fire to the faggots.'[94] Though Lansbury's biographer fastens upon this remark *inter alia* to contend that Bevin had acted in 'a calculated bad temper . . . calculated because the jovial jests with which he commented on his success afterwards seemed to rule out a deep anger',[95] Bevin's biographers convincingly demonstrate that his anger was too white-hot to be a ploy.[96] That anger can be explained by Bevin's intense belief in loyalty and his sense of outrage at such black-legging.

Though the anger seems genuine, calculation entered as well, because Bevin aimed at the discrediting as well as the defeat of the pacifists. To accomplish the former, he had to confront the party, in the words of a perceptive member, with 'the choice between the satisfaction of one's personal conscience and one's duty as a citizen'. Mary Agnes Hamilton recalled her own reaction:

. . . as I came away from the Conference session with George Ridley, I found that he shared my sense of deep relief and agreed that E.B. had pulled the Party out of a sentimental morass into which it had been in real danger of sinking. He compelled a naturally sentimental body to see an issue in larger than personal terms. He had to attack Lansbury to make the issue clear. But it was not the personal attack, but the sense he conveyed of the responsibility of the issue itself that gave force to his speech and carried the conference.[97]

If that was indeed Bevin's purpose, he succeeded overwhelmingly. Lansbury immediately moved to the microphone to protest that he had not been present when *For Socialism and Peace* had been drafted and that he had made known his objections at Margate – only to find that power had been turned off. Less docile than at the TUC meeting, Lansbury threatened to shout loud enough for all to hear, unless power were restored. His anger was compounded by the refusal of anyone on that very Executive which had repeatedly refused to accept his resignation to acknowledge that he had offered it. At the conclusion of his remarks only Herbert Morrison moved to comfort him in what Lansbury considered his hour of denial.[98]

The debate was not concluded until the following morning, when better than ninety-five per cent of Conference supported the resolution which Dalton had moved. The objections of Lansbury, Ponsonby and Cripps, taken together in effect, were sustained by only 102,000. The Labour Party had spoken out unequivocally for collective security under the League of Nations; what had been theory in 1934 was now a recommended practice. That practice faced reality within twenty-four hours, when Italian legions attacked Abyssinia. The National Council of Labour announced to the Conference on 4 October that they had asked for an immediate summoning of Parliament to hear of government proposals in the face of actual aggression.[99]

The debate on 'Italy and Abyssinia', the lengthiest yet in Conference annals, dominated the Brighton assembly almost to the exclusion of all other foreign policy questions; only on one occasion, and then briefly, was Nazi Germany considered. In defence matters, the Executive prevailed against an attempt to put Conference on record in opposition to government proposals for civilian air raid practices, which the mover considered futile and an attempt to arouse public feeling in favour of rearmament.[100] Herbert Morrison replied; the Leader of the London County Council viewed the question pragmatically, holding that if drill would save the life of one child, he would agree to it. Realism did prevail in the counsels of Labour in 1935, but to maintain that the party emerged from its 'great debate' with its 'unity unimpaired'[101] is simply mistaken. One should not equate the size of the majority with unity, for the proportions of their defeat was not likely to convince Labour's left that their views were incorrect. Michael Foot however goes too far in the opposite direction in characterizing as a 'fairy tale' the orthodox view that at Brighton 'Bevin's hammer started to knock the nonsense out of the thick heads of the rank-and-file' and that thereafter he and Dalton were able to open the eyes of the movement to the reality of the fascist peril. 'Brighton, we are often told, marked the water-shed between Labour's post-1931 indulgence in pacifist and emotional extremism and the preparation for the responsibility of 1940. No such glimmering of enlightenment was apparent at the time.'[102]

In the first place, we have seen the eyes of the Labour movement opening to the peril of fascism in 1933; before Brighton, the executives had worked out a theory of resistance to fascist aggression which the Conference in 1934 approved by a considerable majority, and whose application to the situation of 1935 was approved by an even larger majority. Though we can here only anticipate what follows Brighton, Bevin's frontal assault on the pacifists was of great significance; the Christian pacifists were not again to confound Labour policy. We might note that there was even a time when Michael Foot subscribed to a water-shed view of Brighton: along with his *Evening Standard* colleagues Frank Owen and Peter Howard, he wrote in the famous polemic *Guilty Men* that 'henceforth the Labour Party was officially pledged to armaments every whit as much as the Government'.[103] That statement was of course unfounded, because the PLP continued to vote against the Service Estimates until July 1937. Foot now holds the slightly more tenable position that Brighton was drained of any significance because Cripps, Bevan and the Socialist League were two months later proved 'correct' in their prophecy that an imperialist deal would be struck with Mussolini; a revival of the argument for a united front grew out of the left's justified hostility to the National Government. Thus for the Labour left Brighton was no turning point; even in October few had taken it that way. The Tory-oriented *Observer* pointed out that the 102,000-vote minority included the official Labour organization in a hundred constituencies, and its correspondent warned: 'It must not be imagined therefore that the fight is ended. On the contrary, it has only begun.'[104] Foot's judgment, valid for the left, nonetheless exaggerates their importance in the Brighton proceedings; only the events of December put the bite into their arguments.

What Ernest Bevin's hammering had accomplished was in fact the exorcizing of purely pacifist doctrines from official Labour leadership as well as from policy, for the balance of the decade. Since that force had been so strong, the 1935 Conference was indeed a water-shed. Though the stream of Labour policy encountered diversions and rough passages in the years ahead, the decision made at Brighton to apply the theoretical concept of collective security to the realities of the post-1933 era was never overturned in the rapids. The longest debate in Labour Party history had not been conducted in vain.

5

Since their leader was so obviously at odds with policy, the Labour Party had to seek a new one, from the ranks of the PLP, to lead them into the forthcoming election. Those outside that small group regarded this choice as provisional, until such time as the ex-ministers were restored to Parliament. Dalton and Morrison consulted concerning the future leadership; the former had decided not to stand for the leadership, which he thought '... should go to someone, provided he had the necessary qualities, who had not had exceptional opportunities ... a man of working-class origin, who had not been to a public school or university'.[105] Such a formula disqualified Attlee no less than Dalton, of course. Though the two had not been close political allies, Dalton offered his support to Morrison, who was 'a good deal taken aback', but evidently willing. For the moment, however, the decision was out of their hands. On 8 October George Lansbury met the PLP to resign; at first – likely *pro forma* – they refused to accept his resignation, but Lansbury insisted.[106] Since the other Deputy Leader, Cripps, had lately resigned from the Executive, Clement Attlee was an obvious choice. No one then foresaw that Attlee would retain the leadership for two decades, eclipsing even the consecutive endurance record established by Gladstone. In 1935 he was not a well-known figure outside Labour circles.[107] Attlee had confined his activities mainly to Westminster, where he had served as chief spokesman on foreign policy; he had not attached himself to any one cause, in the manner of Lansbury, or to any particular segment of the party, as had Cripps.

On the day before Attlee's selection, the Council of the League of Nations had declared Italy an aggressor in violation of the

Covenant. The Assembly accepted that report on 11 October and established a committee to recommend and co-ordinate sanctions; that group proposed a comprehensive financial sanction, an arms embargo and a limited embargo of certain important commodities – oil was excluded because it was considered not under the control of League members – to operate against Italy. Though some observers were surprised that the League could even set in motion the machinery of sanctions, these measures fell considerably short of the complete and general boycott stipulated by Article 16. Whether the League powers controlled the supply of oil was a meaningless distinction in view of this provision for the immediate severance of all trading and financial relations with the aggressor and also for the prevention of any commercial intercourse between the aggressor and any other state. Such pressures as might lead to war were, however, not applied to Italy.[108]

The British government were anxious to draw the distinction between the League-imposed boycott and war. Hoare informed the House of Commons on 22 October that

... from the beginning of the present deliberations at Geneva until now, there has been no discussion of military sanctions, and no such measures, therefore, have formed any part of our policy ... The action that we have been considering ... is not military but economic ... Nobody in this House can believe that any body in Europe desires a war.[109]

In view of Mussolini's blatant aggression, the last assertion rings rather hollow, but Stanley Baldwin reassured the world of Britain's peaceful intentions in commenting that the government had never had war on their minds: 'I deprecate the use of that word,' added the Prime Minister. Though thus limiting collective security to economic measures, the British government at the same time considered that in the interests of world peace a measure of British rearmament was necessary. Baldwin stressed that unilateral rearmament against a particular country was not involved, but rather '... a strengthening of our defensive services within the framework of the League, for the sake of international peace, not for selfish ends'.[110] Baldwin's refusal to hear mention of war and his profession of the need for strengthening the League militarily '... to meet the risks which are inherent in the situation' appear self-contradictory; Labour did not, however, question the government's approach.

Despite the obvious clue given Labour in Lansbury's welcoming of Hoare's statement[111] – Lansbury was now free to state his personal pacifist beliefs – the PLP did not raise the matter of the possible use of force. Instead George Hicks, the Labour spokesman, endorsed, in effect, the government policy: 'Sanctions should embody law action, and not war action, against Italy. We do not believe that war action against Italy is necessary. International law is so firmly established that if countries are willing to back up the League such law action can be taken.'[112] Obviously law action should come first, but Hicks might have noted the possibility that 'war action' could be involved; his failure to do so represents a retreat from the strong words of Citrine at Margate or Dalton at Brighton. Labour's new leader too was concerned with strengthening the League, but Attlee suggested a rather different approach from Baldwin's. In what could not have been well received by Dalton, Bevin and their like, Attlee maintained that '. . . this occasion should be taken for a great leap forward towards disarmament and not towards increased armaments'.[113] Thus the Labour Party, as represented in Parliament, joined the government in ignoring the possible need for military sanctions. Where the government asked for rearmament on behalf of the League, while refusing to contemplate the use of those arms which they possessed to restrain Mussolini, Labour advocated disarmament as a means of strengthening the League. After the strong stand at Brighton, the PLP position must have disappointed those party members aware that mere resolutions had little effect upon the designs of the dictators.

Meanwhile the British government were apparently committed to a policy of financial and economic sanctions.[114] Simon, shortly before the dissolution of Parliament, assured the Commons that no arrangement with Italy was contemplated: 'We are neither going behind the back of the League, nor have we ever contemplated for one moment doing so . . . we have no intention of wavering in giving effect, as a member of the collective system, to our obligations under the Covenant.'[115] With Great Britain solidly in support of collective security under the League, Stanley Baldwin judged the time ripe for an appeal to the country: the opposition parties would be hard pressed to differentiate their foreign policy from that of the government. The cleverness of Baldwin's timing is obvious, but his foresight in holding the election '. . . in a time of crisis – enough of a crisis to lead people to play for safety . . . yet not a crisis too serious for comfort'[116] can be exaggerated in retrospect. The Parliamentary Labour Party could hardly protest against this opportunity to better their representation too vigorously, although Clement Attlee scorned Baldwin's electoral tactics:

> Where you have politicians who at a moment's notice throw over all their principles and join with the other side thus shaking faith in democracy, and where you have responsible statesmen, instead of giving the country the opportunity of forming a calm judgment on policies, going to the country on stunts of one kind or another, there too you have the destruction of democracy.[117]

Though the timing – traditionally a great advantage to the government, of course – was objectionable, Attlee was clearly most distressed with what he considered Baldwin's appropriation of Labour's foreign policy. The party Attlee now led thus went to the hustings with roughly the same apparent position on the issue of the day as that held by the government; as Mowat so aptly comments, the Conservatives had stolen their clothes, and Labour could only protest that Baldwin would never wear them.[118] Consequently, the party turned its electoral attention elsewhere: fourteen of the sixteen pages of Labour's pamphlet, *The Case against the 'National' Government*, were concerned with domestic matters. Its attack on conditions of unemployment and poverty could not disguise the fact that these conditions had improved since the last Labour government.[119] Nor did inept handling of Labour's national broadcasts aid the electoral campaign: Lansbury's omission emphasized the seriousness of Labour's internal difficulties and deprived the party of a popular and effective speaker,[120] though his inclusion would have been a calculated risk. We should not forget that Attlee was the fourth leader of the party since 1931; a party racked by internal quarrels did not offer the nation a well-known potential Prime Minister, nor even an experienced leader.

Stanley Baldwin, on the other hand, was a widely known and experienced leader of a party which had just resolved its own greatest internal disruption, with the passage of the Government of India Act. An advertising campaign on its behalf had been initiated in the summer, gathering momentum in the autumn with such anti-socialist pamphlets as 'Leaders at Loggerheads', 'Guard Your Savings', 'Your Home to Go: Your Building Society Too!' and, most amazingly, 'The Socialist Policy Means War'[121] Given the historian's advantage of hindsight, one finds it difficult to believe that Labour might have turned out the government.[122] While Baldwin prepared to go to the polls on behalf of collective security, Eden spent a busy month in its advocacy in Geneva; he was however warned in the middle of October by the Foreign Office to go more slowly until Laval's position became clearer.[123] The British refusal to entertain the notion of war was not lost upon the Ethiopian government, which considered that the British attitude was weakening. By 1 November, Eden himself felt that 'any kind of compromise appeared . . . increasingly difficult to reach; it looked like an all-out win for one side or the other'. With so much at stake, Eden grew increasingly frustrated with his own government's unnecessary caution in failing to supply arms to Abyssinia, despite Britain's obligations under the Treaty of 1930. The British government was warned in mid-November that the real danger for Abyssinia lay in her lack of arms and in a potential food shortage, conditions which would go uncorrected under the negative sanctions of Geneva. Eden consequently minuted on 29 November that he thought the Abyssinians had had 'a consistently raw deal from us in the matter of arms'. In general he is critical of the British government's actual foreign policy at the time of the General Election:

. . . our policy was determined by an optimistic belief that Mussolini might still come to terms, by reluctance to do anything which might goad the Duce into some rash act, and by an insufficiently clear view of whose side we were on. In fact, wishful thinking and a desire to appease were already doing their insidious work, with the usual disastrous consequences.[124]

Viewed from within, then, the policy of the British government was less solidly grounded upon the implementation of collective security under the League than their public pronouncements indicate. No matter what contradictions were obvious behind the scenes – a matter which the relevant British documents should clarify – the government campaigned on a policy of collective security, admittedly limited to economic and financial sanctions; on that basis they were returned to office.

The Conservatives could well have drawn a sharp distinction between party platforms had they campaigned more vigorously for rearmament; instead the party, though not all its candidates, kept the issue well out of the limelight. Though urged by Neville Chamberlain to fight the election on defence policy, Baldwin, on the advice of party agents and officials who still lived within the shadow of the Peace Ballot, decided not to unfurl that battle standard.[125] Chamberlain personally stressed the need for measures of rearmament, and he even provided an epigrammatic differentiation between his party's policy and that of Labour: 'Our policy is defence without defiance; their policy is defiance without defence.'[126] Labour could not easily have combated such an assertion, for the party was still riven on the issue of rearmament: the trade union elements anxious for increased defence forces could hardly have enthusiastically advocated Labour's official policy, reflected in the PLP's opposition to the Service Estimates and Attlee's recent appeal for disarmament. Baldwin however chose to cloud over the armaments issue, typified by a chain of Baldwinian *non sequiturs* offered on 31 October:

> You [the Peace Society] need not remind me of the solemn task of the League – to reduce armaments by agreement. But we have gone too far alone and must try to bring others along with us. I give you my word that there will be no great armaments. We are 'bound over to keep the peace', and it may not be an easy task. But we accept it.[127]

There can however be no doubt that Baldwin asked for some measure of rearmament, for his government's record serves as proof. 'Cato's' charge that Baldwin's oft-quoted remark of November 1936 – 'Supposing I had gone to the country and said Germany was rearming, and that we must rearm, does anyone think that this pacific democracy would have rallied to that charge at that moment?' – referred to the 1935 General Election was exposed as a gross fabrication as long ago as 1948.[128] Since the legend persists, even a work concerned with the Labour Party should correct the wrong done to Baldwin. Whether he pressed measures of rearmament sufficiently hard in 1935 is however another question, which Churchill unhesitatingly answers in the negative.[129] Perhaps Baldwin was just too consummate a politician for his country's good in 1935, appealing to all factions with a platform of arms – but not too many.

Labour staged no overpowering comeback at the polls; though the party returned three times more candidates than in 1931, the PLP was barely half as large as that which had formed the minority government of 1929. Among the 154 successful Labour candidates were leaders and debaters who had been sorely missed: Morrison, Dalton, Clynes, Alexander, Shinwell (who had routed Ramsay MacDonald at Seaham), Lees-Smith, Tom Johnston, Pethick-Lawrence, Creech Jones and Chuter Ede head the list.[130] The imbalance of the 1931–5 PLP was also corrected, with the role of the Miner-sponsored MPs decreased in importance. The major result of the General Election was, however, continued Conservative domination, ensured by a majority of 159 over all other parties in the Commons. That majority was never to be overturned in the ten-year course of that 'long Parliament': even in 1940, as German troops swept into the Low Countries, Chamberlain mustered a majority of 80, which fortunately was insufficient for him to continue as Prime Minister.

The results brought disappointment in Labour ranks; especially discouraging was the failure of the younger generation, for the most part contesting the more difficult seats, to break through.[131] Only ten non-trade unionists under the age of forty were successful.[132] In part the younger generation fell victim to the union grip on the safer seats, which meant the placement of a number of superannuated officials who were not much concerned with matters of foreign policy. Yet in general the younger candidates, with all unsuccessful Labour aspirants, fell victim to the balanced appeal of Baldwin's National Government. Churchill maintains that the country paid a terrible price, in the course of the next decade, for Baldwin's triumph.[133] His concern was of course with the failure of the government to campaign for rearmament; the Labour Party can lay no such charge against Baldwin, given its own attitude towards rearmament. It is however possible to flaw the National Government for campaigning on a platform of collective security while seeking a settlement which could vitiate that very system. Did not the government give away the game to Mussolini by openly refusing even to consider the possible use of military sanctions? Here too Labour's posture was not exemplary, but the party had long warned against settlements with dictators which could undercut the collective system. One cannot imagine a Labour government concluding arrangements with Mussolini at the expense both of Abyssinia and the League of Nations; one can, however, see such a settlement prefigured in the diplomatic negotiations of the National Government in October–November 1935.

5   The year of indecision

I

The election of its leader was the first order of business for the new PLP, on 26 November. Hugh Dalton had returned to London ten days earlier to concert plans with Herbert Morrison. The two regarded the latter's chances as 'hopeful'; they recognized his most dangerous rival was Attlee, backed, they judged, by forces of sentiment and inertia.[1] Arthur Greenwood, supported by Ernest Bevin and other trade union elements, also stood for the office. Attlee, evidently heavily supported by those who had sat in the 1931–5 Parliament, led the first ballot with 58 votes; Morrison received 44, and Greenwood 33. On the second ballot, Greenwood's supporters almost to a man turned to Attlee, in a move clearly concerted beforehand; Morrison added only four votes to his poll, and Attlee 30. Dalton attributed Morrison's defeat to a strong and widespread prejudice against him, but also to the feeling that ' . . . if he got the Leadership now, he would keep it, but that, if Attlee got it, there might be a change later'. The latter reason may well be only rationalization on the part of a disappointed partisan; Ernest Bevin had, however, from the first expressed antipathy to Morrison's candidacy, predicting that his victory could well endanger political co-operation between the trade unions and the party.[2] On the other hand, Dalton thought little of Attlee's abilities at the time, commenting in his diary, 'And a little mouse shall lead them!' Subsequently he saw Attlee grow in stature and Morrison little if at all; he was prepared to admit that he had backed the wrong man in 1935. Since Morrison refused the Deputy Leadership, claiming press of business across the Thames, that post went to Greenwood.

Meanwhile the diplomats had continued to search for some manner of resolution of the Italo-Abyssinian war. Eden recounts

119

British willingness to consider the cession of some Abyssinian territory to Italy, but Laval's hopes of offering Mussolini rather more than a third of the country for economic development were quite a different matter. Such proposals clearly would prove unacceptable to the other interested parties, Abyssinia and the League. Eden himself strove to apply an oil sanction against Italy but received little co-operation from his own government and less from the French: 'The handling of the oil sanction was timid and uncertain, while Laval's ingenuity proved more than a match for the British government's tentative methods. As Mussolini saw the danger of an oil sanction approaching, he used every device of propaganda to scare the League and His Majesty's Government.'[3] Laval, who may have been privy to Mussolini's designs,[4] was certainly willing so to be 'scared', and Hoare persisted in the belief that an oil sanction was likely to make the Duce more, rather than less, intransigent. Eden, at Geneva, discounted to his government the possibility of spurring Mussolini into a 'mad-dog act', an assertion later confirmed by the Duce himself.[5] During this period of hesitation by the League powers, Mussolini continued to wage war on Abyssinia, which stood nearly unarmed and quite alone.

Sir Samuel Hoare, the Foreign Secretary, departed for Paris in early December to discuss oil sanctions among other matters with his French counterpart, who had requested such a meeting at quite short notice.[6] He did not set out to discuss possible peace terms; on the contrary he had told the Dominion High Commissioners on 5 December that even the chance of a 'mad-dog act' on Mussolini's part should not deter the members of the League from proceeding with sanctions. Eden records that '. . . the mood was certainly that, having taken our decision to act with the League, we must see the business through. Hoare appeared fully to accept this'.[7]

Such an attitude is also evident in Hoare's portrayal of the government's attitude in the Abyssinian dispute to the Commons on that same day, after Dalton had marked his return to the House by stressing the vital need for an oil sanction. Dalton argued that oil was '. . . the most indispensable of all the modern materials of war' and that the sanction would not be too difficult to apply. He asked the British government initially to stop the export to Italy of the oil which Britain did control and then to strike an agreement with the United States and the Soviet Union as well, because the three powers together could bring over-whelming pressure to bear. Anthony Eden could not but have heard Dalton's conclusion sympathetically:

... it is the duty of the Government and should be easily within their compass, by discussion, with comparatively few powers who are loyal to the object in view, to stop at once and almost completely the supply of oil to the Italian aggressor. If they do not do this they will be responsible for the continuance of war and for a weakening of the collective peace system. On the other hand, if we put the pressure on now, and put it on hard, along the pipe lines of oil, the war will come to an early end.[8]

As for Hoare's imminent trip to Paris, Dalton hoped he would there make clear to Laval the fact that Britain was not interested in any terms of settlement which would allow Mussolini to profit from aggression: 'If the lesson is to be learned that war is wrong and does not pay, there must be no profit for treaty breakers and warmongers, and I trust that in spite of any temptation ... in Paris, he will hold firmly to that view.' If the collective peace system were vindicated, Dalton foresaw the opportunity to take up again the interrupted negotiations for all-round disarmament.

Hoare challenged Labour's proposal of an isolated, unilateral oil sanction as divisive of the collective approach; rather the British government had followed consistently a 'double line' of genuinely collective action under the Covenant and a concurrent search for a peaceful settlement acceptable to the three powers: 'I state these factors once again lest anyone should be so foolish as to harbour suspicions that the French and ourselves are attempting to sidetrack the League and to impose upon the world a settlement that could not be accepted by the three parties to the dispute.'[9] Hoare left no doubt that the settlement should be quickly made, because there existed sufficient difficulties in the world without the added trouble of the Abyssinian dispute. Eden too spoke that day, on a note which sounds hollow since the publication of his memoirs. Though he is now critical of govern-ment policies in the matter, especially in regard to the oil sanction, he then proclaimed to the House of Commons that since he had assumed his office '... there has never been ... the faintest shadow of difference between myself and either ... [Simon] ... or ... [Hoare] ... the more difficult that my situation has

E

been, the more sure have I always been able to be of the most splendid and loyal help of my colleagues at home'.[10]

Under the impression that no peace negotiations were contemplated at Paris, Eden must have seen 'shadows of difference' emerge as Hoare submitted sketchy reports on his week-end dealings with Laval. On Sunday the 8th he learned that the Foreign Secretary had asked for a Cabinet meeting on the following day, but Eden knew next to nothing about the actual arrangements[11] until on Monday morning he read a hand-delivered copy of the peace plan, that document known to history as the Hoare-Laval Pact. Seeing immediately that Ethiopia was asked to surrender about one-half its territory, Eden recognized that the Emperor would not accept such terms, nor could the League. Though he personally felt that Hoare had yielded without playing Britain's strongest cards, he felt, with the Cabinet, confidence in the Foreign Secretary; no one wanted to reject lightly the genuine appeal Hoare had made for acceptance of the terms. Yet not a word of explanation had accompanied the text of the proposals; Eden admits that the Cabinet ought to have summoned Hoare to explain the arrangements, but they were reluctant to question his judgment and anxious not to interrupt the sorely-needed Swiss holiday on which he had embarked from Paris. They took refuge in the hope that the League of Nations might correct the damage obviously done at Paris, for the terms were not to be made public until the League took them up, in three days' time. Eden judged the possibility that the League would amend the terms sufficiently strong '. . . to tempt anxious men'.[12]

Events were, however, fast outpacing the reaction of the British Cabinet, as copies of the document initialled by Hoare and Laval were leaked to the Paris press and prematurely published.[13] What Hoare tersely describes as 'a very awkward political situation' developed in London. The odours emanating from Paris were first noted in the House of Commons at Question Time on 10 December; Baldwin, who according to Eden had no idea that Hoare would sign anything in Paris, lamely replied that any comment would be premature, as the results of the conversations had not yet been submitted to Italy or Abyssinia. Attlee was however quick to retort to this plea for patience: 'We are not in a position to wait, because here, in a crisis like this, is a matter which has been the subject of a General Election, and we understand that proposals, which, in our view, overthrow the whole basis of the League system, are being put forward to settle this question.' Later in the day, Lees-Smith reiterated this argument, adding that if the press reports were even fifty per cent accurate, the National Government had abandoned the foundations upon which they had campaigned and '. . . as a result of which they practically came to an understanding with the British people, and as a consequence of which understanding they sit where they are to-day'. The Prime Minister replied, though under the handicap of 'lips . . . not yet unsealed'; could he but speak freely, Baldwin was certain that not a man would go into the Lobby against the government.[14] The PLP did not accept such a lame retort; from the first they opposed the Hoare-Laval Pact, which they had indeed specifically warned against.

That pact did not long remain a partisan affair, as Eden records: 'The reaction of public opinion was indignant and ashamed. It was said that we should have no part in rewarding aggressors. Many felt the Government had won the election less than a month before on false pretences and Members of Parliament were swamped by a tide of indignant letters.'[15] The British government had given their support, grudgingly it would seem, to Hoare on the night before the proposals were revealed to the press. When Hoare learned of the press leak, he offered to return to London; Baldwin however assured him that he had complete control of the situation.[16] Within a day word from the Foreign Office indicated that the situation had in fact got out of hand, and Hoare resolved to return to face the parliamentary storm. Then, in a tragi-comic upheaval, Hoare 'fell on his nose',[17] breaking it in two places, while skating in Switzerland. His doctor refused to permit his return to England for two or three days, at that very time when the public outcry against the proposals mounted. Hoare was however consoled by the Cabinet's continuing support; Baldwin personally told his Foreign Secretary upon his return to England on 16 December, 'We all stand together.' Neville Chamberlain only the previous day had regarded the clamour for Hoare's resignation as 'of course absurd'.[18] Hoare was still prepared to defend his action by arguing that 'it was for the League to accept or reject a plan that seemed to the French and ourselves to contain the minimum proposals for stopping Mussolini short of the risk of going to war with him'.[19]

Eden had meanwhile left for Geneva on 11 December, where he encountered dismay among the delegates of friendly powers; consequently he worked to extricate Britain from her compromised position, telling the Committee of Eighteen that the proposals were neither definitive nor sacrosanct.[20] Hoare's position was more drastically undercut at home, however: on 16 December Geoffrey Dawson, editor of *The Times* and normally a prop of the Baldwin government, attacked the Hoare-Laval Pact, details of which had been increasingly made known. At least once in the 1930s the 'old thunderer' spoke out against a deal with the dictators; and on this occasion *The Times* spoke for the nation as well.[21] Though Dawson's leader may not have been the precipitating agent in Hoare's subsequent resignation, it at least typified the public reaction which the government could no longer resist. When the Cabinet met on 17 December, Eden, again in London, read to them the draft of a statement prepared the previous day, and shown to Hoare, who was unable to attend. Since this draft sounded the death knell of his peace plan, Hoare was confronted with the alternatives of recantation or resignation; he chose the latter.

Consequently he offered the House of Commons a personal explanation of his action, before the Labour Party moved what amounted to a vote of censure. Hoare's summation of his defence is quite accurate:

The danger of a European conflagration, the need to maintain the Stresa front, the risk to Anglo-French friendship, the critical plight of Abyssinia and the failure of any League State except Great Britain to take military precautions against a mad dog act by Mussolini – these were the points that I tried to bring out. More than once, also, I insisted that my action had never been influenced by any fear or doubt as to our ability to defeat Italy. If there was to be a collective action against Mussolini, we were perfectly ready to take our part, but we did not intend to enter a unilateral war and call it collective action.[22]

He also cautioned the Commons lest Great Britain lead Abyssinia into thinking that the League could do more than in fact it could do, which would lead to Abyssinia's total destruction – a fate worse than that it would have suffered without such British sympathy. Nonetheless Hoare recognized that his resignation was dictated by the evident lack of public confidence. Attlee raised the missing point in Hoare's account, whether the action he had taken squared with the declared policy of the government to support collective security and to make the collective system a success. As for the actual provisions of the pact, embodying a settlement which the government considered just, Attlee was contemptuous:

We say that they misrepresent the people of the country, that to give immense concessions to the wrong-doer at the expense of the victim is not British justice ... that to encourage violence and to allow the aggressor to profit by his wrong-doing destroys the whole foundation of collective security, destroys the League of Nations itself ... And these terms ... are regarded by the people of this country as a betrayal of the electors who were induced to support the Government at the last General Election.[23]

Hoare had argued for the reasonableness of his proposals, but he and the government were liable to such criticism. Though one can see, given the proclaimed British desire to avoid war, Hoare's rationale in concluding the pact, which the German Ambassador in London held did not 'in *principle* ... constitute any reversal of British policy, but ... rather its logical execution',[24] one cannot reconcile that policy with the allegiance paid to the collective system at the election. The German Ambassador saw this contradiction clearly in reporting on 16 December that '... a considerable number of Ministers, and especially Eden ... doubtless take the view that the principles of British policy which have been proclaimed to the country must be honestly upheld'.[25] The Labour Party may well not have known how little the British government had ever inclined towards the implementation of collective security,[26] nor could its leaders have known that Hoare's efforts at conciliation had included discussing terms with Laval which the latter then relayed to Mussolini on the telephone.[27] Such was the actual imbalance of Hoare's 'double policy'. What Labour could see and rightly pointed out was that collective security had not been tried and found wanting; rather it had been abandoned in favour of a deal which rewarded the aggressor. The Leader of the Labour Party was justified in asking an immediate repudiation of those terms to restore Britain's honour among nations.

Stanley Baldwin, whose fabled *rapport* with the British people had for once broken down, had been utterly at a loss with the press ablaze and his postbag bursting full with wrathful letters, until Hoare's proffered resignation had freed him from the spectre of defeat, first in the Commons, then in the country.[28] Now he was free to admit that the provisions of the pact, which the Cabinet had approved out of deference to Hoare, had gone too far; the Foreign Secretary ought to have been summoned back, and Baldwin herein admitted an error in judgment. Noting the country's strong reaction, the Prime Minister assured the Commons that the proposals were obviously dead, absolutely and completely; his government were going to make no attempt to revive them.[29] In view of this assurance, the House of Commons defeated Labour's motion, 297 votes to 165.

Despite its quick death, the Hoare-Laval Pact has found its defenders no less than has the Munich pact. Hoare continued to maintain that the plan was the 'least bad' in the circumstances, offering as it did a good chance – possibly the last – of maintaining the Stresa front against Hitler.[30] Laval too claimed that he had been motivated throughout by a concern for European peace: 'Once Austria fell, Czechoslovakia was bound to go – and, after her, the rest. Only one power could have saved Austria, and that was Italy. But the price was Abyssinia. It was worth paying – a thousand times over.'[31] Vansittart, who had been roped into the Paris discussions while on holiday in Paris, defended the terms on Laval's grounds, commenting that in this inevitable choice between Abyssinia and Austria '. . . option for the more civilised member [of the League] was curiously unpopular.'[32]

The Permanent Under-Secretary of the Foreign Office also raised the question of British military preparedness for possible unilateral conflict with Italy. Such a matter is beyond the scope of our inquiry, but among the responsible naval authorities there was little fear of the Italians; they did, however, object to '. . . committing Great Britain's political and naval strength in a sphere which was of secondary importance for British interests, and withdrawing it from much more important questions, more especially the problem of Eastern Asia'.[33] Hoare himself disclaimed any fear of Italy, and Eden's memoirs indicate no Cabinet concern on this point; the latter states simply that in matched strength British power exceeded Mussolini's.[34] Hoare had not contemplated war, so such measurements were not relevant to his purposes. He yielded to Laval's entreaties for a peaceful settlement in order to preserve the Stresa front. Yet France was every bit as tied to England for her security as was

England to France; she was therefore every bit as liable to British pressures as Hoare was sensitive to Laval's calculated delays. The British government could well have been more resolute in implementing at least the oil sanction, had they simply lived up to their professions of September. The Hoare-Laval Pact exposed the difference between theory and practice, and so Britain had to reap the harvest of her irresolution, as the Labour Party had pointedly warned.

The party surely found some consolation for their strenuous resistance to the pact in Hoare's resignation and the collapse of his proposals, though they would have preferred the fall of what it considered a collectively responsible government. The situation was yet critical, Attlee saw: 'If you turn and run away from the aggressor, you kill the League, and you do worse than that, or as bad as that: you kill all faith in the word of honour of this country.'[35] Only a resolute pro-League policy could save both from that fate. Hopes for such a restoration arose when Baldwin appointed as Hoare's successor that Cabinet minister who had worked hardest to make a reality of collective security in the Abyssinian dispute, Anthony Eden. For Labour, this glimmer of hope must be viewed against the demoralizing effects of the Hoare-Laval pact, however quick its death.

Clearly a damaging effect in the short run was the reopening of the issue brought to a head at Brighton by the Labour left. Cripps argued in the Commons on 19 December that the pact proved the correctness of the left's suspicions: 'I do not know how better you can describe the proposals which were made to Italy and Abyssinia than as an Imperialist deal . . . the very thing which Ministers were disclaiming so vociferously for the purposes of the Election and immediately before it.' He rose to ironic heights in suggesting how the British imperialist mentality reacted to Italian aggression:

. . . after all, she is a capitalist Power; she is an Imperialist, and if she is reasonable we ought to allow her some expansion. We will put on sanctions but . . . they must be such sanctions as will really have no effect, and then we will settle the matter by giving her half of Abyssinia. That is untold generosity on the part of Imperialism. What other instance is there in the history of Imperialism where a backward race has been allowed to keep half of their territory?[36]

Reality seemed to have placed itself at the disposal of the left's argument that the League of Nations was an imperialist sham; the Hoare-Laval Pact served to confirm the argument now put by Cripps that the very economic structure of its member states made impossible effective action by the League. Such reinforcement of the left views on international policy troubled the Labour leadership throughout 1936, for pre-electoral prophecies from that quarter had been fulfilled. Aneurin Bevan had gone on the record at the Socialist League Conference in disbelief that Hoare's word at Geneva would prove the deed; instead he held that Britain and France were negotiating to give Mussolini all he wanted without the necessity of fighting for it.[37] Such a deal had also been predicted by a government critic, 'Vigilantes', in a book on international affairs brought out for the General Election.[38] These predictions were recalled in December:

What the whole commotion did do was to harden the belief on the Left that Baldwin and Chamberlain were utterly untrustworthy in meeting the Fascist menace. The substantial case of the Right wing at Brighton had been that the Government *must* be trusted if the League was to be saved. Baldwin had shattered that claim and the battle of Brighton would have to be fought over again on different terms.[39]

Since the abortive Hoare-Laval Pact did not change the long-term disposition of the British government's policy, one can claim that it more deeply affected the Labour Party than the Conservatives. Distrust of the National Government, long preached on the left, was rekindled in the Labour leadership in December 1935, thereafter to remain a constant in Labour attitudes; the revolt of the left, beaten back at Brighton, surged anew.

2

Eden, taking stock of his legacy at Christmas, 1935, saw the fortunes of the League of Nations rather battered: 'While there could be no going back on the policy of sanctions, I could not believe that Geneva would be, at least for some time to come, an adequate guardian of peace.'[40] Recognizing the need to strengthen the power of the League, he was greatly dissatisfied with the 'miserably weak' state of Britain's military defences and her potential contribution to the League. This two-pronged concept of collective security and rearmament characterized Eden's foreign policy. Meanwhile the League's Committee of Eighteen, which was responsible for the imposition of sanctions, again considered the problem of Italian aggression. At the turn of the year there was some hope that Mussolini had over-extended himself in combat, but shortly thereafter he resorted to the use of poison gas and indiscriminate attacks on hospitals and Red Cross vehicles, in contravention of the rules of warfare; evidently he was not prepared to lose the initiative. Yet Eden learned at Geneva in mid-January that Laval was not at all inclined to press Mussolini to reduce his territorial demands; he would agree only to establish a committee of experts to examine the efficacy of an oil sanction. The report of that Petroleum Committee, published in February, held that given universal application by League members and limitation of US exports to a pre-1935 level such a sanction would require at least three months to become effective; Eden justly comments that this report showed the cost of having missed the chance two months earlier to implement that sanction,[41] a course strongly advised by the Labour Party.

On 24 February 1936 Lees-Smith, with the report of the Petroleum Committee in hand, rose in the Commons to press the government to take the lead in proposing the oil sanction. He was certainly overconfident of the degree of French and American co-operation; Eden, in reply, enumerated the practical difficulties involved in applying this sanction, including – Lees-Smith's confidence to the contrary – tripled exports from the USA. The British government, he added, was nonetheless resolved to secure whatever collective action could be taken under the League.[42] Arthur Henderson, son of the late Foreign Secretary, challenged the government to do no less: '... we have not yet tried the collective peace system in its entirety. We have not even tried the policy of sanctions in its entirety. We have simply tinkered about, afraid for one reason or another to take risks . . .'[43] Attlee argued yet another facet of Labour's case, that more than the future of Abyssinia was at stake:

This matter is of importance in itself, but everyone recognises that behind that question looms a much larger subject. The whole question, not merely with regard to aggression in Africa, but with regard to aggression in Asia or Europe, or anywhere in the world, is whether the aggressor is going to get away with it.[44]

E*

On 28 February the British government finally agreed to impose the oil sanction, should other League members do likewise. France remained a stumbling block; although Flandin had succeeded Laval, Eden regarded their policies as indistinguishable.[45] Early in March the Committee of Eighteen agreed to give the French government yet another chance to come to terms with Mussolini; when the committee met again a week later to assess the results, French concerns were directed elsewhere.

With the League powers in considerable disarray, Hitler moved. When the Abyssinian dispute had first assumed serious proportions in October 1935, the German Ambassador in Rome had pointed out the possible advantages which might accrue to Germany, including the hope that both the League of Nations and the Stresa front would not survive.[46] By February the latter was no more, and the former too was endangered. Mussolini was indeed 'getting away with it', with the progress of his conquest improving considerably in that month. The French government at this time supplied Hitler with a pretext for unilateral action, through the ratification by the Chamber of Deputies of the Franco-Soviet Treaty, signed the previous July. The German government had consistently made known their view that the alliance was incompatible with the French obligations under the Locarno pact.[47] Though Foreign Minister Neurath in July 1935 had informed several German ambassadors that the German objection was not '. . . the overture to a German campaign to enable us to withdraw from the Rhine Pact on the grounds that it has been violated by France, and then to treat the provisions concerning the demilitarized zone as void as well', the French Ambassador in Berlin, after an interview with Hitler on 21 November, reported that this was indeed his intention, at the appropriate moment.[48] Hitler himself wondered in mid-February '. . . if the psychological moment had not arrived now', though he admitted that '. . . militarily Germany was not yet ready . . .' He did not think that the reoccupation of the demilitarized zone '. . . would be answered by military action – though perhaps by economic sanctions; but these had meanwhile become thoroughly unpopular amongst the followers, who served as whipping boys, of the Great Powers'.[49] His military advisers were however thoroughly alarmed at the prospect of the immediate mobilization of some ninety divisions by France and her Polish and Czech allies.[50] That the French were conscious of the possibility was evident in Flandin's declaration that 'they were not going to let themselves again be confronted with *faits accomplis* and had already agreed upon the measures to be taken'.[51] Eden however minuted at this time that it was improbable that the French would fight for the Rhineland; consequently, as far as Britain was concerned, '. . . it seems undesirable to adopt an attitude where we would either have to fight for the zone or abandon it in the face of German reoccupation. It would be preferable for Great Britain and France to enter betimes into negotiations with the German government for the surrender on conditions of our rights in the zone while such surrender still has a bargaining value.[52]

As had happened with the proposed Air Locarno Pact, the German government took, before the western powers had in fact given. On 2 March 1936, orders were issued to the military to prepare for the reoccupation of the Rhineland, which was accomplished five days later. The expected pretext was used, though the French government had throughout been prepared to submit the Locarno Pact and the Franco-Soviet Treaty to the International Court at The Hague for a ruling on their compatibility. Hitler's action was a flagrant violation not only of the Treaty of Versailles but of the Locarno Pact as well, signed freely by Germany in 1925. Since he had consistently maintained that he would fulfil all such voluntary obligations[53] and had failed to test the French willingness to do the same with reference to Locarno, doubts as to Hitler's good intentions were justified after 7 March 1936. Yet he cleverly – and characteristically – used the very occasion of his aggression to issue new guarantees and propagate hopes for a permanent settlement of Europe's problems. He spoke of concluding non-aggression pacts with all European countries save Russia, expressed the hope of bringing Germany back to the League if its Covenant were separated from the Treaty of Versailles and she were given equality of status with regard to colonies, and declared that Germany had no territorial demands in Europe. In the view of the British government, primary responsibility for the maintenance of the demilitarized zone lay with the French, whose army was in 1936 superior to the German in size, experience and equipment.[54] Upon learning of the German action, the British government nonetheless impressed upon the French Ambassador the need to do nothing which would make the situation more difficult, until discussions could be held.[55] They were evidently determined not again to counter public opinion, Eden implies:

The French Government, under Laval, having been cool towards their obligations to the League over Abyssinia, their successors now wished to invoke its authority over the Rhineland. To the British people this was a much more doubtful course. There was not one man in a thousand in the country at that time prepared to take physical action with France against a German reoccupation of the Rhineland.[56]

He therefore urged the Cabinet to resist any French attempt to invoke financial and economic sanctions, asking only for a formal condemnation by the League of Germany's action. Eden's fear of a fiery French response was groundless, for French public opinion was irresolute, even pacifist: Flandin claims that only four ministers favoured war on Germany. Further, despite the warning sounded by the French Ambassador in Berlin four months earlier and Flandin's own assurances, no military plans to deal with this contingency existed.[57] France proved as unprepared for military action as Great Britain was unwilling.

After conversations with the French government in mid-March, Eden announced to the House of Commons on 26 March that Britain intended both to strengthen the Locarno system and maintain her world-wide commitments under the Covenant. Specifically he proclaimed: 'It is a vital interest of this country that the integrity of France and Belgium should be maintained and that no hostile force should cross their frontiers.'[58] In reply to this declaration of policy, Dalton stated Labour's acquiescence to Hitler's *fait accompli*:

It is only right to say bluntly and frankly that public opinion in this country would not support, and certainly the Labour Party would not support, the taking of military sanctions or even economic sanctions against Germany at this time, in order to put German troops out of the German Rhineland ... Public opinion here does, I think, draw a clear distinction between the action of Signor Mussolini in resorting to aggressive war and waging it beyond his frontiers, and the actions, up-to-date at any rate, of Herr Hitler which, much as we may regard them as reprehensible, have taken place within the frontiers of the German Reich. The public here draw that distinction, and it is a proper distinction.

Dalton proposed that Britain forthwith draw the line for Germany's benefit by telling the German people: 'We wish you no ill. We recognize your title to equality, equality in political status, and equality in economic opportunity. We recognise this, but we do not recognise the right of any nation, you or any nation, to an overbearing and brutal predominance in the world.' He raised only one criticism of the government's apparent course, namely their emphasis on the Locarno system; he hoped that they were not drawing a distinction between western and the other parts of Europe. Labour regarded the preservation of peace in the west as of no greater importance than elsewhere on the continent.[59] He was quickly reassured by Neville Chamberlain that the government considered European peace indivisible: 'Under the League we are interested just as much in the preservation of peace in the East of Europe as we are in the West, and our obligations under the League will apply equally whether aggression takes place in the Eastern or Western parts of Europe.'[60] Brave but fleeting words! For the moment, however, a general measure of agreement pervaded the House of Commons. Evidently Eden had not erred in his belief that very few Britons were prepared to go to war to prevent the remilitarization of the Rhineland.

Speakers on both sides of the House stressed their determination that Britain should stand by her obligations under the Covenant. For his recent conversion to the pro-League cause Winston Churchill was welcomed to the ranks of the collectivists by Clement Attlee, who characterized him as a 'repentant sinner'.[61] Ironic that this rare measure of agreement among the government, the opposition and the Tory critics of the slow pace of British rearmament had been provoked by a flagrant violation of two treaties on Hitler's part; all however shared the hope that the occupation of the Rhineland ended a lengthy and troubled chapter in post-war history. The note of hope that a less contentious period might follow was sounded as early as 9 March in a *Times* leader, 'A Chance to Rebuild'.[62] With the collapse of an iniquitous provision of the Treaty of Versailles and the redress of a rankling German grievance, a genuine, functioning system of collective security might be established. In the same manner in which the editor of *The Times*, Geoffrey Dawson, had long since forgotten about the First World War and remembered only the peace treaty, the Labour Party also placed little stock in the preservation of the Versailles system. The *New Statesman* spoke for more than Labour's left in commenting at this time: 'We all have bad consciences about Germany's treatment since the war.'[63] Three years' experience of the evils of Hitlerism, recognized and denounced by the Labour Party, did not deter the party from supporting the redress of German grievances nearly twenty years old.

There seems no reason to doubt Hitler's subsequent assertion that 'the forty-eight hours after the march into the Rhineland were the most nerve-racking in my life. If the French had then moved into the Rhineland we would have had to withdraw with our tails between our legs, for the military resources at our disposal would have been wholly inadequate for even a moderate resistance.'[64] Yet hypothetical speculation of what might have been are in this instance particularly idle, since France was of no mind to march and no party in Britain was prepared to recommend such a course. Our proper concern then is with the impact of the German remilitarization of the Rhineland: few could doubt that the League system had been dealt another damaging blow. Eden argues that the inaction of the League powers in part represents the fading of their conviction that international order must be upheld: 'The growing tendency to find excuses had been fertilized by the Abyssinian failure.'[65]

As Abyssinia had reacted upon Europe, so did European developments ease Mussolini's path of conquest in Africa. He took advantage of the March crisis to regroup his forces and renew his military offensive. France, irresolute over events upon her own door-step, showed no interest in the application of coercion, even in the form of the oil sanction, to Italy. As a result of the Rhineland crisis, however, France won an important recruit to her view of the Abyssinian conflict, in the person of Winston Churchill, who called for the withdrawal of sanctions against Italy in order that Europe might concentrate on the German menace. Attlee refused to accept such an arrangement:

Are you going to sacrifice Abyssinia entirely? I would say that the duty of this country regarding the vindication of the League in the case of Italy is quite as vital as in the case of Germany. It is no good taking action against someone who offends against the League if when the next sinner comes along you give the first sinner absolution and enrol him in your police force if possible.[66]

Though Attlee's logic was impeccable, the Abyssinian cause was all but lost: the northern front broke on 31 March and the Emperor retreated. On 4 April Italian aircraft arrived over the completely vulnerable capital; the Ethiopian Army was crumbling in the face of bombardment and continued subjection to gas. Faced with this deteriorating situation, the British government called for League action, but, according to Eden, 'M. Flandin argued the Italian case with confident cynicism and did what he could to obstruct any action . . . either against the use of gas by the Italians or in favour of pressure for the cessation of hostilities'.[67] Abyssinia, it seems, expiated French frustrations over the Rhineland.

On 20 April the Council of the League of Nations agreed that hopes of conciliation were at an end and agreed to the continuance of sanctions against Italy; Eden advocated these measures, though he realized that the Abyssinian chances were fast fading. How fast probably even the Foreign Secretary did not realize, for on 1 May Haile Selassie was forced to flee his country, ironically in one of the few pieces of armament Great Britain had placed at his disposal, a warship. Four days later Marshal Badoglio led the Italian legions – which had used poison gas in a manner which the Second World War, for all its barbarities, did not repeat – into Addis Ababa. That entry was very much in the mind of the House of Commons, when on 6 May that body met to discuss Supply for the Foreign Office.

Dalton used that occasion to criticize Eden's irresolute policy; he charged the government with failure to carry out their obligations under the Covenant and he maintained that they had abandoned the Abyssinians to a cruel fate, after having encouraged them to resist in the first place.[68] 'We charge the Government further with having discredited the League of Nations and the whole idea of collective security, and we charge them with having betrayed the trust of millions of electors who were foolish enough to vote for them at the last Election in the belief that they were going effectively to support a League of Nations policy.' Labour demanded a continuation and an extension of sanctions to make such a policy effective. Eden, in response, turned sharply on these accusations in arguing that a Labour government would not have followed a different policy towards Abyssinia and Italy. He castigated Labour's concept of collective security: 'The truth is that while hon. Gentlemen opposite profess to support the League with horse, foot and artillery, they really only mean to support it with threats, insults and perorations.'[69] Eden thus called into question Labour's continuing opposition to rearmament.

Since the government were sincere in their belief that Great Britain had done all she could on behalf of the League,[70] abandonment of the futile sanctions became inevitable. Abyssinia was obviously lost to the League, and the rebuilding of the shattered European peace front of 1935 assumed greater importance than any last-ditch resistance. Though Eden was not overly hopeful of preventing Mussolini from moving closer to Hitler through removal of the sanctions, pressures – economic, naval and political – were mounting for such a step; he himself grew less confident that sanctions served any good purpose.[71] Nonetheless Eden felt that the sanctions ought to be removed as they had been imposed, collectively and under League auspices. Consequently he was rather disturbed by Neville Chamberlain's first intervention of note in foreign affairs; the Chancellor had concluded that it was fantastic to prolong sanctions when the war was over. As for the Labour-urged extension and intensification, Chamberlain told the 1900 Club on 10 June: 'That seems to me the very midsummer of madness . . . Is it not apparent that the policy of sanctions involves, I do not say war, but a risk of war?' Chamberlain recognized that he was undercutting official policy; he recorded in his diary for 17 June, 'I did it deliberately because I felt that the party and the country needed a lead . . . I did not consult Anthony Eden, because he would have been bound to beg me not to say what I proposed . . .'[72] Though Baldwin denied that Chamberlain was a spokesman for the government, Britain's long game – it was no more – of economic and financial sanctions clearly was at an end.

Eden announced the inevitable to the Commons on 18 June 1936: '. . . His Majesty's Government, after mature consideration . . . have come to the conclusion that there is no longer any utility in continuing these measures [sanctions] as a means of pressure upon Italy.' Cries of 'Shame', 'Resign', and 'Sabotage' were hurled at him. Arthur Greenwood developed such accusations: 'There was to be a settlement within the framework of the League, a fair and just settlement. All we are to have now is a withdrawal of sanctions against the victor. The primary question remains unsettled. Gangsterism is triumphant and Abyssinia stands as a ghastly monument to the treachery of nations who were sworn to stand by her.'[73] In Labour's view neither the League nor sanctions had failed: 'it is the courage of . . . [Eden] and his friends that has failed.' One can however argue that the failure lay not in the irresolution of the British government in 1936, as Greenwood maintained, but rather in their proclaimed resolution of 1935 that they would not resort to force in settling the dispute. At the time of that declaration, with which Labour sympathized, neither government nor opposition had foreseen that non-military sanctions, imperfectly applied, would not deter an aggressor. Subsequently, the government had not adjusted their thinking to deal with just that situation. Perhaps Labour would have proceeded, first to the crucial oil sanction – with or without France – and then to the military sanction. In both cases Labour would have had to deal with the same unyielding opposition of the French which so frustrated Eden's attempts.

The internationalist Labour Party, which had all along proclaimed the need for genuinely collective security, might well have been forced to act unilaterally in the application of the oil sanction and in the possible closing of the Suez Canal to Italian shipping. Whether such moves would have deterred Mussolini we cannot say, but the Labour Party recommended them to the bitter end. In a censure debate on 23 June Dalton pleaded for the maintenance even of the operative sanctions: '. . . we say that there should be no question whatever of lifting the existing sanctions, not until the rainy season is past, and until we have seen what a few more months of economic and financial pressure will effect upon the minds of those responsible for Italian policy.'[74] The League of Nations, however, shortly abandoned even those sanctions, since the British government had made known its feelings.

Regardless of the possible consequences of Labour's sanctionist policy, the actions of the National Government ultimately stand condemned by the very words of the Prime Minister himself, dating from May 1934:

The moment you are up against sanctions, you are up against war . . . there is no such thing as a sanction that will work that does not mean war, or, in other words, if you are going to adopt a sanction you must be prepared for war. If you adopt a sanction without being ready for war, you are not an honest trustee of the nation.[75]

Two years after that statement, Baldwin's trusteeship was rather tarnished. Labour's defence policy had not yet taken into account such realities as France's refusal to join in the application of a meaningful sanction, which in the weakened condition of the League would perforce have thrown the burden upon Britain's national armaments. Yet Labour's foreign policy dictated an attempt to make effective the sanctions approved by the League, even to extend them. In that attempt the Labour Party might have proved an unsuccessful trustee of the nation; they would not have proved dishonest.

3

To treat the interaction of the Spanish Civil War and the British Labour Party is necessarily a difficult task; fully told, the account would run to several hundred pages. The Spanish Civil War, a sufficiently complex event in itself, raged for nearly three years, an open sore in the European body politic; initially the desire to limit the conflict produced an apparently unprecedented measure of European co-operation, which subsequently degenerated into institutionalized hypocrisy. Swept into the vortex of the war were domestic politics in both England and France; those countries which had put an end to the pedantries of domestic politics – Germany, Italy and Russia – were involved as well. Tested in Spain were the latest methods of warfare, juxtaposed in that troubled land with medieval brutalities and ageless acts such as piracy and blockade running. These developments induced severe strains in the Labour Party: they exacerbated the conflict between the two wings of the party to such an extent that the Edinburgh Conference of 1936 marked the nadir of party unity in the 1930s. Yet the Spanish events forced upon the left a recognition of the threat of fascism from without; in this sense the Spanish Civil War made possible the unity of the Labour Party in entering the war in 1939.

In recent years, the complex phenomenon that was the civil war in Spain has received full and excellent treatment at the hands of two historians: Hugh Thomas' account has re-created the very atmosphere in which the war was waged, while Dante Puzzo has depicted the international complications which stemmed from the conflict.[76] For an understanding of Labour's reaction, the polarization of Spanish politics, among the welter of causes of the war, is most important: in 1936 a multitude of political parties grouped themselves in 'fronts' to stand for election. Those on the left adopted the title of 'Popular Front', a name proposed by the Communists, who at first contributed hardly anything more;[77] the parties to the right more slowly allied in the 'National Front'. The former scored a decisive victory in the first round of elections in February, returning to the Cortes 256 members, as opposed to 143 rightists and 54 representatives of centre parties. Winning an election in Spain was however quite a different matter from governing effectively: complex, interlayered problems of Church versus liberals, landowners versus bourgeoisie on the one hand and working classes on the other, and localists versus the advocates of centralized control defied solutions. The forces of the left, themselves divided into moderate Republicans, Socialists and groups further to the left, proved unable '. . . to transmute the electoral agreement that was the Frente Popular into a political compact from which could come a government of the united Left'.[78] On 16 June, the leader of the Spanish Catholic Party charged that Spain was in a state of anarchy and that the Cortes meeting was the 'funeral service of democracy'.[79] Long before the Popular Front had come into being, certain military leaders had been preparing the interment rites for the Spanish Republic. The military *coup* actually started in Spanish Morocco on 17 July 1936; on the next day the revolt spread to the mainland. The pattern of revolt – an initial uprising by the military garrison, with immediate support coming from the Falange and in most cases the Civic Guard – was repeated time and again; in Madrid, which had teetered on the brink of civil war quite independently of the military plot, the rather timid uprising was overwhelmed on 20 July. The failure of the rightist revolt in that key city, however, triggered a countering socialist reaction.

With these events in mind, we can now survey the reactions of the British and French governments, for those responses in turn played a part in shaping the policies of the Labour Party. Eden claims that his sole immediate response to the news of events in Spain was to ask the Admiralty to order British warships to the more important ports, in order to protect British subjects; though he met with Blum and Delbos, the French Premier and Foreign Secretary, on 23–24 July, the exclusive concern of that meeting was the German problem.[80] Yet by that time Blum had been approached by the Spanish Ambassador in Paris who had asked for export licences for the shipment of arms to Spain; Blum, himself the recently installed leader of a Popular Front government, had replied favourably, on 20 July, to a further appeal for such aid from the Spanish Prime Minister Giral. At about the same time, the French Ambassador in London reported that the British government were alarmed at the French involvement; Baldwin urged Blum to accompany his Foreign Secretary to London for talks already scheduled to start on the 23rd. The French Prime Minister arrived only in time for luncheon at Claridge's, where he was queried by Eden: '"Are you going to send arms to the Spanish Republic?" "Yes," said Blum. "It is your affair," Eden replied, "but I ask you one thing. Be prudent." '[81] Recent biographers of Blum offer a different timing but agree that Blum '. . . found the British Government anxious to avoid any further international complications at a moment when they had just succeeded in sliding out of the sanctions that had been imposed by the League of Nations on Italy . . .'[82]

Directly upon his return to Paris, Blum took the first step in his painful retreat from his desire to aid a legitimate and friendly government. On 25 July he refused to ship arms directly to Spain, though he agreed to effect the shipment via Mexico. Domestic pressures had become intense: his Radical colleagues, especially Chautemps and Herriot, made clear their opposition to the direct flow of war material to Spain. Eden recorded the British government's pleasure: 'He [Blum] and Delbos knew only too well that any other course of action would sharply divide France, while open intervention by the great powers could lead to a European war. We agreed with this French decision of policy.'[83] Who was agreeing with whom is not quite clear: when, on 2 August, the French Cabinet agreed to a proposal for non-intervention they were at least in part responding to what Delbos characterized as 'in consideration of the British position'.[84] At the same time, they authorized the Air Minister to proceed with a shipment of thirty reconnaissance aircraft and bombers, fifteen fighters and ten transport and training planes to the Republic. Political judgment and emotions were in conflict. However, the Blum government could not long persist in such contradictory policies, and on 8 August France suspended all export of war materials to Spain. Once again, British pressures possibly supplemented a course dictated as well by French politics. According to a Spanish Republican source,

... the previous day Sir George Clark, the British Ambassador, had almost presented Delbos with an ultimatum. If France did not immediately ban the export of war material to Spain, and a war with Germany were to follow, Britain would hold herself absolved from the obligation to aid France under the Treaty of Locarno.[85]

Whatever the source – likely a combination – of the French decision to initiate discussions concerning a non-intervention agreement,[86] Blum so bitterly regretted this decision that he was about ready to put the matter to the Chamber of Deputies, which would almost certainly have entailed the fall of the Popular Front government: 'He was only deterred from doing so by the arguments and, indeed, the tears of ... the representative of the Spanish government in Paris, who said that the fall of the Popular Front government in France would be a far more shattering moral blow to the Spanish Popular Front than the practical disadvantages caused by the lack of some material assistance.'[87]

Eden has steadfastly maintained that no British pressure was brought to bear on France. The French proposal of non-intervention on 2 August showed a 'bold initiative' with which the British government sympathized; his memoirs shed no light either upon the origins of that proposal or on the French decision of 8 August, in which British diplomatic pressures may have figured. On 16 August, Eden announced the British embargo upon arms shipments to either side in Spain; within a month a meeting of those powers willing to join in a declaration of non-intervention convened in London. At the end of September the Spanish government's Foreign Minister handed to Eden documents and photographs to prove the extent to which Hitler and Mussolini were violating their undertakings not to intervene, to the disadvantage of the Spanish government. Eden was not moved: 'I gave him no encouragement to think that we would change our policy.'[88] The British government was fully committed to the policy of non-intervention in the Spanish Civil War. The precise origins of that policy remain in the shadows; the publication of the British and French documents is awaited with what might be called suspicion, especially with regard to role of the British Foreign Office.[89] This scepticism finds its historical counterpart in the attitude of the leaders of the Labour Party.

Within forty-eight hours of the outbreak of the Spanish Civil War, Clement Attlee proposed a resolution to a conference of some 1,400 Labour Party and Co-operative delegates gathered at London to discuss methods of resisting new unemployment assistance regulations. Concern was expressed for the outbreak of war in Spain at the instigation of reactionary fascist forces; the delegates declared their confidence in the will of the Spanish government to resist this attack and pledged '. . . all practicable support to our Spanish comrades in their struggle to defend freedom and democracy in Spain'.[90] A week later, the movement's advisory board, the National Council of Labour, spoke out along similar lines and also mentioned possible international consequences: 'The maintenance of representative government in Spain is of the greatest political significance for all other countries concerned with the triumph of democracy over fascism.'[91] Though to the Labour left it seemed that the whole movement was swinging into action with united fervour,[92] the Parliamentary Labour Party was from the first more cautious. On 27 July, Morgan Jones emphasized that Labour was not asking the British government to take sides in the conflict, but he reminded them that '. . . if we have any sort of comfort to give to anyone in Spain, it should be given to the constitutional authority in Spain at the moment'. He also then called to the government's attention the possible shipment of arms to the rebels by Germany and Italy. Philip Noel-Baker reiterated the PLP's position shortly before the summer adjournment: 'We are not urging the Government to intervene . . . We urge them to give to the Spanish Government every facility which the practice of international law allows . . . We urge them, above all, to use their influence to prevent other Powers from intervening on the side of the militarist dictators.'[93] Labour entertained no idea of the use of a

British or international expeditionary force; in accordance with international law, they held, however, that the legal government should be succoured. On this point their recommendation clashed with that advanced by their French comrade, Leon Blum, and eagerly seconded by the British government. Thus the socialist party in Britain had to deal with proposals for non-intervention (i.e. denying arms to both sides) advanced by a left government in France, led by a socialist.

That reaction was shaped not by Labour's political leadership, which had scattered from Swedish Lapland (Dalton) and Russia (Attlee) to California (Alexander),[94] but at party headquarters in Transport House. There, in addition to the party officials – Middleton and Gillies, respectively Party Secretary and Secretary of the party's International Department – the 'proprietor' of Transport House, Ernest Bevin, and the Secretary of the Trades Union Congress, Sir Walter Citrine, assumed a direct role in the formulation of policy; the sole political leader available, Arthur Greenwood, was close to the trade union movement. Not surprisingly, these leaders, reacting to Blum's proposal, adopted a position which was short on emotion, but which they held was realistic. Bevin's feelings may be taken as typical: despite his hatred of fascism and his concern for the Spanish workers, he realized that emotion was not a substitute for policy. Along with Citrine and Dalton he had faced the continuing dilemma of the Labour Party's willingness to aid all those who were attacked by the fascist powers while opposing rearmament. Consequently Bevin could not take lightly the risk of general war in Spain, for that country's fate was not an issue apart, nor could it be treated independently of the general questions of foreign and defence policy.[95] With such considerations in mind, a deputation of five Labour leaders called upon Eden on 19 August to hear his confidential explanation of British policy towards Spain. They were not untroubled about the role of the British government, for Eden relates that at one point

... a member of the deputation interjected that I was perhaps aware of the rumour that the initiative had been taken by the French, but under pressure from the British Government. I replied that there was no truth whatever in this suggestion and my statement was at once accepted. A week later, the same deputation came to the Foreign Office again and, after discussion of other aspects of the war in Spain, asked once more about the origins of the proposed Non-Intervention Agreement, which, according to information they had received from Paris, had emanated from London, probably at the time of the three-power discussions between France, Belgium and ourselves [23–24 July]. I denied this statement, adding that I should have been glad to be able to say that non-intervention was my proposal, as I considered it the best which could have been devised in the circumstances.[96]

With Eden's unequivocal denial in hand, the Labour leaders called an urgent meeting of the PLP, the TUC General Council and the National Executive Committee for 28 August; at that meeting, following Citrine's report on the events of the past five weeks, a declaration of sympathy for the Spanish people was agreed upon. That statement stressed the right of the Spanish government to obtain arms for its own defence but noted that the illegal supply of arms to the rebels had created a new and immediate danger of war. Labour, in view of this threat, came grudgingly to accept the policy of non-intervention, as the British and French governments used the term. Though Citrine has since written that the Labour deputation had '. . . told . . . [Eden] flatly that the policy of non-intervention could not succeed', because no one among them '. . . had the least doubt that both Italy and Germany would go on supporting the rebels with arms, no matter what they signed or others did', the full meeting now endorsed that policy.[97] While regretting that the effect of non-intervention was to place the rebel forces and the legitimate government on the same footing, Labour, in order to lessen international tensions, declared its support for non-intervention, provided that the agreements were '. . . applied immediately, are loyally observed by all parties, and their execution is effectively co-ordinated and supervised . . .'[98] The Labour statement emphasized that the utmost vigilance would be required to prevent the use of the agreements to injure the Spanish government. Cautious endorsement of non-intervention marked the Labour declaration of 28 August.

Before seeking the approval of the 1936 gathering of the TUC for this policy, the Labour leadership sent a deputation to Paris to inquire into reports of Portuguese violations of the agreements and into the attitudes of certain sections of the French Popular Front towards non-intervention. Blum made clear to Dalton, Gillies and George Hicks his own views:

Speaking as head of the Popular Front Government, he insisted that the policy of non-intervention in Spain was *his* policy. It was he and not Eden, as some alleged, who had first proposed it. He was sure that this policy, if fully observed, would help the Spanish Government much more than the free supply of arms on both sides. Even if it was not fully observed, if there were only comparatively small infractions by Hitler and Mussolini, it would still be better for our friends in Spain than opening the floodgates.

Blum asked the Labour deputation ' "to urge my British colleagues to support *my* policy of non-intervention" '. Dalton at least yielded readily to Blum's arguments, for he had no emotional commitment to Spanish democracy:

I value France above Spain, both as a civilised modern state, and as a friend and pledged ally of Britain. I was not an admirer of the Spanish approximation to democracy ... Again, we had many personal friends among French politicians on the Left, and especially among French Socialists. But we knew very little of the Spanish left-wing leaders. Spanish Socialists did not, until now, often attend meetings of the L.S.I. And there were other elements in the Spanish Left, including Anarchists, who did not inspire much confidence.[99]

Like Bevin, Dalton also saw a potential danger in the slogan 'Arms for Spain', if this meant that Britain was to supply arms which would otherwise have been kept for her own defences; he was very much concerned with the terrible insufficiency of British armaments in the face of the German danger. This note of calculation characterized the document which was presented to the Trades Union Congress in its September meeting. None other than Citrine offered a four-point defence of Labour's support of non-intervention, which was based upon the French initiative, concern that a general war might otherwise ensue, the desire that Italy and Germany should be restrained from supplying munitions to the rebels and the hope that the European powers would not be divided into two blocs. Though the decision to support non-intervention was distasteful, the General Council recommended it as the sole practicable policy. They would not however yield to the jibe that they were simply taking their policy from the socialist-led government of France or, worse, from the National Government. Citrine, to the contrary, declared: 'We decided our policy, unpopular though it may be with large masses of our own people who do not understand perhaps the niceties of the question, because we believe that that policy is right . . .'[100] Historians have however questioned such a view: 'Thus, the National government first imposed non-intervention on Blum; he imposed it on the Labour leaders; and they imposed it on their followers – all in the name of European peace.'[101] Though the first part of that statement is open to question, the essential point about the second clause is that the Labour leaders were quite willing to be imposed upon.

Not so the Labour left, which at Congress asked for arms for the Spanish government; they argued that non-intervention would only make more difficult the defence of Spanish democracy, by encouraging fascism to greater acts of aggression. Left spokesmen disbelieved the possibility of fascist observance of international agreement. Especially cutting was their attitude toward the collections taken up by the Labour movement for the benefit of the Spanish workers: 'If you decide that the best policy for the Labour Movement to adopt at present is to send round the hat among your colleagues and collect a few pence – if that is going to salve your conscience in connection with the Spanish workers, then God help you.'[102] Only 51,000 supported the left challenge, while representatives of three million trade unionists voted for the policy of non-intervention. Such an overwhelming vote never served to silence the left, however.

To anticipate, non-intervention failed as a policy because intervention was permitted under the guise of the former; the concept of non-intervention has consequently become one of opprobrium, not unlike that of appeasement. Yet to treat non-intervention as nothing more than a sham on the part of the governments involved, and, in consequence, to view the Labour Party's initial acceptance of the concept as a base betrayal of the Spanish workers, is to miss the force of the argument for effective non-intervention in August and September 1936. Had the policy been strictly observed and enforced, it could well have proved in the general interests of Europe and the particular interests of the Spanish government, since the rebels would have been more damaged by the cessation of support from Hitler and Mussolini than the Republic hurt by the proscription of aid from France and Russia. Considerably before the last power intervened, just at the time Blum began his retreat, the German Ambassador in Spain reported: 'The development of the situation since the beginning of the revolt consequently shows distinctly increasing strength and progress on the part of the Government and stand-still and retrogression on the part of the rebels . . . Unless some-thing unforeseen happens, it is hardly to be expected that in view of all this the military revolt can succeed . . .'[103] Equal treatment favoured the Republic, which '. . . could even win if both sides received foreign aid, or if both were denied it. The rebels had a chance only if they received foreign aid, while the Republic received none or very little . . .'[104] But the unforeseen occurred, in the covert violation of the precepts of non-intervention. A policy which in theory made possible – even likely – the defeat of the insurrectionists ought not to be confused with the practical failure of statesmen to ensure its success. Even on the Labour left the appeal of non-intervention was recognized. The *New Statesman*, constantly critical of the Labour leadership through-out the decade, concurred with Blum's decision for non-inter-vention, on the grounds that a general war should not be risked at a time when British public opinion seemed rather indifferent to the issues at stake – yet another consideration for the Labour leadership.[105]

The Spanish Civil War however captured the emotions of the left and converted them into enthusiasms, such as a renewal of the appeal for a British popular front. Several observations about the temper of the left wing of the Labour Party should clarify its reaction to the challenge posed by that conflict. In the first place, the Spanish Civil War provided an opportunity, long denied the left, to do something against fascism, a psychological release as it were. More than five hundred Britons, by no means all Com-munists, laid down their lives on the battlefields of Spain in availing themselves of that opportunity; Hugh Dalton has written of their sacrifice, 'though cut off in their prime . . . [they] found self-fulfilment'.[106] More than resistance to fascism was, however, involved; in the Spanish conflict the *New Statesman* saw a class war,[107] with the forces of the left standing as one. The slogans which were so difficult to implement at home were all applicable in Spain. The left's course of action is explicable, and reasonable, given their beliefs and frustrations. Spain was the spark, and the preservation of Republican Spain became their crusade. Any truck with the fascist powers was repugnant to the left on emotional, ideological and logical grounds. Strategic considerations were adduced, as in Bevan's concern for a point normally the concern of right-wing Conservatives; since the Tory right was strangely silent, it remained to Bevan to warn that 'should Spain become Fascist, as assuredly it will if the rebels succeed . . . then Britain's undisputed power in the Mediterranean is gone'.[108] Emotional repugnance for non-intervention however ran deepest; that spirit is captured in the assertion that the Labour left '. . . saw the timid hesitation of Transport House silhouetted against the heroism of the Spanish people'.[109] They turned against their own leadership no less than the British government. The depth of the commitment to the Spanish Republic felt on the Labour left can be gauged by Bevan's first response to the outbreak of the Second World War, as described by his wife, Jennie Lee:

. . . for once too excited for words . . . [Aneurin] stopped walking up and down to rummage in a corner among a disorderly pile of gramophone records. He found what he was looking for. He found records we had not dared play for more than a year: the marching songs of the Spanish Republican armies. Now we may listen to them again. We need not be ashamed. They ring triumphantly through the cottage. We are on our way back to Spain. We are bringing arms this time. We are coming fully armed.[110]

The intense belief that Spain's cause was the cause of democrats everywhere led to a bitter intra-party clash at the Edinburgh Conference in the autumn of 1936. The delegates had another controversial matter to deal with: in addition to the question of arms for Spain there was the matter of arms for Britain.

4

In 1935 the Labour Party had announced its willingness to wage war in the cause of collective security, yet in Parliament the party had continued to oppose rearmament. Central to this refusal was uncertainty about the use to which the National Government would put those arms. On the very day that Hoare left for his meeting with Laval, Labour's A. V. Alexander criticized the duality of the government's foreign policy: '. . . we never seem to know on which leg they are standing, whether on the leg of policy which stands solely for the maintenance of a collective peace system, or whether on the leg of policy which stands solely for the right to take unilateral action, either in regard to international negotiations for treaties or in regard to the provisions of actual national defence.'[111] The Hoare-Laval Pact provided all too clear-cut an answer to Labour's query; detecting in that action the temper of the National Government, Labour's opposition to rearmament under their auspices was confirmed.

We have seen that the reasons for such opposition were deep-rooted. In addition, the suspicions entertained concerning the intentions of the National Government, stemming from 1931, had only recently been confirmed. To arm the government returned to office by an electoral ruse would be an act of folly, and a dangerous act as well, because of the inherent place of war in the capitalist system. The *New Statesman*'s comments typify Labour's resolve not to be tricked again by that government's proclaimed intentions to adhere to the Covenant and collective security. Rearmament assumed a sinister guise:

In private the idea that British armaments might be used for any other than an exclusively Imperialist purpose is not taken seriously in the Conservative Party. They are wanted because the Government does not believe in the League and knows that Europe is returning to the old system of the Balance of Power. And, in spite of the recent improvement in our relations with Russia, the assumption in armament and die-hard circles is still that we are arming in order that Germany may more certainly eschew Western ambitions with the understanding that we shall not object to any Eastern adventure.[112]

Four months later that journal ruefully noted the decision to terminate sanctions: 'We may, indeed, roll up the map of Europe ... Collective security for the time being is dead.' Though regrettable, this development at least enabled Labour to '... refuse, and ask everyone to refuse, support of a rearmament designed not for genuine collective security but for a balance of power policy which means war'.[113] The implications of the government's rearmament policy were also spelled out for the trade union membership by Norman Angell in the journal *Labour*: '... the sinister fact in the situation is that armament increase receives its strongest support from those who are bitterly opposed to the Covenant. The Rothermeres and Beaverbrooks

... believe ... that these vast national armaments can be made, not the instrument of a truly international order, but an alternative thereto.'[114] As for the National Government's appeal for rearmament, that was received in many quarters of the Labour Party, especially on the left, as yet another sham:

How could they [British Socialists] see the tormentors of their people suddenly translated into stout defenders of working-class liberties? For Bevan, that would have implied a betrayal of a whole lifetime's experience and struggle. British Capitalism, not German Fascism, was the enemy on his doorstep, as ancient as the industrial revolution itself, as modern as the latest Means Test infamy. It was Tory rule which decreed that there should still be two nations and it was doing so as brutally as in the days of the Chartists. To suppose that the nation could overnight be made one, by a patriotic cry, was the most cruel of frauds.[115]

Such negativism, while comprehensible, did not offer any practical solution to the problem of defence so long as that hated National Government remained in power; in 1936 their mandate ran for another four years. To be sure the Labour left attempted to shorten that mandate by once more agitating for a front powerful enough to bring down the government, but meanwhile distrust of the government perforce outweighed all considerations of defence. A. L. Rowse, then active in Labour activities, shows that distrust was present in all sectors of the party:

After that [Abyssinia] coming after the experiences of 1931 and 1924, no Labour man would take anything from a Tory ... I well knew the atmosphere of complete and justified distrust. I thoroughly understood it and shared it ... The tragedy of all this was that after 1935 no Labour man would accept anything that came from the Tories – *even when they were right*. And this is where I criticise the Labour Party. In spite of everything, when danger threatened, we ought to have pocketed our humiliation, our pride, our distrust, everything for the sake of the country and all that depended upon it.[116]

Distrust was not easily dispelled from Labour ranks, nor were patterns of thought lightly broken: disarmament had been argued from Labour platforms too long and too persuasively to be cast out overnight. Rearmament remained beyond the Labour pale.

In rebutting the charges which Labour had brought against the Hoare-Laval pact, Neville Chamberlain had satirized the party's defence policy:

You will not get peace, he [Attlee] said, by running away. Well, then, the corollary of that is that you must be ready, if necessary, to fight. Where will he and his friends stand if presently we come to say, 'Now we ask for the authority of the House to repair the gaps in our defences'? We can see now where they stand. (Hon. Members: 'Not a penny.') There are the intellectuals like the hon. Members who say 'Get on with your sanctions whatever the cost', and the hon. Members behind who say 'The Tories it is who want war'. But all join together to say 'Above all do not let us have any armaments'.[117]

The PLP however offered one positive suggestion for the government's proposed defence schemes: they continued to advocate the creation of a Ministry of Defence, in the name of the efficient performance of that function.[118] Evidently increased Service Estimates did not meet that test, for in March 1936 the PLP opposed them, though not without some internal strife. Baldwin on 9 March 1936 – coincidentally following upon Hitler's reoccupation of the Rhineland – laid before the Commons a White Paper on Defence; at that time he solicited the support of all parties for those measures of defence considered necessary by the government. He appealed especially to the trade union leaders in the Labour Party, whom he knew well enough to be confident that they would not shirk the responsibility inherent in the declaration they had approved at the Margate TUC, nor willingly leave the country weak in defence or ill-prepared to deter an aggressor.[119]

There was method in Baldwin's appeal, for the TUC General Secretary, Citrine, had only recently commented that 'it may be that, in pursuance of Labour's policy, we may find we cannot resist a certain measure of rearmament'.[120] The publication of the White Paper on 3 March had precipitated considerable discussion within the Labour Party. Dalton records his own participation in a number of meetings which considered Labour's reaction: 'On the three days March 2nd, 3rd and 4th, I attended no less than nine meetings (several of these bodies met more than once) of the National Council of Labour, the National Executive, the Parliamentary Executive, the full Parliamentary Labour Party, the International Sub-Committee of the National Executive and a Grand Jamboree of all members of our Three Executives.'[121] The *Morning Post* of the 4th detected a rift in the socialist camp, reporting that the industrial wing did not share the parliamentary opposition in principle; that paper, ever eager to point out division in Labour's ranks, maintained that the TUC intended '. . . to co-operate with the Government in furthering the programme while seizing every opportunity of improving their position'.[122] Reports in *The Times* and the *Manchester Guardian* confirm the existence of this rift and agree that while the political wing was concerned with competitive national rearmament and the British government's evident distrust of the collective system, the industrial wing was interested in such consequences of rearmament as the organization of industry.[123] The General Council were hopeful, *The Times* reported, that discussions of the problem would enable them to advance employee interests; as yet the government had not offered to consult the GC, however.[124] Dalton, hopeful of trade union pressure for rearmament, regretted that Baldwin had made no such direct approach:

> Those of us who sensed the peril of German rearmament got no help from the Government in our efforts to wake up our colleagues. If some hard facts about Hitler's doings had been officially disclosed in the first instance to our Trade Union colleagues, these facts would certainly have influenced them and very soon, through them, a wider circle.[125]

Since Bevin and Citrine were certainly aware of the German peril, Dalton's reference most likely is to the trade union-sponsored MPs who seldom concerned themselves with matters other than domestic.

The view of the political wing again prevailed in 1936; both the PLP and the National Council of Labour – though nearly half its membership came from the TUC General Council – opposed the measures of rearmament requested by Baldwin. Dalton recorded in his diary:

> We *are* unfit to govern. 'He who darkeneth counsel by words without knowledge' abounds among us . . . The Party won't face up to realities. There is still much mere anti-armament sentiment, and many more are agin' our own Government than agin' Hitler. Pretty desperate.

To the disapproval also of Bevin, who had worked with Dalton to bring about their colleagues, '. . . the amendment moved by Attlee in the Commons debate [on the White Paper] might well have been copied unchanged from any Labour Party manifesto of the past fifteen years'.[126]

That point was not lost on Sir Samuel Hoare, when he pointed out to Labour that their attitude assumed that everything was normal in the world, as if no great changes had taken place in past years, or even in recent days. Labour spokesmen might well have retorted that Hoare had himself presided over one of those changes for the worse, but his point is well taken. Attlee however held that rearmament would only worsen the situation, since the British action would provoke other countries to rearm in response.[127] Labour's approach, he reiterated, was to maintain such defence forces as were 'necessary and consistent' with membership in the League; yet he did not consider what forces the League might be able to deploy, after its failure to supply any for the defence of Ethiopia. Hoare's criticism of Labour's defence policy might have been profitably applied by the party leaders, but following his disastrous stay at the Foreign Office 'no Labour man would take anything from the Tories', least of all from Hoare.

Herbert Morrison concluded for Labour, proclaiming that they would go unitedly into the opposition lobby on the White Paper:

... we disagree with, we regret and we condemn the whole foreign policy, practically speaking, of this Government since it came into office. We do so, not only because of the wrong things which it has done, but also because of the good things which it has refrained from doing and its general lack of grip and competence in the conduct of diplomacy and the leadership of the world.[128]

One can explain and understand the reaction of the Labour Party to the request for additional armaments by a government which they loathed and distrusted; however, other criteria, such as that of national interest and the preservation of peace, also demanded consideration. Labour's weighing of those several criteria seems in error: by focusing their attention upon the faults of the National Government, the Labour Party could not but distract from concern for the international menace of fascism. It is interesting to note that the opposition Liberals had grasped this point in the autumn of 1935; Samuel, then their leader, had laid bare the logical end of continued opposition to rearmament: 'If the peace-loving democratic powers, like Britain, France and the United States, were to disarm, and if the militarist powers were to increase their armaments, the affairs of mankind would be handed

F

over to them. Peace must have its realists as well as war.'[129] In this elemental sense the Labour Party was less than realistic in 1936.

Opposition to the White Paper dictated resistance to the particular Service Estimates. Typical of Labour's approach to the problem of Britain's defences was Alexander's opposition to the Naval Estimates. This ex-First Lord simply reckoned up the naval forces of good and evil and decided that those of the former were sufficiently superior: the combined tonnage of French and British naval forces was very nearly 2,000,000 tons, while the German Fleet totalled only 300,000.[130] When several years later the British were forced to attack and destroy the French fleet so that it would not fall into German hands, when the Japanese fleet had driven the British back into the Indian Ocean, and when German and Italian control of the air in the Mediterranean dictated that the British life-line to the Middle East stretch around the Cape, Churchill's First Lord of the Admiralty, A. V. Alexander, may well have rued his precise calculations of 1936.

In response to demands from his left and right for a Ministry of Defence, Baldwin had established the office of a Minister for the Co-ordination of Defence; the PLP expressed disappointment with the government's action, since the powers of the new post, given to the former Attorney-General, Sir Thomas Inskip, fell considerably short of those envisaged by Labour. Though Inskip's qualifications for the post were open to some doubt, Labour based its criticism upon the 'responsibility divorced from authority' which it found incorporated in the new office.[131] This criticism proved most perceptive; because of the circumscribed nature of the post, '... no living man – not even Winston Churchill – could have made a success of the appointment...'[132]

Hugh Dalton attempted to minimize the impact of Labour's moving token reductions to the various military estimates by arguing that such a procedure lay within long-established parliamentary traditions. The manœuvre initiated debate which would reveal whether the armaments were intended for use within a scheme of collective security and whether '... as between the demands for the different Services, there was any scheme of intelligible co-ordination so as to get the best results from a given expenditure'. As these criteria were not met, Dalton continued,

Labour divided on behalf of the token reduction; defeated in each instance, Labour did not then challenge the main Estimates, which passed without division. The only thing wrong with Dalton's careful exposition of the tactics of Labour's opposition to rearmament was that in the following month the PLP made a mockery of it. On 20 July 1936, just days after the outbreak of the Spanish Civil War, the Labour Party in fact divided against the total Supplementary Estimates for the fighting forces; a week later, they voted against the final stages of the total Supply Estimates. Dalton's technical defence of Labour's procedure was fractured; no longer could the party deny Baldwin's charge that they had voted '. . . against every vote for the Navy, every aeroplane for the Air Force, and every proposal for the production of an extra shell for the Navy'.[133] Yet in no sense does this lift the onus of responsibility in matters of defence from the government: throughout the decade, the House of Commons without exception sanctioned whatever measures the government requested. No aeroplanes or shells were lost to the nation because of Labour's opposition.

Not everyone in the Parliamentary Labour Party agreed with such total opposition: Dalton resisted, but he received the support of only three other members of the PLP Executive and of thirty-eight MPs. Fifty-seven MPs decided to oppose the total Estimates, and some sixty took no stand at all.[134] The PLP announced its decision on 25 July to oppose the full Estimates '. . . in order to mark its entire opposition to the international policy of the Government, of which the rearmament programme is an integral part'.[135] They stipulated that a vote against an Estimate was not a vote for the abolition of the service involved but rather a vote in opposition to the policy of which the Estimate was the expression. Dalton regarded this assertion as a 'lame excuse', and he and a number of his colleagues invoked the conscience clause generally monopolized by the pacifists to abstain on the final stages of the Estimates. That group did not, however, '. . . sit ostentatiously in our seats in the House when the vote was called, and others went into the lobby, so that our names should be noted by the Press'.[136] Regarding that as a form of parliamentary exhibitionism, they simply left the House, saying nothing to the press.

To discover the size and composition of this group, one must consult the division lists in *Hansard*. What Dalton does not relate is that this technique of passive opposition had originated a week earlier, before the PLP statement. On 20 July the party moved a token reduction, voting 134 in favour; after that defeat, only 116 voted against the Supplementary Estimate. By consulting division lists for that day and for the 27th, when the main Estimates were taken up, we can isolate eight Labour MPs who were consistent abstainers in the final stages – Barnes, Bellenger, Dalton, Fletcher, Leslie, Mathers, Price and J. Henderson. In addition, Alexander, Clynes and Green abstained on the 20th, though they cannot be definitely placed in the Commons on 27 July.[137] Since Alexander and Clynes were with Dalton the only members of the PLP Executive among the eleven, they must certainly be included among the pro-rearmament group. No striking generalizations emerge concerning the eleven, except that only four were trade union-sponsored, none, surprisingly, by Bevin's TGWU.

The attitude of the leader of the Labour Party was of some importance in the decision to oppose rearmament totally; as late as 1937 Clement Attlee opposed rearmament, despite his recognition that the aggressive policies of the fascist powers posed genuine dangers: 'To say what the Government is doing is necessary for the defence of the country is to beg the whole question. I do not believe that the entry into a competition in arms will give security. On the contrary, I think that it is leading straight to the disaster of another world war.'[138] Attlee took care to maintain that the level of British rearmament was not necessarily adequate, but rather that that proper level was impossible to ascertain, because the British government's foreign policy was so uncertain. In such a dangerous situation, one would prefer to find Labour erring on the side of caution; yet Attlee found the greater danger in an arms race. He seemed to regard fascist rearmament as an aspect of some international arms race rather than as national phenomenon: 'Do not compete with the fascists in arms,' he apparently reasoned, 'and they will not rearm.' Nothing was further from the truth. It was he, and the party he led, which begged, if not the whole question, then the major one.

To the ranks of the eleven parliamentarians who had tacitly rejected such reasoning, there was shortly added the Secretary of the Labour Party's International Department, William Gillies, who reviewed the European situation on 1 September 1936 in a document probably intended for circulation among the leadership.

We may also have to consider whether we can go on assailing Fascism, urging our Government to take a strong line in foreign policy, advocating an anti-fascist bloc of the peace-loving nations, and expecting that bloc to call the Nazi and Fascist bluff (if it be a bluff), and at the same time appear to oppose the adequate rearmament of our own country. It has to be examined whether the rearmament of Great Britain is not essential merely on the grounds of ordinary prudence.[139]

Ernest Bevin developed what he considered would be the results of such a re-examination for the benefit of the 1936 TUC meeting, later in September. Noting that this extensive undertaking should properly be carried out by the new General Council and Labour Party Executive, he commented bluntly:

In this examination it will be necessary for this Movement to take new responsibilities ... The question of collective security is in danger of becoming a shibboleth rather than a practical operative fact ... We are ... satisfied that we are not going to meet the Fascist menace by mere resolutions ... [nor] by pure pacifism ... If in certain respects it means uprooting some of our cherished ideals and facing the issue fairly in the light of the development of Fascism, we must do it for the Movement and for the sake of posterity.[140]

Bevin's views were of more than passing interest, for he was to chair the General Council in the following year. 'Ordinary prudence' was coming to the fore; Bevin and Dalton had both made clear their support for rearmament even under the National Government, and the next year was to provide them with the chance to work together for that measure. Yet meanwhile the leadership had to enter the Edinburgh Conference before that re-examination was undertaken, with what amounted to no agreed international policy.

5

On 5 October 1936 the Labour Party met in Conference at Edinburgh, a setting which Dalton did not like from the first.

Though he offers a geo-political explanation,[141] it is likely that his discomfort stemmed less from the absence of the usual soothing sea-side than from the rancour of the Conference deliberations. Controversy centred about three topics – rearmament, non-intervention in Spain and the United Front. No agreed resolution on Labour's international policy, including the question of British rearmament, had been presented to the Plymouth TUC; the National Council of Labour however produced a temporary formula on which the delegates at Edinburgh might unite, before the new governing bodies could take up their planned re-examination. The actual drafting of this formula was in the hands of a sub-committee consisting of Attlee, Morrison, Dalton, James Walker of the Ironworkers and Susan Lawrence. Once more the Tory press expected that a pro-rearmament statement would result.[142] The *Observer* reported confidently: 'The sub-committee is really a face-saving device. There is not the slightest doubt about the content of the resolution to be submitted to the Party conference. It is the sugar [coating] that is now important.'[143] That fact was evidently not so apparent to the drafters, for their resolution contained only what Bevin had characterized as 'shibboleths': it reaffirmed Labour's policy to maintain such defence forces as were consistent with Britain's responsibility as a member of the League but stipulated, because of the deplorable record of the National Government, '. . . the Labour Party declines to accept responsibility for a purely competitive armament policy'. Debate upon this resolution ranged through nearly a day, but the various speeches classify themselves into four categories. The pacifists and the Labour left persisted in the arguments heard before; thus the significant conflict at Edinburgh was between the views of the two majority factions which, though they agreed on the resolution, differed on its meaning.

Dalton, speaking for the Executive, initiated the discussion; he stressed the brutal facts of German rearmament, which meant the possibility of a direct aerial attack upon the British Isles – more vulnerable to such an attack than any other great country in the world. The conclusion he considered inescapable:

. . . a Labour Government, if it came into power to-morrow, and was faced, as it would be, with the present world situation, that such a Government – pending an international agreement to reduce and limit armaments – and such a Government would strive to its utmost to negotiate such an agreement – pending that, a Labour Government would be compelled to provide an increase in British armaments.[144]

Gasps greeted this bluntness, but Dalton had deliberately spoken of what Labour in power would do, not of how Labour in opposition would vote;[145] unfortunately Dalton gives no reason for this tack. Possibly he wanted someone else to speak of the position of the Labour Opposition, since his own views were those of a minority. He did refer to Labour's continued opposition to a competitive arms policy, if only to show that Labour's rearmament would be accomplished within a planned system of collective security. Dalton had then been bold for rearmament, but only under conditions which were rather removed from reality.

Herbert Morrison, like Dalton a member of the Executive and the drafting sub-committee, spoke to the point of Labour's attitude to rearmament while in opposition. Though he first stipulated that the PLP alone had the right to say whether it would vote against Service Estimates as a whole or divide only on token reductions, he regarded the meaning of the temporary formula as unequivocal:

... what the resolution does not contemplate being done, is lining up behind the Government and voting for its rearmament programme, because directly you do that you have not only voted for its competitive national rearmament programme, you have thereby become implicated in the whole of its foreign policy. You cannot possibly separate your considerations of armaments policy from your consideration of foreign policy.[146]

Labour's opposition to rearmament under the aegis of the National Government was made all the more clear in Morrison's assertion that the resolution was '. . . in no way a departure from the policy that this Party has approved for a number of years past'. Morrison's statement, however, did not contradict that of Dalton; the two were talking about different phases of Labour's policy, the one in opposition, the other in power. Stafford Cripps interjected the point that the former role should be the party's sole concern – a reasonable argument, though no one had talked more of the millennium than had Cripps. He asked Conference not to try to 'slip out' of making the decision that opposition alone mattered, by accepting a resolution which could be interpreted in such widely divergent ways as those of Dalton and Morrison.[147]

Although Ernest Bevin more often than not clashed with Cripps, he now felt himself in sympathy in sensing that the National Executive was asking the delegates to 'pass the buck' to the PLP; he chose to single out Morrison's speech for criticism, as one of the worst pieces of tight-rope walking he had ever witnessed in Conference. Bevin had taken the resolution to mean '. . . a clear departure on the armaments side of the policy; not what has been declared at the [past Labour Party] Conferences – that is burking the issue – but a departure from the votes that have been given in the House on the Estimates during the past few months'. Since Dalton had avoided the question of Labour's attitude in opposition, Bevin might well have criticized the irrelevancy of that speech as well, but he probably recognized that Dalton's personal views paralleled his own. Whether he then wished to lay the blame upon his old foe Morrison is problematic, but Morrison had hardly burked the issue. Thus Bevin compounded the confusion of the meaning of the Executive resolution, but he made his own views again plain:

. . . I believe that if this great Movement says to Hitler: 'If you are going to rely on force . . . we will stand up four-square to it ' . . . I am afraid . . . that we may have to go through force to liberty. With the philosophy of Fascism in the world, I feel that unless it is checked it will be inevitable. Therefore, I ask this Conference to get a clear declaration from this platform as to what it means.[148]

Though Bevin's biographer maintains that Attlee, speaking for the Executive, failed to supply that answer, Attlee's reply seems unequivocal: 'There is no suggestion here', he commented, 'that we should support the Government's rearmament policy.'[149] Further, he sketched the consequences of such support: 'It will lead you to demand after demand being made on your liberties. It will in effect lead to a demand that you shall accept Fascism practically, in order to conquer Fascism. We shall be no party to that.' Here was the answer Bevin sought; Labour's leader, the voice of the PLP, refused national rearmament against an acknowledged danger, because the remedy was as dangerous as the disease. Yet G. D. H. Cole, in his history of the Labour Party, accepted Bevin's reading of the equivocal 'buck-passing' attitude of the Executive; he held that the resolution '. . . failed to tell the delegates what they really wanted to know – whether the PLP meant to go on opposing the Government's estimates for rearmament or not'.[150] We cannot so indict the Executive, for their view of Labour's role in opposition was clear, if unfortunate. Morrison and Attlee refused to acknowledge that the British contribution to the collective task of resisting aggression could no longer be based on the assumption that there in fact existed such a collective system. Even Dalton, who had created confusion by his reference to Labour's role in power, did not disown that assumption, though he had not been enthusiastic about the possibilities of League action. Thus the Executive's position was neither contradictory nor equivocal; neither was it decisive, nor particularly relevant. The resolution was carried by 1,738,000 votes to 657,000 but, because of the debate, few could judge the possible impact.

Edinburgh was not a happy hour for Labour's leadership in another regard as well. On the first day of the Conference, the Executive recommended a policy of non-intervention; subsequently, severe pressure from delegates forced them to make that stand rather more conditional. Thus while the question of rearmament was settled in one day, Spain was the centre of attention on the first, third and last days of the Conference. The Executive had not so planned it, for certain party leaders regarded Spain as simply a part of a larger problem. Yet there were present at Edinburgh those to whom nothing mattered besides Spain.[151] The months which had passed between the outbreak of the civil war and the assembly in Edinburgh had not narrowed the internal breach over the question of arms for Spain. During September rumours of acts of intervention had come to the attention of Labour spokesmen; though details on German and Italian actions were sketchy, presumably their intervention had provoked Blum's dispatch of aircraft to the Republican forces before the non-intervention agreements were to take effect, an action he had justified to a visiting Labour Party deputation.[152] We now know that as early as 24 July Hitler agreed in principle to support the Spanish rebels; the well-organized German aid may well have been crucial in securing the Nationalist gains in the summer.[153] Throughout September, after the non-intervention agreements had become effective, German and Italian supplies reached

Franco's forces, enabling him to advance against Madrid on 6 October. On the other hand, Stalin apparently did not decide to supply the Republicans until 21 September, when the failure of the Western democracies to supply arms had created a vacuum which Soviet Russia could partially fill, to her own advantage.[154] These developments were of course more nebulous in September 1936, when they took the form of rumours. That one's willingness to credit rumours is a function of his predisposition towards the subject of those rumours is illustrated by the debates at Edinburgh, where the left was far more inclined to argue the 'fact' of German and Italian intervention.

The Executive's case initially was put by Arthur Greenwood in a most apologetic fashion; he characterized non-intervention as 'a very, very bad second best'. His claim that the alternative was free trade in arms to both sides was not an overwhelming argument to those who held that the struggle of democracy and fascism which was being waged in Spain concerned all Europeans; nor would they accept his assertion that free trade in arms would favour the rebels in an overwhelming fashion.[155] Greenwood also declared that the National Council of Labour would be ever vigilant for violations of non-intervention; perhaps in response to the widespread rumours, he stressed that proof would be required. Major trade union leaders – Bevin, Charles Dukes and George Hicks – supported Greenwood, but vigorous opposition came from Charles Trevelyan, Aneurin Bevan and others, mainly to the left.

Opposition was based both on practical and emotional grounds. Judging the situation pragmatically, Christopher Addison took as established fact that for which Greenwood had asked proof:

We know perfectly well – those of us who have first-hand information from Spain, and I have no doubt that my friends who supported it [non-intervention] have first-hand information – that the supply of aeroplanes and munitions is four or five times more now than six weeks ago, and those supplies, we know well enough, have come from Fascist countries ... there is a wholesale leakage going on every day to the assistance of the rebels in Spain.[156]

Philip Noel-Baker, no leftist, also accepted the validity of that information, which alone could explain why what he styled a 'handful of adventurers' were defeating a government backed by the vast majority of the nation. Consequently he wanted Conference to press the British government to announce that, since the agreements were being violated, they would suspend the arms embargo on the Spanish government. Such a suspension, he claimed, would not embarrass the French government, nor could it give Hitler a pretext for an international war; on the contrary, it would very quickly end the war in Spain. A more emotional note was sounded by William Dobbie, a Labour MP who had recently visited Spain, where a militiaman had told him: 'With us it is victory or death. Take the message to your people, and ask them to give us, not help, but the opportunity to buy the things necessary for us in defence of democracy, not only of ourselves, but of all the free peoples of the world.' Bevan endorsed the emotional view – though he doubted that the point of view espoused by Greenwood and the trade unionists could be called pragmatic – because grave and practical consequences would stem from the defeat of the Republicans. The height of emotional fervour was reached in the remarks of Sir Charles Trevelyan, who condemned the 'playing for safety' which would, however, lead to the creation of another fascist state and bring war in its course. The man who had opposed all wars at the Labour Party Conference of 1933 now turned his wrath on the leadership which shied from intervening in war: 'You are beggared of policy at this moment . . . When the last great war that is looming comes and when Japan and Germany crash in to try to destroy Soviet Russia, I hope then that the Labour Party will have some other policy to offer than their sympathy accompanied by bandages and cigarettes.'[157] A huge derisive cheer from the floor smashed against the platform, and Ernest Bevin reacted, 'God help the Labour movement.'[158] Cheers notwithstanding, the resolution was approved, 1,836,000 to 519,000; the matter had neatly been settled before the special Spanish fraternal delegates addressed the Conference.

Those two were given the floor on Wednesday the 7th; they were well aware of the vote – perhaps some on the Executive regarded it as a *fait accompli* – and the first to speak, de Asna, was not prepared to ask the delegates to change their vote. Nonetheless he reminded them:

. . . We are fighting with sticks and knives against tanks and aircraft and

163

guns, and it revolts the conscience of the world that that should be true. We must have arms. Help us to buy them somewhere in the world . . . Is it too much to ask that in this fight against the Fascisms of the world, the democracies shall allow us to buy the arms we need to fight this battle, which we are certain we can win for democracy and for the peace of the world.[159]

Coupled to this appeal to the radical conscience was specific proof of the continuing violation of non-intervention; de Asna cited not only the material recently presented to the League of Nations, but also seven known instances of such action since early September.

Emotion followed upon exposition; his colleague, Señora de Palencia, 'a proud Amazon straight from the Spanish battle-fields',[160] spoke in English, unlike her colleague. She reminded the delegates of her Scottish descent, recalling that as a child she had walked those very streets of Edinburgh, peopled 'with the characters of Walter Scott and echoing with the music of Robert Burns's poems'. Of late those memories had returned to her, but they were confused with the nightmares of the present in Spain. Nonetheless she could take leave of the Conference greatly comforted:

We know that we are holding your hand over the distance. But let me tell you, if you wish this atrocious war to end soon come and help us as you have been asked, whenever you can. Think of the difference in the price of lives of two months to one year. Think of the precious gift that is being wasted – of the lives of our youth. Do not tarry. Now you know the truth. Now you know what the situation is. Come and help us. Come and help us. Scotsmen, ye ken noo![161]

In response the delegates rose to their feet and sang the 'Red Flag', to which the Spaniard returned the clenched fist salute. How ironic that the apogee of Labour emotionalism in the decade came in the address of a Communist to a Labour Party which resisted any and all CPGB entreaties for co-operation in the face of fascism!

Labour's calm resolution of two days earlier paled in comparison; the NCL recognized this fact, and after lunch they announced that Attlee and Greenwood were to proceed (or shall we say beat a hasty retreat?) to London to discuss the Spanish situation with the acting Prime Minister, Chamberlain. As a result, Attlee moved for the Executive on the last day of Conference a resolution designed to implement the policy towards Spain which Labour had consistently followed, he claimed. Under its terms they would press for an investigation of the alleged breaches of non-intervention; if the Non-Intervention Committee failed to act with the utmost speed, the Executive would demand the restoration to the Spanish government of the right to purchase arms. Though Attlee was justified in arguing that no departure from past policy was involved, certainly the tempo had dramatically altered. At the same time Attlee went to unaccustomed lengths to warn the party: 'It has got to be made quite clear that if we demand that the Government of this country should take action to end this Agreement, we must be prepared to face any risks that may attend this action.'[162] The Edinburgh Conference unanimously agreed to run that risk; their earlier opposition to rearmament must have seemed rather inconsistent to its proponents. Perhaps Hugh Dalton had just this in mind in recording the mood of wild excitement of the delegates on Friday: 'They were wallowing in sheer emotion, in vicarious valour. They had no clue in their mind to the risks, and the realities, for Britain of a general war.'[163]

Though the left had successfully agitated for a more critical approach towards non-intervention, they were unable to budge the Edinburgh Conference from opposition to Communist affiliation and to any domestic version of the Popular Front. Late in 1935, Harry Pollitt had once again applied for Communist affiliation to the Labour Party; he had stressed their willingness to work to win a majority of working-class representatives in all local governmental bodies and in Parliament. Anticipating denials of Communist sincerity, he stated that the CPGB was prepared '. . . to do this, not as a manoeuvre or for any concealed aims, but because it believes that this would unite the working class and make it better able to face the immediate fight against the National Government, against Fascism and against imperialist war'.

Pollitt might well have spared himself the apologetics, for the Labour Party refused to grant any such sincerity of purpose to the Communists; in addition, the Party Secretary reminded

Pollitt that the fundamental difference between a democratic policy and one of dictatorship, which the CPGB had been created to promote, remained irreconcilable.[164] In order to review their arguments against granting affiliation to the Communists, the Executive asked the NCL to draft a report. The result, 'British Labour and Communism', discussed such fundamental differences as ideas on democracy, Soviet subventions and conspiracies: the 'United Front' sought by Pollitt they labelled a product of the Communist failure to secure a substantial membership in their own party. The report inverted the existence of such a front in France as an argument against the Communists, who had increased their parliamentary representation six times over as a result but had refused to share the responsibilities of the Blum Government. In any case, why offer such an opportunity to the CPGB, whose historic contribution had been minimal?

> Communist principles, Communist propaganda, and Communist organization have clearly made no helpful contribution to the advance of British Labour. On the contrary, Communist influence in Britain has been a serious drag upon the Labour Movement wherever and whenever it has been exercised ... Communist association will only serve to distract the Movement, mislead the electorate generally, and store up difficulties against the day of Socialist victory.[105]

The summer of 1936 witnessed a great upsurge of left sentiment, fed by the Spanish Civil War, running contrary to the views of the Labour leadership. Their decision to accept nonintervention flew in the face of this sentiment, which turned elsewhere for a means of expression. The Communist appeal for a united front against fascism gained new adherents. At the same time, the Left Book Club, established by the publisher Victor Gollancz in May 1936, supplied a forum for such agitation, which the Labour leadership had refused to do. With all shades of left support, club groups were set up throughout the country, attracting large numbers of the politically unattached, for the most part young; they were thereafter given a steady diet of propagandist books,[166] issued at the low price of 2/6. A high proportion of the books published were quite in accordance with the Communist 'party line', and nearly all the discussions of the international situation concluded with a plea for some sort of a united front as the only way to stop Hitler.[167] Such an ideological bias is all the more surprising since not one of its editorial committee – Gollancz, Harold Laski and John Strachey – was a CPGB member, although all were committed leftists. The success with which the Communists utilized the Left Book Club to serve their own purposes, without ever possessing actual control of its operations, might well have served as a warning to those who would co-operate with the CPGB in any endeavour. Through the Left Book Club, Spain became the beginning of politics for many a British intellectual.[168]

This upsurge of sentiment on behalf of Spain however had little influence upon the attitude of the Labour Party delegates to the entreaties of Pollitt. Since exigencies of time forced a shortening of debate on topics other than rearmament and Spain, the Communist bid for affiliation received scant attention: a delegate protested against the partisan approach of 'British Labour and Communism', which missed the central point that there should be a single co-ordinated fight against capitalism. The Executive in effect stood by the arguments of that special report, while a Labour MP indicated that a fear of the electoral consequences of such an action also operated; the Labour Party might gain perhaps 10,000 new members, as opposed to the loss of the '. . . support at the next General Election of probably millions of folks who otherwise would be willing to vote for us'.[169] Though affiliation was rejected by 1,728,000 votes to 592,000 – 400,000 of which were contributed by the Miners' Federation – the supporters of the United Front raised that matter as well; they maintained that as co-operation with the CPGB would be limited to one specific matter, entirely different considerations from those of Communist affiliation operated. Once again the cry resounded, 'We have got to bother more about the thing we are marching against, rather than the comrade we are marching with,' but the vast majority of the delegates refused to trust that particular 'comrade' from Communist ranks. William Mellor of the Socialist League, protesting against the proscription of Communist auxiliary organizations at the same time as Labour leaders shared platforms with right-wing Tory groups for specific purposes, asked, 'Are we not bone of bone and flesh of flesh of the working-class leaders who are not part of this Movement? Are we not linked more essentially with them than with people who have for years fought the very principles on which we stand?'[170]

Conference evidently felt not, as only 435,000 favoured the unity proposals.

No one emerged pleased with the results of Conference; the very concentration of debate upon these contentious issues forced a number of important constitutional reforms, particularly favourable to the Labour left, from the agenda.[171] Reactions to the Conference neared despair on all sides, from frustration and resentment on the left to bewilderment and fear among the Labour right. Ernest Bevin was greatly troubled by the irresponsibility of the debate upon defence, his friend Francis Williams records: 'After the Conference Bevin came nearer I think to believing that the gulf between the trade unions and "the politicians" was unbridgable than at any previous time in his life despite his not infrequent hostility to the political wing at earlier times.'[172] Another trade union leader, George Ridley, explained his own unease in the journal *Labour*: 'One of the things that troubled me most about the discussion was the fact that the most vociferous demands for intervention came from people who, for the sake of a gesture, were prepared to defy half Europe without being willing to equip themselves with the instruments of defence.'[173] Thus did the trade union wing apply the very same criticism to Labour's left wing which the Conservatives had long brought against the entire Labour Party.

The left were even more grieved with the Edinburgh proceedings, because the Executive had retained firm control of the party, though they had retreated somewhat on Spain. Bevan's wife, Jennie Lee, present as an ILP observer, was struck by Labour's hypocrisy in singing the 'Internationale' at the Conference's conclusion. Unable to bear their proclaiming 'Then comrades, come rally,' she fled the hall and

... stumbled into Aneurin. He looked haggard and careworn ... ill anyhow at the time ... he looked as if he had just dragged himself from the torture chamber. And he was not the only delegate who felt like that. Out they came, singly and in groups, the most unhappy, guilty-looking collection of people I have ever seen. Their very misery made me hope again. If they felt like that something could perhaps still be done.[174]

Harold Laski failed to detect even this glimmer of hope; he wrote his old friend, Felix Frankfurter, that the Labour Party

... goes so directly the road of German Social Democracy that it turns my hair gray. After a long fight, those blasted trade union leaders decided on non-intervention though they know this meant a sure rebel victory in Spain. They turned down all and every suggestion for a united front; and they made the foreign debates at Edinburgh the worst mess since 1931 ... I have never seen such blindness in a body of leaders since I began to be interested in politics.[175]

The verdict on the Edinburgh Conference rendered by *The Times* – 'The Conference showed the Labour Party to be a party adrift in a stormy world, with a committee of divided leaders uncertain how or where to steer'[176] – is endorsed by such diverse reactions no less than by the proceedings.

Yet such an interpretation overlooks one of the basic elements in the problem faced by the Labour Party as it emerged from Edinburgh: though the Executive was collectively adrift, certain of the leaders had set their courses. Bevin and Dalton offered one policy; Cripps and the left shortly evolved an alternative approach. Only the Executive, and indeed the Leader, remained to be won. Attlee was justifiably concerned with the preservation of party unity and consequently acted more the part of moderator than of leader. The Parliamentary Labour Party, which alone could implement the policy decisions of the party, remained opposed both to rearmament and to arms shipments to the Spanish Republic. The pressure of events of course would influence their position in both regards, but more important, elements within the Labour Party, to the right as well as the left, were shortly to organize attempts to capture the collective leadership and the PLP for their policy. Cripps backed a Unity Campaign; Dalton and Bevin meanwhile sat as joint chairmen of the National Council of Labour.

The year of indecision was fast drawing to a close.

6   For Spain and rearmament

The left's discontent with the decisions reached at Edinburgh did not quickly abate. G. D. H. Cole, for one, protested against the 'Conference steam-roller', that ever-present block vote of the trade unions which was used to suppress all deviations to the left:

> The change in this respect is due mainly to two things – the appearance in the Trade Union movement of two men who have turned the Trades Union Congress from a not very effective forum for debate into a very positive instrument of policy, and the distrust of 'intellectuals' and all non-official-unionist leadership which is the aftermath of the defection of Mr MacDonald and Lord Snowden in 1931.[1]

Cole further deprecated the increase of trade union influence, exercised of course by Citrine and Bevin, upon Labour Party policy, effected by the marshalling of a collective trade union view in Congress; the decisions made there were simply 're-registered' at the party Conference. If the entire working-class population were to be rallied in a united left, Cole argued, a political rather than an industrial appeal would be required. Implicitly then, Cole wished to weaken trade union influence to ease the way for a popular front.

Official Labour, in the person of Hugh Dalton, replied that Cole read too much into the proximity of Congress and Conference; in fact TUC resolutions were drafted only after consultation among the General Council, the National Executive Committee and the PLP Executive. Nonetheless the NEC were anxious to alleviate misunderstanding and so were prepared to change the date of the party Conference; only the lengthy attention given to Spain at Edinburgh had prevented them from bringing this reform to fruition in 1936. Dalton also challenged Cole's assertion that the trade union block vote passed measures opposed by the local Labour parties: for instance, the latter groups had opposed Communist affiliation by a ratio of no less than 5:3, he claimed.[2] He raised as well the matter of Labour's electoral prospects, which he considered so good as to obviate the need for a left front. Others were not however so optimistic; A.L.Rowse refused to accept Dalton's contention that a turnover of 1,750,000 votes would be likely to return a Labour majority at the next general election. An advocate of an arrangement with the Liberal Party, Rowse correctly asserted that Dalton's calculation was based upon an even distribution, whereas Labour's success depended entirely upon how that turnover was distributed.[3] Rowse disagreed with Labour's continued electoral isolation, but where Cole had looked left, he looked right.

While the row over Edinburgh continued in the pages of the *New Statesman*, Stanley Baldwin had overcome his usual indolence to move to save the nation, not from the fascist threat, but from the irreparable harm of King Edward's resolution to wed a divorced woman. Mercifully we can spare ourselves a detailed account of that event, though its effect upon matters of international import should be noted. Baldwin had taken up 'the King's matter' on 20 October, though the crisis did not break in the London press until 3 December. Attlee was informed of the affair on 16 November, and thereafter the Labour Party posed no difficulties to the British government. Their reaction is of some historical interest; Dalton maintains that if they had come out in support of the King the Labour Party would have been 'split and smashed'.[4] Though grateful to Edward VIII for several sympathetic gestures toward the working-classes, the leaders realized that public opinion was almost completely against him. Labour was not prepared to counter that opinion, nor did the leaders care for the prospect of a king defying the advice of his ministers. A.J.P.Taylor to the contrary,[5] the Labour leadership would probably have followed a course like that of Baldwin's.

Where the National Government's foreign policy was in virtual abeyance during the period when the ministers concerned themselves only with the constitutional crisis,[6] the foreign policy attitudes of the Labour Party were affected in probably only one respect. Before the crisis broke, a number of trade union leaders were participants in the abortive campaign on behalf of 'Arms and the Covenant'. Churchill, who organized the project, described its purposes as 'the most rapid large scale rearmament of Britain, combined with the complete acceptance and employment of the authority of the League of Nations'. A massive Albert Hall rally of many of the leaders, which included right-wing Tories, the leaders of the League of Nations Union and the Liberal Party, chaired by Churchill's opponent of the General Strike, Sir Walter Citrine, met on 3 December. Churchill comments: 'We had the feeling that we were upon the threshold of not only gaining respect for our views, but of making them dominant';[7] however, by the time of the meeting Britain's attention was elsewhere. Churchill was quickly swallowed up in his work for a King's party – which incidentally lowered his parliamentary influence to nil – while the forces of the Covenant campaign were quickly estranged and the campaign soon dissolved. As for those members of the Labour Party involved, Dalton maintains that the continuing association with members of other parties would have undermined their influence within their own party.[8] The effect of the failure of the campaign was to divert the pro-rearmament activities back to the conversion of the PLP to the acceptance of rearmament. In that sense the failure of 'Arms and the Covenant' conceivably was a boon to the Labour Party.

Meanwhile Hugh Dalton had assumed the chairmanship of the National Executive, an office of potential power as well as prestige. He was of course committed to rearmament, yet because of his inclination towards team-work in party as well as government,[9] Dalton had to move cautiously. He did not take his task lightly:

> The Party, I judged, was in a bad way, disappointed by the small advance made at the General Election, unsure of itself, of its Leaders, of its programme, of its constitution, and some sections of it, unsure whether, fighting alone and by democratic methods, it could hope ever to win power. But I also judged that most of this malaise was curable, provided that the National Executive and its Chairman, and the whole Transport House machine, bucked up and showed some originality and initiative. The widespread complaints that we were all very slow and stodgy had some justification.[10]

Dalton's vigour was not appreciated in all quarters of the party: what has been described as his 'ferocious distaste for self-conscious freelances and eccentrics whose self-satisfaction varies in proportion to the distance they can get from centre opinion'[11] won him few friends on the left. Patricia Strauss, wife of Cripps' colleague, maintained that for all his ability and intelligence, he was never master of an audience: 'His booming voice assails their ears, but their hearts and brains are left unaffected.'[12] Dalton's effect upon the minds, if not the hearts, of the Labour leadership in the course of 1937 made him no new friends on the left; in using his new position for the propagation of ideas which in his view would strengthen the Labour Party, he quite clearly risked his popularity with the rank and file.[13]

Fortunately for his purposes, Dalton did not lack allies; Ernest Bevin of course held similar views in matters of international policy and even stronger views on the subject of party loyalty. In their joint chairmanship of the National Council of Labour the two collaborated closely; each strove to ease the misunderstanding between the political and industrial wings of the movement. They agreed that the most important job they had to do was to bring the party to take a more realistic view on defence.[14] Citrine too was of such a mind; from what has been said about his attitude, one is tempted to conclude that he and Bevin had worked out their position in concert, because for a decade they had agreed on all major issues facing the trade union movement. In such diverse topics as the Mond-Turner talks, the crisis of 1931, foreign policy and the need for rearmament 'they had been in agreement and their combination of talents in pushing a policy through the TUC was invincible'.[15] Citrine, with his shorthand notes, his note-books crammed full with facts, and his ability to turn an argument on its advocates, acted as the dispassionate expositor of General Council views. Bevin's speeches were subjective and personalized, and consequently they carried a sense of deep commitment to his listeners, which Citrine's rational presentation could not convey. Though the patterns of thought and presentation were different, the conclusions were more often than not strikingly alike.

Curiously enough, though, that agreement was not pre-arranged. Indeed Citrine has written, 'The occasions on which Bevin and I discussed policy outside the [General] Council chamber might be counted on one hand, certainly on two.'[16] Nor did they meet socially; those temperaments which enabled them to present, in sum, such a well-rounded case to the GC or the

Congress did not make for such intercourse. Citrine's recent account leaves open the question whether they even cared for each other: he records the fact that on only one occasion did Bevin ever pay him a direct compliment – and that in 1919![17] Their relationship has been incisively characterized by Bevin's biographer as '. . . one of the most successful involuntary partnerships in modern politics'.[18] Despite his participation in that partnership, Citrine has not hitherto received as much credit as he deserves for his role in bringing the Labour Party to recognize, first, the menace of fascism, and, second, the need for rearmament to confront this threat to life and liberty.

Behind the scenes, the Advisory Committee on International Questions was also struggling with the problem of Labour's international policy: the name of Leonard Woolf in particular may be added to those who urged a recognition of the realities of the world situation. In December 1936 he and Ivor Thomas submitted a draft to the ACIQ, which sent it largely unaltered to the National Executive. Labour's leaders were told:

> It is now obvious that there is no Government in the world prepared to rely for security on the League. Without formal abrogation the provisions of the Covenant for the prevention of war have become null and void. They will not be exercised. This is a disagreeable fact to everyone in the Labour Party, and, indeed, to most people in the country, but that it is a fact cannot be denied. The sooner it is recognized the better. To pretend that the argument for 'collective security' has been unaffected by the events of the last few years; to maintain that the Governments and peoples of this and other countries can still rely on the League for security is to ignore irrefutable facts. The task before the Labour Party is nothing less than a revision of its whole peace policy.[19]

These outspoken views did not impress all members of the committee, including its chairman, Charles Roden Buxton. He maintained that the stumbling block to world peace remained the privileged position of the western powers, written into the Treaty of Versailles; consequently, 'collective security is attainable, but not without a drastic revision of the *status quo*. The League of Nations has only "failed" because it has not realized the inseparable connection of these two things.'[20] Long-overdue revision would ease the underlying cause of the aggressiveness of Germany, Italy and Japan, which was economic. The voice of post-war radicalism was not yet stilled within the Labour Party.

Yet the majority of the ACIQ were no longer satisfied with such an explanation of the international situation; they were not, however, prepared to endorse rearmament under the National Government. In April 1937 the committee attempted to square the circle, by proclaiming 'rearmament there must be, but the Government's plan of arms and yet more arms, without any relation to foreign policy, is suicidal'.[21] This dilemma was difficult enough in itself, but the problems of the ACIQ were complicated further when an influential member indulged in retrograde criticism of the position on the League of Nations adopted the previous December. Philip Noel-Baker, who had been ill for several months, had only lately read No. 473A, whose contents filled him with consternation:

If I may say so with all respect, it seems to me to be founded on a total disregard of the true history of international affairs in the last six years ... If the ... memo were to be adopted by the National Executive or the Annual Conference as the official policy of the Party, I should not have the slightest hesitation in resigning my membership of the Party and of the House of Commons. Perhaps I may say that I have talked to other members of the Parliamentary Party who share this view.[22]

How a 'true history of international affairs' would restore the League to a position of primacy Noel-Baker unfortunately did not explain. His reaction however demonstrates the continuing ferment within the Labour Party on the possibilities for collective security and the need for rearmament, at that time of year when the PLP again had to consider the question of rearmament, given the existence of the National Government. Only the Dalton-Bevin-Citrine grouping so far had made clear their support for rearmament under that government. The critics of the Labour leadership on the left had meanwhile advanced quite another solution to the problems of international policy.

2

Where the Dalton-Bevin-Citrine block increasingly saw only one issue at stake in 1937 – the rearmament of Britain – the Labour left refused to agree that the problem could be so simply defined.

They were not blind to the menace of fascism, but, as in the case of Leonard Woolf, who recognized the destruction of the collective system but opposed rearmament under the National Government, they would not trust that government with arms. So it was with Bevan, no pacifist and very much aware of the fascist peril; nonetheless he opposed rearmament under their auspices, because he feared any association with the policies of that government:

> If Labour tacitly agreed to the defence plans of the Government, its case on foreign policy would go by default. It would be telling the public, by implication, that the Government which stolidly refused to mobilize the peace forces of the world could be relied upon in the last resort to perform this essential task: and that would be 'black treachery'.

With these considerations in mind, Bevan retorted to those who held that armaments must be voted to a National Government since a subsequent Labour government would require them: 'It is no argument that because I may need a sword in the future that I should therefore put a sword in the hands of my enemy now.' He apparently did not take into account the length of time required to forge such a sword; perhaps the left thought that a Labour government would have the moral strength to wrench their Excalibur from a stone. Bevan and the left with him simply could not shake the spectre of the enemy at home; events in Spain served to prove the British government's collusion with the fascist dictators, so that British rearmament would have meant a capitulation to neo-fascist forces.[23] In their weighing of the potential for evil of the National Government as opposed to the fascist régimes, the Labour left exhibited poor judgment.

Fear both of the fascist menace and of rearmament under the Tories underlay the attempt of the left to construct an alternative to government policy in the form of a united front of the working classes in 1937. Its leaders recognized that a necessary instrument for such a campaign was considerable publicity; during the final stages of the frustrating Edinburgh Conference, Cripps, Bevan, Laski, George Strauss, William Mellor and several others decided to proceed with a project which they had considered before, the launching of a new socialist weekly. Dissatisfied with the trade union orientation of the *Daily Herald*, they founded *Tribune* as a forum for left causes. With the wealthy socialists Cripps and Strauss supplying £20,000, the bulk of the capital, *Tribune* first appeared on 1 January 1937; Mellor served as editor, and Cripps, Strauss, Bevan, Laski, Ellen Wilkinson and Noel Brailsford composed the controlling board.[24] The journal immediately set about propagandizing for the Unity Campaign, which was launched on 24 January jointly by Cripps, Mellor, James Maxton of the ILP and Harry Pollitt of the CPGB.

Just a week earlier, the Socialist League had decided to participate directly; a Special Delegates' Conference, recognizing that such action rendered the League liable to disaffiliation by the Labour Party, had agreed nonetheless to support the unity proposals, 56 votes to 38, with 23 abstentions. Labour's National Executive reacted quickly, resolving on 27 January that as the League had directly defied a Conference decision, it should be disaffiliated. In a manifesto issued to the press, the NEC claimed that repeated party decisions dictated this regrettable action, adding '. . . unless a small minority is to be permitted to defy the will of the majority, there is no alternative'.[25] They expressed the hope that the Labour supporters of the Unity Campaign would abandon that disruptive effort and join loyally in the constructive efforts of the Labour Party.

Bevan however felt that the intention of the Unity Campaign was not divisive: 'We have not come to make discord, but to bring peace to Labour and a sword to our enemies.' Nor could he accept the argument that because a minority had failed to carry its view it must cease advocacy; was not Dalton persisting in his advocacy of support for the government's rearmament programme, in defiance of the Conference decision? Bevan's biographer admits that his criticism of the leadership may sound splenetic, though it really reflects his impatience: 'To the leaders opposition meant a more or less sedate presentation of their case in the House of Commons, coupled with the development of a practical programme to be offered at the next election.'[26] To the inflamed left, opposition however entailed 'the politics of the street'; the spirit of revolt against the parliamentary style of the government was directed against the Labour leadership as well. At root was the familiar question whether the Labour opposition was to act the part of a party looking to power or to play the role of a party of protest, regardless of the electoral consequences. A recent commentator, exuding the spirit of 1937, has severely criticized the failure of official Labour to utilize all the means at its disposal to organize effective resistance to the British government's disastrous policies:

> There were many things the Labour leaders could have done ... they could have used, indeed abused, their parliamentary opportunities to harass the Government, to obstruct its business, to refuse to participate in that sedate parliamentary minuet which was the Government's best guarantee against effective challenge. They could ... have sought to mobilize their industrial strength and used that strength as a means of pressure upon the Government ... And they could have sought to bring about a grand alliance of all those who opposed the Government so as to break the frozen political mould in which Britain was imprisoned.[27]

The Executive, however, demonstrated anything but inertness in reacting to the action of the Socialist League. Why did they clamp down so severely on the Unity Campaign? Partly the explanation lies in the very weakness and division of the Executive: still divided on the perilous question of rearmament, they could unite to oppose the Unity Campaign and strengthen their control of the Labour Party by that very act. On the other hand, to permit the Socialist League rebellion to continue could only weaken their leadership. Nor was their action arbitrary, for – as if in reply to Bevan's question – they claimed that they were not asking the Socialist Leaguers to abandon their views, but rather to cease the attempt to bring about their goal in common with a proscribed and anti-democratic party.

Nor should one deny that the Executive also acted from a sense of justified frustration with the continuous revolt among the left of the Labour Party. This feeling was especially strong among the trade unionists, as a letter of Bevin to G. D. H. Cole made clear:

> You talk about driving Cripps out. Cripps is driving himself out. The Annual Conference came to certain decisions. If I did not accept the decisions of my own union I know jolly well what the members would do with me. That does not stop me from being loyal and at the same time advocating within our own circles any changes I may think desirable.[28]

What Bevin did not perhaps recognize was that where he had a reasonable prospect of convincing the TGWU to change its mind, Cripps had little hope of convincing the Labour Party without bringing outside pressure to bear upon it. Nonetheless, the left

could not be permitted a privileged place within the party, simply
because of their minority position. Nor could the NEC look with
any favour upon the object of Cripps' affection; Dalton was
grieved that in the midst of the Executive's own constructive
work, '. . . Cripps and his Socialist Leaguers were still nattering
about a United Front with the Communists and the ILP. . . . It
was a piece of clotted nonsense anyhow, and was, to me and
others, a most exasperating diversion of the Party's mind and
energies.' He further resented the fact that the Socialist League
had defied an appeal from the Executive to the movement on
12 January not to take part in the proposed Unity Campaign.
Cripps' intemperate language also nettled; Dalton cites one of his
remarks during the campaign: 'The reactionaries of our Movement are keen to prevent Socialists from coming into it. The last
thing anyone should do is to pander to the reactionaries by staying out. James Maxton and Harry Pollitt should be the Leaders
in the Labour Movement today.'[29] On the same day that Cripps
made that slur upon the leadership, Ernest Bevin retorted in
kind: 'I saw Mosley come into the Labour Movement, and I see
no difference in the tactics of Mosley and Cripps.'[30] Feeling in
the Labour Party ran deep when a left spokesman proclaimed his
preference for Pollitt, and a trade union leader in turn compared
Cripps to a fascist.

Not all advocates of a left front approved of the tactics of the
Unity Campaign. No one was more prolific in his agitation for
such a front than G. D. H. Cole, but he preferred a loose, informal
collaboration among those forces sympathetic to such a front to
any specific agreement which would alienate the Labour Party.

The first task of the apostles is to create the will: the instrument comes
later, as something secondary, however essential to the effectiveness of
the will in action . . . The People's Front will come, when political
leaders see it has to come – or when, if they fail to see it, new leaders of
greater vision are enabled, by your help, to thrust them aside.[31]

Cole did not sign the Unity Manifesto because he did not want
to be expelled from the Labour Party if he could avoid it; since
the 'will' had not been created, Cole considered it of more importance to influence the party from within. However, 'if it comes
to a show-down, I am with Cripps, and against Transport House;
but I prefer to work against exclusiveness from within the Party,

179

and I do not propose to give Transport House more chances than I must of kicking me out'. Cole's pragmatic approach was validated by the actions of Transport House as the Unity Campaign proceeded: on 24 March the Executive determined to expel all individual party members who continued to belong to the disaffiliated Socialist League after 1 June.[32] The League began to crumble in the face of the Executive's resolve, for the majority of its members – now confronted with the situation foreseen by Cole – did not wish to be read out of the Labour Party.

The Socialist League had then to reap the bitter fruits of its refusal to heed the warning issued by the NEC, even before the Unity Campaign had formally opened; a Whitsuntide conference dissolved the League, while announcing that the adherents of unity would continue to support it in their private capacities.[33] Cripps himself had not initially inclined to such a compromise; rather he had proposed that the Socialist League should carry on the campaign, with its members prepared to suffer whatever penalties the Labour Party chose to impose.[34] Yet Cripps, who risked political extinction by this resolve, found little support or encouragement from those two parties – the Communists and the ILP – which he had worked so diligently to bring together in the pursuit of unity. The CPGB strongly advised him to yield to the dictates of the Executive; their purpose of course was co-operation with (or subversion of) the Labour Party, not with a handful of Socialist Leaguers. Fenner Brockway of the ILP maintains that the obvious disharmony between his party and the Communists may have influenced Cripps' ultimate yielding: 'He might have been willing to face expulsion from the Labour Party if he felt that a real spirit of unity existed between the three sections participating in the campaign, but when two of them were engaged in fierce dispute he probably came to the decision that the sacrifice would not be justified.'[35] William Mellor and Aneurin Bevan made it clear that they did not want to leave the Labour Party if some means could be found of working for the Unity Campaign from within. With such factors to consider, Cripps agreed to the dissolution of the Socialist League.

The NEC welcomed this decision, while warning all members of the Labour Party against further joint activities. The ex-Leaguers however formed a 'Committee of Party Members sympathetic to Unity', which carried on its own campaign until the National

Executive banned it as well. That the leadership was frankly fed up with the endeavours of the left was reflected in its invocation of the 'three years' rule' (whereby any matter ruled upon by an annual Conference could not again be raised for that period of time) to ban any discussion of a working-class front at the 1937 Conference.[36] Though legitimate in itself, the Executive ruling quite contradicted their appeal to the left elements to work within the party to secure the acceptance of their proposals by Conference. Activists could hardly be expected to await a ruling by the 1939 Conference. The NEC action had in the interim broken the back of the Unity Campaign; without the cementing properties of the Socialist League, the ILP and the Communists did not long hold together.

Few tangible gains had crowned the efforts of the unity campaigners. One note of hope however could be found in a statement by the leader of the Labour Party in a book published at this time by the Left Book Club. Though Attlee had argued that there was no use in patching up a sham unity between parties which differed fundamentally – as he considered the Labour Party did with Liberals, on ends, and the Communists, on methods – he wrote: 'I would not myself rule out such a thing [unity] as an impossibility in the event of the imminence of a world crisis. It might on a particular occasion be the lesser of two evils . . .'[37] By implication then, Attlee did not regard such a crisis imminent in 1937. The Labour left certainly disagreed; though badly battered in their campaign for unity, they doubtless agreed with the *New Statesman*: 'There are moments when it is criminal to wait for General Elections – moments when the fate of democracy is hanging in the balance.'[38]

3

After Edinburgh, the Labour left continued its assault upon the policy of non-intervention, for which it continued to cite breaches of the agreements. So flagrant were these that Maisky, the Russian representative on the Non-Intervention Committee, announced to that body on 23 October that his government could not consider themselves bound to its agreement 'to any greater extent than any of the remaining participants'.[39] That the Soviets meant this was evidenced in the circulation a day later by Lord Plymouth, chairman of the Committee, of a note accusing Russia of three breaches of the agreement, while Italy was cited for only one. Stalin had hesitated for several months, but on 29 October 1936 a Russian tank formation took the field against Nationalist forces. Though now resolutely committed to a policy of intervention – if only to stave off a fascist victory which could conceivably result in Russia's isolation[40] – Russia continued to participate in the work of the Non-Intervention Committee, probably because a denunciation of the agreements could mean a diplomatic breach with France and Great Britain. Though Russian vacillation was at an end, her hypocrisy persisted.

While the Soviet Union had decided upon intervention, the Labour Internationals – the IFTU and the LSI – similarly saw the futility of non-intervention. In a meeting at Paris on 26 October, with Greenwood, Gillies and George Dallas representing the British Labour movement, which had requested the meeting, those bodies unanimously agreed that the fascist determination to aid the rebels and the impossibility of effective supervision had undercut the hopes for non-intervention; therefore international labour requested the restoration of complete commercial liberty to Republican Spain.[41] British Labour quickly pressed this view upon the government, in a declaration drafted by the General Council, the National Executive and the PLP Executive. In that statement of 28 October, the Labour movement abandoned its support of non-intervention; they stressed the continuity of Labour policy stemming from the Plymouth TUC and the Edinburgh Conference, for those bodies had resolved only upon conditional acceptance of non-intervention.

There were those in the Labour Party who regarded that this somewhat tardy decision vindicated their earlier opposition to that policy. Among the leadership, Herbert Morrison had opposed non-intervention from the first. Though he had publicly made known that sentiment, as a member of the Executive he '. . . did it in a way calculated to cause the Party a minimum of inconvenience'.[42] The left however gave Morrison no credit for his prescience, for his failure to lead a revolt against the Executive indicated that he valued party loyalty above the dictates of his own judgment; they now regarded him as Ernest Bevin's political counterpart. Their consistent denunciation of non-intervention had not been designed to save the Labour Party embarrassment. The repudiation of that policy signalled to them the correctness of their view; within three weeks of the Edinburgh Conference, not a shred of the arguments presented there by the Labour leaders survived.[43] The turnabout of the leadership only strengthened the left's conviction that here were men trailing after events.

The Parliamentary Labour Party forced a debate on the Spanish question when Parliament reconvened on 29 October; Eden initiated that debate with a government statement which the opposition would have in the main accepted just a few weeks earlier. He admitted shortcomings in the working of the agreements, but the British Foreign Secretary maintained that taken together these complaints paled into insignificance beside the decision to limit the risks of a general European war.[44] To establish their case against non-intervention, the Labour leaders had to circumvent this argument that intervention would lead to general war, a thesis which they had earlier accepted.[45] Greenwood attempted to do that by appending an important reservation to the thesis: '. . . whether it is an arguable position or not really depends upon the effectiveness of non-intervention . . . now that arms have been supplied and non-intervention is not 90 per cent effective, the dangers of this policy of non-intervention are much greater than would have been the dangers if the supply of arms had been permitted at first.'[46] Though Greenwood can be credited with a desire to show the consistency of Labour's Spanish policy, the logic of his argument is rather difficult to comprehend. Certainly the covert supplying of arms to the opposing sides in Spain did not pose the same threat of escalation as overt involvement would have entailed. The tacit violation of the agreement, by Russia as well as Germany and Italy, would not cause the same polarization of the powers, nor would it entail the same depth of commitment, as the outright abandonment of the arrangements.

Though the rigour of Greenwood's argument was less than compelling, the party's decreasing concern with the prospect of general war can be understood: what was more persuasive was the danger of a Republican defeat. By the end of October, with Madrid besieged, that was all too likely a possibility. Labour saw the violation of non-intervention as the major factor in Republican reversals; thus what Greenwood had regarded as 'a very bad second best' policy at Edinburgh had within three weeks become the worst policy. The Labour Party evidently was now prepared to risk general war on behalf of the Spanish Republic, which the British government refused to do. We cannot overly concern ourselves with what might have happened had that government's displeasure grown apace, but the possibility certainly exists that Germany would have shied from such a struggle. Nearly a year after the outbreak of the Spanish Civil War, the Director of the Political Department in the German Foreign Office minuted: 'Germany refuses to permit the Spanish crisis to lead to war . . . our goal now should be the prevention of a general conflict rather than the unconditional and complete victory of the Franco party in the Spanish Civil War.'[47] Mussolini too may have been unwilling to risk war.[48] Whatever the likely result of Labour's willingness to run the risk, the parliamentary spokesmen viewed the government's acceptance of non-intervention as very much a part of the wider context of the history of the five years past, in which Britain had retreated on one issue after another. Attlee argued that the ultimate result could only be a world in anarchy.[49] The Labour Party, he continued, did not desire yet another case in which the finger of scorn could point to Britain as wanting in a time of crisis; they wanted a turn from that course, to accomplish justice for the Spanish people.

In this debate of 29 October 1936 were drawn the parliamentary lines which were to persist for the balance of the Spanish Civil War; Baldwin then, as Chamberlain did later, regretted Labour's 'reversal' of policy and altered the government's policy not a whit. The Labour Party thereafter remained critical of the British government's policy, whenever foreign affairs were debated. What follows is by no means a complete account of that opposition; even less is it a treatment of that government's policy or the workings of the Non-Intervention Committee. Rather the intention is to show Labour's persistent – and fruitless – protests against the course of events in Spain and the international reaction. The Labour Party consistently opposed legislation which they judged would damage the cause of the Spanish government: the first instance was their resistance to a 'Carriage of Munitions to Spain' Bill, which Noel-Baker argued Labour could support only if non-intervention were made effective for both sides; Labour's opposition was characterized across the floor of the House as 'the gun-runners' lament'.[50] The British government, having banned the export of munitions to Spain in British bottoms, next proceeded to ban the recruitment or volunteering of British citizens for the conflict. At the same time, on 19 January 1937, Eden defended the recent Anglo-Italian agreement – inappropriately styled the 'Gentleman's Agreement' – in which both parties recognized the other's interests in the Mediterranean and disclaimed any desire to modify the *status quo*. Attlee scoffed at this *de facto* guarantee of the territorial integrity of Spain, which amounted to shaking hands with a party in the midst of aggression; he also protested against the ban on volunteers as 'a sop to Mussolini and Hitler'.[51]

Since Mussolini was prepared to practise non-intervention only in direct proportion to the success of rebel arms,[52] continual Italian violation of the agreements formed the basis of the PLP's complaint on 25 March. Again on 14 April the party attacked the policy of the British government; in this instance they were provoked by the timid reaction to the Spanish Nationalist proclamation of a naval blockade of food supplies from Republic-held areas on Spain's northern coast. Hitherto the British government had deliberately refused to recognize the warring factions as belligerents, which meant that any British ship could ask for the protection of the Royal Navy if they were interfered with outside the three-mile territorial limit. Yet in April the British government responded to the Nationalist blockade by asking British merchant shipping not to proceed to Basque ports; in this way they hoped that dangerous confrontations could be avoided. Baldwin explained to the Commons that there were risks against which it was impossible to protect British shipping, for the Navy (presided over by Sir Samuel Hoare) considered the blockade effective.

Attlee moved a Vote of Censure in a carefully documented speech: 'We hold that this action is a surrender of the rights which this country has always maintained on behalf of our shipping, and is an acquiescence in a grave breach of international law.'[53] The effect of the government's action was that 'the greatest maritime country in the world, which keeps a great Fleet for the express purpose of protecting British shipping . . .' had allowed ships engaged in peaceful commerce to be turned back by rebels and had subsequently asked them not to dock in Bilbao. He asserted, 'General Franco may not be able to make an effective blockade, but the British Government will oblige him by doing so.' The Labour Party asked that government not to permit Franco to defeat by starvation a people whom he could not otherwise conquer. In defence of the government's action, Sir John Simon was, as always, well stocked with legal precedents, but the Liberal leader, Sinclair, challenged their application in the present situation.[54] Further, he regarded the government's acceptance of the blockade as, in effect, an act of intervention. No reasoned case, not even the barbed taunt of Noel-Baker that for the first time since 1588 the British stood in fear of the Spanish fleet, could budge the government or reduce their crushing majority. Thus Eden concluded the debate with the hope that British merchant ships would not attempt to run the blockade because '. . . in view of reports of conditions we do not think it safe for them to go'.[55]

What all the arguments of the massed opposition could not accomplish one intrepid seafarer could. Five days after the debate, the *Seven Seas Spray*, Captain Roberts master, ignored frantic shore messages and cleared St Jean de Luz; disregarding the warnings of a British destroyer, he proceeded to Bilbao, without a single sighting either of mines or Nationalist warships.[56] The overwhelming reception given him by the hungry Basques resounded even to Westminster, where A. V. Alexander noted the exploit on 20 April. His parliamentary sailing was equally clear, for Roberts' feat had proved wrong the British government's estimate of the efficacy of the Nationalist blockade.[57] With justice, Alexander argued that the only blockade of Bilbao had been that imposed by the British government. He warned of the danger of pursuing further that policy which the government had followed for two years, typified by the Bilbao affair: 'We have allowed these countries over and over again to bluff us . . . You cannot have permanent peace without justice and you will not secure justice among nations by giving way in such cases as this.'[58] Peace would not come from submission to the designs of the dictators, the Labour Party warned.

Though they could see more clearly than ever that nothing

would jar the British government from its policy of non-intervention, the Labour spokesmen, to their credit, persisted in pointing out violations of the Non-Intervention Agreements and in protesting against such arrangements as that which left German and Italian ships patrolling the east coast of Spain, where they showed habitual disregard for the practice of non-intervention. Meanwhile, on the northern coast, the British played the game by the rules. Labour commented upon the rather different approaches.[59] Neville Chamberlain, now Prime Minister, claimed that non-intervention had succeeded in its primary function of confining war; Attlee however retorted that the ending of the Spanish conflict was an equally important function, and therein non-intervention was a failure. He then asked two questions of the National Government: when did they propose to stop giving way to the dictators, and what would they at last stand for? Labour's query received no answer for two long agonizing years, though the party heard a harbinger of things to come in the words of Anthony Eden, who commented that although the government would not agree to 'peace at any price', they were content to secure 'peace at almost any price'.[60]

On 15 July the British government indicated a willingness to pay the price of a grant of belligerent rights to Franco, in return for the withdrawal of foreign troops supporting him. Labour regarded such a brazen deal as unthinkable,[61] and the PLP consistently opposed such a proposal through the Commons' adjournment for the summer recess; the Non-Intervention Committee had meanwhile taken up the matter. Attlee however showed that Labour placed little stock in that body's operations, because the fascist powers persisted in violating the Agreements.[62]

Such an outline of the PLP's protests in the months from October 1936 to July 1937 should suffice to show their vigorous advocacy of the cause of Republican Spain. Yet these genuine efforts did not overly impress the critics of the Labour leadership: G. D. H. Cole all but holds them responsible for the fact that Labour '... did not persuade the Governments concerned to give up the policy of non-intervention'. He regards official Labour's organization of relief measures and Red Cross services for the Republican forces as a salving of conscience and asserts, 'the Labour Party continued to protest; but it did not go beyond protests'. Cole cites only two specific instances of this 'failure', however. In the first place, he charges that when in November 1936 Blum sent a deputation to London to seek British support if the French were to denounce the Non-Intervention Agreement, 'the British Labour leaders held off, because they could not assure the French of British Government support, and were hesitant about invoking the war danger which stronger pressure, if . . . successful, would have involved'.[63] Yet surely no one could expect the Labour leaders to assure the French about the government, while their parliamentary utterances contradict Cole's postulate of their fear of general war. To assess the significance of the French mission is difficult, because no mention of it is found either in the National Executive's report or in the accounts of Dalton and Eden. It was not, however, the British Labour Party which required conversion to the French viewpoint. Cole also cites Labour's failure to initiate a national campaign on behalf of the Republican cause, apart from the war relief. The assertion is correct, but it conveys the mistaken impression that Labour waged its protest only in Parliament. On the contrary, no event in the 1930s so touched off Labour Party pamphleteering as the Spanish Civil War and the fascist violation of non-intervention: no fewer than five pamphlets and a like number of leaflets were published between October 1936 and October 1937. The former sold 90,000 copies, while 1,750,000 leaflets were distributed.[64] The party's failure to mount a more formal campaign can be explained by their concentration upon publicity for *Labour's Immediate Programme*, a document published after extensive preparation in March 1937. Considerable difficulties of finance and organization would have been posed in conducting two national campaigns simultaneously. Cole's criticisms are thus hardly overwhelming.

Yet those arguments have been echoed by other left-inclined critics of the Labour leadership;[65] like Cole, they are faced with the task of digging rather deeply to uncover damaging material. Michael Foot, for instance, attacks the caution exhibited by a March 1937 meeting of the two Internationals, which Bevan regarded as a return to the 'discredited temporising of Edinburgh'. He also cites the wilting of the parliamentary leadership after their initial attack upon the 'Carriage of Munition to Spain' Bill; ultimately only seventeen divided against that Bill, in defiance of Labour Party Whips. Of greater import was the support of the *Daily Herald* (which Ernest Bevin liked to call 'my paper') for the continuance of non-intervention in the midst of the Bilbao debate in April 1937. The last episode fed fuel to Bevan's suspicions, and the three taken together led Foot to conclude that in regard to Spain 'the Bevin-Dalton leadership looked feeble almost to the point of deceit'. The primary concern of those two was however not with 'Arms for Spain', but with 'Arms for Britain'. The Spanish conflict did not stir them in the way it affected the Labour left, but the PLP worked enthusiastically for the Republican cause. After all, Foot might have recalled that in March 1937 the 'Bevin-Dalton' leadership was of a minority group. The leadership of the parliamentary party lay with Attlee, Greenwood and Morrison; that group waged a tenacious though vain struggle against the iniquities of non-intervention.

4

At the Edinburgh Conference, Morrison had reserved to the PLP the question of their response to specific rearmament proposals of the British government. Before the Estimates for the Fighting Services were introduced into the Commons, traditionally in March, the Chancellor of the Exchequer, Neville Chamberlain, had on 17 February given some indication of the scope of the government's proposals. Warning that defence expenditures over the next five years would total no less than £1,500 millions, he requested authorization to raise a £400 million loan for purposes of rearmament alone in that period.[66] Concurrently the government published the third annual White Paper on Defence, which in their view justified the requested loan; Chamberlain so coupled the two in his remarks about the 'abnormal and exceptional circumstances' confronting the British government. The Labour Party was no more pleased with this White Paper than it had been with its predecessors; Pethick-Lawrence complained that there was no

... suggestion of correlating this vast, amorphous mass of expansion to any clear conception of international policy. There is not a single word about the League of Nations, not a single word about collective security, no suggestion of any kind that the defences of this great

Empire are affected for better or for worse by the fact that the Government are pledged up to the hilt to the electorate to respect the conception of collective security.[67]

Labour also opposed the very idea of what amounted to a war loan in time of peace, advocating instead a pay-as-you-go policy, then an economically fashionable idea. Labour spokesmen reiterated these two arguments throughout the course of the debate, in various degrees of detail, but eventually their dual objection was easily outvoted.

Labour's challenges had not gone unanswered, as government spokesmen defended both the policy and the financial method. In considering the former, Sir John Simon lodged the usual deft criticism of Labour's coupling of collective security with opposition to British rearmament:

> You cannot treat collective security as though it were an arrangement by which you are going to receive a contribution without making one. When I hear that argument I am always reminded of the passage in Lewis Carroll's famous book 'The Hunting of the Snark' in which he describes a man who
>
> 'At charity meetings stands at the door
> And collects – though he does not subscribe.'[68]

Though there were those among the Labour Party who appreciated the force of this argument, the PLP, in the March debates, reiterated its view that criticism of the government's failure to work for the collective system could best be expressed by a protest against the Estimates.[69] Labour consequently moved token reductions, but the party did not then divide on the main question. The debates showed that government and opposition were still stalemated with regard to defence policy: the Labour Party refused to support a concept of unilateral rearmament because it was not tied to the collective system; the British government argued that rearmament would benefit both that system and the national interest. As the fascist threat grew, Labour was bound to have the worst of this argument, for defences – of any sort, for either purpose – were increasingly necessary.

The PLP, in addition to this basic difference with the government's defence policy, was also critical of other aspects. They were hostile to the private manufacture of, and trade in, arms; Philip Noel-Baker, on 26 May 1937, deprecated the government's refusal to carry out the proposals of the Royal Commission which had examined the matter and reported the previous September. Noel-Baker felt that the Commission ought to have moved even further away from private control than they had, but as it was the government had rejected their moderate proposals almost *in toto*. Evidently the government reasoned that the profit motive worked in the national interest; recalling however that at Gallipoli British soldiers had been killed by British-made guns, Noel-Baker wondered how such a situation was in the national interest. The Minister for the Co-ordination of Defence, Inskip, countered that the government had accepted the main conclusion of the Royal Commission, namely that manufacture and trade in armaments should be left in the private sector of the economy. Positions on this issue had not altered since the debate of February 1934.[70]

When in June the British government introduced a proposal for a National Defence Contribution, in the form of a tax upon profits from armaments manufacture – those very profits which Labour had long attacked – the party received it quite without enthusiasm. Dalton, noting that the levy would be only 9d to 1/- in the £ of profits, treated it as a farce and a humbug: '. . . the gravest objection against this tax is the ludicrous inadequacy of the yield and the contemptibly small contribution to the cost of National Defence . . .'[71] Charging as well that the revenue which the tax would yield was overestimated by the government, so that in fact it would fall far short of bridging the gap between income and expenditure, Labour carried its opposition to a division. Subsequently, Labour renewed its objection to the limited powers of the Minister for the Co-ordination of Defence, in a debate initiated by the opposition Liberals.[72] Once again the case put by the opposition was supported by such right-wing Tories as Amery and Churchill.

Of far greater importance than these Labour decisions was the action of the PLP on 27 July 1937: in the final vote on the total Service Estimates, the Labour MPs, instead of trooping into the Opposition Lobby, abstained. Dalton and his cohorts had attempted to accomplish this in 1936; when that move failed, a small band had then abstained. The Labour Party had consistently maintained that their vote against armaments was a parliamentary tactic rather than a vote of principle against armaments; no matter what its place in parliamentary procedure, their vote against Service Estimates was open both to misrepresentation and to certain sound objections. These objections were increasingly clear by 1937, as Hugh Dalton indicates: '. . . after twelve months of Spain, the Party's policy being "Arms for Spain", it became more and more impossible, in the view of many of us, to justify a vote which, whatever pundits in Parliamentary procedure may pretend, means to the plain man "No Arms for Britain".' The PLP's attitude was pregnant with great consequences for Dalton: 'This decision might make all the difference between victory and defeat at the next election, and between Peace and War for the world, and the accomplishment or failure of our dreams of Socialism in this Country.'[73]

What was so clear to Dalton was evidently less apprehensible to other Labour MP's, for their decision to abstain came only with the greatest difficulty. The month of March heard rumours of such a change, but such rumours had proved unfounded in 1935 and 1936; again such headlines as 'Socialists Split on Defence' were featured in the Tory press. The PLP at that time reserved decision until the final stages of the Estimates were considered in July; the matter was discussed at a meeting on 21 July, but no decision was reached despite the Parliamentary Executive's recommendation that the party oppose.[74] *The Times* reported the Executive's belief that '. . . it is the duty of the Opposition to vote against the Government's foreign policy, regardless of whether or not their attitude is understood in the country'. Pressures were however brought upon the membership of the PLP; Bevin not unsurprisingly lent 'strong support' to Dalton's advocacy of rearmament within the parliamentary ranks. Citrine has judged that Dalton could have got nowhere without the considerable pressures exerted by the TUC.[75] In part the TUC attitude stemmed from economic and social considerations which the PLP subordinated to political, but the trade union leaders were genuinely concerned with the threat of fascism abroad. At one point the TUC, whose members supplied the vast bulk of Labour Party membership, announced that it had never abandoned its own right to make political decisions, a not-overly subtle pressure which was immediately understood by Labour MPs. In addition Citrine credited the political wing with an increasing recognition of the worsening international situation, which more inclined them to the measures advised by the trade union leaders. Citrine quite properly maintained that this support of measures of rearmament was not a blind one; rather, as he told the 1937 Congress: 'Some risks are inevitable, and it is a question of measuring the relative risk and measuring the danger . . .'[76] He concluded that if the movement considered some measure of rearmament necessary under the present circumstances, then that rearmament could not await the advent of a Labour government. In his measurement of the relative risks, the external fascist menace clearly came first.

Within Transport House, William Gillies, Secretary of the International Department, also exerted pressure on behalf of rearmament. Sometime before the PLP caucused to decide its stand, Gillies surveyed what he considered a 'very ugly and dangerous' international situation as prelude to a discussion of Labour's defence policy. If Great Britain were not to continue retreating, he concluded, the country would have to risk a showdown with Germany and Italy. All but assuming that Labour would choose to stand, he commented:

Most of us . . . believe that a Labour Government coming into power tomorrow and faced, as it would be, by the present international situation, would be compelled, pending a halt in the arms race, to go on increasing British arms. Further, since arms are not made, nor their future production planned, nor new recruits trained, in a day, the arms which are being made now, and the recruits who are being trained now, will be needed by the next Labour Government, if we win the next election, and needed to support a policy of collective security.[77]

Gillies noted two other factors favouring British rearmament: Socialists on the continent had welcomed it as a deterrent to aggression and Labour's own ACIQ had recently stated that British rearmament had reduced the risk of war in Europe.[78] Regarding the latter assertion, he recognized that 'we might not care to say so publicly, and we are under no obligation to say so. But it may be true.' Labour did not care to admit this, but the PLP's decision reflected the possibility of its truth. Gillies also met head-on the left's argument against rearmament, in a manner like Citrine's: 'It is sometimes said that we cannot trust this

Government with arms . . . an alternative reply is that, little though we trust the British Government, we trust Hitler and Mussolini still less.'[79]

Dalton thus had some prominently placed supporters when he pressed for a redefinition of Labour's defence policy, first upon the PLP Executive and subsequently upon the entire parliamentary party. On the former he could count on support from Alexander, Lees-Smith and the absent Clynes; Noel-Baker, Pethick-Lawrence and Greenwood at first expressed interest but ultimately voted against his proposal, along with the other eight members. Two days after his defeat, Dalton took his case to the Labour MPs, on 21 July. Dalton admitted in the course of the two-day discussion that the policy he recommended, abstention, could be misrepresented, just as the negative vote had been.

But . . . the practical question was, which form of misrepresentation would be more serious. Morrison had said that, if we abstained, the Tory Head Office would at once issue a most damaging leaflet. I was not much afraid of this, but I asked Morrison the question: 'How do you think the Tory Head Office would like us to decide today?' I myself had no doubt that they should like us to go on voting against all arms.[80]

Dalton also posed electoral considerations for the PLP, claiming that there was no chance of 'turning over' the two million voters needed for a Labour victory if the party continued to vote against arms. Greenwood's rejoinder, for the Executive, Dalton characterized as 'very halting and unhappy' (the Deputy Leader once again was defending a 'very bad second best' policy), though he supplied only a few details of his opponent's case.

In the PLP balloting, Dalton received the support of all the Co-operative MPs save one, of all the Railwaymen and the Lancashire Miners, and of some of the Durham Miners, though the Yorkshire and South Wales Miners opposed him. Following seconding speeches from James Walker of the Ironworkers and Ernest Thurtle, a local Labour Party MP, Dalton amassed 45 votes; the Executive's recommendation was backed by 29. Labour's parliamentary opposition to rearmament was thus reversed on 22 July 1937. One is somewhat surprised that in such an important decision only slightly more than half the Labour MPs cast ballots, but Dalton assures us that a larger attendance would only have increased the margin of victory: 'If I had polled all my promises, the majority would have been nearly 30.' Dalton could not then have been surprised with the results, but a section of the minority, the South Wales Miners led by Jim Griffiths and Arthur Jenkins, were surprised and outraged; their attempt to form a Miners' block to oppose the Estimates were, however, frustrated. Attlee scrupulously refused to entertain a manœuvre to reconsider the decision, and the defeated Executive asked only of Dalton that he not emphasize his point of view before the actual division of the House and that he keep his troops, specifically the trade union leaders on the General Council of the TUC, quiet as well. The PLP rallied to the majority decision; when the Service Estimates were voted upon on 26–27 July, only six Labour MPs – Barr, Salter, Messer, McGhee, Silverman and S. O. Davies – joined four members of the ILP and a single Communist in opposition.[81] Dalton was most gratified: 'This, in view of the strong feelings of many of our colleagues, was a most remarkable display of loyalty and discipline. It was a great disappointment to the Tories in the House.'[82] Though Herbert Morrison had threatened to raise the matter at the annual Conference, nothing was heard of this in October at Bournemouth; perhaps in the interim he recalled that he had reserved this decision to the PLP.

One does not expect that the left would welcome this reversal of policy, but in view of the circumstances, Michael Foot's description of Dalton's campaign is rather surprising:

> This was as skilful a piece of backstairs intrigue as even Dalton had ever executed. He lobbied his own friends without putting his opponents – they included a majority among the party leaders – on their guard. None but the eventual victors knew that so momentous a decision was to be taken at the meeting.[83]

Perhaps the party leadership did not expect to lose the vote, but surely they, and any MP who cared to know, were well aware that the vote was to be taken: the *Daily Express* of 22 July had duly noted, 'Today a decision must be made.' That paper concluded with the *Manchester Guardian* and *The Times* that the Executive would probably prevail in the balloting.[84] The Labour left were not tricked; rather, as so often in the decade, they were outvoted, despite the fact that the leadership shared their distrust of rearmament. After the PLP decision, the editor of the *New*

Statesman, Kingsley Martin, protested against the new tactic of abstention: 'I would rather explain opposition on a platform than abstention, which sounds as if the Party could not make up its mind, as if it were glad to wound but afraid to strike.'[85] Dalton had already countered this particular argument, when Morrison had advanced it at the PLP meeting. Probably he was willing to exchange the criticism of the Labour left for the approbation with which such persistently critical journals as the *Morning Post*, the *Daily Telegraph* and the *Observer* greeted the Labour reversal, typified by the judgment of the first that 'our Socialist Opposition has had a sudden determination of common-sense to the head, and has rejected the advice of its leaders'.[86]

So long as we remember that abstention is, in parliamentary effect, tacit acceptance,[87] we must recognize that the Labour Party travelled a considerable distance along the path of national defence between 1936 and 1937. Opposition to rearmament under the National Government was scrapped completely in the process; a silent revolution had overtaken the Labour Party. The quietness of the demise of Labour's opposition to rearmament, embodied in the form of a parliamentary abstention, reminds one of the lines

> This is the way the world ends
> This is the way the world ends
> This is the way the world ends
> Not with a bang but a whimper.

5

The PLP's decision to abstain on the Service Estimates, important though it was, constituted no defence policy in itself. The leaders of the National Council of Labour had, however, undertaken a re-examination of Labour's international policy, doubtless with the Edinburgh fiasco in mind. According to Ernest Bevin, the report drafted by the NCL was prepared quite independently of the views of the PLP; the former were not influenced by the latter's decision to abstain, because by that time their report was practically completed.[88] In conducting that re-examination, the NCL noted that the support for the League of Nations so evident when *For Socialism and Peace* had been drafted in 1934 had been called into question by Labour's Advisory Committee on International Questions, which had observed in December 1936 that the League had proved unable either to deter an aggressor from resorting to war or to prevent him from fulfilling his objects in war.[89] The ACIQ had advised the Labour Party to look elsewhere than to the League of Nations for the instrument of its international policy. While their re-examination was still in process, in March 1937 the National Council of Labour had issued a short statement of Labour's intentions, *Labour's Immediate Programme*. In that statement they declared that Labour would seek to strengthen and reinvigorate the League as an instrument of international co-operation and collective security,[90] but despite the title of the document the NCL had no policy to recommend while the League remained unreconstructed. In matters of defence they stated what a Labour government would do but said not a word about the role of a Labour opposition. Partly this approach was inherent in the form of the statement, which offered a programme for a government, but nonetheless the statement was of little help to the party in facing the realities of 1937.

Labour's long-awaited comprehensive statement, published in July[91] under the title *International Policy and Defence*, sprang directly from a memorandum on 'Foreign Policy and Defence' prepared by William Gillies, whose recognition of the need for rearmament we have noted. Those particular arguments were not included in the statement issued by the NCL, but Gillies' comments upon the international situation were utilized nearly word for word; only concluding paragraphs on 'Policy and Defence' were appended. *International Policy and Defence* traversed the course of international developments since 1919 in an orthodox Labour fashion; as a result of those events, the NCL now agreed that 'the League of Nations, for the time being, has been rendered ineffective'.[92] They hoped for its reinvigoration and for peaceful economic change as well, which would greatly ease the difficulties of Germany, Italy and Japan; they were however determined that such concessions as equal access to colonial resources and frontier revision would be granted only to those countries which were prepared loyally to accept the League system and agree to all-in arbitration. The NCL remained convinced that '. . . the "Next War" can be prevented . . . the Arms Race can be stopped . . . the League of Nations can be made strong again, provided that a

British Government soon comes to power which will base its policies on the declarations of the British Labour Movement'. They recognized that such a government would have to be equipped to defend the country; thus that government '. . . until the change in the international situation caused by its advent has had its effect, would be unable to reverse the present programme of Rearmament'. Evidently the question of rearmament under the National government was left to the PLP. Viewed in the context of 1937, when the term was not one of opprobrium, appeasement figured prominently in this important revision of Labour's international policy; throughout, however, Labour's advocacy of the appeasement of genuine grievances was contingent upon the deprived powers' acceptance of certain political conditions, e.g. a cessation of the arms race and the negotiation of a general disarmament treaty. Labour's concept of appeasement was not the 'peace at any price' variety.

Did this policy statement provide an unequivocal lead to the movement? For G. D. H. Cole it represented 'most inadequate guidance';[93] though he does not indicate why, probably he meant with regard to the present rather than the future. Once again, Labour's leadership had supplied a programme for a Labour government, at the expense of one for an opposition; nothing was said of how they proposed to influence affairs in the interim, before that government could be established. Perhaps we ask too much of them in looking for a considered statement of their parliamentary resistance, which would detail their position as well as sketch methods of bringing pressure to bear upon the government; yet a doubt remains whether the leader's sights in 1937 may have been too much trained on the general election likely two or three years hence.

Left discontent with *International Policy and Defence* was shortly registered at the Bournemouth Conference; meanwhile the pacifist element of the party, whose activity we have not surveyed since their rout at Brighton in 1935, had taken to extra-party approaches to present their alternative policy. For our purposes Lansbury's work with Canon 'Dick' Sheppard of St Paul's on behalf of the Peace Pledge Union is peripheral, as is his personal quest for peace, which found him journeying from capital to capital urging upon statesmen the Biblical precept, 'Ye must be born again'.[94] Clearly Lansbury's sincere activities militated against his acceptance either of the Labour abstention on the matter of rearmament or of the philosophy of *International Policy*. In fact he led a revolt of Labour MPs, gathered with some 1,100 delegates at a National Convention of the Parliamentary Pacifist Group, which resolved that Labour's recent manifesto

... commits the country to a policy of militarism, assumes that Fascism can be defeated by war, makes the adoption of conscription by Great Britain inevitable, and, by dividing nations into hostile groups, is in complete opposition to the principles on which the League of Nations was founded.[95]

Supporting Lansbury were five Labour MPs, three of whom had divided against the Service Estimates in July, and four Labour peers, including Lord Ponsonby.

Press reaction to *International Policy*, voiced in September, was on the whole favourable, though some serious reservations were expressed by the non-Socialist newspapers. The *Daily Herald*, Labour's own, trusted that the manifesto would '... remove all misunderstandings and check all misrepresentations of Labour's decision to withdraw opposition to the rearmament programme', and expressed pleasure that Labour could now fight the government's foreign policy, not with one hand tied behind its back, but with full force. The *Daily Telegraph* and the *Morning Post*'s sentiments were accurately reflected in their headlines, respectively 'Truth Dawns on the Socialists' and 'The Socialists' Canossa', though both were critical of the NCL's treatment of the record of the National Government. Only *The Times* judged Labour's 'a policy of despair', in its reckless conversion from pacifism to power politics. In a commentary which revealed more about *The Times*' own hopes for appeasement than about the Labour statement, that journal criticized the emphasis Labour placed upon 'the power of restraint'.[96]

We know little of the deliberations of the National Council of Labour upon Gillies' basic draft, though Bullock contends that it represented the most which Bevin and Dalton could get out of the National Council. Though he regards it as a far from incisive policy statement, Bullock correctly adds that '... as so often in the Labour movement's discussion of foreign policy and defence, the debates at the two autumn conferences made clear what the resolution left unsaid, that acceptance of the report meant the abandonment of opposition to rearmament'.[97] It was however Citrine who most forcefully expressed that sentiment at the 1937 Congress:

We cannot wait for that time [of a Labour government] before framing our policy and indicating to our people, despite the possibilities and probabilities of misrepresentation, that we have a moral duty to perform, and that, recognizing the disturbed state of the world, this Labour Movement will not be indifferent to the defence of its own shores.[98]

The trade union leadership read resolute purposes into the less convincing language of *International Policy and Defence*. If one policy had ended in a whimper, another was not to be conceived in ambiguity.

6

The Labour Party Conference of 4–8 October 1937 gathered at Bournemouth, by the sea, which its Chairman, Hugh Dalton, regarded as conducive to harmonious proceedings. Nonetheless that gathering faced harsh and foreboding reality, as Dalton made clear in his opening address:

... in this most grim [international] situation, not of the Labour Party's making, our country must be powerfully armed. Otherwise we run risks immediate and immeasurable. Otherwise, a British Labour Government, coming into power to-morrow, would be in danger of humiliations, intimidations and acts of foreign intervention in our national affairs, which it is not tolerable for Englishmen to contemplate.[99]

The delegates could not have asked for a quicker lead on the interpretation of *International Policy and Defence* than the resolute course set by Dalton. The manifesto itself was not discussed until the fourth day, when Clynes, who had supported Dalton in the Parliamentary Executive in 1936 and 1937, reiterated the argument that in view of the threats posed by fascism, British Labour could not leave every preparation for resistance until the attack had begun. He carefully defended the manifesto from the expected left criticism:

Those who say they would only offer armed resistance to protect a

Socialist State should remember that millions of Socialists in Britain will be in need of defence if Britain is attacked. It is untrue to say that this Report commits us to a policy of militarism and to a mere defence of the present Government.[100]

A left spokesman, Sidney Silverman, nonetheless moved a condemnation of rearmament under the auspices of the National Government, using the traditional argument that war was bound to be imperialist. Before Aneurin Bevan continued the exposition of the left's case, the pacifists Ponsonby and Lansbury pleaded their cause. The ex-leader again summoned the Bible to support his refusal to accept war under any conditions. From the floor the pacifist case was quickly challenged; R. H. S. Crossman asserted: '. . . I believe Mr Lansbury's aims for universal pacification can only be achieved by a Labour Movement which faces the fact that it believes sufficiently in the justice of its cause to take the responsibility upon itself for the use of force if necessary.' Ernest Bevin, as usual concerned only with countering the potentially effective arguments, paid no attention to the pacifist case; rather he told the Labour left that they were too obsessed by the National Government and too little concerned with the international obligations of socialists. In the latter connection the NCL had recognized that 'a lot of the Labour Movements in . . . [European] countries began to wonder, not where the National Government in England stood, but where the Labour Movement in England stood, and whether in a crisis they could rely on us'.[101]

After luncheon, Aneurin Bevan, in a clever speech which his biographer claims won the biggest ovation of the week,[102] inquired where the manifesto stated explicitly Labour's support for the government's rearmament programme, as both Citrine at the Norwich TUC and Clynes had taken it to mean. Bevan was quite justified in his protest, for the manifesto had not considered the matter. Leaving this point aside, Bevan reiterated the left's willingness to support with arms a socialist international policy, but stated '. . . what we are not prepared to do is to tie the Movement behind a National Government which will betray our policy. That is the real issue before us.' Bevan outlined the consequences of Labour acquiescence, involving the emergence of a 'united nation' concept which would militate against industrial or political action on behalf of Labour's goals. 'Along that road', he commented, 'is endless retreat, and at the end of it a voluntary totalitarian State with ourselves erecting the barbed wire around.' For the left much more than international policy was involved in the Conference's decision: implicitly the independence of the working-class movement was at stake. Bevan offered on their behalf an approach which would save the soul of the movement:

> We should conduct throughout the country such a campaign against the National Government, against its armament programme and against its foreign policy as to make our position quite clear; we should say to the country we are prepared to make whatever sacrifices are necessary, to give whatever arms are necessary in order to fight Fascist Powers and in order to consolidate world peace, but we are not going to put a sword in the hands of our enemies that may be used to cut off our own heads.[103]

Even the imagery was carried over from year to year, as the left continued its agitation for active protest.

The National Council of Labour and the parliamentary party had however chosen a position of responsibility based upon a consideration of reality and a careful weighing of relative risks. The touchstone of political leadership is responsibility, and the Labour leadership acted in a responsible fashion, reacting to the grim exigencies of the international situation confronting the nation, rather than to the ideological conviction that Labour's most threatening enemy was British capitalism. James Walker, a Dalton supporter, concluded the Executive's case: he was evidently of no mind to permit the left's criticism to pass unchallenged, assuming the role normally taken by Bevin or Dalton, or, in domestic matters, Morrison. He pointed out that Bevan's case amounted to the assertion that because the government did not do everything he wished, therefore the country should be left defenceless; also Walker stigmatized Bevan's implicit theory of instantaneous generation of armed forces upon the assumption of power by a socialist government.[104] Conference overwhelmingly supported the Executive's position in rejecting the left resolution, 2,167,000 votes to 228,000.

By comparison with Edinburgh, the Bournemouth gathering was mild-tempered; in no topic of debate was the difference in tone more apparent than in that on Spain, which in 1936 had raged in fierce partisan exchanges. By 1937 the left's criticisms had become orthodox Labour tenets, and the Executive had no trouble in accepting Sir Charles Trevelyan's motion that Conference declare its support for the Spanish people and instruct the Executive to launch a national campaign to compel the government to abandon the so-called Non-Intervention Agreement. In response to Trevelyan's rather pointed hope that the new Executive would not sit back content with general resolutions but strive to force its will on the government, George Lathan noted that they had no need to apologize for their attitude towards the Spanish struggle since its outbreak, for 'no opportunity has been missed of indicating our views and the views of the Movement generally in regard to what has been happening . . .' Though no organized campaign had been waged, he reminded the delegates that every meeting the party had held had been turned into a demonstration on behalf of the Republic, noting that one of his Executive colleagues had in the past year addressed no fewer than sixty meetings called for the purpose of dealing with Spain. While accepting the resolution, Lathan commented that a nation-wide campaign might be beyond Labour's means: 'We have another campaign in view, but . . . you may be sure that we shall not relax our efforts to secure justice for our comrades who are fighting in Spain.'[105]

The Executive had not, of course, reversed its position on any united front since Edinburgh; rather they had destroyed the Unity Campaign and had refused to permit the matter to be raised in Conference except in the form of a reference back of the Executive's Report. Sir Stafford Cripps used that small opening to argue against the Executive's action; he resorted to the usual question, asking why the right of association claimed by the Labour right to associate with the likes of Churchill, Lord Cecil and the Archbishop of Canterbury, '. . . three as bitter opponents of the working class as you could find in Great Britain', was denied the left. Thus the Executive's action reflected not only prejudices but also a denial of Labour's traditional tolerance of divergent opinions on certain issues. If the Executive were to continue in that course, then '. . . the Labour Party is going to become a lifeless automaton, repeating only the things it is allowed to repeat and not endowed with that fire of conviction and enthusiasm which is essential if we are ever to win victory and power'.[106] Harold Laski took up this oft-heard theme in stating that '. . . truth may begin, even in this Party, in a minority of one'. J. R. Clynes challenged the assertion that the Executive were persecuting a minority; rather they were acting under Conference instructions to oppose any form of association on the part of party members with the CPGB, a point, he noted, which Cripps had cleverly avoided. Perhaps for the hundredth time, the Executive declared that they were acting not against the left's point of view but their associations.[107] On this issue the clash of left and leadership remained on two levels which never interacted: the left pleaded minority rights, while the Executive protested the constant unconstitutional abuse of majority views. The annual resolution of that conflict in Conference found only 373,000 votes favouring censure of the Executive's action.

Yet the left leaders emerged from Bournemouth in reasonably good spirits, even confident that the Labour Party would shortly move to the left.[108] The sole tangible reason for such optimism was the internal reform approved by the Conference, which resulted in the election of three left-wingers – Cripps, Laski and D. N. Pritt – to the National Executive. Those reforms were not however dictated to the leadership by the overwhelming force of the left exerted in 1937; they had been scheduled for consideration at the Edinburgh Conference but were displaced on the agenda by the recurrent Spanish question. How justified then was the left's optimism?

In the first months of his chairmanship, Hugh Dalton had recognized the nearly universal demand by the constituency parties to elect their own representatives to the Executive; hitherto the entire Conference had balloted for the five constituency representatives as well as the twelve trade union and five women representatives – in effect the trade union block vote could return whomever they pleased to represent the local Labour parties. Anxious to conciliate the most active constituency workers, Dalton however saw that vested interests were involved: 'Some of the Trade Union Section were strong in opposition and so, fearing for their seats if they had to face this new and unknown electorate, were one or two in the Constituency Party Section [of the Executive].'[109] Nonetheless the NEC approved the change in June 1937, at the same time advocating that the constituency representation be increased from five to seven – partly to give greater recognition to the importance of the local parties and partly to make less likely the displacement of incumbent constituency representatives.[110] The Executive proposed also that the new method of election be made operative at the Bournemouth Conference, if first approved by that gathering. The most cogent argument against these proposals was offered, not by the vested interests, but by *The Times*:

... the proposals undoubtedly undermine the principle of the collective responsibility of the executive to the conference; they will be liable to perpetuate in the executive the sectional constitution of the conference and the differences of the sections, whereas now the Executive is unified by its election by the whole conference and its responsibility collectively and individually to the conference.[111]

The Times also appeared concerned that an increment of strength would be granted to 'the ambitious restlessness of the Left wing leaders who are wary of the steadiness which characterizes the trade union leaders'; no doubt the trade union leaders also were concerned with that possibility.

Those leaders were themselves divided with regard to the Executive's proposals: Dukes, of the General and Municipal Workers, and Marchbank, of the National Union of Railwaymen, spoke against them at Bournemouth; the Railway Clerks and the Distributive Workers indicated approval, as did the Miners. Ernest Bevin admitted that the TGWU was itself divided; he added with a touch of irony that the trade union block was not in prospect. Bevin expressed his own concern with the increase in representation and the immediate implementation of the new voting arrangements, preferring to delay the latter a year.[112] Dalton's year of close collaboration with Bevin yielded dividends during the luncheon recess which followed the latter's remarks: the TGWU agreed to support the Executive on the main matter of constituency election, while the Executive gave up support for immediate implementation; however, the two failed to compromise their difference over the increase in constituency representation. In the event the TGWU support proved less vital than anticipated: separate sectional elections were approved, 1,814,000 votes to 658,000; the increase of two local party representatives was carried, 1,408,000 to 1,134,000; despite the Executive's withdrawal of support for the third proposal, that too was carried from the floor even more decisively. Dalton comments that this last decision represented Dukes and Marchbank 'getting their own back on Bevin' for his support of the main proposal.[113] Thus the supposedly monolithic trade union vote shattered on the question of party reform, while the constituency delegates cheered excitedly. Also of note during this debate was Dalton's ruling that the party's desire to move its annual Conference forward to Whitsuntide, so as to avoid following too closely upon Congress, could be implemented either in 1938 or 1939, as the new Executive saw fit; the delegates left Bournemouth not knowing whether they would meet again in, roughly, six or eighteen months' time.[114]

The left then and subsequently claimed victory at Bournemouth, because of the Constituency Party Section's choice of Cripps, Laski and Pritt, along with Dalton, Morrison, Dallas and Noel-Baker. While the local parties clearly showed some sympathy for left views through these selections, the reform could never have been accomplished without Dalton's initiative and the acquiescence of a major portion of the larger trade unions. The Labour left were themselves powerless to force through such a reform; the Executive had acted to redress a widely held grievance, though they realized that the result might benefit the left's causes. The *New Statesman* argued that the leadership was actually conceding very little; in resisting *The Times*' contention that the Labour Party was moving to the left, the periodical argued that what power the trade union leaders had given up on the Executive they maintained on the National Council of Labour, which was emerging as the real arbiter of party policy.[115] Certainly the left forces gained several positions of influence within the party, however.

The leadership, too, had reason to be encouraged by the Bournemouth Conference, since they had won clear-cut, decisive majorities for their international policy and in resistance to blandishments for a united front. Dalton did not engage in empty rhetoric when in his concluding remarks he maintained that the party went forth from Conference united to a degree which they had not known for many a long year. Doubtless his last words rang through the Pavilion: 'Now in the ears of a Movement, confident as it had not been for a long, long while, the trumpets had sounded for the great advance.'[116] Even if that great advance were eight years distant, Dalton had every right to be proud of the progress made under his chairmanship: the Labour Party had truly come to terms with responsibility. Since Labour left and right derived satisfaction from the Bournemouth proceedings, their struggle was for the moment considerably eased, and a greater cohesion settled upon the movement.

With our longer perspective, we can claim that with the Bournemouth Conference the Labour Party had reached a decisive turning-point – and had turned. Granted, this situation came uncomfortably late in the decade and it affected the hold of the National Government not a bit. As an active member and persistent critic of the Labour Party wrote at the time:

... the Labour Party has little to be proud of in the opportunities it has missed and the showing it has made in this period [to 1937]. There are reasons for this, chiefly the impossible situation that the Party was manœuvred into over armaments, and the uncertainty of its leadership right up till the last year.[117]

We have surveyed the reasons for Labour's internal irresolution and sectional warfare and the effects these problems had upon the party's foreign and defence policies. After Bournemouth, we need no longer search about for such explanations, because Labour advocated a firm and honourable international policy, buttressed at last by a commitment to rearmament. Disagreeable lapses there will be, and perhaps a missed opportunity as well, as the Labour Party worked for peace – but not peace at some other nation's expense.

7

Before we turn to consider European developments in 1938, we should review events in the Far East, which was the very first matter dealt with by the Bournemouth Conference. Attlee moved an emergency resolution condemning the deliberate and unprovoked acts of war by Japan against China over many years and calling upon the British government to co-operate with members of the League of Nations and the United States in imposing '... measures of economic and financial pressure designed to bring Japanese aggression to an end'.[118] Labour's Leader stressed his concern that actions rather than words be used: 'We must remember that this has been a long continuing outrage, that the original attack of Japan on China was the first step in the descent of the world to war.'

That particular descent we have followed in the Far East to the Tangku Truce of May 1933, which was followed by a lengthy lull; no serious fighting took place in 1934. Though disturbances occurred increasingly in 1935, neither side was as yet prepared to resume a trial by force. In the course of the next year, the Chinese spirit of resistance strengthened, but, more important, the Japanese militarists were impressed with the success of aggression elsewhere and the consequent preoccupation of European statesmen with their own affairs. Further, they had linked their expansionist policies with those of Germany in the Anti-Comintern Pact of 26 November 1936; thus, '... by 1937 the trend of events was moving towards a situation where a violent collision was probable'.[119] Throughout this period, Eden was far from confident that the Japanese appetite had been sated, because small slices of Chinese territory had steadily disappeared into the Japanese maw. The Foreign Secretary also recognized that the only way to halt the process was for the United States and Great Britain to act together in the Far East; progress towards mounting a joint policy was however very slow, because both of America's resistance to the idea of alliance and of the heritage of suspicion stemming from the exchanges of Simon and Stimson. By his own testimony, Eden worked to dissipate that mood, and his government strove also to strengthen the Chinese economy, through a grant of credits coupled with a reform of the Chinese currency.[120] Such measures could do no more than shore up the Nanking government; the initiative in the Far East remained with the Japanese.

Once again a railway incident provided the spark for the outbreak of hostilities, which this time would in due course merge into the general conflagration of the Second World War. As with the Mukden incident, the origin of the exchange of gunfire between Japanese and Chinese troops at the Marco Polo bridge in July 1937 was disputed; yet there can be no doubt that the Japanese took immediate advantage of the situation to strengthen their position in northern China. By the end of the month

Japanese reinforcements – moving too quickly to convince anyone of their spontaneous reaction – occupied both Tientsin and
Peking. From this time forward, though war was not officially
declared, for all practical purposes Japan and China were again
at war.

What was the British reaction to these events? Eden had immediately inquired of the American Ambassador, Bingham, about
the possibility of joint action, but Washington instead proposed
mediative roles for both countries. Eden regarded this as 'bad
news', for in his view only joint action would deter Japanese
aggression. In September, the British Foreign Secretary hoped
for effective international action along the lines of an economic
boycott, but Neville Chamberlain rather than the State Department discouraged this particular idea. Eden nonetheless discussed
sanctions in November 1937 with the American Norman Davis;
upon reporting this to the Prime Minister, he was told that on no
account would Britain impose a sanction. He had then encountered two rather formidable obstacles to effective action against
Japan; given the attitude of his own government and the resolve
of the United States to avoid firm action, the Nine-Power meeting at Brussels, boycotted by Japan, could agree only upon what
Eden characterizes as '. . . an anodyne resolution deprecating the
use of force'.[121] In December Japan intensified her military
efforts by attacking British and American shipping on the
Yangtse. Cordell Hull testifies to Eden's attempt to secure joint
action as a result of the sinking of the US gunboat *Panay*:

> He [Eden] believed that the dangerous character of the Japanese
> military was such that a show of possibilities of force on a large scale
> was necessary to arrest their attention, their movements, and their
> policy of firing upon the citizens and warships of other countries in a
> most reckless, criminal and deliberate manner. We did not feel, how-
> ever . . . that joint action was the solution, or that any show of force on
> a large scale was possible.[122]

The American response continued to be short of decisive; Eden
had to content himself with the improvement in Anglo-American
co-operation evident in the latter part of 1937.[123]

Meanwhile, how had the British Labour Party reacted to developments in the Far East? Attlee had raised the matter on 30 July,

before the Commons adjourned for the summer recess: he expressed Labour's concern with treaty violation in that part of the world, considering this a matter which should be brought before the League of Nations. In the Far East as elsewhere, '... unless there is a feeling that the world will not sit by and see innocent States suffering from aggression, it will be a continued incitement to those gambling and adventurous elements, and will weaken the position of all those elements, whether in Japan, Italy, Germany or other States, who are against this kind of aggression'.[124] The National Council of Labour too denounced Japan's latest invasion of Chinese territory as yet another act of aggression following upon those which the Labour Party had protested in 1931–3; the Council urged the British government to concert measures with League powers or those with obligations to China, especially the United States, to secure Japan's respect for international law and treaty rights.[125] The Labour Party Conference supported the protests of the PLP and NCL; at that time Attlee promised the Bournemouth gathering that he would press for an early meeting of Parliament, in order to urge Labour's views upon the government. In that endeavour he was quite unsuccessful, for the Commons did not reconvene until 21 October; Attlee then was heartened to hear that the United States was going to join in discussions under the Nine-Power Pact. He maintained that only resolute action on the part of Britain was lacking:

> I believe this adventure of Japan's is only undertaken because of the attitude of this and other Governments in always letting the aggressors get away with it ... If one tithe of the consideration which is shown about British shipping in the Mediterranean was shown about the Japanese invasion of China, I believe that this invasion would stop.[126]

Attlee specified the means of bringing this about – economic pressures applied collectively. The Labour Party, in dealing with the Far Eastern crisis, was nothing if not consistent: they had urged economic sanctions against Japan five years earlier.

When in November Labour continued its attack upon the government's attitude, Eden utilized as a guiding precept of their policy a statement made by Herbert Morrison shortly after the war had erupted. 'He [Morrison] used certain words which were to this effect. Would we in this dangerous and difficult Far

Eastern situation "go as far as the United States, in full accord with them, not rushing in front but not being left behind?" I wholly accept that definition as our guide.'[127] Eden's assertion was of course in good faith, for he had striven to work out a policy in common with an American government which could not commit itself to such an arrangement. Nonetheless, the failure of the Brussels conference, the Japanese capture of Shanghai and their drive on Nanking, and their barbarous practices in what remained an undeclared war, combined in early December to give the Far Eastern crisis a new urgency, although the British government refused to admit a suggestion that British possessions in China were in grave danger.[128]

Following the fall of Nanking on 13 December, the Labour Party again pressed upon the government a greater concern for the rule of law in the Far East. Eden replied with a reminder to the opposition:

We are told that in the Far East today we ought to be upholding the rule of law . . . If hon. Members opposite are advocating sanctions . . . I would remind them that there are two possible forms of sanctions – the ineffective, which are not worth putting on, and the effective, which means the risk, if not the certainty of war. I say deliberately that nobody can contemplate any action of that kind in the Far East unless they are convinced that they have overwhelming force to back their policy.[129]

Eden maintained that the League powers did not possess any such overwhelming force. The Labour spokesman, Alexander, forgoing the chance to point out that the National Government was expert at ineffective sanctions, retorted that in the event of an attack by Japan arising from an economic blockade imposed by Britain, resistance would of course be required. Further, 'I do not agree, on the strategic case, from a naval point of view at any rate, that that is impossible.'[130] Labour came no closer than this oblique reference to arguing the case for military sanctions, however. Their brief for economic and financial sanctions was of course far more detailed; yet in the implementation even of those sanctions a Labour government would have been no less dependent upon a measure of international co-operation than was Eden. Probably then they would have encountered the same stone-wall resistance on the part of the United States, although a Labour Prime Minister could conceivably have influenced the

American government toward a more active role than did Chamberlain, whose negativism hindered Eden's efforts. Whether a Labour government could have successfully carried out the sanctionist policy recommended by the party remains a hypothetical matter; would they have dared go it alone, if need be, or would they too have used the American position as a convenient excuse to dissociate Britain from the Far Eastern crisis? It would have been no easy question to face.

There had been dissent within the Labour Party on its Far Eastern policy, though the disputation was conducted quietly in the Committee rooms of the Palace of Westminster. The Chairman of the Advisory Committee on International Questions, C. R. Buxton, had long been pleading the economic case of the aggressor powers, Germany, Italy and Japan. In October 1936 he had argued that 'frustration and restriction in the sphere of trade has had the effect of forcing Japanese policy in the direction of aggression on the mainland'.[131] Though his view that China, among others, must offer concessions to Japan to overcome her sense that the world was hostile, did not pass the Committee unchallenged, Buxton persisted in his economic interpretation of the Far Eastern situation; in July 1937, he maintained that Japan's 'whole Continental policy is bound up with, though not entirely motivated by, this conception of economic self-sufficiency in the face of a hostile world'.[132] While its chairman solicited understanding of Japan, the ACIQ, now confronted with the renewal of Japanese aggression, proposed an economic boycott: the dual purpose of such a sanction would be the exhaustion of Japanese means of purchase in foreign markets and that of foreign supplies essential to the Japanese war effort. Buxton dissented from this recommendation, arguing that forcible pressure would not solve the problem; he admitted that Japan must respect international law, but Buxton held that the British government must also recognize and move to ease the unviable *status quo* in the realm of trade.[133]

At the same meeting at which Buxton signalled his dissent, he resigned the chairmanship of the ACIQ, as befitted the fact that in his desire to conciliate the Japanese, he was clearly out of step, not only with the Committee, but with the Labour Party. That resignation was conceivably late in coming, because even in December 1936 he had opposed the Committee's draft on the international situation, minuting to it sentiments fashionable in 1938 among the appeasers: 'I submit that there is no evidence that the "dictatorships" are beyond the reach of diplomacy; and that there cannot be any such evidence, until a suitable policy has been proposed and rejected.'[134] The appeasers, as history has come to style them, were not all in government circles, but significantly, those who pleaded the cause of the dictatorial powers within the Labour Party saw in 1937 that they were indeed out of step with their party.

Despite his earlier strictures upon the ACIQ views, Philip Noel-Baker succeeded Buxton as its chairman. Meanwhile, since the government refused to impose an official boycott upon Japanese goods, Labour sought to marshal public opinion on behalf of a private boycott; the National Council of Labour organized in October 1937 a campaign of national demonstrations protesting against Japanese aggression and seeking to obtain public co-operation in the boycott.[135]

Japanese aggression in China continued to the outbreak of war in Europe, but in 1938 the Far Eastern crisis, which had in late 1937 assumed importance in Labour ranks second only to that of the Spanish struggle, faded in importance – not because the crisis eased, but rather because more immediate crises had supervened. To these European events we must now return; the Sino-Japanese war henceforth will be viewed within the general context of appeasement, a course on which Neville Chamberlain was no less resolved than C. R. Buxton. Unfortunately, however, Chamberlain had the weight of the British government to devote to the cause.

7 'A far away country...'

'Appeasement' is the term which will forever be applied to characterize the plummeting path which the western democracies trod in the year 1938. But how distinguish between the pursuit of peace and appeasement?

> ... it is whether the agreement for which they [a government] are working will serve only to relax tension for a while, or whether it is in the true interests of a lasting peace. We must not perpetuate an injustice in order to get a little present ease; and the Government has to consider whether their decision gives peace, not just for an hour or a day or two, but in their children's time. That is the difference between appeasement and peace.[1]

Anthony Eden was well qualified to comment upon the problem, but his description serves only to confuse the student of the 1930s. In presuming that appeasement is a term of opprobrium, and that its practice negates the interests of lasting peace, Eden distorts the primary meaning of the word, 'to bring to peace, settle ...' The historian must work with that primary meaning rather than the subsidiary definition, 'to pacify, by satisfying demands', if he is to explain the widespread support which Chamberlain's efforts received in 1938. Eden's comment typifies the process in which the second meaning has driven out the first: the semantic equivalent of Gresham's Law has debased the very concept of appeasement. If Neville Chamberlain failed in his general project of appeasement, he at least succeeded in changing the meaning of the word.

Throughout the 1930s, the Labour Opposition and the National Government had disagreed over the meaning of appeasement; Chamberlain, however, brought to the concept a new consistency and rigour of definition, which precipitated resignations even within his own Cabinet, and which widened the political dispute on the theory and practice of appeasement. For Labour, appeasement had once been a thoroughly legitimate tool of diplomacy; as proof of this, we have the statement in an official biographical sketch of Arthur Henderson that '. . . the hardest part of the decision Mr. Henderson had to take in the events preceding the Labour Government's resignation was that he must leave unfinished the great work of international appeasement and constructive organization of the world for peace by handing back the seals of the Foreign Office'.[2] The Labour Party, however, recognized realistic limits to the project of international appeasement, as the editors of *Labour* asserted in September 1933: 'This policy of appeasement was politically sound whilst Social Democracy determined the attitude of the German Government. But the old, sabre rattling spirit animates the present German Government . . .'[3]

The policy of appeasement was yielded up only grudgingly by the Labour movement, because it was based in part upon the pacifist sentiments present within the party, and the nation as well. A contemporary observer shrewdly noted: 'She so hated the thought of war that she could not believe that it was going to happen, and the appeasement policy gave her confidence that this hope had some basis.'[4]

More basically, Labour's hopes for the success of appeasement were rooted in socialist ideology. Since the party had long regarded war as the product of capitalism's search for markets, Labour's leaders examined closely the problems posed by the existence of colonial empires and the resulting inequality of economic opportunity in the colonies. In 1936 the Labour Party published a lengthy pamphlet dealing with these problems, which had been prepared jointly by the Advisory Committees on International Questions and Imperial Affairs.[5] Though those bodies proposed the re-establishment of the principle of the 'Open Door' and the equality of trading opportunities in all the dependencies, they specifically cautioned against the exchange of territories, for they believed that such political measures could not solve the economic problems of imperialism. The obvious implication was that economic measures alone could break the cycle which culminated in imperialist war. In socialist eyes, there existed a clear distinction between political concessions and economic measures concerning colonial possessions. In such a vein, the *New Statesman* commented late in 1937:

Hitler proposes, with a cynical eye on our recent history, that we should continue the process of selling the weak countries to the strong. Amongst other objections to this policy of keeping off wolves by throwing babies to them is that they will grow fatter and stronger on the babies and that the supply of babies looks like giving out . . . We might at least first try an offer of some of those economic concessions which could be granted without shame and even with mutual advantage.[6]

The socialist preoccupation with economic concerns led the Labour Party into arguments for redress of grievances which political considerations would have denied.

Nor was this attitude characteristic only of the Labour left. Ernest Bevin, too, held that the root of the international problem lay in economic problems, such as access to raw materials, which could be resolved neither by diplomacy nor by war. He told the Bournemouth Conference: 'The mere revision of the Versailles Treaty will not do. Is it too much to dream that we might yet change the name of the British Commonwealth to one of the European Commonwealth and open up avenues without destroying the political institutions at all?'[7] Such a commonwealth, he wrote in *The Record* of January 1938, would make for greater security than any attempt to maintain the balance of power. If Germany could be attached to such an arrangement, Bevin mused, she would slowly develop a less introspective, more expansive attitude, over the course of a generation or two.

Yet Bevin, as we have seen, never forgot that the Nazis were in control of Germany. Thus the Germany he looked to build was a war as well as a generation away, as his words of February 1938 indicate: 'I have never believed from the first day when Hitler came to office but that he intended at the right moment and when he was strong enough, to wage war in the world. Neither do I believe, with that kind of philosophy, that there is any possibility to arrive at agreements with Hitler and Mussolini.'[8] For Bevin, Nazi control of Germany delayed the time at which economic appeasement could be instituted; international developments forced Bevin to withdraw from the practice, though not the theory, of economic appeasement. The Labour Party subscribed with him to the belief that legitimate economic grievances existed; appeasement of those grievances was not so much designed to satisfy German and Italian demands as to create conditions in which such demands would be superfluous. Adjustment of genuine – if exaggerated – economic grievances would remove the imperialist drives which led to war; international co-operation would expunge the spectre of capitalist competition.

Fringe elements within the Labour Party were prepared to offer territorial concessions even to Hitler, though again on economic grounds. Charles Roden Buxton argued for a far more systematic redistribution of territory than Neville Chamberlain ever contemplated; his biographer comments that 'he supported Mr. Chamberlain as far as he went, but . . . the Prime Minister's policy of mere "appeasement", of yielding concessions piecemeal, seemed so trivial and so unworthy to be called a policy at all, that it hardly surprised him when Germany and Italy should not be taking it seriously'.[9] How many party members agreed with him is unknown, but they were in a very small minority, recruited almost exclusively from pacifist and unilateralist circles. The majority of the party viewed the matter of political negotiations with the dictators in a harsher light; in so doing, the party acted consistently with its espousal of appeasement at a time when the concept was as yet untainted by Chamberlain's variety. Labour had above all striven for appeasement within an economic context – socialist ideology had shaped the party's view here as in other aspects of its international policy.

2

The National Government's pursuit of appeasement was not, of course, based upon a belief in the inevitability of war within the capitalist system; rather they saw the root of war in the failure to redress the specifically national grievances of the vanquished or frustrated powers, in the years following the Great War. The government were now prepared to satisfy the territorial grievances, voiced by fascist régimes, in order to accomplish their grand design of permanent peace: appeasement was the means to that end. Though Chamberlain systematized its application, the design was nothing new. At the time of the German reoccupation of the Rhineland, the Foreign Secretary had assured the

House of Commons that '. . . it is the appeasement of Europe as a whole that we [the Government] have constantly before us'.[10] Eden significantly omits this assurance from the extract of his speech which he publishes in his memoirs, which serves to remind us of the altered meaning of the word appeasement; in the context of his remarks, the word was used in its primary, and honourable, meaning.

Only events following upon his remarks in 1936 have given to appeasement the invidious connotation which he even now associates with it. Surely the definition had been debased by 1940, when Harold Laski claimed that the Labour Party had '. . . always stood four-square against the policy of "appeasement".'[11] The process through which the notion of appeasement altered so dramatically is the necessary background for a consideration of the Labour Party's international policy in 1938 and 1939. They shared with the Prime Minister the will to peace, but the Labour Party did not debase the practice of appeasement in the manner of Neville Chamberlain.

Eden was in no way initially dismayed by Chamberlain's expressed intention to take a greater interest in foreign policy than had Stanley Baldwin, whom he succeeded in June 1937: 'We both knew that no one could have taken less.'[12] Nor had he reason to suspect that the new Prime Minister would pursue an apparently Germanophilic policy; though Chamberlain had not spoken publicly, in private he had expressed throughout his life a dislike and distrust of Germany, which was intensified by the Nazi seizure of power.[13] Yet upon his assumption of office, Chamberlain subordinated his own feelings to strategic considerations: he coldly remarked that if only he could get on terms with the Germans, he would not 'care a rap' for Mussolini.[14] When his initial approaches to Berlin received no response, the Prime Minister decided to test the solidarity of the Axis powers at the Roman end. Two major problems barred the way to Anglo-Italian rapprochement: the Italian conquest of Abyssinia, as yet unrecognized by the British government, and continuing Italian intervention in the Spanish Civil War.

Since the latter problem had in a formal sense eased, as a result of Mussolini's ban upon Italian 'volunteers', in February 1937, Chamberlain attempted to resolve the former and in the process to test the Duce's protestations of good intentions. In July 1937 the Prime Minister went behind the back of his Foreign Secretary to accomplish his project: his 'greater interest' in foreign policy was assuming unforeseen proportions.[15] The Foreign Office's scepticism grew, because precisely at this time Mussolini's pirate submarines were attacking shipping in the Mediterranean. Though Chamberlain complained that such distrust of the Italian régime would get Britain nowhere in her efforts,[16] he recognized that the submarine menace would have to be ended first. The Nyon Conference accomplished that purpose, when Italy subsequently agreed to abide by its arrangements. Those in England who advocated a hard line toward the dictators took heart,[17] but Chamberlain saw that this success had been won at the expense of Anglo-Italian relations, which he again set out to repair.

Meanwhile the Prime Minister renewed his courtship of Berlin, sending Eden's deputy Halifax to Berchtesgaden to achieve his diplomatic object of '... creating an atmosphere in which it is possible to discuss with Germany the practical questions involved in a European settlement ...'[18] Chamberlain took the trouble to record in his diary the emphatic declarations both of Hitler and Goering that they had neither the intention nor the desire to wage war: ' ... I think we take this as correct, at any rate for the present.' What neither he nor Halifax could know was that only two weeks before the latter's trip Hitler had informed his principal military advisers that Germany's problem could only be solved by means of force; the questions were when and how.[19]

Eden had grown increasingly concerned with the direction of Chamberlain's policy; adding to his discomfort at the Foreign Office was Halifax's agreement with the Prime Minister that talks leading to some form of *de facto* recognition of the conquest of Abyssinia ought to be opened. The Foreign Secretary lost a further grip on the control of policy when he left on holiday early in 1938. During his absence, President Roosevelt forwarded to London his imprecise plan of aligning America in sentiment though not in alliance with the European democracies. Chamberlain quickly expressed no interest in a scheme which he thought would create the appearance of hostile blocs of powers. Especially galling to Eden was the Prime Minister's decision to send a discouraging reply without consulting him or any other member of the Cabinet; he was '. . . outraged and uneasy at the way in which this opportunity had been handled . . . if we were not careful, we would lose all that we had gained in the last two years in our relations with the United States'.[20]

His protestations were ineffective; Chamberlain countered that the Foreign Office was not sufficiently sincere in its approaches to the dictators. By mid-January 1938 Eden had resolved upon resignation if Chamberlain did not soon see the paramount importance of good Anglo-American relations, but he really did not expect such a dramatic reversal; he noted in his diary on 18 January: 'I fear that fundamentally the difficulty is that Neville believes that he is a man with a mission to come to terms with the dictators.' Just a month later, Eden recognized that Chamberlain was not to be deterred from his mission. In an outrageous joint interview with the Italian Ambassador, the Foreign Secretary found his position persistently undercut by the Prime Minister; when Grandi left, Chamberlain was even more pointed: 'Anthony, you have missed chance after chance. You simply cannot go on like this.'[21] Two days later, Eden resigned; Chamberlain had cleared another obstacle from his path of appeasement.

On the following day, 21 February, Eden explained his action to the House of Commons; the Opposition was of course likely to be sympathetic. Yet Eden gravely disappointed the hopes of the PLP; with ample grounds for severe attack, he chose instead tepid criticism. By limiting the issue to whether official negotiations with Italy ought to begin immediately, Eden enabled the Prime Minister to retort that only a matter of timing was at stake. Only near the end of his remarks had Eden suggested that fundamental differences in the broad range of foreign policy were involved in his resignation:

Of late the conviction has steadily grown upon me that there has been too keen a desire on our part to make terms with others, rather than that others should make terms with us. This never was the attitude of this country in the past. It should not, in the interests of peace, be our attitude today.[22]

Viscount Cranborne, the Under-Secretary at the Foreign Office who had resigned along with Eden, was both more forceful and more specific in refuting the contention that they had over-reacted to a matter of detail; on the contrary, 'I think that it is . . . a matter of fundamental principle . . . the principle of good faith in international affairs.'[23] Eden implicitly recognized the futility of his own remarks in noting that Chamberlain's tack '. . . left the House bewildered as to the real difference between us', but the burden of responsibility was his own. It was the weakness of Eden's speech which played directly into the hands of those who wanted to minimize the difference between the two views.

The Labour Party attempted to focus upon that difference and its far-ranging implications. To be sure they wished to bring Chamberlain's administration into disrepute, but they were in deep sympathy with Eden's action. Attlee commented that Eden and Cranborne had '. . . taken the line that the representatives of a British Government ought to take in foreign affairs. They had taken the line of courage and the line based on principle'. He criticized the government for following the line of expediency, which was bound to betray the cause of peace and the security of Great Britain:

> It is perfectly ridiculous, after our experience during the last 18 months of dealing with Signor Mussolini, for the Prime Minister to come here and say that everything is going to be wonderful because he has a promise from Signor Mussolini that at some time or other he will come to an agreement which at some time or other he may carry out.[24]

The diplomatic procedure advised by Labour – '. . . first principles are laid down and assurances were given and performances are forthcoming'[25] before formal negotiations were opened – was of course precisely that for which Eden had sacrificed the seals of office.

Though Eden undercut the force of Labour's position by his own weak remarks, the party pressed a vote of censure upon those policies which had led to his resignation; in asking for a general election, Arthur Greenwood charged that the government had repeatedly abandoned the principles upon which they had been returned in 1935. The Prime Minister as much as admitted the allegation, though for him the fault lay with the League of Nations, which since then had been tried and found wanting. Consequently, Labour's position was both unrealistic and anachronistic: 'The party opposite seems to me to be the worst kind of die-hards. They keep on repeating clichés and phrases which once had some significance but have none to-day.' Correctly assessing the strength of the League, he continued, the government had concluded that Great Britain had to talk to those with whom she disagreed. In contrast, Labour's policy '. . . of holding their hands and turning their backs, of making speeches and doing nothing . . . [was] a policy which must presently lead us to war'.[26]

After attacks on government policy mounted by Lloyd George and Churchill – critics hardly noted for holding their hands or turning their backs – Morrison scorned Chamberlain's criticism of Labour and insisted that it was the Prime Minister himself who was playing the game of the fascist powers in saying 'Do what you will, there will be no war so far as we are concerned'.[27] His comment was probably the most perspicacious of the debate, for 1938 was to prove the year of peace at any price.

The Labour Party supplemented parliamentary support of Eden with several leaflets issued to the public. It is likely that the enconiums were strained, but Eden's resignation served to illustrate Labour's long-held tenet that the way to peace did not lie along the path of concessions to the dictators. Rather the party sought '. . . a clear declaration that Britain stands for the enforcement of treaties against lawless force, and against aggressive interference in the internal affairs of independent States'.[28] The Labour Party specifically demanded such a guarantee for Czechoslovakia. And they cautioned that if the peace were to be saved, Chamberlain would have to be turned out of office.

Eden was equally aware of the stakes of the conflict, but, unlike the Opposition, he made no move to rally the Prime Minister's foes. If his vision was so clear, if his convictions were as deeply held as his memoirs indicate, why did he not take his case to the country? The parliamentary debate had offered one opportunity, and his address to his constituency Conservative organization, several days later, a second. That he failed to seize either is painfully clear in a letter which he later received from Neville Chamberlain:

You had to say enough to justify your resignation, and to vindicate your views, and the easiest, and perhaps the most popular, way would have been to emphasise differences and to call for support. I have no doubt that you have been urged to do this, perhaps by some who would not be sorry to attack the Government. Anyhow, whatever the temptations, you have resisted them.[29]

The Labour Party had every reason to regret the performance of this paper tiger, though Eden was to disappoint time after time. Aneurin Bevan, obviously spoiling for a parliamentary rumpus, had expected the most exciting sitting of the House of Commons since 1931, because when Eden rose to address the House, no verdict had been reached in advance. Hoping for Chamberlain's political ruination, Bevan was deeply grieved when Eden instead '... proved once again how much there was to be said on the other side of the question. Instead of widening the issue to embrace the realities of the European scene, he narrowed it almost to a point of diplomatic finesse.'[30]

Labour's hopes were dashed. Where they had sensed a boiling up of the political waters, calm instead prevailed; few then recognized the deceptiveness of the calm, for Great Britain had entered the eye of the hurricane.

With Eden gone, Lord Halifax was given the unhappy task of carrying out Chamberlain's mission. His noble rank at least spared him the full brunt of continued Labour attacks upon the practice of appeasement; a renewed wave of attacks, centred in the House of Commons, came during the Austrian crisis of spring 1938. That had been precipitated by the fateful trip in February of the Austrian Chancellor, Schuschnigg, to Berchtesgaden. At that time Hitler had literally shouted down the Austrian leader's objections to drawing the two countries closer together, and thereafter he kept pressure on the Schuschnigg government through the newly appointed Nazi Minister of the Interior, Seyss-Inquart. Though Schuschnigg decided to gamble on a plebiscite to maintain Austria's independence, in the crucial pass he refused to contemplate military action in defence of Austria's free choice.[31] The last hope of avoiding *Anschluss* passed; the way to German annexation of Austria – 'the proudest hour of my life', Hitler commented – lay open. Further, the success of his bullying tactics reinforced Hitler's belief in the utility of such procedures in international relations.

The initial stages of the Austrian crisis had coincided with the final stages of Eden's breach with Chamberlain; though secret information received shortly after the Berchtesgaden meeting indicated to Eden that Hitler was determined upon *Anschluss* and that Mussolini had acquiesced, there is no reason to believe that the Austrian situation played a decisive role in precipitating his resignation.[32] When pressed by the PLP, which also had heard about the Berchtesgaden meeting, Eden had acknowledged Britain's commitment to Austrian independence, under the Stresa declaration. Labour's fears were not so easily stilled; the party raised questions concerning Schuschnigg's voluntary participation in the Berchtesgaden meeting and also voiced concern that Article 88 of the Treaty of St Germain, which forbade any type of union between the two countries, was called into question.[33]

Neville Chamberlain took a rather optimistic view of the talks between Hitler and his Austrian counterpart; he pointed out that no juridical matters were involved, as the two statesmen had merely '. . . agreed to certain measures being taken with a view to improving relations between their two countries'.[34] In fairly short order, however, he had to admit that this improvement of relations had been accomplished in an unorthodox fashion, by the loss of Austrian sovereignty. Nonetheless he maintained that Britain had fulfilled her treaty obligations by protesting, in common with France, against the *Anschluss*. The Prime Minister explained that 'the hard fact is . . . that nothing could have arrested this action by Germany unless we and others with us had been prepared to use force to prevent it'.[35] Though Chamberlain's lack of concern for breach of treaties is appalling, his government's inaction is excusable: the Austrian government had refused to solicit British support in the country's dying days.[36]

Labour voiced the belief that in view of the intensification of the sense of insecurity in Europe, Chamberlain's professed desire to review British defence programmes was an insufficient response to the German challenge. Attlee argued that the British government's attempt to deal with the dictator states on the assumptions which usually prevailed in international relations was futile. With an eye to recent events, he held that the *Anschluss* had proved Eden right, and Labour as well:

He was, in fact, stating what we have urged on these benches again and again ever since the rape of Manchuria. Each successive instance of bad faith, each successful act of aggression leads to another ... Manchuria, Rhineland, Abyssinia, Spain, China, Austria – what next? In this progressive deterioration of the world situation there must come a time when it is necessary to stand firm unless all Europe is to be thrown into the melting pot.[37]

The lesson was clear: separate bargainings with the dictators could not maintain the peace, so the British government must return to principles and policies based upon the League of Nations. In his belief, the world could yet be rallied to stand for a collective system of law and justice.

Winston Churchill was quite at one with Attlee in protesting against the British government's policy, asking '... how much shall we throw away of resources now available for our security and the maintenance of peace?'[38] For a future course Churchill recommended the creation of a Franco-British-Russian alliance. Attlee had spoken of a League policy, but since the nucleus of any such League grouping would be found among those three great powers – the only great powers left in the League of Nations – the Labour Party's scheme of collective security was not far removed from the proposals advanced by such dissident Conservatives as Churchill and Amery.[39]

The great gap came between such collectivist policies and Chamberlain's individualistic pursuit of peace; the dichotomy became all the more clear in the weeks following the German *coup*. The Soviet government reacted quickly by proposing a conference, attended by Britain and France among other nations, to concert practical arrangements demanded by developments. Such a procedure remained anathema to Chamberlain, who maintained that such exclusive groupings of nations would prove inimical to the prospects of peace.[40] Not only did the British government refuse to entertain the Russian proposal, but Chamberlain refused as well to give a prior guarantee of involvement in a war occasioned by some incursion upon the integrity or independence of Czechoslovakia. Though pressed by Labour, the Prime Minister would go no further than to remark that any war in central Europe could probably not be confined to those nations which had assumed legal obligations. Yet he expressed no concern with matters of right or wrong in international relations, nor with the League of Nations and its obligations.

H*

Attlee could detect only a postponement of war in the course followed by the government; their policy was essentially negative:

We have had a rejection of the Soviet Russian proposal for a conference, and the Prime Minister has rejected the suggestion we made for a meeting of the League of Nations. There is a rejection of every attempt to bring this matter before the nations so that they can discuss and try to save the situation before they all fall into this gulf. Our indictment against the Government is that it is not sufficient to say that we are going to keep out of war, while at the same time we are steadily sliding down to war.[41]

Though the Labour leader could not know it, his nation had more reason to fear a determined policy of accommodation on Chamberlain's part. The Prime Minister, however, privately expressed discouragement with the *Anschluss*, but his hope in breaking off negotiations with Germany was simply to register British determination not to be bullied. There remained one substantial ray of hope, he wrote on 13 March: 'If we can avoid another violent coup in Czechoslovakia, which ought to be feasible, it may be possible for Europe to settle down again, and some day for us to start peace talks again with Germany.'[42] His actions for nearly a year were a gloss upon this statement.

Once again temporarily frustrated in Berlin, Chamberlain typically hoped for success in Rome. Mussolini had his own reasons for Anglo-Italian rapprochement, and in April the two countries set aside the debris of history which had kept them apart. A bargain was consummated which would lead to British recognition of the conquest of Abyssinia, in return for the withdrawal of Italian troops from Spain; Mussolini further disclaimed any intention of seeking a privileged position in Spain.[43] His belated willingness to evacuate Spain may only have reflected the fascist belief that a quick settlement of the Spanish conflict was in the offing, since Franco had just severed the Republican territory; events however belied the expectation.

Chamberlain was in fine fettle in asking for parliamentary approval of the Anglo-Italian agreement, on 2 May; he voiced his conviction that Mussolini's promises were given in good faith. Labour's opposition he could then label factious, and even more important, his project of conciliation was validated: '. . . I repudiate the idea that it is impossible to come to terms and understandings with States where authoritarian ideas prevail. This Agreement proves the contrary . . .' The Labour spokesman, Herbert Morrison, however, stressed other consequences of the agreement: the sacrifice of Abyssinia and the violation of the precepts of the Covenant of the League of Nations. He argued effectively that five of the eight annexes to the pact were reaffirmations necessitated only by Italy's violation of earlier agreements, thus serving to prove Italian bad faith. His party could find absolutely no justification for the agreement, which dealt yet another heavy blow at the League, the rule of law and the collective organization of peace; only Franco and his Italian and German masters could extract satisfaction from Chamberlain's work.

Attlee concluded for Labour in much the same manner as Morrison, but he added at least one important item to Labour's growing catalogue of displeasure with the actions of the Prime Minister: on a personal level, they found his parliamentary manners offensive. Attlee specifically complained of Chamberlain's 'usual sneer at the Opposition', expressed in his ostentatious asides during Morrison's speech and his failure to attend the first part of the speech of the Leader of the Opposition. Whether philosophically or ironically, Attlee added: 'We are getting rather accustomed to that sort of thing now.'[44] Unlike the amiable though tricky Baldwin, Chamberlain had managed throughout the decade to provoke the Labour Party needlessly. Not surprisingly, the troubled relationship dated to the time of the General Strike:

His letters and diaries [c. 1926] begin to fill first with expressions of his exasperations and then of his contempt for them. For their [Labour's] part no chance was let slip to torment him. And so a gulf opened and widened . . . almost by accident a disastrous personal relationship was begun which was to leave its mark on the history of the next dozen years. Lloyd George and Chamberlain could see no good in each other, and they were both wrong. Nor . . . could the Labour Party and Chamberlain, and again they were both wrong.[45]

A portion of the misunderstanding is traceable to the Labour Party, but surely Chamberlain's refusal to bend to parliamentary customs when he assumed high office is the major exacerbating factor. His unflinching honesty of mind and arrogant disposition suited him poorly for dealing with the Opposition. That the

Prime Minister was no model parliamentarian surely added yet another measure to Labour's brimming cup of dissatisfaction with his policies.

In this assessment of appeasement, in theory and practice, we have come to the eve of the Czech crisis. In the Labour Party we have found a widening recognition that force alone would deter the aggressors, coupled with a steadfast opposition to the granting of political concessions to them. The party had turned its back on appeasement even before Chamberlain debased the concept.

3

To recognize that force would be required to deter aggression is one matter; to provide and organize the force required to combat actual aggression is quite another. In 1937 the Labour Party had at last bridged its dichotomy in these two vital matters; in the following year the party continued to act in a responsible manner, expressing sympathy with certain measures of national rearmament but voicing criticism, in Attlee's words, of any 'competition in armaments divorced from foreign policy'. He stressed Labour's commitment to rearmament, though much of the responsibility for that regrettable necessity Attlee traced to the disastrous foreign policy pursued by the British government. For that reason, the Deputy Leader of the Opposition warned the government against expecting his party to play the role of yes-men in discussions of defence policy.[46]

That redoubtable critic of the inadequacy of the government's defence policies, Winston Churchill, underscored the Labour Party's recently found role of constructive critic in defence matters; in December 1937 he had complimented the Opposition, and more particularly the trade unions, upon the assistance they had given the strength and unity of the country through support for measures taken to repair Britain's defences.[47] What is somewhat ironic in this developing rapport is that Churchill, probably more than Chamberlain, earlier had been an inveterate enemy of the Labour movement. Yet by the late thirties both he and the Labour Party had risen above their past difficulties, in a manner which Chamberlain and the party could not. The Labour

Party's fateful decision of May 1940 to refuse to enter a coalition government under Chamberlain, followed by acceptance of office under Churchill, certainly stemmed from past relationships as well as from Chamberlain's inadequate conduct of the war.

The Prime Minister refused to credit the Opposition with a responsible role in defence debates generally. He refused to take at face value Labour's criticism of the lack of co-ordination in strategy, administration, and supply and the party's protest that immense armaments were necessitated by the government's unsound foreign policy. Ever the parliamentary cynic, Chamberlain chose instead to view these strictures as an attempt to mask the obvious, namely that Labour really wanted to vote against defence provisions but did not think it prudent to inform the electorate.[48]

The Opposition concentrated its attention upon all too obvious shortcomings in air defence. Attlee used the occasion of the issuance of yet another White Paper on Defence in March 1938 to show how little had actually been accomplished in air defence measures: 'Everything seems to be thought of, but nothing seems to be done . . .'[49] Before the government's Air Estimates were approved by the Commons, something in fact was done: the Secretary of State for Air, Lord Swinton, was sacked, victim of a barrage of criticism. In mounting this successful attack, the PLP played a significant role, though the opposition of Tory back-benchers, led by Churchill, was probably more telling.

In the initial stages of the Air Estimates, Labour had requested an independent inquiry into the wasteful procedures at the Air Ministry, but Chamberlain heatedly denied the need for such an action.[50] Needless to say, the Prime Minister's assurances did not still the Labour criticism: Stafford Cripps, in a rather unconventional posture, argued that the Ministry was incapable of organizing the vast production needed for the RAF; he proposed the creation of a system paralleling the Ministry of Munitions of the Great War.[51] The House of Commons, however, rejected his proposals.

In April, Hugh Dalton, absent from Parliament since mid-December because of a trip to the Antipodes, returned to England; he received from Attlee shocking accounts of aircraft production. Dalton immediately urged upon Attlee a double-edged attack, because he saw that '. . . this failure of the Air

Ministry, and of private enterprise, to give us aircraft was the biggest single issue at the present moment, both in the national interest and as political dynamite . . .'[52] Attlee probably had hoped for such a reaction on Dalton's part; he placed the voluble Dalton in charge of the accumulation of materials relating to British air defences.

Dalton used the research facilities of Transport House, but he found far more useful the willingness of a few RAF officers to supply accounts of the serious deficiencies and long delays in the government programme. Acting in the conviction that they were serving the national interest, a team of three officers brought the same information to various government critics, one to Dalton, the second to Churchill and the third to the Liberal leader, Sinclair.[53] Though Churchill was aware that 'the many great and valuable expansions and improvements which Lord Swinton had made could not become apparent quickly,' he also felt that 'the whole policy of the Government lacked both magnitude and urgency' and so joined in pressing for an inquiry into the state of the British air programme.[54] To complete the solid front of opposition, the Liberals asked for a committee of inquiry when a stage of the Air Estimates was debated on 12 May. The RAF team had done its work well.

With Swinton in the Lords, the defence of the air programme in the Commons fell to the lot of Earl Winterton, who had assisted Swinton at the Ministry for only ten weeks. The more experienced Churchill challenged Winterton's ill-informed satisfaction with projected production. Attlee too remained unpersuaded, commenting with words that ring true: 'The Government, ever since it was first brought to their knowledge that there was a great air force being built up in Germany, have been guilty of an entire miscalculation of the situation.'[55] Though the Liberal motion was defeated, Swinton's stewardship remained an open question, and in short order he was dismissed from the Ministry.

Churchill and his cohorts were for the moment satisfied with this remedial measure, and they declined to press an inquiry upon the new Minister, Kingsley Wood. The Labour leadership, however, reasoned that as the purge had proved their point, the inquiry should follow. In speaking to this point, Dalton argued that 'on any view of foreign policy . . . in this danger zone that we are now traversing an emphatic inferiority of British to German air power is for this country a most grim and most unwelcome relationship'.[56] Though Dalton recalled that Baldwin had opted for air parity in 1934–5, the better to establish the government's failure he did not point out Labour's resistance to that course at that time. For Dalton – and most of the party as well – that past was quite dead: the paramount concern now was the means of defence from air attack.

Chamberlain still wanted no part of what he described as a 'sort of fishing and roving' investigation which he contended would distract the Ministry from its essential work.[57] Churchill, on the other hand, had withdrawn his motion for that inquiry, but he was by no means prepared to accept Chamberlain's optimistic views; Dalton, he noted, had made a formidable case. With the RAF officers in mind and tongue in cheek, he added: 'I cannot challenge any substantial part of the statement he made.'[58] Consequently he – and Eden as well – abstained on the Labour motion, which Chamberlain treated as a vote of censure; not a single Conservative supported Labour's bid for an independent inquiry.

The PLP nonetheless was united in its defence posture. In regard to Dalton's effort, Aneurin Bevan somewhat grudgingly judged that, from a parliamentary point of view, it had been a brilliant success: 'It was true that he was batting on an easy wicket, but he scored all the runs that could be got'.[59] Thus the PLP, given the disastrous policies of the government, could score easily enough, but they could never win the parliamentary match – the 1935 General Election had queered the pitch.

Despite the apparent futility of their efforts, Labour had played a responsible and constructive role in the air defence discussions of 1938; perhaps Swinton was sacrificed unfairly,[60] but in this vital area strong pressures had to be brought to bear upon the government. Labour may have taken up the cry for air parity belatedly, but even belated attention to air defence may have made quite a difference in the Battle of Britain. Labour's efforts in the direction of rearmament are commendable; the party was prepared to combat actual aggression.

4

Upon his return from Australia in April, Dalton received another piece of disturbing news; as he tersely summarizes this development, 'Cripps was at it again'.[61] His reaction was typical of that of Labour's leaders, who were grievously disappointed that the elections of Cripps and Laski to the National Executive had not satisfied the demand of those critics who called for unity. As their disillusionment turned to rancour, these leaders sensed deliberate factionalism where there existed only a desire to broaden the base of a domestic anti-fascist movement. In reacting in this fashion, they – and Hugh Dalton in particular – created a myth concerning the agitation of 1938.

What the Labour leaders failed to understand was that no Executive balloting nor even Conference's repeated rejections of proposals for working-class unity could destroy the enthusiasm of past campaigns nor contain the sentiment to do 'something' on behalf of the forces struggling against fascism, particularly the Spanish Loyalists. Men who were more thorough-going socialists than the majority of the Labour leaders – G.D.H.Cole, for example – were by 1938 prepared to forgo the goal of socialism in order to deal with urgent international matters. In Cole's mind the People's Front existed '. . . in order to save democracy from overthrow by the forces of Fascism, and to pursue a constructive policy of economic recovery and social and political reform'.[62] He preferred any moderate government of the left to the continuance of one of the right.

Other groupings on the left had come to share Cole's belief that if such a left government could be secured it was criminal and suicidal to resist. In 1937 the Communist Party, faced with the collapse of the Unity Campaign, turned to the idea of a broad left front, which it had so far spurned. There developed in Britain in the winter of 1937 a demand for the widest possible coalition of anti-fascist, anti-government forces; only at this point did the supporters of a British 'Popular Front' aim at a base as broad as that of the Spanish and French models. Reacting to disturbing international developments, symbolized by Eden's resignation, an increasing number of Liberals joined in the campaign to oust Chamberlain and install by pressure of public opinion a government which would stand up to the aggressors.

Scattered sources offered support in the early months of 1938. *Reynolds' News*, with an appeal primarily to the Co-operators, advocated a 'United Peace Alliance', based on the Labour and Co-operative movements but including those Liberals and even those Tories who were critical of Chamberlain and accepted the need for collective security. *Reynolds'* saw its recommendation carry the day at the Easter conference of the Co-operative Party. Another newspaper, the *News Chronicle*, had taken up the demand for some sort of a popular front on much the same basis. In the constituencies, a number of popular fronts were created, mainly through the efforts of Labour intellectuals, progressive Liberals and supporters of the League of Nations Union, the National Peace Council and other non-partisan bodies.

In all this nebulous agitation for a broad-based front, there is no visible trace of the hand of Stafford Cripps; unlike earlier campaigns, that of 1938 lacked either a definite organizing centre or even a single focus.[63] What is particularly ironic is that Cripps' newspaper, *Tribune*, might well have supplied that focus; however, in early 1938, *Tribune* was in the throes of an internal crisis. Its editor, William Mellor, had severed his close political alliance with its major proprietor, Cripps; more doctrinaire than his colleagues in regard to the matter of co-operation with other political parties, Communist or capitalist, Mellor refused to support the popular front agitation. Cripps eventually fired him in July 1938 but meanwhile *Tribune* had conspicuously failed to focus the front agitation.[64] Nor can Cripps' personal role justify the allegations brought against him: unlike his extensive efforts in front campaigns both in 1937 and 1939, only once did Cripps publicly undercut Labour policy, in commenting on 23 April 1938 that the chance of altering British foreign policy was worth the temporary abandonment of the concept of working-class control.[65]

Though Cripps specifically denied that such an alignment could be permanent, no doubt the spectacle of one of their number endorsing front agitation, even in a passing and qualified fashion, infuriated the Labour Executive. Frustrated and annoyed as he no doubt was at that time, Dalton nonetheless erred – it seems deliberately[66] – in alleging in his memoirs that Cripps was once again systematically 'at it' in 1938. Perhaps Dalton was simply unable to believe that Cripps was not directly involved;

more likely his intention, even twenty years after the fact, was to discredit Cripps and the various fronts in one fell swoop.[67]

What must above all be kept in mind if the motives of those who backed the front activities of 1938 are to be understood is their concern with Spain. Aneurin Bevan, then as earlier, held that all else must be subordinated to the necessities of the Republican cause. The reverses suffered by the Spanish government forces in 1938 made the popular front more essential than ever, Bevan contended on May Day:

> If the National Government remains in office another two or three years we shall rue in blood and tears that we did not take action sooner. The country is faced with two alternatives – the establishment of a Popular Front in this country, under the leadership of the Labour Party, or drift to disaster under the National Government.[68]

What was the size of the group within the Labour Party prepared to follow Bevan's lead? Calculations are necessarily guess-work: possibly a third of the party's militants (some 30–40,000 in 110,000) favoured left proposals generally; yet this group constituted not even one in ten of those Labour Party members who can be characterized as politically interested (approximately a half-million).[69] More than likely, then, the leadership had little to fear from open discussion of the front proposals. In fact, however, the Executive acted as if they feared such discussion; they afforded little opportunity to the active party members to influence party policies.

Since no Conference was scheduled for 1938, the Executive were in an unassailable position. Basing their stand on the several past Conference decisions not to weaken Labour policy in order to accommodate other political elements, the Executive refused to convene the party to discuss the front proposals. Instead they asked all party members to withhold their support from '. . . movements which are bound to weaken the Party's organisation and electoral power by association with other political bodies that do not share the Party's policy or its determination to achieve its democratic Socialist objectives'.[70] Thus domestic socialism continued to take precedence over the fascist threat.

And so too did the Executive persist in the argument that the party's means of redress of the policies of the National

Government was electoral. They reminded the movement that Labour had fallen only nineteen seats short of a majority in 1929; they believed that 'the capture of power' could be achieved if Labour's electoral independence were unsullied. A number of constituency parties, more concerned with the dangers of 1938 than the election results of a bygone era, initiated steps to form local councils of action, and to support the popular front, despite the Executive's appeal. The leadership threatened, and in some cases resorted to, expulsion of the dissident local Labour parties. In the Executive's measured judgment, the party could not agree even to a temporary loss of independence, '. . . unless they were convinced that such sacrifice was the sole condition for the preservation of peace and democracy. We do not believe that condition exists.'[71]

Diametrically opposed was the view of the front supporters that the condition indeed existed and the time to act was in the present; their growing impatience with the Executive's failure to alter their stance as the international situation deteriorated can be appreciated. In May 1938 the degree of that deterioration was not yet apparent: the Executive's policy was defensible, though short-sighted. What these leaders could not grasp was that their refusal to compromise Labour's stance appeared to others to place socialist ideology above the country's vital interest – to overthrow Chamberlain and to stem the external fascist tide. Of course they wanted badly to bring down the detested National Government, the deformed child of 1931, but they insisted upon doing it on Labour's own terms, terms which necessarily limited the appeal which they could make to the British people. As the months passed, and the year turned, this flaw in Labour's policy loomed increasingly large.

The Labour left despaired at what they regarded as the leadership's inertia in the face of impending calamity. What was needed they argued, was the unorthodox, extra-parliamentary methods that the unemployed had used so effectively:

The aim was to produce such a ferment of opinion, such hostility to the appeasement policy of the National Government, such a pressure in Parliament that British policy could be diverted from its dangerous course before much damage was done. The truth was that no one could gauge what would be the magnetic effect of realignment of forces on the Left; the claims of both the official leaders and the rebels were

235

unprovable. Maybe the Popular Front was always a desperate, forlorn hope. But what other card in the Socialist hand was there left to play?[72]

If the Labour Party ever held another card, the leaders never played it. Unable to defeat Chamberlain in the Tory House of Commons, they refused to risk the loss of their political identity by turning outside Parliament and leading the popular front.

When the Executive refused even to convene the Conference which had been promised to the party – if events warranted – they effectively deprived the front agitation of the focus which was so desperately needed. There were those on the Executive who were troubled by this refusal, though their own report glosses over the matter in its usual show of unity. Nonetheless one meeting of the NEC found nine in favour of a special conference and nine opposed; since nine represented only one-third of the full body, the Chairman, George Dallas, adjourned the matter to the next meeting.[73] That meeting decided to consider the request again in September, when they would concurrently review developments in central Europe and Spain. *Reynolds'* correspondent reported that the Executive were not opposed on principle to such a special party conference but felt that the timing was not yet right; he noted Dallas' assertion that 'whenever we think that the emergency requires it, there will be no hesitation about our attitude'. In the interim, the Executive's action deprived the front agitation of any chance of securing a mass following.

Without Labour's support, the popular front faltered and collapsed, by mid-1938. Despite the efforts of its supporters, including the Left Book Club, the burdens of organizing and leading a broad anti-government front without the Opposition's support were too great. In June the Co-operative Congress overturned the Co-operative Party's endorsement of the United Peace Alliance by 4·5 to 2·4 million votes, a decisive reversal; the National Union of Railwaymen too looked askance at the proposal, as did the National Conference of Labour Women. Thereafter, with the exception of one parliamentary triumph secured after Munich, the popular front agitation of 1938 simply petered out.[74] Though a variety of reasons can be advanced to explain the faltering of the campaign – disillusionment with the behaviour of the Communists in Spain and in the continuing Moscow purge trials, the diversion of attention from Spain to central Europe, the discredit attached to a disorganized campaign which coupled a vigorous anti-fascist policy with opposition to rearmament under the National Government (an unwelcome feature of the front) – the decision of the Labour Executive is clearly the decisive factor. That body would have no part of a popular front or any other front for that matter, at least not until the international situation worsened.

5

Deterioration in fact marked the European scene in the summer of 1938, as the Czech crisis assumed major proportions. The Labour Party had long been aware of the problems posed by the creation of this multiracial state in the heart of Europe. Indeed they had, right after the war, protested against the cession of the predominately German-settled Sudetenland to Czechoslovakia; the party Conferences of 1920–3 had passed resolutions favouring the revision of boundaries established by the Paris settlement. Subsequently, however, Labour's concern shifted away from such territorial revision. In the case of Czechoslovakia, the Labour leaders were impressed with the development of democratic institutions. Hugh Dalton commented in May 1935: 'I have recently spent three weeks in Czechoslovakia, to-day by far the freest and most civilized land in Central Europe. I wish that more of my fellow countrymen, venturing abroad, would take that road . . . [to see] the simple decencies of democracy maintained, amid the surrounding decadence.'[75] Dalton saw that the country faced formidable problems, though he did not include Henlein and his Nazi-like German Party among the foremost; and he contended that the various national minority groups were better treated than national majorities under most dictators. Dalton did not deny that the Sudeten Germans had genuine grievances. He rejected any large-scale revision of Czech frontiers as a panacea for Czechoslovakia's problems, but, under certain conditions, he concluded '. . . it would not be impossible here and there to cut away the German rind from the Czech cheese, and if this were to be regarded as a final settlement, leading to good and

237

neighbourly relations . . . accompanied by a diminution of trade barriers, there would be much to be said for it'.[76] Since the international developments of 1936–8 made the likelihood of such a lasting settlement slim indeed, Dalton was not heard recommending severance of the German 'rind' in 1938. Prime Minister Chamberlain, however, put precisely this idea into operation, though on a much larger scale than Dalton had envisaged three years earlier.

The Labour Party had meanwhile watched very closely the development of the crisis: the Advisory Committee on International Questions had the Sudeten question under constant surveillance in 1938. In April Arnold Forster's memorandum argued forcefully on behalf of a British guarantee to Czechoslovakia, which in his view would end the 'flight from collective security'. He cautioned that Labour should be chary of pressing the British government too severely, because the party could not know the precise state of readiness of the British defence forces; the government conceivably might feel that the danger of crying 'halt' in 1938 was greater than it would be in 1940.[77] Yet the ACIQ kept Labour's options open: they examined a tortuous plebiscitary plan drawn up by a Labour MP, John Parker, in the hope that the settlement of just grievances would decrease the importance of frontiers, and so dampen the crisis. He proposed that any areas recording a less than three-quarters sentiment for autonomy remain Czech.[78] The hope of those within the Labour Party who looked to a settlement along autonomous lines was graphically depicted by Lord Noel-Buxton, the brother of C. R. Buxton: 'To refuse autonomy in such circumstances might be to risk the loss not only of their [Czech] German-speaking territories, but of the independence of their whole country.'[79]

The National Executive of the Labour Party was well acquainted with the discussions of its Advisory Committee, whose discussion of legitimate grievances and autonomous status brought the Sudeten question well within Labour's ken. The threat to the integrity or independence of Czechoslovakia was discussed publicly as well: *Labour* featured articles in January 1937, May 1938 and June 1938, dealing with various aspects of the situation. All in all, Czechoslovakia was hardly a far-away country of which little was known – not for the Labour Party. Nor were the unsettling consequences of the *Anschluss*, particularly in regard to the neighbouring country of Czechoslovakia, lost upon the Labour leaders.

Yet undeniably it was Winston Churchill who best recognized these strategic considerations, which he discussed on 14 March, with heavy-handed irony:

To English ears, the name of Czechoslovakia sounds outlandish. No doubt they are only a small democracy, no doubt they have an army only two or three times as large as ours, no doubt they have a munitions supply only three times as great as that of Italy, but still they are a virile people, they have their . . . treaty rights, they have a line of fortresses, and they have a strongly manifested will to live, a will to live freely.[80]

Here was a formidable ally.

Yet Chamberlain refused to extend to Czechoslovakia a British guarantee, the pleas of his critics notwithstanding; the British government instead pressed upon the French guarantors of that state '. . . a solution of German minority questions as would be compatible with ensuring the integrity of the Czechoslovak State, while retaining that minority within the frontiers of Czecho-slovakia'.[81] As the negotiations initiated by France and Britain late in April to find a solution to the Sudeten question – which led eventually to the conference table at Munich – form the best-known chapter of inter-war diplomatic history, detail is not here in order. What is vital is the attitude of the Labour Party to the Czech crisis and its reaction to Chamberlain's course, which cul-minated in his assurance to Hitler that he would obtain 'all essentials without war, and without delay'. By that time, the integrity of the Czech state had long been forgotten.

When Chamberlain addressed a House of Commons about to rise for the summer, on 26 July, the Czech Government had already survived what they claimed had been an attempted German *coup*. In this so-called May crisis, a surface display of Anglo-French unity secured its purpose, for no *coup* was hazarded and the crisis quickly eased. However, it seems likely that Hitler was not yet prepared to move;[82] consequently he was outraged at the humiliation of what seemed his hasty retreat, in the face of Anglo-French warnings. From his 'black rage' of that week '. . . sprang the venomous hatred with which he referred to

President Benes, and an inflexible determination to obliterate the very name of Czechoslovakia.'[83] Chamberlain too had been shaken by the events of May, which had revealed to him the danger of war. Where Hitler had however determined upon war as a result, the British Prime Minister resolved only to avoid any such military confrontation in the future. Clearly then Czechoslovakia would have to pay the price of Chamberlain's determination.[84]

By late July, Chamberlain voiced cautious optimism, claiming that the European atmosphere was lighter and the tension less than six months earlier. He was buoyed by the dispatch of Lord Runciman as a special adviser to the Czech government on minority questions, because he considered that country the key to the settlement of Europe's problems:

If only we could find some peaceful solution of this Czech question, I should myself feel that the way was again open for a further effort for a general appeasement – an appeasement which cannot be obtained until we can be satisfied that no major cause of difference or dispute remains unsettled.[85]

Speaking for the Labour Party, Morgan Jones wished Runciman well in his difficult and intricate mission, which he held should be that of an adviser rather than of an adjudicator; he welcomed the Prime Minister's assurance that the Czech government should determine the extent of the concessions which might be offered the Sudeten German minority.[86] Nonetheless he chose to remind the government that the Czech government, which had in no way departed from proper standards of international conduct, were entitled to Britain's complete sympathy and, if possible, support. The outspoken Labour back-bencher, Colonel Josiah Wedgwood, supplemented Jones' reminder with the warning that if through the instrumentality of the British government the whole of Czechoslovakia were placed in what amounted to Nazi hands, then

... we shall have scrapped one more of our friends and allies, weighted the balance once more against democracy and freedom. We may congratulate ourselves that day that for another three months, or until another July or August comes, we have secured peace, but it will be a peace which is even more precarious than it is at the present day, a peace which can only be maintained ultimately by a war into which we shall go shackled and handcuffed . . . Every time you sacrifice one of your potential allies to this pathetic desire to appease the tyrants you merely bring nearer and make inevitable that war which you pretend you are trying to avoid.[87]

The consequences of Chamberlain's policy were for a moment laid bare in the House of Commons, alas in vain. The appeals of the critics of that policy were not heeded: Runciman set about his task, criticized by one prominent Labour spokesman for spending more time in German castles than Czech flats.[88]

Labour's National Executive became aware by mid-August that the Germans were massing armed forces close to the Czech frontier; early in September, the NEC met in joint session with the General Council and the PLP Executive at Blackpool, to draft a joint declaration to place before the annual Congress gathering. The result, 'Labour and the International Situation', declared that 'the British Government must leave no doubt in the mind of the German Government that it will unite with the French and Soviet Governments to resist any attack upon Czechoslovakia'; the Labour movement also asked that Parliament be immediately summoned.[89] With the world standing on the brink of war, the Executives maintained that the weakness so far shown in dealing with the dictators had been an incentive to aggression; unfortunately the British government bore a heavy responsibility. In the present situation, Labour repudiated the right of the British or any other government to bring pressure upon Czechoslovakia to accede to German demands; the party refused also to acquiesce in the destruction of the rule of law by aggression. 'Whatever the risks involved, Great Britain must make its stand against aggression. There is no room for doubts or hesitations.'[90] The annual Trades Union Congress accepted this statement, following George Hicks' lengthy explanation; on 8 September – four days after President Benes had in fact yielded to nearly all the demands of Henlein's Sudeten German Party, responding to the direct pressure of the French and British governments, he told Runciman[91] – Hicks commented that the Czech government had gone to the limit of their powers in accommodating the Sudeten demands. All diplomatic pressures designed to force Czechoslovakia further along this path of accommodation should cease. Neville Chamberlain, perhaps beginning now to see the end of that road, paid no heed to the Labour declaration. Further, he judged that the moment was not an opportune one for calling Parliament together.[92]

Small wonder he felt this way – at this very time Chamberlain had resolved upon an ultimate attempt at personal diplomacy. On 13 September, he signalled his willingness to fly to Germany on the following day to try to find a peaceful solution.[93] No matter what the cause of this key decision – whether his own inclination (he had considered the proposal about two weeks) or the desperate pleas of the French Foreign Minister, Bonnet, that '. . . peace must be preserved at any price as neither France nor Great Britain were ready for war' – Chamberlain had set his dangerous course.[94] On the 15th he flew to Berchtesgaden, in what his biographer regards as '. . . an act of faith, a policy which clearly cannot exist if doubts are always being cast upon it in public . . .'[95] The Labour Party had been among those honest doubters; their questioning of the type and consequences of the political appeasement which Chamberlain now personally implemented reflected well upon their role as an opposition. Nor was a lapse of patriotism inherent in their questioning of Chamberlain's course: no less than he were they impelled by considerations of national interest; and where they were realists, Chamberlain acted only on faith. He might have spared himself much trouble and salvaged his reputation as well had he recalled the doubting words of his late half-brother, Austen:

While something is offered to Germany, it is vital. If you say, We will give it to you, and now your relations will, of course, be on a satisfactory footing, it loses all value from the moment they obtain it, and it is taken by them merely as a stepping-off place for further demands.[96]

On 17 September, the Prime Minister made known the results of his Berchtesgaden meeting with Hitler to a delegation from the National Council of Labour, composed of Citrine, Morrison and Dalton. Their accounts agree that Chamberlain noted Hitler's claim that everything depended on whether the British government would admit the principle of self-determination for the Sudetenland.[97] Chamberlain had replied that he would have to consult his colleagues; no doubt he told them, as he told the Labour leaders, that Hitler otherwise planned to move against Czechoslovakia between the 20th and the 28th of August. In such a situation, the Prime Minister continued, a real difficulty had been posed by the crumbling of French resolution. Against such a carefully constructed case, Dalton, by his own account, warned Chamberlain of the consequences of submission to Hitler's demands:

> It is said that some of *us* take the view that now or never is the time to take a stand against Hitler. Whatever we may feel, I think you have been confronted with this choice, and have chosen never. I hope you have chosen it realising all it means. I don't believe that this will be the last of Hitler's demands.

Citrine pressed the Prime Minister whether he believed that Hitler wanted a peaceful settlement. After a pause, Chamberlain replied: 'If we accept the challenge now it means war. If we delay a decision something might happen. Hitler may die.'[98] The delegation remained justifiably unimpressed; they reiterated Labour's belief that unless Britain stood firmly against the dictators without delay '. . . we might be too late'. Three days later, the full National Council of Labour publicly declared that the reported dismemberment of Czechoslovakia, based upon the threat of German military action, was '. . . a shameful betrayal of a peaceful and democratic people and constitutes a dangerous precedent for the future'.[99]

Such dismemberment was, however, concerted by Czechoslovakia's allies and friends. Autonomy was forgone; even worse, self-determination was denied, since Daladier and Chamberlain agreed that any district containing an absolute German majority should be directly transferred to Germany – without plebiscite. The severe and divisive terms were forwarded to the Czech government on 19 September. Their reluctance was well known, at a time when the Labour movement again condemned this rumoured dismemberment and reaffirmed belief that '. . . enduring peace can be secured only by the re-establishment of the rule of law and the ending of the use of lawless force in international relations'.[100] Such protests proved as much in vain as the anguished Czech outcries; relentless Anglo-French diplomatic pressure was brought to bear upon the unhappy Czech government.[101] In the face of what the British and French representatives in Prague admitted had the '. . . character of an ultimatum in the sense that it represented final advice of our Governments and in their view the last possible moment for acceptance of their advice, if this country [Czechoslovakia] was to be saved',[102] President Benes capitulated to the Anglo-French proposals. Grudging though his acceptance was, Benes' action enabled Chamberlain to satisfy the demands put to him at Berchtesgaden.

The Labour Party had already striven to protect the democratic state of Czechoslovakia from falling into the Nazi maw; their declaration of uncompromising resistance to the rule of force Winston Churchill had greeted as doing honour to the British nation.[103] As Chamberlain prepared to return to Germany to implement the proposals which he and Daladier had forced upon the Czechs, the Labour Executives rebuked his course of action in harsher terms. More than the callous sacrifice of a gallant democratic country was involved, they declared in a statement of 21 September, deprecating the British government's setting aside of 'all considerations of freedom, equality and justice', a path of dishonour which could not secure peace. 'Hitler's ambitions do not stop short at Czechoslovakia. There is no longer a frontier in Europe which is safe . . . With every surrender to violence peace recedes.'[104] The parliamentary leaders, Attlee and Greenwood, had conveyed Labour's abhorrence of the proposals to the Prime Minister before he left the second time for Germany. According to Attlee he had told Chamberlain in the midst of a disagreeable interview, 'You have abandoned these people completely. You have made an absolute surrender. All Eastern Europe will now fall under Hitler's sway. We are full of the most profound disgust. This is one of the biggest disasters in British history.' No wonder then that Chamberlain had no desire to receive a six-man deputation from the three Executives later in the day; that chore fell to Halifax, whom Dalton characterized as sharing Labour's sense of shame but convinced that the government were choosing the lesser evil.[105] One damaging admission extracted by the deputation from the Foreign Minister was that there had been no contact with the Soviet government in two weeks, despite the crisis.

Chamberlain flew to Godesberg on 22 September with Czech assent as well as umbrella in hand, there to be greeted by Hitler's declaration that '. . . he was sorry, since those [Anglo-French] proposals could not be maintained'.[106] 'And with these words he pushed his chair back from the table, crossed his legs, folded his arms and turned to scowl at Mr. Chamberlain,' an observer reported.[107] Was Austen Chamberlain's warning returning to haunt the peace-making efforts of Neville, with Hitler simply asking for more now the first demands had been met and Czechoslovakia badly compromised? In a form, yes, but more likely Hitler supplied the rather odd explanation, when he commented to the Prime Minister at the end of their first meeting at Godesberg: 'He never believed himself that a peaceful solution could be reached, and he admitted that he never thought that the Prime Minister could have achieved what he had.'[108] Possibly since his humiliation in May, Hitler desired the destruction of the Czechoslovak state by force, so that the Sudeten demands served only as a means to that end. Now he was confronted with the cession of the Sudetenland as an end in itself. Possibly again looking to a Czech refusal which he could use to precipitate war, Hitler at Godesberg demanded the immediate occupation of the areas to be ceded to the Reich. Though Hitler's timetable was subsequently delayed, the Munich agreement in effect incorporated even this new demand.[109]

For the moment, however, Chamberlain's plans had been dramatically upset. The Czech government reaffirmed their willingness to abide by the Anglo-French proposals, harsh though they were, but regarded Hitler's latest demands '. . . absolutely and unconditionally unacceptable'. On the following day, 26 September, Chamberlain informed Hitler of the Czech position and hinted at the likelihood of general war if Germany resorted to the use of force; on the other hand, he reminded Hitler that '. . . the only differences between us lay in the method of carrying out an agreed principle'.[110] All parties, the Czechs included, agreed that the Sudetenland was Hitler's, if only he would take it peacefully.[111]

The Labour leaders knew not which way the Chamberlain administration would move; Dalton comments that his own estimate of the prospects for peace or war '. . . swung violently from day to day and hour to hour'. Until he had learned, on the 25th, of the details of Hitler's Godesberg demands, he felt that the Anglo-French pressure would accomplish a dishonourable peace; once he had seen those terms, however, he was certain that the Czechs could not possibly accept them; he also detected a stiffening in public opinion on their behalf. Labour attempted to increase that resolution by means of a letter to the Prime Minister which was subsequently published in the press; at the same time the PLP, with only half a dozen pacifist dissidents, approved the course which their leadership had so far followed in the crisis.[112] The British Labour Party recognized that the breach in European relations was wide; the democracies and Germany stared at each other across the abyss.

At a time when Hitler's willingness to commit the German army to an invasion of Czechoslovakia was questioned by his military leaders, Chamberlain's foreign policy adviser, Sir Horace Wilson, had indicated to the German Chancellor that Britain would feel obliged to support France if she went to the aid of the Czechs.[113] While Hitler had to take into account these developments – and perhaps more important, the mobilization of the British Fleet, which could only evoke memories of 1914 in knowledgeable observers – Chamberlain took to the radio to inform the British people in this hour of peril. At a time for resolution, the Prime Minister instead offered what must be called prevarication. 'How horrible, fantastic, incredible it is that we should be digging trenches and trying on gas-masks here because of a quarrel in a far-away country between people of whom we know nothing,'[114] he commented. Yet his claim to know nothing of the peoples involved was demonstrably false; further, he knew that the question at issue was not the dispute between the Sudeten Germans and the Czechs, but rather the territorial demands of Hitler. After all he had gone to Germany, not Czechoslovakia, in his attempts to settle the matter. Even to grant Chamberlain his argument of lack of information would be to damn inexcusable ignorance on his part; others, the Labour Party prominent among them, had repeatedly proclaimed the facts in the Czech crisis and had stressed its importance – militarily and symbolically – to the causes which Great Britain had long held dear.

Later in the evening of that fateful speech, the Prime Minister heard from Sir Horace Wilson that Hitler evidently wished Chamberlain to persist in his efforts to bring the Czech government to reason.[115] Despite the fact that Hitler had offered no modifications of his Godesberg demands, Chamberlain was emboldened to try yet another approach, which did not involve further reasoning with the reluctant Czechs. He replied to Hitler that same night: 'After reading your letter I feel certain that you can get all essentials without war, and without delay . . . However much you distrust Prague Government's intentions, you cannot doubt the power of British and French Governments to see that promises are carried out fairly and fully and forthwith.'[116] At the same time Chamberlain informed Mussolini of this last appeal and asked support in bringing Germany to the conference table, there to be joined by representatives of Czechoslovakia and France and Italy as well, if Hitler so desired.[117] Thereafter the Prime Minister set about composing the speech which he would deliver in the House of Commons that very day, for the hour had passed midnight.

So it had for the Czech state as well, though when Chamberlain rose to speak the issue of peace or war still hung in the balance. Nearly at the end of his detailed but incomplete remarks[118] he received word through one of the Parliamentary Private Secretaries, Lord Dunglass, that he, along with Daladier and Mussolini, had been invited by Hitler to come to Munich.[119] Apparently deciding immediately to accept the exclusion of Czech representatives from the conference,[120] Chamberlain quickly concluded: 'I need not say what my answer will be. Mr. Speaker, I cannot say any more. I am sure that the House will be ready to release me now, to go and see what I can make of this last effort.'

Attlee's impromptu acceptance of adjournment was to the point; he commented that everyone would welcome this fresh opportunity to prevent war, but Labour's Leader stressed the need for '. . . preserving peace without sacrificing principles'.[121] Whether Attlee would have stretched those principles to cover the Anglo-French proposals which the Czech government had already accepted, we cannot know with certainty, for he failed to consider the matter; although Labour had severely criticized the pressure brought upon Benes, it seems unlikely that in view of the Czech acceptance the Labour Party could subsequently reject the proposals. They did however protest against the Godesberg terms which Chamberlain was now prepared to grant Germany, in essentials if not in timing. Alone in the House of Commons the Communist deputy, Gallacher, stipulated that no peace ought to be based upon 'the cutting up and destruction of a small State'.[122] Though Attlee had spoken up on behalf of principle, a doubt must remain whether a Gladstone – given the National Government's past record – would have acquiesced so readily to their seeking an arrangement with Hitler in which the Czechs were not heard.

How did the Parliamentary Labour Party respond to the Prime Minister's dramatic announcement, amid a scene the likes of which that venerable chamber – within three years, a victim of enemy air action – had seldom witnessed? Descriptions have outpaced reality: later that evening, Harold Nicolson told the nation over the BBC that '. . . the whole House rose as a man to pay a tribute to his [Chamberlain's] achievement'.[123] Yet Nicolson, long a critic of the Prime Minister's policies, had himself remained seated, though hissed at and urged by a Tory, 'Stand up, you brute!' In the general pandemonium, with Members on their feet, cheering and throwing order papers in the air, Eden left the House pale and shaken, and neither Churchill nor Amery took part in the emotion-laden scene.[124]

It is unlikely that the PLP rose to a man to cheer the Prime Minister; reports from the correspondents of *The Times* and *Manchester Guardian* note a greater rising response to Attlee's reply than to Chamberlain's statement,[125] which suggests that a number of Labour MPs took their lead only from Attlee's response. A Labour MP asserted retrospectively at the 1939 Conference that 'when Mr. Chamberlain went to Munich we did not stand and cheer him'.[126] In the excitement of the occasion some Labour MPs may have been carried away, but the party's representatives did not rise collectively to cheer Chamberlain on to Munich and a betrayal of the Czechoslovak nation. Neither did the PLP protest or hinder his trip in any way, though for weeks Labour's leaders had agitated ceaselessly against the course which the single-minded and obstinate Prime Minister had pursued.

No Labour MP welcomed the prospect of war; all desired no less than Chamberlain to avoid that self-destructive course. Yet where appeasement had been a distinct part of Labour's policy, it was the whole of Chamberlain's. By subjecting everything to that one end, the Premier made the success of that policy a plaything in the hands of the dictators. Before his departure, the Labour leaders hastened to inform the British government once again that they objected to any further sacrifices on the part of

Czechoslovakia.[127] Attlee and Greenwood thus made to Halifax
the case which they might better have made in the Commons, if
Chamberlain were to be deterred: they deplored the absence of
any Czech representatives at the forthcoming conference and the
lack of any reference in his remarks to the role which the United
States and Soviet Russia might play. Their dissatisfactions and
misgivings, expressed – alas privately – before Chamberlain left
for Munich, were validated in the next few days.

6

That few documents are '. . . more banal, even more unimportant . . .'[128] than the Munich agreement which capped the
peace-seeking efforts of the British Prime Minister is a supreme
irony. In terms of its ultimate importance, the Munich meeting
was not in fact particularly consequential, but in its immediate
context the terms were hardly banal to those Czech officers who
took their own lives rather than retreat from the elaborate forti-
fications in the Sudetenland. And at that time Chamberlain was
not so interested in the precise terms as he was in the spirit of
conciliation which he expected to flow from Munich; nothing was
more important to his hopes for general appeasement than the
preservation of the spirit of peaceful negotiation. For this reason
he attached considerable significance to the supplementary
Anglo-German declaration, which stated that '. . . the method of
consultation shall be the method adopted to deal with any other
questions that may concern our two countries . . .'[129]
     Yet the real spirit of Munich lay in the terms of the settlement,
which must be viewed in relation to Hitler's Godesberg demands,
which Czechoslovakia had refused to accept and which Britain
and France had declined to recommend. In certain ways that
'ultimatum'[130] was modified, but Hitler was given his military
occupation, on the instalment plan, as it were, rather than in one
move, as he had demanded. In theory the final line of German
occupation was to be determined, not by Hitler, but by an international commission; in the event, Hitler controlled the commission, for the western powers had already sold the pass. For
his part, Hitler offered certain minor concessions, which he soon
overlooked or revoked: the idea of plebiscites in disputed ethnic

I

regions went the way of the once-held concepts of Czech territorial integrity, autonomous status and self-determination – into
the rubbish bin of history. Thus on balance '. . . the divergences
from the original Anglo-French proposals were more striking
than from the Godesberg memorandum'.[131] Eight hundred
thousand Czechs lived on the lands now ceded to the Reich (by
comparison, two hundred thousand Germans remained within
the new Czech boundaries); the nation lost her system of forti-
fications; she suffered crippling industrial losses, coupled with
the disruption of her railway system: such were the 'banal' terms
agreed to by Chamberlain and Daladier at Munich.

The importance of the debate on the Munich pact is illustrated
in the length of parliamentary time set aside – four days, com-
mencing 3 October. In the House of Commons the Prime
Minister had first to deal with the resignation of the First Lord
of the Admiralty, Duff Cooper, who had protested that the
British government had failed to convince Hitler that they were
prepared, in certain circumstances, to fight. Through this failure,
they had broken with the traditional foreign policy of Great
Britain, which dictated that no one country should dominate by
brute force the continent of Europe. Chamberlain reserved comment on that allegation; instead he chose to defend his own
course, commenting that he felt no shame with Munich – only
sympathy for the Czechs.[132]
    Attlee countered strongly for the party he led:

    The events of the last few days constitute one of the gravest diplomatic
    defeats that this country and France have ever sustained. There can be
    no doubt that it is a tremendous victory for Herr Hitler. Without firing
    a shot, by the mere display of military force, he has achieved a dominat-
    ing position in Europe which Germany failed to win after four years of
    war. He has overturned the balance of power . . .[133]

Labour recognized the great exertions of Chamberlain in the
name of peace, but Attlee likened the Prime Minister to a ship's
captain who had disregarded all the rules of navigation and run
his ship into great danger – 'watchers from the shore, naturally
impressed with the captain's frantic efforts to try to save something from shipwreck, cheer him when he comes ashore and
want to give him a testimonial'. What was instead required was

an inquest, for the shipwreck had claimed victims. How had the vessel got so far off course? Attlee answered that question by arguing that the rudder had been badly handled since 1931. The cause of the Czech crisis lay not in the existence of minorities, but in Hitler's decision to take another step forward in his design to dominate Europe. He had been able to accomplish this step because the western powers had failed to deal in time with the political and economic questions arising from the follies of the peace treaties, or with the use of force against those settlements. In contrast, 'we on these benches have, again and again, shown the danger of a policy which failed to restrain aggression, which failed to face the issue, which neither stood firm against aggression, nor tried to deal with causes'.[134]

Attlee's concern went beyond the government's past actions; he faced the problems of the present and future in the light of Munich. He deplored the cold-shouldering of the USSR during the Czech crisis and wondered aloud if that country would be brought into any future negotiations. The British attitude, coupled with France's recent course, left the nation in an un-enviable diplomatic position: 'We are now left isolated. The USSR may well hold aloof in future when it considers that little trust can be placed on the Western democracies, and we shall be left alone with France; all our potential allies are gone; and France, which in my view has the greatest responsibility for this debacle of policy, finds herself in the position of a second-class State.' Though Attlee exaggerated the Soviet Union's altruism, his prophecy was all too accurate: a frightening future faced a faltering and discredited western alliance.

Though his criticism of the Munich pact was both temperate and incisive, Attlee had little to offer by way of a policy. He had singled out resistance to aggression as the missing element in the government's foreign policy, but he did not develop any idea of waging war against Hitler. Instead Attlee concentrated upon the need for a new, all-in peace conference, '. . . to deal with the causes of war that are affecting this world, the wrongs of the Versailles Treaty, the wrongs of minorities, to deal with the question of raw materials, to deal, above all, with the great economic question, the condition-of-the-people question'.[135] Such a demand, however, ignored Attlee's own assertion that these matters had not precipitated the Czech crisis. His hope that Hitler would now rejoin the League of Nations, since he could at last enter on a basis of equality, verged on the ridiculous. The Labour Party's spokesman thus faltered at the very last, in imagining that a peaceful settlement of Europe could be built upon the ruins of Czechoslovakia – that after all had been Chamberlain's purpose in going to Munich! The long-range causes of war were no longer central; the problem of confronting the aggressors was. Attlee failed to assert that the alternative to Munich was war, and war alone.

As the debate developed, scattered criticism of the Prime Minister's action was voiced on the Tory back benches; Labour leaders learned on the first day of the existence of a body of opinion within the Conservative Party which opposed the Munich pact and was anxious for some form of concerted protest with the opposition parties.[136] Possibly Churchill had such a liaison in mind as early as 20 September, when he had praised highly a Labour declaration, only to elicit from Attlee the reply, 'I am glad you think so.' Dalton records straightforwardly:

I heard later that Churchill intended his compliment to be an overture for some form of concerted action, and was vexed that Attlee did not make a warmer response. My own view was that that openly concerted action between our Party and other critics of the Government would be less useful at this stage than outwardly separate action. Alexander was inclined to differ, but I warned him of the danger of upsetting a large number of people in our Party . . .[137]

Even in the face of Anglo-French diplomatic pressures upon the Czechs, a broad-based anti-government coalition remained anathema to the Labour leadership. Two weeks later separate action had proved singularly ineffective, and consequently Dalton was more amenable to back-bench overtures to act together in the vote of censure which Labour intended to move in the course of the Munich debate.

The initiative was taken by Harold Macmillan, who brought Dalton the news that some Cabinet ministers were anxious for an immediate general election, to capitalize on the country's gratitude to Chamberlain. The dissident Tories were disturbed at the possibility that the vote on a motion commending the government's action might be used as the pre-election test of party loyalty, precipitating another coupon election. Macmillan proposed that Dalton and Attlee meet with Churchill and some others to discuss the terms of the Labour motion; Dalton, pleading the press of time, met instead – apparently on his own – with Churchill, Eden, J.P.L.Thomas, Brendan Bracken and some others '. . . anxious to organize the maximum Tory abstention, both on the Government's motion and our amendment . . . [who] therefore hoped that the latter would not be too patently a vote of censure'.[138] Several possible drafts, centring about collective security, were discussed. To one that referred to 'national unity and strength', Dalton retorted, 'That is not our jargon.' Churchill tellingly replied that it was jargon they might all have to learn.

Labour's amendment expressed relief that war had been avoided for the time being; the party, however, disapproved of the sacrifice of Czechoslovakia to the threat of armed force and of the great danger to which the Munich arrangements exposed Great Britain. Labour demanded that the government support collective security through the League and also through the summoning of a world conference to consider the removal of economic and political threats to the peace. Arthur Greenwood added to these points a deprecation of Chamberlain's acceptance of Hitler's word and sincerity.[139]

That speech however pales by comparison to Churchill's great philippic, delivered that same day. Churchill described the course of the negotiations at Berchtesgaden, Godesberg and Munich in a strikingly simple metaphor: 'One pound [£1] was demanded at the pistol's point. When it was given, two pounds were demanded at the pistol's point. Finally, the Dictator consented to take £1 17s. 6d. and the rest in promises of good will for the future.' He announced his agreement with Attlee that Britain had sustained a total and unmitigated defeat, for the western powers had been weighed in the balance and found wanting. His proposals for remedial measures however diverged from Attlee's, as Churchill warned the Commons:

. . . do not suppose that this is the end . . . This is only the first sip, the first foretaste of a bitter cup which will be proffered to us year by year unless, by a supreme recovery of moral health and martial valour, we arise again and take our stand for freedom as in the olden time.

Though their accents were different – and Churchill's closer to the stresses of reality – the dissident Tories and the Labour Opposition clearly shared important goals. Yet Churchill, in his account of the events following directly upon Munich, does not mention the hearing which Labour gave the appeal of the Tory dissidents; on the contrary, his only reference to their role in this historic debate is that both oppositions '. . . now so vehement for action, had never missed an opportunity of gaining popularity by resisting and denouncing even the half-measures for defence which the Government had taken'.[140] The Labour Party had abandoned opposition to rearmament, which had been based upon considerations other than popularity, some fifteen months before Munich, and the opposition Liberals years before that. Surely both parties deserved better of Churchill than this ungracious and misleading reference.

When the debate neared its conclusion, Chamberlain announced that there would be no general election, because he did not regard relief and thanksgiving as party matters,[141] a decision which reflects favourably upon his integrity. Directly, the pressure upon the dissident Tories eased, though some were subsequently attacked in their constituencies by the central Conservative organization. Some thirty or forty government MPs carried out their resolve to abstain, both on the Labour censure motion, which was defeated 369–150, and the encomium moved by the government. Among those who abstained were three future Conservative Prime Ministers, Churchill, Eden and Macmillan.

On the day of these votes, Stafford Cripps urged Dalton that Labour should make common cause with the anti-Chamberlain Tories: he expressed a willingness to put aside socialism if they could work out an agreement to preserve Britain's democratic liberties, rebuild collective security and control economic life.[142] Only then did he learn of Dalton's behind-the-scenes consultation with the dissidents three nights earlier; evidently encouraged, Cripps commented that he looked to Dalton, Attlee and Morrison to concert a national agreement with Churchill, probably Amery, perhaps Eden and Sinclair as well. Envisaging a tremendous response, Cripps hoped to persuade the Labour Executive but was prepared to break out if that attempt failed. 'This, he said, was a new and desperate situation. The Labour Party alone could never win. He regarded the old Popular Front idea as dead, but this move had much bigger possibilities. On the last point I agreed with him. To split the Tory Party would be real big politics.' Dalton surely had motives beyond those of 'big politics'; he agreed to attempt such negotiations, after pointing out to Cripps the uncertainty as to which Tories would go along, and the difficulty in carrying along the suspicious trade union leaders. 'How far we should get remained to be seen. But in this grim situation, where everything must be looked at through fresh eyes, I was sure it was worth trying.' At least he did not think that Cripps was 'at it again'.

Dalton accordingly raised the matter once more with Macmillan, who persisted in speaking about a '1931 in reverse'. The young Conservative, however, recognized the difficulties in welding the dissidents together: Eden and some other moderates desired 'national unity' with everybody, while Churchill and Duff Cooper were anxious to overthrow Chamberlain and were inclined to join with anyone to accomplish that. Dalton expressed his preference for Churchill in a scrap, though he foresaw difficulties in the preparation of a programme; Macmillan replied that the Conservatives had better sort out their own problems before meeting Labour. With Cripps in agreement that the Tories could not be rushed, Dalton did not resume conversations with Macmillan until 12 October, when he learned that the dissidents were still divided on the question of tactics. According to Dalton's account, Eden's refusal to throw in his lot with an anti-Chamberlain grouping was crucial.[143] Once again, as in February 1938, Eden's inaction undercut attempts to fell Chamberlain, because few of the dissidents were willing to move faster or farther than he. Dalton concluded that in view of this refusal, the negotiations should be closed, because a major Tory rupture was not in sight. Despite the success of a 'Popular Front' candidate, Vernon Bartlett, at a by-election following Munich – the constituency Labour Party had supported him instead of the candidate proposed by Transport House – the Labour leaders agreed with Dalton that only a major Tory break-away would invalidate their stand against the Popular Front. Retrospectively Attlee asserted that to make a go of such a front in late 1938 'about forty or fifty Tories would have had to take it very seriously'. In his view, the root of the problem lay in the dissidents' failure to vote as well as talk against the government: 'You

255

could never get them to stand. It was the surprise of my life when eventually I did see some of them marching into our lobbies in 1940.'[144] What Labour's leader apparently did not recall in the months after Munich was his own assertion that the imminence of a world crisis – not a Conservative revolt – was the precondition of Labour support for a broad front.

Possibly the very success of Bartlett caused the Labour leadership to think once again about their tacit acquiescence to such Front candidacies:

They saw quite clearly that two or three similar contests would break the power of the [party] machine. The experiment had been too successful and the dead hand of the officials clamped down upon any suggestion that there should be a repetition. War or peace was a minor issue compared with the preservation of Labour Party discipline.[145]

Such an allegation is too sweeping by far, particularly since no evidence is offered to validate the conjecture. Nonetheless the breakdown in parliamentary negotiations may not have been completely the responsibility of the dissidents: Leo Amery criticizes the Labour Party's attitude towards National Service, a position which troubled the PLP considerably in 1939. Amery had talked privately to Attlee on 21 October 1938, but they had got nowhere:

He insisted, without rejecting the principle [National Service] on merits, that nothing would induce them to look at anything of the sort so long as Chamberlain was Prime Minister. They feel they have been tricked again and again (and I had to admit that 1935 was, in fact, if not in intention, a real leading up the garden) and they are convinced Neville truckles to the dictators because he likes their principles . . . Apparently he [Attlee] accepts disaster as inevitable and, whether he would wish to or not, does not feel capable of making his Party take a larger view.[146]

Although the reluctance of the Eden moderates to move openly against the government must be taken as the principal factor in the failure to bring about a parliamentary front, Labour's attitude toward National Service dissuaded men such as Amery from closer co-operation. For their part, the Executive's failure to foster popular pressure in the form of electoral alliances, which could conceivably have forced closer co-operation upon the parliamentarians, also played a role.

No inquiry into the Labour Party's position on the Munich pact would be complete without some estimate of the possible consequences if their point of view had prevailed. Was the party's continuing criticism unrealistic? In the first place, did the party take into account the French abandonment of the Czechs, to whom they were bound by alliance, and, second, did Labour recognize the overwhelming opposition of the Commonwealth countries to a policy which would have involved them in war?[147] To take the second point first, a Labour government in office in 1938, having long proclaimed collective security, would obviously have had to act on the basis of a *de facto* alliance with France and Russia; perhaps the Commonwealth countries – certainly South Africa and Eire – would not have joined in, but Labour had always looked more to an international order than to a Commonwealth founded on imperialism. Thus the problem of the attitude of the Commonwealth seems not insuperable: resolute leadership, grounded upon the principles of respect for law and justice, might well have brought the doubting members along. If not, perhaps the European powers could themselves have settled the German problem in 1938, as they were unable to do after the acquisition of Czechoslovakia gave Hitler a predominance of power on the continent.

To pursue the hypothetical, could a Labour government have persuaded the French government to act as if they possessed a backbone? Or would knowledge of French irresolution have made a Chamberlain of Attlee? The first question is the more difficult; the second can be answered with more certainty, because of the factual evidence that Labour's discovery of irresolution on the part of their French colleagues did not adversely affect their own determination.[148] Possibly the responsibilities of government would have given these leaders cause to pause, but there exists no reason to indicate that they would have altered their position; even a trip to Paris for conversations, on 22 September, did not shake their conviction. Although a British lead would not necessarily have produced a strengthening of the French attitude, it is difficult to imagine that France could have stood out alone, had Britain and Russia taken up arms against German aggression. Whether Russia was prepared to do so remains an open question,[149] though there are those who express greater confidence in the willingness of the Soviet Union to do battle than in His

Majesty's Opposition. Thus John Wheeler-Bennett maintains that the party's failure to interrupt Chamberlain's speech of 28 September in order to protest against the acceptance of the Berchtesgaden terms illustrates its avoidance of the central issue of peace or war, as does Labour's failure to declare in the House of Commons during the Munich debate that the terms ought to have been rejected, even at the cost of war.

The party had in fact faltered in these two instances: yet their pre-Munich declaration had faced the reality that war against Hitler could prove necessary: 'The time has come', that statement had read, 'for a positive and unmistakable lead for collective defence against aggression and to safeguard peace . . . Whatever the risks involved, Great Britain must make its stand against aggression.' Given the responsibility of government, the Labour Party would have faced the issue of peace or war: in view of its past record and its commitments, no Labour government could have refused succour to Czechoslovakia.

What then? What if the course advocated by Labour had in fact been followed? In the morass of controversy over what might have resulted from a strong British lead, two questions are most relevant. Would war have resulted? If so, would the conditions of conducting war in 1938 been more to Britain's advantage than the war which came a year later, but burst over western Europe only in the spring of 1940? In speculating about the first, if Hitler's own resoluteness for war explains the increased demands made of Chamberlain at Godesberg, then Anglo-French obstinacy apparently would have led directly to war. Yet a number of Hitler's influential military advisers were opposed to war at this time: testimony at Nuremberg established the existence of a generals' plot to take Hitler prisoner upon a declaration of war against Czechoslovakia. The plotters pleaded that their plans were upset first by Chamberlain's flight to Godesberg and then irreparably by his agreement to negotiate at Munich. Given the record of such plots in the twelve-year Reich, no one can say with certainty that the generals would have acted had Chamberlain refused to prolong his search for peace.[150] The possibility remains to intrigue the speculative mind.

Nor can we possess full certitude with regard to the second question. Hugh Dalton follows the rough-hewn Churchillian line in claiming that Chamberlain, far from gaining a year for the rearmament of Britain, actually lost that year.[151] Dalton missed a particular irony of the Conservative argument centring about that alleged year of grace: it was not a contemporary view; the original defence offered by Chamberlain and his coterie was that 'peace in our time' had been secured. Only in the ruins of Chamberlain's project was the Munich pact hailed as an astute act of diplomacy by which the Prime Minister had cleverly bought time to complete British defences.[152] Is this retrospective defence of Munich correct?

Divergences of opinion exist whether Britain should have fought in 1938.[153] Churchill's contention was that the year's 'breathing space' left Britain and France in a worse position relative to Germany's than they had been at the time of Munich; only in the admittedly vital sphere of aircraft production did Britain improve her relative position – yet even so there was no possibility of a decisive air battle of Britain until the Germans occupied air bases in the Low Countries and northern France. Such a feat he held beyond the capabilities of the German army in the context of 1938.

On the other hand, Chamberlain's apologists contended that Britain's weakness in air strength virtually dictated Chamberlain's trip to Munich: 'If Chamberlain had fought in 1938 he would have been playing into Hitler's hands . . .'[154] A principal weakness of this case is the failure to take into account the vast increment in Hitler's power thrust into his hands by the Western leaders at Munich.[155] They are perhaps on sounder grounds in asserting that above and beyond the military consequences, the effect of the 'Munich year' upon the will to fight both of country and empire was clearly beneficial. Again, a two-headed coin is being manipulated: the effect of Munich upon Hitler was most dangerous. The most successful German Chancellor since Bismarck could hardly be blamed for thinking that those powers which had abandoned a strong moral and political position with regard to Czechoslovakia would do likewise to Poland. As Munich then lessened the chances of avoiding war, the pact was a poor object-lesson to offer the Fuehrer.

The controversy about the consequences of war in 1938 will continue, for there can be no final answer. Labour's interest in such historical conjecture is basically peripheral, though the party stands to benefit from the acceptance of the Churchillian position, somewhat the stronger of the two. What is important in an assessment of Labour policy is that, given power, Labour would have reaped the consequences of war in 1938: the party could not but have gone to war in defence of Czechoslovak integrity. Though Attlee faltered briefly in forthright opposition to the British government's partisan arbitration of the dispute, in power neither he nor any other Labour leader could have sacrificed the Czech nation in the name of appeasement. The concept of peace at the price of some other nation was, after all, alien to Labour's international policy.

8   The last months of peace

1

Nineteen-thirty-nine witnessed the final restatement of those Labour themes which we have heard throughout the decade. Chamberlain's sweeping diplomatic revolution of March did not affect Labour's conception of foreign policy; rather, through his action the British government accepted those concepts enunciated by the Opposition at the time of Munich. In 1939 Labour continued to offer constructive criticism of the government's re-armament policy, though the party tenaciously resisted the intro-duction of conscription. One can, however, maintain that in this regard Labour's opposition was but a variation on a familiar theme, the deep-rooted distrust in which the party held the policies and personnel of the National Government. That decade-long distrust of the right found its counterpoint in Labour's revulsion from those to its left, in 1939 as earlier. Once again Cripps unfurled the banner of a popular front; this time, however, Labour's Executive expelled him and certain of his colleagues from the party. Though no responsible Labour spokesman could deny that the long-foreseen world crisis was upon Britain, this realization did not jar Labour's antipathy toward a broad anti-government coalition.

As in earlier years, the forum of a party Conference serves to focus the major themes of Labour's foreign and defence policies and its internal conflicts as well. Yet in the last months of peace, following upon that Conference, the shriller themes which had sounded through the decade were muted: the final defeat of the popular front eased internal conflict; defence policy, following Labour's wrong-headed resistance to the introduction of con-scription, became less contentious; most important, the British government embraced, in name at least, the foreign policy advo-cated by the Labour Party. Great Britain at last – at the very last – stood in the name of collective security and the rule of law against fascist aggression.

Though the efforts to forge a group comprising those forces opposed to the appeasement policy of the British government had widened its appeal over the years, that appeal still fell upon the deaf ears of the Labour leadership. To be sure, they had negotiated in good faith with the dissident Conservatives in the aftermath of Munich, but these conversations had led nowhere. Attlee and Dalton – resolute opponents of earlier fronts – remained in contact with Chamberlain's outspoken critics; at the end of 1938, yielding to the pressure of international events, Attlee was in touch with the Tory, Amery; at the same time, Cripps urged the inclusion of the Communist Party as well. The more optimistic foresaw the broadest of anti-government fronts, ranging from Amery and Churchill on the right to Pollitt and Maxton on the left. Yet this coalition was never brought to pass, because the major linkage – close co-operation between the dissident Conservatives and the Labour Opposition – was never closed.

The advocates of such a front, within and without the Labour Party, refused to accept the stalemate. Viewing Vernon Bartlett's by-election victory of November 1938 as proof of the electoral efficacy of the popular front, and alarmed by the deteriorating prospects of the Spanish Republicans, the forces of the left resolved upon another effort to transform the British political scene. Cripps and Bevan believed that 'leadership must come from the Left if there was to be any true national alternative to the Government of Chamberlain'.[1] Both recognized that the renewal of front proposals would not sit well with the National Executive, which had the overwhelming support of Conference decisions for its position. Aware of the hazards of his course, Cripps prepared a carefully balanced assessment of public opinion, striving for the type of objectivity required for a legal brief.[2] With this in hand, he requested, on 9 January 1939, a special meeting of the Labour National Executive.

Cripps prefaced his appeal, which the Executive reluctantly[3] agreed to entertain, with the assurance that he would not seek such a combination with non-socialists in normal times; however

... the present times are not normal. Indeed they are absolutely

262

unprecedented in their seriousness for democratic and working-class institutions of every kind. In such times it is absolutely impossible to overlook the fact that a too rigid adherence to Party discipline and to traditional Party tactics may amount to losing the substance of working-class freedom and democracy for the shadow of maintaining a particular type of organization which is, as a mere machine, in itself of no value.[4]

Cripps took care to document his assertion that only a broadly based front could secure victory at the next general election; buttressing his statistical calculations lay the belief that '. . . one of the greatest assets of such a combination would be its appeal to the unpolitically minded electorate, because the party leaders so joining together had shown themselves ready to drop the aims peculiar to their parties to meet the dangers besetting Britain'.[5] Historically, such an appeal had won a great response, Harold Macmillan had reminded Dalton in speaking of accomplishing a '1931 in reverse'. The Executive showed no interest in reversing anything, whether 1931, the disastrous drift towards war, or the party's policy: they refused to accept Cripps' calculations and to admit that such a coalition as he proposed was practicable or tolerable for the Labour Party. In acting in this fashion, the Executive were responding to historical rationale: the troubled experiences of the minority Labour governments of 1924 and 1929–31 discouraged the idea of coalition; Cripps' repeated dissension undeniably sapped the party's unity; frequent combat with left-led fronts had become an unpleasant fact of life for the party leaders. Apparently the Executive concluded that the situation early in 1939 was not so dramatically different from that of pre-Munich days that they need alter their reliance upon history and precedent. Habit, alas, involved little thought.

Cripps had anticipated their negative response and had provided against this contingency. He stole the pass from the National Executive by circulating immediately a statement of his appeal to Labour MPs, parliamentary candidates and secretaries of affiliated organizations. Only on the day following their decision (reached by the overwhelming majority of 17–3, with D. N. Pritt and Ellen Wilkinson supporting Cripps) did the Executive inform the press that they had rejected the front appeal; since Cripps had seized the initiative, the Executive's 'great resentment' is understandable.[6]

The Executive met again on 18 January to consider Cripps'

latest challenge. Their options were few: either they would have to censure his action in circulating his memorandum or, failing that, permit a renewed diversion of the party's energies to matters which in their belief had been decisively settled at past Conferences. Hugh Dalton, perhaps because he himself had been involved in negotiations along lines proposed by Cripps, strove to avoid an intra-party struggle. Though personally opposed to Cripps' proposal, he suggested that a special National Conference be convoked, to settle the front business once and for all; at the same time, the Executive would seek party approval to expel anyone who, following the ultimate decision, sought to renew the agitation. Cripps, never one to compromise when convinced of the correctness of his position,[7] refused to agree to the notion of a final, irrevocable decision; Dalton concluded that Cripps '. . . showed no interest in the argument that he was harming the Labour Party. He seemed almost to welcome the prospect of expulsion, as a martyr's crown. So we got nowhere.'[8]

On the grounds that Cripps refused to submit to majority rule, Dalton voted for the expulsion of Cripps, on 25 January, along with seventeen of his Executive colleagues; Ellen Wilkinson alone dissented. The Executive stated that they had not invoked the Constitution and Standing Orders of the party, stipulating that each member must 'accept and conform to the Constitution, Programme, Principles, and Policy of the Party', to discourage dissent within the party; rather, in Cripps' case, the Constitution was invoked only because no Executive member should participate in campaigns whose objects conflicted with Conference decisions. His actions '. . . display an indifference to the welfare of the Labour Party and a demand for a degree of liberty incompatible with loyal membership'.[9]

Foreseeing his expulsion, Cripps was quite prepared to pursue his proposal by carrying his campaign to the public. Nonetheless he insisted that any member of the Labour Party had a right to circulate his personal view within the movement. What he considered personal liberty the Executive could regard only as 'an act of political treachery' bound to provoke dissension and discouragement in Labour ranks.[10] In these opposed views we find the kernel of the problem which had divided the party through most of the decade – the concept of loyalty. In January 1939 the Labour Executive resolved that problem, in favour of its belief that loyalty had to be accorded a majority decision, if the Labour Party were to prove an effective political force; Cripps had reiterated the dissident view that ultimate loyalty lay with one's conscience. The divergent points of view had long been held, but the deteriorating international situation had not brought about a reconciliation. On the contrary, that deterioration was taken to confirm the correctness of whatever view was held: '. . . it seemed just as misguided to Cripps that Bevin should stand on Party loyalty in the face of national danger as it seemed misguided to Bevin that Cripps should abandon Party loyalty in the face of the same danger.'[11]

The Executive went to quite questionable lengths in compiling an official party pamphlet summarizing the case against their late colleague.[12] A section devoted to Cripps' more outspoken, contradictory and oft-mistaken comments of the past seven years was irrelevant: perhaps the Executive failed to recall that Cripps supposedly had not been expelled for his political views. Criticism of the Executive's expulsion of Cripps was vocal. R. H. S. Crossman, in the *New Statesman*, commented that the older generation represented on the NEC failed to understand the temper of the younger Labour members, who in the world of 1939 were unwilling to wait for the promised millennium of undiluted socialism. For that reason, many who had disagreed with Cripps in the past now judged his policies correct:

He knows the urgency of the situation and realizes that Labour cannot jog along to victory in the old traditional way. It may be tactically wise – by pre-war reckoning – to leave the responsibility for the mess to Mr. Chamberlain and reserve for Labour the pleasant position of a Socialist opposition for the next five years, but such tactics look to us like suicidal mania in the present international crisis.[13]

The *New Statesman* judged that the driving force of the front appeal lay in the Labour Party's signal failure to lead the country as it might; many in the party shared the uneasy feeling that the party itself did not appear capable of serving as an alternative government.[14] Thus those who sympathized with Cripps thrust aside the constitutional niceties propounded by the Executive. What really mattered was the political situation: the world crisis demanded a drawing-together of all possible sections of anti-Chamberlain opinion to pull down his government before that government pulled down the world.

Cripps' appeal was widely and favourably received: the chairman of the Co-operative Party, George Barnes, and the leader of the Liberal Party, Sir Archibald Sinclair, both endorsed the memorandum. Sharing a platform with Cripps on the very day of his expulsion were such diverse – and committed – personages as Vernon Bartlett, Victor Gollancz, the leaders of the International Brigade, and Ebby Edwards and Will Lawther of the Miners' Federation, along with some others who had not previously engaged in united political activity. Cripps formed an *ad hoc* National Petition Committee, and the swift response convinced his supporters, for a few exultant weeks, that the miracle could be accomplished.[15] Seven MPs – Bevan, George Strauss, S. O. Davies, John Parker, Cecil Poole, Phillips Price and Ben Riley – joined with Labour candidates and other prominent Labour members, such as G. D. H. Cole and Crossman, to protest against Cripps' expulsion. They commented succinctly:

We regard it as in keeping with the failure of the Executive to mobilize effectively the opposition to the National Government which exists in the country among members of all parties and among those who belong to no party. There is a grave danger that this failure, if continued, will reduce the Labour Party to political impotence.[16]

The style of the Cripps appeal may well have alienated some potential support. The *News Chronicle* reported the proceedings at one petition meeting:

Rolling drums, four white spotlights across the darkened hall, and tremendous applause as he [Cripps] ascended to the white, solitary rostrum . . . To the strains of stirring music and with their movements precisely arranged, miners from Harworth led a march of unity, carrying pit-lamps in their hands and wearing black pit-helmets on their heads. With spotlights on them, and carrying banners, they marched round the hall, followed by railway workers, busmen, printers, writers, artists and office workers.[17]

The ascetic barrister does not quite fit into such a Mosley-like scene, nor does the gathering much resemble a British political rally. Why the petitioners embarked on such panoply remains an open question.[18]

Convenient though our distinction between criticism of Cripps' tactics and sympathy with his proposed ends may be, Labour's

Executive could not make any use of it. Given his aims, Cripps could not but alienate the leadership, whatever his tactics. One can understand their root-and-branch condemnation; yet one must regret that mistaken action. The overriding consideration ought to have been the existence of a grave world crisis, which threatened the democratic system of government. Yet in the case of Labour's leadership, the challenge of fascist aggression and Chamberlain's ingratiating acquiescence did not beget the response which circumstances demanded. Those arguments used by the Labour leaders, so empirically demonstrable in ordinary conditions, lost significance in the face of the international situation. The Labour Party may well have had an election to lose as the result of collaboration with other political parties and extremist groups; they had as well a world to save from Nazism.

Others within the party took up Cripps' attempt to win Labour for the popular front, though they were under no illusions that they could long retain their own membership; Aneurin Bevan acknowledged as much in declaring that 'if Sir Stafford Cripps is expelled for wanting to unite the forces of freedom and democracy they can go on expelling others . . . His crime is my crime'.[19] Though Bevan and his colleagues avoided sharing a platform with proscribed Communists, the NEC charged that they were violating the conditions of their party membership, in exceeding the limits of permissible internal controversy: 'No Party can permit such activities and agitations and at the same time gather strength to fight for power.'[20] Controversy by correspondence ensued, but the Executive refused to hear the views of Bevan and Strauss in particular, unless they first withdrew from the front. Late in March Cripps' voluble supporters, protesting at the iniquity of the proceedings, were also expelled from the party. The Executive decided upon this drastic course, which could not be justified by reference to the responsibilities of a member of the Executive, over the objection of seven of its members, after narrowly defeating another attempt to come to terms directly with Cripps.[21] Sir Charles Trevelyan, who was among those expelled, best captured the sentiments of those who shared Cripps' fate:

It is an inexpressible tragedy that at this moment, when the influence of the Executive ought to be used for drawing together by inspiration and reconciliation all possible sections of anti-Chamberlain opinion, it should be spending its time by disintegrating the Labour Party by threats, expulsions and anathemas ... What future can the Party have which professes to be the bulwark of democracy but whose leaders spend their time in finding excuses for destroying freedom of speech and discussions?[22]

The viewpoints of the Labour left and the Executive were irreconcilable.

The resolute action taken by the Executive in expelling those who refused to give assurances of proper conduct – Cripps, Bevan, Strauss, Trevelyan and two parliamentary candidates – broke the back of the front movement. Sir Stafford had been the first to admit that any such agitation would fail unless the Labour Party participated; shortly after his own expulsion, he commented that he was '. . . as convinced as ever that that great organisation must be the core and centre of every anti-Fascist drive . . .'[23] His hope that his allies within the Labour Party could work for unity from within as he would from without was of course dashed by the Executive's action. Though Cripps was granted one final appeal to Conference, the popular front was by that time moribund.

International events ironically contributed to that demise: the front movement had long been linked to the saving of Republican Spain, but by March 1939 there was no longer a Spain to save. According to Cripps, Winston Churchill offered a different explanation later in the year, commenting that 'but for Chamberlain's switch on foreign policy after Prague's occupation by the Germans the Popular Front movement would have swept the country'.[24] Cripps also surmised that Churchill would have backed it. Yet the Executive's relentless opposition had predated these international developments; they had simply had their fill of front agitation and the divisive activities of Cripps. Nor has their decision lacked defenders, who invariably invoke the inclusion of Communists in any such front. Thus Roy Jenkins argues that the passage of time justified the attitude of Labour's leaders, because in 1940–1 the CPGB did its best to hinder the war effort. Since 'dangerous allies had been wisely rejected', the Labour Party was mercifully free from the embarrassment of unnecessary political alliances in the General Election of 1945.[25]

In the light of those events, one can easily disparage the concept of working together with the Communists; in 1939, however, the threat to peace came from the fascists, and the Communists were an anti-fascist force. David Marquand has justly commented: 'The intellectuals who joined them, or who worked for close association with them, were duped. But there are times when it is as honourable to be duped as it is to keep one's head.'[26] More than a question of intellectual honour is, however, involved. Certainly the Communist Party might have caused considerable difficulties in any non-Labour front, because of their organization and single-minded devotion; whether the CPGB could have posed such problems for a Labour-led popular front is a matter of speculation. It is difficult to imagine the Communists, who were few in number, playing an important role in a front including the Labour Party, the Liberal Party and Churchill and his cohorts; the CPGB could well have been relegated to a minor role, in which they could neither divert nor disgrace the movement.

Labour's National Executive evidently felt otherwise. This implicit lack of confidence in their own ability to direct such a front against fascism is the measure of their failure to confront that threat early in 1939.

2

Since Chamberlain had removed what he regarded as the Czechoslovak canker-sore from the European body politic in the fall of 1938, he moved quickly to complete the pacification of the continent. On 2 November 1938, he asked the House of Commons to signify assent to bringing into force the Anglo-Italian Agreement of 16 April, whose terms the Commons had already approved. Now in the restrained euphoria of his post-Munich mood, the Prime Minister judged the time ripe for its implementation. Mussolini, he informed the Commons, had saved the peace at Munich; further, Italian troop withdrawals meant that the Spanish imbroglio was no longer a menace to Europe. His major concern – to win the friendship of Mussolini – went unmentioned, though few could have failed to recognize the ulterior motive.[27] Within his general project of appeasement, the Anglo-Italian Agreement was of course a logical and comprehensible step.

Yet its implementation was a step which had to be taken in the face of a continued Italian stake in the insurgent cause in Spain. For all that Chamberlain might make of Italian troop withdrawals, in fact the Italian Foreign Minister, Ciano, had on 27 October informed the British Ambassador that for Mussolini to effect more than the symbolic withdrawal of 10,000 troops would look '. . . as if Italy was deserting General Franco and such an attitude after Italian losses and Italian expenditure in Spain would be more than difficult to justify'.[28] In his quest for better relations with Italy, Chamberlain was prepared to overlook such discomfiting reminders of reality.

Not so the Labour Party: though not privy to Ciano's comment, Arthur Greenwood stigmatized Mussolini's gesture as a trick; consequently Chamberlain's policy was one of concessions without return. Philip Noel-Baker added details of Italian military involvement in Spain, Italy's protestations to the contrary. Thus the British government were giving up their sole means of restraining Mussolini, which was the refusal to implement the Anglo-Italian Agreement: 'In effect, he [Chamberlain] is giving him a free hand in Spain, and saying: "Do what you like, I shall not trouble you any more about it".'[29] The PLP, in December, expressed considerable unease concerning Chamberlain's forthcoming trip to Italy; Hugh Dalton pointed out the danger involved in such a trip, namely that lately the Commons had not been taken into the government's confidence until after the event. Nor were British relations with Italy alone the cause of Labour's discomfort; Dalton was concerned with signs of deterioration both in Spain and Czecho-Slovakia, and he saw danger signals raised with regard to Poland as well.[30]

Chamberlain was particularly angered by Dalton's inference that some cause would be betrayed or some principle abandoned during his Italian visit; he regarded this as '. . . not only insulting to us but highly discourteous to our hosts as suggesting that they will invite us to do any such thing'. Confident and combative as ever, the Prime Minister declared that if he were to live over again the past eighteen months he would not alter his policy a jot: even if the policy were ultimately to fail, he regarded it right to attempt that course.[31]

In the continuing pursuit of that goal, Chamberlain and Halifax proceeded on their state visit to Rome. Thereafter, the

Prime Minister expressed satisfaction with the results of that trip. Attlee asserted, however, that the conversations had in fact accomplished nothing and, in view of the Italian performance in Spain, that he could not understand the Prime Minister's strengthened conviction in Mussolini's good faith. Only one explanation was possible:

The Prime Minister's conviction does not rest on facts; it is pure faith. Here one touches the essential vice of ... [his] attitude ... to announce generally to the world that anybody can do anything they like and count us out, is not the way to promote peace.[32]

Chamberlain retorted that he saw no other way to negotiate with Hitler and Mussolini, unless he accepted their word. Labour's warning, on the other hand, he quite discounted.

In short order Chamberlain added Franco's name to those whose word he accepted. Because the material of war had been denied to them under the provisions of the Non-Intervention Agreements, the Republican forces were in a state of advanced decay, though they still held a third of Spain, including Madrid and Valencia. Discouraged and at last stripped of their illusions – with any hope of succour from the western democracies crushed by the realization that the bastion of Czechoslovakia had been surrendered without a shot fired in its defence[33] – the Republican elements finally asked terms of Franco. 'The Nationalists have won,' he retorted on 18 February, 'the Republicans must therefore surrender without conditions.'[34] Upon reconsideration, he announced that tribunals would be set up after the Republican surrender to deal only with criminals, since reprisals were alien to the Nationalist movement.

Chamberlain accepted this declaration, coupled with a telegram from Franco which stated that his own honour as a gentleman, his patriotism, and his generosity were the finest guarantees of a just peace, as proper grounds for British recognition. On 27 February the British and French governments acknowledged Franco's as the *de jure* government of Spain. In this action, Chamberlain reflected the sentiments of many as well as his own design for peace:

... on no conclusions was Conservative opinion more united than on these; that this had been a civil war, that 'non-intervention' with all its falsity [a point however never admitted by the British government] had stopped it becoming European, that recognition is a question not of ideology but of fact, and that Franco was, if we allowed him to be, well disposed.[35]

In obvious anger, Clement Attlee deprecated this recognition of the insurgent forces, an action which constituted '. . . a deliberate affront to the legitimate Government of a friendly power . . . a gross breach of international traditions . . . and a further stage in a policy which is steadily destroying in all democratic countries confidence in the good faith of Great Britain'.

Setting aside for the moment the question of justice, Attlee argued that, in exchange for recognition, the British government should have extracted binding conditions from Franco: settlement of British claims against the Nationalist forces, involving the loss of twenty-five ships and forty-five lives; clemency for the Republicans; withdrawal of all foreign troops from Spain. Instead Chamberlain had nothing to show for his callous action, which the Prime Minister had cloaked in his '. . . usual hypocritical plea that this is all being done to prevent further suffering and loss of life'. Hypocrisy fittingly capped two and a half years of the sham of non-intervention. Yet this recognition of Nationalist Spain represented another step in the government's abandonment of the permanent interests of Britain: 'They do not do anything to build up peace or stop war, but merely announce to the whole world that anyone who is out to use force can always be sure that he will have a friend in the British Prime Minister.'[36]

Chamberlain deprecated this personal attack – the like of which the Commons had not heard in some time – but he chose not to reply to the censure; instead he defended recognition, which constituted only '. . . a formal act which brings the relations between this country and General Franco's Government into relationship with 'reality'. Labour MPs disputed the reality of Franco's victory,[37] but the government's case was, in its own terms, indisputable. For thirty months the British government had not been so much concerned with which side won as with ending the war. The fortunes of war, with a mighty boost from fascist violation of non-intervention, had given the nod to the Nationalist forces, and Chamberlain was prepared to murmur a grateful 'Amen'. The Labour Party had all along quite a different stake in the conflict,

and its members refused to adjust so quickly to what Chamberlain accepted as reality. With the Government and Opposition as
far apart as ever, the House of Commons virtually ended its many
long disputations over the Spanish Civil War, which itself
terminated on 31 March; no foreign issue since the French
Revolution had so claimed its attention.[38]

Though Labour felt this decisive set-back deeply, their worst
fears never came to pass, for Franco's Spain proved no blind ally
of Nazi Germany. Labour erred in the prediction of dire strategic
consequences of the Nationalist triumph. Yet the party's persistent denunciation of the façade of non-intervention and
advocacy of the Republican cause reflected credit on Labour.
Chamberlain probably regarded the abuse of the Non-Intervention Agreements a small price to pay in order to accomplish
general appeasement. Nearly three decades after his death,
however, Chamberlain's willingness to pay that price means
continued suppression of Spanish freedom; only in the Iberian
peninsula has fascism survived the cataclysm to which it gave
birth, the Second World War.

Chamberlain's ends were no sooner attained in Spain than the
general scheme which they were designed to support collapsed in
ruins. The British government had been informed early in
December that all questions arising out of the Munich agreement
were being decided at Nazi dictation; Ogilvie-Forbes, in Berlin,
also cautioned them that 'it is the general conviction in Germany
to-day that Herr Hitler is now about to embark on the third stage
of his programme, namely, expansion beyond the boundaries of
the territories inhabited by Germans'.[39] By February 1939 critics
of the British government noted the deterioration in the Czech
situation; even more so than the Labour Opposition, Harold
Macmillan and Duff Cooper made the point that all hope
of creating a free, independent, economically self-dependent
Czecho-Slovak state from the ruins of Munich had vanished.[40]
Yet Chamberlain remained confident that he had secured a lasting settlement at Munich; on 19 February he commented that
'all the information I get seems to point in the direction of
peace'.[41] In March he informed Lobby correspondents that Italy
and France were mending their disputes and that he saw much
hope in the forthcoming visit of the President of the Board of

Trade to Berlin; he even mentioned the possibility of the convening of a disarmament conference later in 1939. On the same day, 10 March, Sir Samuel Hoare denounced the 'jitterbugs' who were predicting war. He had the vision of a golden age in which the three dictators – Franco having been admitted to that select circle – and the leaders of France and Britain would accomplish not merely the preservation of peace but standards of living never before possible.[42]

Only Hitler's co-operation was lacking for the attainment of Hoare's ecstatic vision. Whatever the degree of Hitler's military preparation for the absorption of the rest of Czecho-Slovakia,[43] events played into Hitler's hands when the Czecho-Slovak President, Hacha, dismissed the Slovak state government; four days later, a German-inspired declaration of Slovak independence followed. Hacha made one final effort to save his country from the German maw by appealing directly to Hitler; he emerged shaken from the encounter and agreed to a German hegemony for his fallen country.[44] Once again, as in the cases of Austria and the Sudetenland, German troops entered Prague on 15 March under the guise of legality.

Just the previous day, Attlee had raised the question of the British guarantee of Czecho-Slovak territorial integrity, since what he described as 'influence' was being utilized to separate Slovakia from the rest of the state. He accused the British government of awaiting a *fait accompli*. The Prime Minister replied with apparent assurance that 'the proposed guarantee is against unprovoked aggression on Czecho-Slovakia. No such aggression has yet taken place.'[45] This exchange was reported to Berlin without comment – what comment was needed? – by the German Embassy in London,[46] before Hitler threatened Hacha. On 15 March Chamberlain of course had to deal with the *fait accompli* which Attlee had warned against; while German troops for the first time occupied non-German lands, the British government professed indifference. Chamberlain announced that developments had simply outpaced the British guarantee to Czecho-Slovakia:

In our opinion the situation has radically altered since the Slovak Diet declared the independence of Slovakia. The effect of this declaration put an end by internal disruption to the State whose frontiers we had proposed to guarantee ... His Majesty's Government cannot accordingly hold themselves any longer bound by this obligation.[47]

Though he bitterly regretted this development, Chamberlain was not at all inclined to give up his hopes for a peaceful settlement in Europe.

A Labour spokesman, David Grenfell, effectively contrasted the Prime Minister's 'calm mien' to the tragedy which had overtaken the Czech people, who in six months had witnessed the occupation of their country, the violation of their liberties, the liquidation of their sovereignty and the destruction of their independence. Grenfell recalled certain provisions of the Munich Agreement – and the results: 'Guarantees – nothing remains; options – forgotten; plebiscites – completely repudiated ... Czecho-Slovakia is now being occupied, under threat and intimidation, in exactly the same manner as she would have been occupied had there never been a Munich Agreement.' For all the force of his remarks, Grenfell missed one essential point: Czechoslovakia might well have resisted Germany's actions in September 1938, had it not been for the participation of Britain and France in her dismemberment.

Grenfell pointed out that the result of the British government's policy was a steady and violent disintegration of the European system: '. . . appeasement, instead of modifying or retarding that disintegration, only gives an added impetus to it.' Clearly by this point, Chamberlain's practices had given appeasement its new post-Munich meaning. Grenfell expressed concern for the future: Poland, Hungary and Rumania had been placed at a tremendous military disadvantage by the German occupation of Czecho-Slovakia. What, he asked, did the British government propose to do? For his part, the Labour MP hoped for a gesture signifying Britain's willingness to stand by those nations which would defend democracy and freedom; he looked to the United States and the Soviet Union in particular to respond to a rallying of those forces working for good will and peace.

Hugh Dalton subsequently reminded the Government Front Bench of the likely alternative, if Grenfell's recommendation went unheeded: 'Either we are to join with other nations to seek by common action to arrest it [the German advance] or it will flow on and on, first in this direction and then in that, until it

275

has reached almost to the shores of this little island itself, and until we are left to resist it, having allowed the dice to be heavily loaded against us.'[48] At this critical moment, debate in the Commons turned against the National Government: though the fourteen members who savaged Chamberlain's policy all sat on the other side of the House, only three back-benchers, along with Sir John Simon, defended without reservation the Prime Minister's recent conduct of foreign affairs; a distinct group followed Eden's lead in coupling moderate criticism of Chamberlain's past policy with the recommendation that he form an all-party government.[49] Unrepresentative the sampling of parliamentary opinion may be; nonetheless Chamberlain's critics were noticeably more anxious to catch the Speaker's eye than were his supporters.

Yet those critics did not much catch the Prime Minister's attention, nor did the strong criticisms of the German occupation voiced by *The Times*, the *Daily Express* and the *Daily Telegraph* on 16 March; that afternoon Chamberlain admitted that no British protest had been lodged in Berlin, nor could he assure Parliament that such a missive would be sent. Shortly after these unfortunate remarks, Halifax, the Foreign Secretary, informed Chamberlain that he faced revolt within the Conservative Party, in the House of Commons and the country too, unless he committed Britain against further German aggression, without equivocation.[50] Finally admitting that 'it was impossible to deal with Hitler after he had thrown all his own assurances to the winds', the Prime Minister changed the draft of a speech scheduled for delivery in Birmingham the following day; only at this point did he formulate the question as to Hitler's intentions which his critics – the Labour Party conspicuous among them – had been asking for months, even years: 'Is this the end of an old adventure, or the beginning of a new? . . . is this, in fact, a step in the direction of an attempt to dominate the world by force?' There followed in the wake of this questioning what Chamberlain described as 'bold and startling' proposals, involving diplomatic guarantees to small nations. In its first form this venture entailed declarations by Britain, France, Russia and Poland that they would act together in the event of further signs of German aggressive ambitions.[51] He did not call this bold proposal by its proper name, collective security, possibly because the Opposition had so long insisted that only such a policy could save Europe.

Chamberlain was not one to credit the contributions of the Labour Party.

Poland, however, posed a stumbling-block to a general system of guarantees, because its leaders refused any such arrangement with the Soviet Union. Chamberlain sympathized with the Polish distrust of Russian intentions; when confronted later in the month with the rumour that Germany planned to launch an attack, he resolved to guarantee, together with France, Poland's independence. The Prime Minister moved a great distance in a short time, although his public remarks at Birmingham would hardly strike terror into the hearts of the aggressors. Nonetheless from those careful, near-prosaic remarks there eventually emerged the system of guarantees which brought Great Britain to war. He announced the new British commitment on 31 March, expressing the hope for maximum co-operation with Russia which he privately thought unlikely.

When the House of Commons discussed this diplomatic venture, Arthur Greenwood entered Labour's *caveat* that this Anglo-French guarantee was only the nucleus for what must be a broader system of mutual aid. A genuine system would have to include Russia, regardless of ideological objections, because that Communist power could well prove the decisive factor in maintaining peace. Greenwood assured Chamberlain that if even now he would press on in his efforts to rally the nations to a system of mutual aid, Labour would not begrudge him the laurels of success: 'We shall have been proud that the policy for which we have consistently stood has borne fruit in establishing enduring peace in the world . . .'[52] Thus Greenwood seemed to detect the first glimmering of a new dawn for the concept of collective security, which had vanished into a long night in December 1935. Chamberlain, his own policy a diplomatic failure, rather peevishly refused to admit Labour's interim advocacy of the concept to which he now turned.

What Greenwood's measured and sensible advice failed to convey was the intra-party strife concerning Labour's response to the British guarantee. The root of Labour's indecision lay in Chamberlain's reaction to the Russian proposal of 18 March that a six-power conference meet to arrange measures of resistance to German aggression; the British Prime Minister, claiming that some quicker action was required, declined participation and suggested instead a four-power declaration.[53] When that approach had proved abortive, he resolved upon the direct guarantee to Poland.

The Labour leaders were disturbed that Russia had been altogether left out; they were also disquieted by press glosses upon the British guarantee – especially ominous was the *The Times'* leader stressing that Poland's independence rather than her territorial integrity had been guaranteed. Labour's leadership, to a man convinced of the vital importance of attaching Russia to the arrangements, divided on the question of supporting a guarantee to Poland to which Russia was not a partner: some wanted to hold out for Russian inclusion, while others saw the guarantee as a first instalment of collective security, following upon which every effort should be made to broaden its base. Dalton held the latter view, regarding the consequences of the former with some horror: 'To have spoken or voted against the guarantee would have delighted the Germans, dismayed the Poles and French, and appeared in Britain as yet one more example of Labour's irresponsibility in foreign affairs and defence.'[54] This point of view prevailed within the PLP.

Whatever Chamberlain's motives in opting for the Polish guarantee on a bilateral basis – recent commentaries suggest that his 'diplomatic revolution' reflected more a change of technique than of principle[55] – on the surface he brought government policy into closer accord with Labour's recommendations. Labour's foreign policy in the first months of 1939 remained consistent with that enunciated earlier in the decade. The Spanish cause was lost, though Labour advocated the Republican cause to the depressing end; Czechoslovakia too had fallen to fascism, but Labour took consolation in what they hoped would prove the rebirth of a system of collective security. Anglo-Russian relations became the touchstone of their concept of foreign policy.

3

In the sphere of foreign policy, Labour had consistently acted in a responsible fashion, as the party's endorsement of the bilateral guarantee to Poland showed. In defence policy, which had troubled the party throughout the decade, Labour's record in 1939 betrays a lapse of this sense of responsibility. Conscription was steadfastly opposed from the Labour benches: the party's rejection – if inappropriate to the menacing course of events – was deeply rooted in Labour's history. Yet in other respects, Labour's defence posture was sound: the PLP's lengthy campaign for a Ministry of Supply bore mutant fruit in June 1939. When the British government belatedly took this step, their spokesman credited Winston Churchill with prophetic advice dating to 1936, although he maintained that only developments in the past three months (especially the decision to double the size of the Territorial Army) had transformed the problem of supply into one best handled by a separate ministry. Though Labour welcomed the principle, Hugh Dalton flawed the bill, because basically it failed '. . . to establish an immediate and unified control of all the supplies necessary for the Defence Services under conditions which will ensure prompt assembly and delivery and stop further profiteering'. He also pointed out – correctly[56] – that Labour had anticipated Churchill's suggestion by two full years; accordingly he thought that the Opposition might have been more generously treated. Labour's objection that an all-service Ministry of Supply was preferable to that of Army supply, in effect proposed by the government, was echoed in other quarters of the Commons, but Chamberlain's ministry persisted in their small but significant step towards the organization of a war machine.

In another crucial segment of national defence, Labour's record was roughly on a par with that of the National Government, with whom the party shared a 'Maginot mentality'. The PLP in fact opposed an increase in the Army Estimates in March 1939, which the government had asked in order to provide for a British Expeditionary Force. Lees-Smith argued that modern warfare had moved in an opposite direction; he cited Liddell Hart's belief that the defence now held an immense advantage over attacking forces. 'If that be so,' and his party assumed it was, 'and that is applied behind lines which are properly fortified in advance, it is possible that it will be found that the Maginot line already is so powerful as to be well nigh impregnable.'[57] Labour's war-time planning envisaged economic warfare and naval control of the sources of raw materials as of paramount importance. Interestingly, Liddell Hart influenced the Labour Party directly, for at this time he was meeting frequently with Dalton and other party members who took a special interest in defence problems; when the successful German offensive of 1940 gave the lie to his theory of defensive predominance, Liddell Hart lost the confidence of the Labour leaders.[58]

Where Labour failed to act responsibly was with regard to conscription, which was no new issue in 1939; in fact the party had throughout the post-war years opposed the principle. Not until 1939 did the National Government see fit to challenge the large body of working-class resistance to the concept. Labour's response, hardly one of the prouder chapters in the party's record – Eden has characterized this as 'the worst mark' in Labour's conduct before the war[59] – is explicable, if not justifiable.

The PLP had warned of their opposition to conscription: in May 1938 they thought the British government had hinted at the existence of plans for conscription. The mere thought of such a plan outraged Aneurin Bevan:

... once you have conscription, the generals and the brass hats will be in charge of the whole of the resources of the country, and we already know how abysmally stupid they will be in circumstances of that kind. It is interesting to note that one of the principal means for defending democracy in this country will be immediate abandonment of democratic rights on the part of the population.[60]

Bevan believed that conscription was not required to provide the military resources needed to carry on a war, but rather to keep the civilian population docile; his conviction that modern warfare did not hinge upon a large conscript army was of course one shared with many members of the party.

In fact Bevan, whose remarks were not normally typical of PLP opinion, was at one with his colleagues in this matter, in which Labour stood united against the principle of conscription. From the right wing came such staunchly moderate voices as that of James Griffiths:

We have now been told that the plans are ready which will destroy the trade union movement and bring in industrial conscription, for that is what they mean in effect . . . [Inskip] said, 'We are appealing for your help now, but our plans are ready and you will be conscripted when the time comes.'[61]

Griffiths documented his fears with reference to the events of the Great War, in which the British government had made promises to the trade unions which had not been kept. Thus the Labour Party made clear its opposition to conscription on ideological, strategic, industrial and historical grounds. Its leadership expressed confidence that in the event of war, the British people would support a voluntary system of enlistment for defence forces; the only conscription required was that of wealth.[62]

In the weeks following Munich, pressures for rearmament and expanded civil defence brought the National Government squarely up against the problem of manpower, industrial as well as military. Appalling lack of any central direction of civil defence led to the appointment late in October of the respected civil servant Sir John Anderson as Lord Privy Seal, with responsibilities for this now vital area.[63] In little more than a month, he introduced proposals for National Voluntary Service, serving two major purposes: to secure sufficient recruits for the essential services, including civil defence, and to compile a register of vital occupations stipulating which workers would remain in their own trades and which could be spared for more vital work.[64] Since these proposals could be viewed as the thin edge of the wedge of conscription, Labour had not signalled its assent when Anderson rose to assure the Commons that '. . . there is no scope for compulsion in peace-time when the manpower available is so much in excess of actual requirements and when the selection that has to be made can best be effected by relying on voluntary efforts'. Despite Anderson's attempt to dispel suspicion, Greenwood voiced Labour's concern for possible industrial dilution and the lack of consultation with the trade unions. Consequently, 'I would say that while the trade unions to-day are sincerely desirous of playing their part and have no wish to burke their responsibilities, they are determined not to allow their members to be "led up the garden path" again . . . "Once bitten, twice shy" is a truism.' He also repudiated outright the idea of military conscription:

Labour does not believe that forced service can inspire a democratic community or deepen its faith. Nor does it believe that conscription

K

can save liberty against external attack. We repudiate the view that compulsory service abroad and the slave state abroad are necessarily to be met by similar methods in this country . . . We do not believe that even partial slavery is the way to freedom.

Labour's leader, Attlee, typically and tersely exposed another facet of his party's suspicions: 'We have no reason to trust the Government.'[65]

Nonetheless the movement agreed to discuss Anderson's proposals, reasoning that if the TUC were to stand aside, it would shirk its industrial responsibilities.[66] Labour subsequently resolved to support a National Service scheme, if it were voluntary in spirit as well as letter, democratically inspired and controlled. Bevan objected'to such co-operation: 'We ought to preserve our rights of independence and keep ourselves detached and aloof, so that we can discharge our proper functions to our own people and not bind them hand and foot and hand them over to their enemies.'[67] Aghast at Labour's agreement, he and ten other MPs voted against the scheme, in defiance of party whips. His biographer explains Bevan's reasoning:

At last, the class Government needed to appeal to the nation. It could not do so, at least with full effect, without Labour's blessing. And yet would-be militant Labour, smarting from all the offences which the Chamberlain régime had committed in foreign affairs, asked nothing in return . . . Nothing could make . . . Bevan angrier than the spectacle of the elected leaders of this mighty force reduced to the status of flunkies or, what was worse, batmen.[68]

Ernest Bevin, no man's flunkey, favoured the proposals, because he believed that the trade unions should do everything they could to make a success of the voluntary scheme, thus avoiding any need for conscription: he agreed to serve on the central committee administering the scheme.[69]

Probably reasoning along similar lines, the National Council of Labour spoke out in favour of National Service: yet they refused to agree until 'important assurances and improvements had been obtained' from the National Government; and further, while stating that suspicion was understandable, 'there is no question that some recruitment effort is immediately necessary, whatever Government is in office, to provide against very real dangers that are a menace to everyone'.[70] Where the Labour left, consistent with its past attitude, remained more troubled with the 'enemy' at home than with the means of defence against the enemy abroad, the leadership agreed to shoulder the very real responsibility of co-operating with a government whose foreign policy remained suspect. Even if Labour's leaders are censured for their failure to hazard a popular front which might overturn a disastrous foreign policy, they ought to be credited with a response to the entreaties of those in power to co-operate in the name of British preparedness.

Despite their differences over voluntary schemes, Labour left and right agreed in opposition to any involuntary projects; George Hicks, an influential trade union leader, warned the government that '. . . if people get the idea that conscription is mixed up with it [National Voluntary Service], then we shall riddle it to the best of our ability and frustrate the evil designs of those who support such a policy'. In March 1939 the National Council of Labour reiterated the party's absolute rejection of conscription, which they held unnecessary alike for armed forces, civil defence and industry.[71]

Meanwhile the British government had suffered the shock of Hitler's entry into Prague; Chamberlain's guarantee to Poland had been followed in short order by similar measures for Greece, Rumania, Denmark, Holland and Switzerland. Although the latter two refused British protection, by mid-April 1939 Britain's military obligations stretched from the Black Sea and the Aegean to the North Sea. In the wake of these commitments revised military arrangements followed: on 29 March the complement of the Territorial Army was doubled. Further, Hore-Belisha promised that in the event of war an Expeditionary Force of nineteen divisions would embark for the continent – in September, four were sent – but the French remained sceptical of the British commitment. The arch-appeaser Bonnet urged that Britain '. . . should adopt in some form, whether direct conscription or otherwise, national service', in order to bolster her military strength.[72] Roosevelt too urged upon the British government conscription, a step which might save the peace.[73] In fact, conscription was fast becoming a test of British resolution.

Chamberlain encountered strong domestic pressures as well: on 29 March a group of thirty-six dissidents centred about

Churchill and Eden put down a motion for the immediate introduction of conscription. The Prime Minister, however, recognized that the controversy which the measure would engender might reveal to Britain's foes a nation divided, or possibly retard aircraft production by industrial unrest.[74] In mid-April Hore-Belisha, risking his political office, again urged conscription upon the Prime Minister; in recording Chamberlain's opposition, the Secretary of State for War noted that '. . . it seemed to me that what really influenced him was the attitude of the Labour Party and the Trade Unions'.[75]

On 26 April Chamberlain announced to the House of Commons the introduction of conscription for men aged 20–21; he recalled the pledge of his predecessor, Baldwin, not to resort to such a step in peacetime but contended (as the Opposition had argued for some months) that April 1939 was not a time to which that term could be meaningfully applied. At the same time, he announced the imposition of a tax upon what might be called war profits, a measure which he imprecisely equated with conscription of wealth. Labour's rage was not eased by this clumsy salve: Attlee's rhetorical reply caught the flavour of the party's reaction.

Is the Prime Minister aware that this decision will break the pledge solemnly given to this country and reaffirmed only four months ago, that compulsory military service would not be introduced in peacetime [a reference to the debate initiated by Sir John Anderson], that it will increase the already widespread distrust of the Prime Minister, that, so far from strengthening the country, it will be sowing divisions in the ranks of this country and will gravely imperil the national effort, and that this departure from the voluntary principle will meet with strenuous opposition?[76]

Chamberlain replied to these questions, first by dismissing the importance of the earlier pledge: 'Nothing could be more stupid, more likely to lead the country into disaster, than that the Government should refuse to change their mind when changed conditions required it.' With the failure of appeasement in mind, MPS may well have rued that this precept had not come to the Prime Minister's mind earlier!

In building the case for conscription, Chamberlain stressed that more than symbolic importance was involved: 'The Government reluctantly came to the conclusion that this measure was necessary . . . for the safety of the country and to ensure the success of the policy which we are pursuing with the approval and, I might say, the active instigation of the party opposite.' Such rare and unusual credit from the Prime Minister, for Labour's advocacy of the collective system, reflected his conciliatory approach to the Labour Party, whom he asked not to persist in '. . . an opposition which I cannot help thinking is based upon views which they have long held, but in very different circumstances from these, and not so much upon the actual proposals that we are putting forward'.[77]

No matter how sincere his appeal, Chamberlain's course of action was open to objections on several counts. Even those government supporters who welcomed the action recognized that the Prime Minister had broken a solemn promise, a fact which he was apparently unable to fathom. The independently minded MP Harold Nicolson recorded in his diary:

. . . if I had been Prime Minister I should have ended my speech by saying that the breach of a pledge was not a thing that any Prime Minister could commit, and that once this thing had gone through, I would retire from public life. I think it is the combination of real religious fanaticism with spiritual trickiness which makes one dislike Chamberlain so much.[78]

Nicolson was too harsh, for any country would have a plethora of retired former premiers if observance of every pledge were required of them. Where Chamberlain can be castigated was in his failure to communicate officially his decision to the Opposition beforehand; Churchill recognized this omission as a needless ineptitude, and one is beggared to offer an explanation – Chamberlain could not hope to catch the Labour Party off guard on such a vital issue as this. Churchill, however, held no sympathy for Labour's assertion that the government ought to hold an election rather than break their pledge. He could see only divisiveness and harm in a campaign fought on the issue of conscription and feared the prospect of a Labour victory in the matter – '. . . if the Opposition won and they established the principle of no compulsory national service . . . the whole resistance of Europe to Nazi domination would collapse'.[79]

Attlee refused to grant Chamberlain a scrap of his arguments:

Labour viewed the introduction of conscription not only as unnecessary – the voluntary approach having succeeded remarkably, under trying conditions – but as harmful to the country. Though Hore-Belisha subsequently met Attlee's request for information concerning the technical reasons for conscription, Labour was not be be swayed; the PLP divided against the introduction of conscription.[80]

In this matter, Labour had been united as on few matters in the entire decade. Ernest Bevin, who had worked unstintingly for rearmament and the voluntary scheme, angrily refused to support military conscription; he saw in Chamberlain's shattered promise a decisive step toward the spectre of industrial conscription, narrowly averted in the First World War. Bevin regarded the argument of military necessity as specious, designed to obscure the government's failure to provide sufficient arms; he also found reiterated the Tory preference for compulsion in any emergency – where he believed in the response of a free man to a just cause.[81] Thus distrust of the National Government's aims and methods played a very decisive role in Labour's response to conscription; Chamberlain's suggestion that Labour's opposition was based upon outmoded tenets ignored the reality of the party's historical distrust of his actions and his Cabinet. Events as distant as 1931 were distinctly relevant in determining Labour's response to Chamberlain's appeal. Though the world situation had altered drastically, the National Government had not; the Labour Party occasionally lost sight of the priority of the first.

Aneurin Bevan, who had constantly given priority to the other, found that position reinforced: the voluntary system had been scrapped in favour of the involuntary, which revealed anew the untrustworthiness of the National Government. To accede to Chamberlain's appeal was unthinkable:

> No Labour leader of that age, even if he had wanted to, could have recommended this course and retained any influence with his followers. It would have involved a repudiation of every argument for the voluntary system which Labour had deployed . . . a bare four months earlier.[82]

Certainly the risk of a rank-and-file rebellion may have frightened a leadership which had been much troubled by the popular front. And yet the test of leadership is to lead, not to follow, and the party's leaders failed to set Labour's priorities right in April

1939. Chamberlain had broken a solemn (and well-remembered) pledge. Can we ask the same sacrifice of consistency on the part of the Opposition?

Colleagues did, and party leaders too have questioned the wisdom of this decision. At the time of their decision, the Labour leaders were probably aware that the French left generally deplored '. . . the inconceivably foolish and unpatriotic attitude of our [British] Opposition'.[83] Retrospectively, Labour leaders have sensed an opportunity missed: Dalton records the technical arguments raised by the party, but he characterizes these as '. . . not nonsense, but not, in present [1939] circumstances, very convincing'.[84] And he saw as well that France, Poland and Russia – not to mention Germany and Italy – had conscription and would not understand why Britain should refuse. Attlee too has conceded that Labour's attitude was 'a mistake', but rather disingenuously he remarked that the issue was of little importance, as in a few months' time Britain was at war and Labour then supported a far more comprehensive measure of compulsory service.[85] His biographer's comment on the speech in which Attlee rejected conscription – '. . . it cannot be said to have been a speech distinguished by its prescience'[86] – can certainly be applied to the attitude of the party which he led.

Some within Labour ranks spoke out at the time in criticism of this decision. R. H. S. Crossman sympathized with the reasoning, though he regarded the decision proper as one which revealed the divorce between Labour's foreign and defence policies. The dichotomy was this: '. . . the only logical consequence of Labour's attitude is appeasement: the only logical consequence of its foreign policy is the demand for the mobilization of the nation's man-power, finance and industry for peace or war.'[87] Such a contradiction, Crossman sensed, had characterized much of Labour's post-war history, for the problems of defence had too seldom been related to a 'highly realistic' foreign policy based upon collective security. The contradiction was of course more complex than Crossman could convey in a few pages, but his insight was precise: Labour's decision to cease opposing rearmament had eased the problem, but rejection of conscription opened it anew, in April 1939.

Albeit briefly. Though the PLP opposed the Military Training Bill from inception to final passage, the party made no subsequent attempt to oppose its operation, as Chamberlain had feared. For all his bitterness, Bevin exerted his influence to oppose any move to withdraw Labour support on general defence matters; nor would he entertain talk of industrial action to resist conscription, because he recognized the gravity of the situation.[88] This acceptance of the implementation of conscription closed the gap between Labour's foreign and defence policies: the National Government would not lack the manpower to carry out the foreign policy which Chamberlain had credited in some measure to Labour. Once again the Labour Party had chosen to confine its deeply felt opposition to the parliamentary framework.[89] By May of 1939, it was well that they had so chosen.

4

The long-awaited annual Conference of the Labour Party, which convened at Southport on 29 May 1939 – some twenty months after the Bournemouth gathering – devoted the major part of its attention to Cripps and the popular front and to the party's foreign and defence policies. No revolutionary verdicts were rendered: Labour's position in the last months of peace stemmed instead from decisions reached earlier on behalf of collective security and rearmament and against a broad-based anti-government coalition. Challenges from the left reproduced only a semblance of past controversies; the Southport Conference was quieter than most. Such quietude – marred only by division concerning Labour's reaction to the introduction of conscription – reflected both the unity and the helplessness which events had forced upon the party.

Stafford Cripps was given one final hearing at Southport, when the delegates agreed (though only by a small majority, which boded ill for the success of his appeal) to suspend the Standing Orders to hear a non-party member. Recognizing that a discussion of the merits of his proposal would abuse the permission given him to speak on the matter of his expulsion, Cripps reduced the constitutional question to his right to circulate his memorandum among the movement. If free discussion were prohibited, he asserted, 'any democratic organization must become static, lifeless, and, eventually, dead'.[90] Cripps' legalistic approach doubtless disappointed his more emotional supporters.

Hugh Dalton, assuming what was regarded as an unpopular assignment, recapitulated a familiar case: Cripps' opinion was not at issue, rather it was his refusal to give the Executive two undertakings, the first reaffirming allegiance to the party and the second withdrawing his memorandum. Were these reasonable? The NEC, Dalton argued, felt that they had no choice but to expel Cripps, because failure to act would have spread disintegration and demoralization throughout the movement.[91]

The debate was perfunctory: minds had long been made up, and most in favour of expulsion – 2·1 of 2·5 million; even the constituency parties voted against Cripps, in the ratio of three to two.[92] An interested observer characterized Conference's mood:

The [Cripps] issue was dead; those who could have stood up to the Executive were outside the hall; many who were friendly to Cripps had been alienated by the Petition campaign; and most of the rank and file were in a state of bored irritation. The difference from Bournemouth or Brighton was staggering.[93]

Such a mood influenced the flaccid debate, later in the week, on the popular front; no one doubted its outcome, including J. T. Murphy, the ex-Communist, ex-Socialist Leaguer mover of a pro-front resolution: 'I know what the vote is going to be, but please listen to a case.'[94] Only 248,000 supported the front; Dalton, finding only 70,000 Constituency Party votes among these, concluded that they must have opposed the proposal in a ratio of six to one, an important facet of an overwhelming defeat.

The popular front was interred with this vote; Cripps presided at the funeral rites in *Tribune*, on 9 June. At that time, he applied for readmission to the party, which some of his backers considered a precipitate surrender. To that criticism Cripps replied that 'if the decision to rejoin is right, then the sooner done the better'. Yet Cripps refused to subscribe to the condition for his readmission, an expression of regret for the campaign, and so remained outside the party for years. With his political passing that of the Labour left went hand-in-hand: Southport marked the end of an epoch in the pre-war politics of the left.[95] As a result, the Labour Party could face the next general election united behind its leaders; the ally-less and uncompromised party

K*

289

in fact won a greater electoral triumph than any had dared hope, but alas six years and a world war intervened.

The Southport Conference also discussed the international situation, which had continued to deteriorate even after Chamberlain's declaration of 17 March. On 7 April – 'and on Good Friday, too' Halifax supposedly protested[96] – Italian troops invaded Albania, expelling King Zog and taking over the country in a day. Though the British government had been warned of this possibility (while Mussolini meanwhile assured them to the contrary) they responded only indirectly, extending guarantees to Greece and Rumania.[97] Chamberlain could find no harsh words for Mussolini's action; rather he defended the agreement which he had reached with the Duce in 1938, though ironically this had stipulated the preservation of the *status quo* around the Mediterranean. At that time Attlee had criticized Chamberlain's good faith in Italy, for the Italian invasion had the same effect upon the Anglo-Italian Agreement as the destruction of Czechoslovakia had upon the Munich pact: in both cases, a policy based upon the idea that one could establish a firm settlement with people who would not keep their word had been utterly discredited. Attlee had urged upon the British government, in consequence, a policy of genuine collective security; if they were not prepared to take that stand, then they ought to give way to those who would.[98]

The Southport Conference reinforced this firm Labour tenet, signalling assent to a resolution which stated that 'imminent danger of war can only be averted by the formation of a strong group of peaceful powers bound together by pacts of mutual aid against aggression'. The delegates agreed with its expression of deep concern at the prolonged delay in working out an unequivocal pact along such lines with France and the Soviet Union and its demand for the closest contact with the United States.[99] Thus Labour had nothing new to offer in the field of foreign policy, save the wish that the National Government would get on with the task of implementing Labour's foreign policy.

The left refused to believe that Chamberlain's government would deliver; Konni Zilliacus warned that the party must be prepared to dissociate itself from 'war preparations' if its precepts in foreign policy were in fact denied.[100] The minority petitioned for the divorce of foreign and defence policies, when the two had only recently again been reconciled!

The Southport Conference also took up the report 'Labour and Defence', a compilation of the various Labour suggestions for the improvement of the effectiveness and efficiency of the armed forces. Only a lone voice from the left protested against the implicit support for the British government and capitalism which he found reflected in that document. Yet when the Executive's decision to continue party co-operation in the voluntary system was reviewed, a storm of criticism was loosed. Herbert Morrison had recognized that some objections would be raised, for the voluntary system incorporated more than Air Raid Protection; nonetheless he held that only an 'artificial distinction' was involved. Further, Labour's most powerful figure in local government reminded Conference that opposition to co-operation between local Labour councils and departments of state ' ... would be interpreted by the country, not unreasonably, as an active and positive hindrance to the reasonable defence of this country in the case of attack from the air by a hostile Power'.[101] He also pointed out the trade union leaders' preference to remain within the framework of the Voluntary Service in order to protect union interests; Morrison concluded that the decision not to play 'tit for tat' with the National Government was a responsible action.

The floor mounted an assault upon the platform, in which the spectre of a pro-fascist government utilizing the voluntary principle to accomplish industrial conscription was invoked. As a result, Labour should cease all support for the system, save in the field of ARP. Not surprisingly, ideology was the keynote of the mover's reasoning: 'We are sick and tired of getting circulars only telling us that we are going to be protected against air raids; it is protection against Chamberlain that we want.'[102] That this attitude was widespread in the left wing is clear in the very similar sentiments of William Mellor, who had told the Brighton Conference in 1935 that Labour's enemy was at home; though much had happened since then, he declared at Southport: 'The enemy we fight is not Germany only, but is here.'[103] One at a time was a wiser course in 1939.

And it was a course which the majority accepted. A delegate spoke of the favourable response of the people to the voluntary scheme: 'Many of these people do really, in their hearts, in their quiet thinking moments, fear Fascist aggression, and they fear the consequences of panic and disorganisation. Where would we be as a great Labour Movement if we were going to let those people down?'[104] Nonetheless the dissidents secured 729,000 votes against continued Labour support; though outvoted five to two, they composed a sizeable minority, particularly in comparison with the smaller numbers of those who supported other left causes in 1939. Certainly their size serves as a reminder that had the Executive accepted conscription, Conference approval was hardly automatic.

Speaking in place of the ailing Attlee, Arthur Greenwood urged the party to great exertions in the impending general election, which was generally expected in the spring of 1940. He refused to hear of any sacrifice of Labour principles for the opportunity of office:

I would never myself, if I were called upon to do so, take office in any Government that was not prepared to implement the 'immediate Programme' of the Labour Party because I know the international situation and our domestic situation demand bold and courageous steps.[105]

Within the year, Greenwood had changed his mind, for he then joined the War Cabinet of Churchill, whom he had stigmatized in 1939 as 'the grim figure . . . who tried to beat us in the General Strike'. His remarks typified Labour's long memory, in 1939 as throughout the decade; and they reveal as well the shorter foresight of the party. In part, this restricted view of the future stemmed from Labour's necessarily ambiguous relationship to Chamberlain's government, which Labour had to trust in matters of defence while uncertain of their foreign policy. Until Chamberlain called the general election, the party could only continue to criticize the National Government's policy where appropriate and bring to bear pressure in order to change disagreeable policies. In this latter regard, however, the party leaders refused to activate a broad-based anti-government coalition, which deprived the party – and the country with it – of a last chance to influence the agonizing question of war or peace. The Labour Party had long been unable to influence the government: in the early 1930s that inability had meant little; in 1939 it meant everything.

Perhaps the recognition of this self-imposed helplessness accounts for the repetitiveness of themes which mark the Southport

Conference. A party unable to influence the actual course of events had to spend much of its time discussing matters over which it had little if any control. Having rejected the only possible means of bringing down the National Government before the next general election, the Labour Party could but wait upon Chamberlain's moves; the question of war or peace was not its to answer.

5

Yet Labour possessed an answer to the question of peace or war, in the salutary effect which the creation of a genuine peace block would have upon international relations; the party considered that Russia's participation was essential. The National Council of Labour emphasized this belief in a manifesto issued shortly after the occupation of Prague; they called upon the National Government '. . . to take the initiative without delay in making a peace pact with France and Russia and all other nations that will join with them for the purpose of defending peace by collective efforts to resist any further act of aggression by Germany'.[106] On 3 April, in the House of Commons, Dalton asked the government to accomplish a Russian alliance or get out. Simon replied that the Opposition underestimated the degree of difficulty of such negotiations; they tended to rivet all attention upon Russia when other powers also were involved. Nonetheless he assured the Commons that the government would strive to conclude an agreement with Russia.[107]

Ten days later, when Chamberlain announced the British guarantees to Greece and Rumania, he did not so much as mention an alliance with Russia; the Labour Party pressed the matter only to receive the reply, couched in Chamberlain's 'famous formula of triple negatives', that if he had not mentioned Russia, it did not mean that the government were not keeping in closest touch with the Soviet representatives.[108] The statement was not untruthful, for on the next day the British government – probably in response to the growing demand in the country for the peace bloc – requested of Russia a unilateral guarantee of its European neighbours. The Soviet government replied on 18 April with the proposal of a pact of mutual assistance among Britain, France and Russia, coupled with a military convention and a guarantee to the

Baltic countries and the other border countries stretching to the Black Sea.[109] Poland and Rumania shortly notified the western powers that they were reluctant (to say the least!) to permit the Red Army into their countries; Estonia and Latvia disclaimed the need for any such military assistance, for they saw no danger of war. Instead these two countries concluded non-aggression pacts with Germany, a step Lithuania had previously taken. Though the Foreign Office had evidence that the '. . . German Government are trying to extort from smaller countries assurance that they do not feel threatened by Germany',[110] neither the British nor the French government brought diplomatic pressure to bear upon those countries reluctant to accept the joint guarantee – in marked contrast to their treatment of Czechoslovakia the previous year. Citing this reluctance, the western powers declined Russia's full partnership in a military alliance; the British government thought the Soviet proposal took '. . . too little account of practical difficulties and would require a very long time for its negotiation . . .' This decision, which came within a week of Hitler's denunciation of the German-Polish Non-Aggression Treaty and of the Anglo-German Naval Treaty, possibly cost Maxim Litvinov his position as Russian Foreign Minister; Halifax noted that Stalin may have been disgruntled by the response of Britain and France and was moving toward a policy of isolation.[111] Whatever Stalin's motives, the advocate of the collective system was replaced by Molotov, who reiterated Russia's proposals of mid-April. A month's negotiations, hesitations and declinations had led nowhere.

Parliament did not much concern itself with these negotiations, for the heated debates concerning the introduction of conscription were then in process. Indeed, foreign affairs received no comprehensive attention until Lloyd George demanded an explanation of where Britain stood, on 19 May. Attlee wished to know more of the diplomatic negotiations: he commented that what was known indicated that the Soviet government sought collective security, the very concept to which the British government was pledged. He was concerned that they would again prove reluctant to act in accordance with the principle of collective security:

They consider all those [foreign] questions in the light of what they regard as British interests, and . . . they have a narrow conception of British interests. They have their points where they are prepared to resist aggression, and the fact that they have those points means that, in other places, they are prepared to condone aggression, and the history of the last few years has shown that this is so.[112]

Chamberlain retorted that his critics failed to see that '. . . the direct participation of the Soviet Union in this matter [multi-lateral guarantees] might not be altogether in accordance with the wishes of some of the countries for whose benefit, or on whose behalf, these arrangements were being made'. By insisting upon the voluntary collaboration of all the border states, the Prime Minister sought to undercut Attlee's criticism; the consequence, however, was that Chamberlain's system would be built at the expense of military alliance with Russia, which alone could make the concept efficacious. Winston Churchill quickly seized this point: 'The Government must realise that none of these States in Eastern Europe can maintain themselves for, say, a year's war, unless they have behind them the massive, solid backing of a friendly Russia, joined to the combination of Western Powers.'[113]

Labour's criticism might better have been centred upon this point, rather than upon continued mistrust of Chamberlain's intentions: the Prime Minister probably by this time had come to recognize the need for a system of mutual aid, but he remained yet to be convinced about the lynch-pin, the Soviet Union. The Executive subsequently moved in this direction in recommending to the Southport Conference a resolution expressing deep concern with the 'prolonged delay' in the conclusion of a definite and unequivocal pact with France and the Soviet Union.[114] Thus the Labour Party and Churchill pursued the same goal in British foreign policy: the man who had given his all to 'strangle Bolshevism in its cradle' and the party which had helped frustrate that aim, now agreed that Russia and Britain must ally to thwart Hitler's purposes.

The fate of that alliance, however, rested with neither, but with a National Government in which '. . . antipathy towards Russia rivalled misjudgment of Nazi Germany', in the view of one of their former colleagues.[115] In Chamberlain's case, this antipathy stemmed from a combination of ideological and practical objections, as he outlined in a letter of 26 March 1939:

I must confess to the most profound distrust of Russia. I have no belief whatever in her ability to maintain an effective offensive, even if she wanted to. And I distrust her motives, which seem to me to have little connection with our ideas of liberty, and to be concerned only with putting everyone else by the ears. Moreover, she is both hated and suspected by many of the smaller States . . .[116]

Though Russia's ideas on the subject of liberty seem a strange criterion on the part of a man who had committed 800,000 Czechs to Hitler's totalitarian régime, Chamberlain's suspicions have proved well grounded. His government was in no enviable position, facing the possibility that under the cloak of the multilateral guarantee Russian troops might simply occupy the border countries, committing aggression on an even larger scale than Hitler's. Yet did not the German menace pose the greater danger to Europe in 1939? If Russia were unable to sustain an offensive, could the Red Army occupy and administer countries from the Baltic to the Black Sea? Halifax apparently thought not, for he had told Poland's Beck on 4 April that '. . . the Red army might be efficient for purposes of defence, but not for purposes of offensive operations'. At that time the British Foreign Secretary gave no indication that he understood the gravity of the German menace, for he also deprecated the fact that '. . . some members of the Labour Party believed that, if Great Britain and the Soviet Union could join hands, the world would be safe for ever more'.[117]

If Chamberlain's suspicions alone determined his actions, he may be credited with considerable foresight if not a proper sense of proportion. There remains the possibility, however, that the Prime Minister had not yet given up all hopes for the success of appeasement and believed that the conclusion of an alliance with Russia would void that project and so bring about war.

What is here of greater importance is the question whether Labour's policy was in fact viable. Might the alliance with Russia which Chamberlain rejected have been successfully negotiated? It is important to pose this question at this early stage, rather than after a consideration of the actual though abortive Moscow negotiations in August, precisely because possibilities were better earlier than later; the Russian inclination towards such an alliance probably weakened in this brief period. Nonetheless, a Labour government might have been handicapped in conducting the negotiations by a mistrust of Russia which the party leaders shared with Conservatives; a historian has suggested that had the two parties' roles been reversed, Labour might have proved no more eager in the approach to Moscow and that such an approach would have met with no more success.[118] Labour's mistrust, however, was not of Russia, but of Moscow's creations, such as the Comintern and the Communist Party of Great Britain. From 1917, the Labour Party had shown friendship for the Russian state and its people and had supplied aid to them when they came under attack.[119] To associate Labour with the National Government's Russophobism does less than justice to the party. What Labour could not have accepted was an extension of Russian power in eastern Europe, for the party opposed aggressive international communism and defended the national rights of other nations.

For this reason, the question of Russian intentions is central, but Russian intentions, in Churchill's classic formulation, were 'a riddle wrapped in a mystery inside an enigma'. No documents reveal Stalin's purposes in offering the tripartite alliance and military convention in April. Since he had commented only a month earlier that Russia did not propose to pull anybody else's chestnuts out of the fire for them, perhaps the subsequent German occupation of Prague caused him to recognize that the non-fascist forces had after all better hang together – if they were not to hang separately. Whatever his intentions, Labour could not easily have ignored a number of the objections which Chamberlain raised to Stalin's proposal: the application of severe pressures upon smaller countries to permit the transit of Russian troops would have demanded a great deal of tact from those who had criticized the National Government for the ungentle arts of persuasion which they had practised on Czechoslovakia. Yet Labour would have more resolutely striven to bring Russia to terms, because their entire foreign policy demanded such an arrangement. In such a vein Dalton commented upon Stalin's offer: 'Here was surely a most dazzling prize to be seized instantly, with both hands, and triumphantly displayed to the world.' Churchill quite agreed, implying that the problem of guarantees to reluctant states should have been avoided:

There can, however, be no doubt, even in the after light, that Britain

297

and France should have accepted the Russian offer, proclaimed the Triple Alliance, and left the method by which it could be made effective in case of war to be adjusted between allies engaged against a common foe ... When events are moving at such speed and in such tremendous mass as at this juncture, it is wise to take one step at a time.[120]

Churchill theorizes that such an alliance might have struck sufficient fear into Hitler to deter him from war. The Labour Party, judged by past policies and present declarations, would have followed that straightforward but hazardous path marked out by Dalton and Churchill from opposite sides of the political divide.

If in fact the key British decision against a genuine system of collective security, involving Russia, was taken in May, the futile negotiations of June, July and August figure only as *dénouement*; yet the pace and sense of purpose of those dealings is important, if Labour's continuing criticism of the actions of the British government is to be assessed. Following the heavy criticism of his policies voiced in the Commons in mid-May, Chamberlain gave way and instructed the British Ambassador in Moscow to agree to a pact of mutual assistance in which Soviet and western guarantees were kept quite separate, though of equal importance. Molotov responded with a modification of the Anglo-French proposal which specified a joint guarantee of certain countries, whether or not they sought such protection.[121] In an attempt to reconcile this difference and to solve the problem of indirect aggression, the Foreign Office sent William Strang, head of its Central Department, to assist the British Ambassador in the negotiations. In announcing Strang's dispatch to the Commons, Chamberlain spoke of the British desire for full reciprocity but warned that difficulties would have to be surmounted.[122]

In view of the frequent travels of British Foreign Secretaries since Hoare's unfortunate visit to Paris in December 1935 and of the Prime Minister's three flights to Germany in September 1938, the question whether the British government made a mistake in negotiating with the Russians at a lower level than they had with the fascists is an apt one.[123] The suggestion that they may well have considered the risk of failure too great to proceed at the Foreign Secretary level[124] can easily be inverted: so great a risk of failure in such a crucial matter demanded negotiations at or near the summit. Another possible explanation is that Halifax would not have been welcomed in Moscow after speaking in the House of Lords on 8 June against the division of Europe into politically hostile groups. Yet when the Foreign Secretary proposed to Germany the idea of a conference for the adjustment of rival claims, including the German claim to *Lebensraum*, what chance could Strang have in Moscow?

Two weeks after Strang's arrival in Moscow in mid-June, the National Council of Labour deputed Citrine, Dalton and Morrison to inquire of Chamberlain and Halifax about the progress of the negotiations. Evidently they were not satisfied, for Dalton sought to 'raise the temperature' in the House of Commons by deploring the fact that the negotiations had dragged on for three months. That there was no great sense of urgency concerning the negotiations may be explained by the prevalent belief among government supporters that Soviet Russia and Nazi Germany were irreconcilable enemies.[125] Strang has since asserted that the British negotiators were not blind to the possibility of such an unholy alliance: 'It was known that the Russians and Germans were in contact, indeed the Russians made no secret of it. What was not known was the extent and timing of the conversations.'[126] What Strang does not record is that the British deputation had the field to themselves until 26 July. Russo-German trade negotiations, under way since May, had been broken off at Hitler's order on 30 June; they were not resumed for nearly four weeks, during which time Strang was not bidding against a German hand.

At nearly the same time when Hitler decided upon resumption, Chamberlain attempted to sidestep the impasse caused by the problem of indirect aggression.[127] On 25 July he agreed to the Russian request for concurrent military staff conversations. Yet the Anglo-French Joint Staff Mission was only slowly assembled, and then not in the form hoped for by the Soviet Union: according to the Russian Ambassador Maisky, the Soviet government asked Arthur Greenwood to convey to the British government their hope that a prominent military figure – Gort for instance – would head the delegation. Greenwood was informed that Gort could not leave at this time; Maisky comments on the appointment instead of Drax: '. . . it would have been difficult to find a candidate more unsuited to conduct negotiations with the USSR than this elderly British Admiral.'[128] The government not un-wisely refused to send such a deputation by train across Germany; yet instead of substituting air transport or cruiser, the French and British chartered a boat capable of only thirteen knots.[129] Not until two weeks after Chamberlain's decision – on 11 August – did the mission arrive in Leningrad. On the following day, they sat down with their Russian counterparts; the British representatives learned that, unlike their colleagues or the Russians, they lacked written credentials![130] Such a situation provides a moment of comic relief in the midst of high tragedy, for the Anglo-French deputation had but a short time for negotiation. Hitler was now suing for Russia's oft-spurned hand.

What was Labour's reaction to the leisurely pace of the negotiations? On 31 July, when Chamberlain announced the dispatch of the military mission, Dalton attacked four and a half months of floundering diplomacy by the British government; he charged that 'those who have been responsible for this gross procrastination have also been responsible for gravely endangering peace in Europe during these weeks and months that have passed'. Reiterating Labour's demand for a 'grand alliance against aggression', he proposed that Halifax should make personal contact with Molotov. Nor did he miss the obvious precedent: 'The Prime Minister used to believe in diplomacy by personal contact ... Has he lost all faith now in the desirability of opposite numbers meeting?' Chamberlain retorted that the government had been labouring to construct the 'Peace Front' since March. Dalton, however, looked to too narrow a segment of that front: '... for him the Peace Front includes one Power and one Power only of any account, and that is Russia. He is interested in Russia, and he is interested in no other country.'[131] Though Dalton challenged this assertion – as he had every right to do – the Prime Minister paid him no heed. The British government, it is clear, were not prepared to admit the paramount importance of Russia.[132] Talk of a 'Peace Front' in the summer of 1939, without such a recognition, was blather. No military mission could succeed where that recognition was lacking.

The Labour Party also protested against the government's desire to adjourn Parliament for the months of August and September; such a practice was conventional, but one may well inquire whether August 1939 was a time for such orthodoxy. Labour did not consider that such a dispersal at a time of such negotiation was in the best interests of the nation. Greenwood frankly explained why: 'A considerable number of Members of this House, not confined to my colleagues on these benches, do not trust this Government.' Continued parliamentary vigilance was required, lest the government throw in their hand on the Russian negotiations.[133] Though even Conservative stalwarts appealed to Chamberlain to change his mind – one argued that a victory over his proposal would be 'a great victory for democracy'[134] – nearly to a man they trooped into the government lobby.

As the House of Commons meekly agreed to disperse, Hitler decided upon a resolute course of action, and on 26 July reopened the Russo-German negotiations; on that evening, Schnurre, in charge of eastern European commercial relations in the Wilhelmstrasse, took the Soviet Chargé and the head of a Soviet trade mission out to dinner. In the course of that fateful meal, he posed to them the questions which were to prove vital in the negotiation of the Non-Aggression Pact:

What could England offer Russia? At best, participation in a European war and the hostility of Germany, but not a single desirable end for Russia. What could we offer, on the other hand? Neutrality and staying out of a possible European conflict, and if Moscow wished, a German-Russian understanding on mutual interests which, just as in former times, would work out to the advantage of both countries.[135]

Schnurre concluded from his conversation that Moscow had not yet decided upon its course; quite rightly he added that 'from our point of view it may be considered a noteworthy success that Moscow, after months of negotiation with England, still remains uncertain as to what she ought to do eventually'. The ensuing negotiations were largely a gloss on Schnurre's questions, which were more in the nature of an inquiry than a proposal. On 29 July the German Ambassador in Moscow, Schulenburg, was instructed to sound out Molotov: if the Soviet Foreign Minister reacted favourably, Schulenburg's instructions continued, 'the idea could be advanced that we will adjust our stand with regard to the Baltic in such a manner as to respect the vital Soviet interests in the Baltic'. On 3 August the German Ambassador notified Berlin that Molotov had been unusually open; yet in his opinion 'the Soviet Government is at present determined to sign with England and France if they fulfil all Soviet wishes'.[136] That condition remained unfulfilled when, four days later, Strang left Moscow; the diplomats had not resolved the problem of indirect aggression.[137]

The military conversations had barely got under way, when on 14 August Ribbentrop moved to outbid Britain and France; he initiated ten days of almost indecent – but effective – pursuit of the loathed Bolshevik régime. Schulenburg was instructed to convey to Molotov the Reich government's opinion that '. . . there is no question between the Baltic and Black Seas which cannot be settled to the complete satisfaction of both countries'.[138] Ribbentrop, claiming that the clarification of Russo-German relations could be achieved only slowly through normal diplomatic channels (he did not add that Hitler's military timetable called for the invasion of Poland in two weeks' time), volunteered to come to Moscow. The German ace had been played, but Stalin and Molotov were dogged in their desire to see the balance of the German hand – the details of a general arrangement of eastern Europe. The German Foreign Minister all but pleaded that the Russians agree to see him by the 18th or 19th; finally the Fuehrer himself appealed to Stalin to receive Ribbentrop by the 23rd.[139] On 21 August came the decisive word from Stalin that the Foreign Minister might proceed to Moscow to sign a Non-Aggression Pact, after the final details were resolved. Hitler's way to Poland – and Europe's path to Armageddon – lay open. While the Anglo-French Military Mission continued tortuous negotiations, German diplomacy secured in a month what the western powers had failed to obtain in five. The different tempi were continued by Ribbentrop's arrival in Moscow within two days, and in the final settlement, accomplished within twenty-four hours.

If the pace of the Russo-German negotiations presents in the abstract a welcome change from that of the Anglo-French-Russian, the terms most certainly do not. The second major diplomatic realignment of 1939 – in consequences, more far reaching than that of March – parcelled out eastern Europe, that very area which Britain and France had lately undertaken to guarantee. At the cost of the Baltic region (striking repayment this, for those countries which had signed pacts with the Reich!) Germany obtained Russian neutrality in the event of war with Poland; Hitler had Stalin's assurance that he would not join with Poland's guarantors in resisting Nazi aggression.

Obviously the Labour Party could not have agreed to such a territorial settlement as that which Stalin won from Hitler. Labour had been too critical of the German absorption of Austria and Czechoslovakia ever to agree to like treatment of other European countries, at the hands of either Nazi Germany or Soviet Russia. The argument of Chamberlain's defenders that no British government could have matched Hitler's offer must be granted.[140] Britain's options were strictly limited; in her Foreign Secretary's view, Russia desired precisely what Britain and France could not provide.

One [factor] was the strong desire to see the recovery by Russia of territories lost after the first war, so that the dictator of Russia's policy would appear to his people as the Peter the Great of the twentieth century. The other compelling thought in the mind of the Kremlin in 1939 must surely have been the imperative necessity of buying time [against German aggression] . . . For these reasons I gravely doubt that anything that we or the French could have said or done would have had the smallest effect in leading Russia to accept a position calculated to invite sharp and early reaction from the German side.[141]

In view of such considerations George Kennan concludes that Stalin '. . . chose, as he had perhaps secretly known all along that he would choose if he had the opportunity, for Hitler'.[142]

Such a pessimistic interpretation of the options open to the British government does not hold the historical field unchallenged, for there are those who regard Stalin's alliance offers to the western powers as genuine. A. J. P. Taylor asserts that, above all, Russia desired to be left alone and that the best method to attain this was through a demonstration of united opposition to Germany.[143] The slow response of Britain and France – Taylor shows convincingly that, if dates mean anything, the western powers spun out negotiations from April to August, while the Russian pace indicated an anxiety to conclude an agreement – had convinced the Russians, by the end of July, that the western hope was to lure them into war with Germany while they remained neutral. He concludes: '. . . we may safely guess that the Soviet government turned to Germany only when this alliance proved impossible.' Bolstering such a contention, we might recall, is Schulenburg's belief, expressed in early August, that Stalin preferred an arrangement with the western powers. Then too it is quite possible that Stalin had not made up his own mind, and that western replies determined him upon the choice of Berlin.[144] If one thing is sure, it is that the vital question of Soviet intentions will divide historians until – if ever – the relevant Soviet documents are published.

Meanwhile, a judgment of the viability of Labour's persistent demands for the Russian alliance depends partly upon the resolution of the latter question. Only partly, though, for by any objective standards Labour's calls for the inclusion of Russia as the keystone of the collective system were justified; no one could reasonably foresee Nazi-Soviet *rapprochement*. To reiterate, no Labour government could have given Stalin the Baltic states in August 1939, thereby preventing the Non-Aggression Pact. Possibly however – depending upon Stalin's intentions – a Labour government might well have forged an alliance in April. Some may object that an agreement with Stalin in April would eventually have entailed the same fate for the Baltic states as that of subservience spelled out in the August pact, because Stalin could use the pretext of 'indirect aggression' to intervene as he saw fit. Again we can only speculate; however, it seems unlikely that Stalin, having committed himself to the tripartite alliance, would have ridden roughshod over his allies' objections. Stalin was able to maximize his gains precisely because he was available to both the western powers and Germany in August; British diplomacy might have limited Stalin's acquisitions either by taking him off the market, so to speak, or by exposing the fraudulent nature of his dealings with Britain and France, in April. To leave the last words to the man who was to forge in the crucible of war that 'Grand Alliance' denied to Europe in the last months of peace, '. . . history might have taken a different course. At least it could not have taken a worse.'[145]

6

When Ribbentrop set out for Moscow, Hitler summoned together his military leaders to inform them of the unusually favourable circumstances which dictated immediate action against Poland; especially important was his belief that the Non-Aggression Pact made slight the possibility of Anglo-French intervention.[146] On the same day, 22 August, when Hitler largely discounted the possibility of western intervention, the British Cabinet gathered to discuss the immediate reconvening of Parliament. The government were anxious to secure approval of an Emergency Powers Bill, because of the deterioration in German-Polish relations. At this time they considered the report that the German and Russian governments were about to conclude a pact of non-aggression; *The Times* reported that 'they [the British government] had no hesitation in deciding that such an event would in no way affect their obligation to Poland, which they had repeatedly stated in public and which they are determined to fulfil'.[147] To emphasize that determination (and doubtless to prepare for the worst) the government began to call up reservists; Chamberlain also dispatched Nevile Henderson, the British Ambassador to Germany, with a personal letter to Hitler. That letter demonstrated a sense of history as well as determination:

It has been alleged that, if His Majesty's Government had made their position more clear in 1914, the great catastrophe would have been avoided. Whether or not there is any force in that allegation, His Majesty's Government are resolved that on this occasion there shall be no such tragic misunderstanding. If the case should arise, they are resolved, and prepared, to employ without delay all the forces at their command, and it is impossible to foresee the end of hostilities once engaged.[148]

A resolute government prepared to meet Parliament.

Nor did the Labour Party waver in the face of Stalin's betrayal of the concept of collective security among peace-loving nations: on 23 August the National Council of Labour reiterated 'the determination of the Labour Movement that there should be no weakening in its declared policy . . .'[149] They stood by Britain's obligations to Poland, despite their shock at the Non-Aggression

Pact. Greenwood had not learned of the possibility of its signature until 22 August, when Chamberlain so informed the Opposition. At that time the Prime Minister asserted that he had had no prior information about a Russo-German agreement: the first word had come only that day, from the British Ambassador in Washington.[150] The *Daily Herald* took the message of the Labour leaders to the British people on 24 August; the caption of its article, 'In This United', indicated the wide measure of agreement between Government and Opposition in response to the Nazi-Soviet pact. Labour of course had not forgotten that the government had committed grave errors of policy in the past, which had contributed substantially to the seriousness of the present international situation:

These errors cannot be minimised or excused. But let no nation make the mistake of thinking that the profound criticism of this Government's past record in national and international affairs which Labour has made and still makes means a division in the ranks of Britain in the event of war. There will be no such division. In their determination to stand by Poland if she is attacked the leaders and the members of all Parties are united.[151]

Asserting that the government had expressed Britain's resolve admirably, the *Daily Herald* hoped that Hitler would take note and draw back from war.

The same sentiments were voiced in the House of Commons upon its reassembly later in the day. Chamberlain noted that the deterioration in German-Polish relations, which had led to the movement of German troops towards the Polish frontier, had dictated further measures of British military preparation. To that end the government had decided upon the reassembly of Parliament when 'a surprise of a very unpleasant character' had been superimposed upon the Polish question. Britain's guarantee held good, but Germany need only show good intentions to establish the confidence and trust which were required for a peaceful solution of the question. Though he had recommended to Germany the observance of her international obligations and the renunciation of the use of force, her government had given no assurances. Since Germany had thereby placed in jeopardy principles to which Great Britain attached great importance, the Prime Minister considered British defensive moves justified.[152]

Greenwood seconded the Prime Minister's resolve and indicated general approval of the Government's policy with regard to Poland, since the April guarantee. As that policy was not a matter of party conflict, no study of the progressive deterioration of German-Polish relations in the summer of 1939 is here necessary.[153] Two back benchers, however, dissented from Labour's acceptance of government policy. Fittingly enough, Lansbury voiced a last appeal for a world conference to find a way out of Europe's mad plunge to war:

Peace can come only when the nations of the world are prepared to do justice by one another. I believe that our people are prepared to make great sacrifices for peace, not mere war for peace, but sacrifices of prestige and possession. I believe that they are willing to do that. But what they want is somewhere in the country a body of men who will give them the lead.[154]

Lansbury had striven all his days – he was now past eighty, and death was only months distant – to give that lead, but the gospel of force had overridden that of love in this troubled decade. No one could begrudge him this last intervention for the cause he served.

The harsh words of Aneurin Bevan were far less welcome; this Labour rebel flew in the face of Chamberlain's appeal for a short debate, in this time of national danger. He recommended new talks with the Soviet Union, charging that the British government had thrown away its proffered assistance. Consequently he told the Conservatives that if they were in earnest to resist aggression, they should get rid of the Prime Minister, to whom the fiery Welshman pointed in scorn: 'He is the man upon whom Hitler relies; he is the man responsible for the situation.' Nor was Bevan impressed by the leaders of the Labour Party: 'No opposition could be kinder. It has prophesied this month for four or five years. It has fought against it at every stage of the journey, and, at the end of it, abstains even from saying to the Prime Minister, "I told you so".'[155] Bevan's history was correct and the leaders might well have indulged in recriminations for past events; instead they looked to the present peril and responsibly chose to emphasize not division, but unity. A prominent Labour Party journalist, Francis Williams, typified this sentiment, writing in the *Daily Herald*:

No man or woman in Britain wishes war. We would with all our power avert it – if it can in honour be yet averted. But if a war comes we shall face it as a united nation – a nation more united on this than at any time in our history, as was shown in the grave session of Parliament yesterday.[156]

Williams' reaction to the Nazi-Soviet pact also differed sharply from Bevan's: already he suspected that secret clauses were attached 'almost certainly'; even if they were not, '. . . there has taken place in Moscow one of the most indefensible and shocking reversals of policy in history. If there is a war of aggression against Poland, heavy indeed will be the burden of Soviet guilt.'

The British diplomatic response, a final signature to the long-negotiated Anglo-Polish Pact of Mutual Assistance, indicated resoluteness where Hitler had hoped for acquiescence to the *fait accompli*. At the same time the Fuehrer learned that his attempt to detach Britain from Poland had failed, Mussolini indicated his unwillingness to march to war in step with Germany. Consequently the scheduled German invasion of Poland was postponed. Hitler fell back upon negotiations designed to attain his solution to the Polish problem; in these dealings with Rome, Paris and London he made use of a confusing variety of agents and approaches.

Parliament met again on the 29th; Chamberlain informed the Commons that the international situation had changed little if at all in five days. Though he acknowledged continuing negotiations with Germany, he stressed that the government would '. . . abate no jot of our resolution to hold fast to the line which we have laid down for ourselves'. Though the ultimate issue of war or peace remained undecided, the British attitude in the Polish matter remained unequivocal, he asserted. Arthur Greenwood added: 'In the most emphatic words I wish to say that, so far as we are concerned, aggression must cease now. Poland will not be allowed to follow to the grave those nations that were martyred by the aggressors.'[157] Both spokesmen left ajar the door to peaceful settlement, though Labour's opening was so slight that Greenwood proposed measures of civilian evacuation before any blows fell. Unreflected in Greenwood's remarks was the current of mistrust of Chamberlain's purposes which had found expression in the PLP caucus which had preceded the session. Dalton sympathized with that feeling but he pointed out to the PLP the greater importance of making evident Labour's continuing resistance to aggression.[158]

The Labour Party also made one last attempt to express British determination to the German people; on 28 August the National Council of Labour issued a statement for publication and broadcast, 'British Labour's Message to the German People'. The practice was not a new one: at the height of the Czech crisis Labour had appealed to the German people to '... raise your voice as we have raised ours against this use of force and violence in the settlement of international disputes ... Refuse to accept responsibility for a world calamity.'[159] This familiar idea of a people's (i.e. workers') strike against war had long since faded from Labour's political arsenal as far as the British role was concerned, though the TUC still had among its Standing Orders enabling powers to lead such a movement. Hitler's emergence and aggression had lessened the likelihood of Labour's opposing British involvement in war; just as surely his consolidation of power within Germany had removed any chance of a strike of the German people against war. Labour's differentiation between the desires of the German people and their rulers and its appeal to the former were in 1938 and 1939 futile gestures.

Only on 31 August, the last day of the inter-war period, did the Labour leaders learn that Chamberlain's negotiations were disturbing the Polish government. The Polish Ambassador informed Greenwood and Dalton of this concern with the trend of British correspondence with Poland, which indicated that Hitler's protestations of good will towards Britain were being taken at face value: '... Raczynski felt that Poland was being manœuvred into a position where, when she refused some German demand, our Government would encourage the British public to say: "Look at those Poles. How unreasonable they are!" '[160] Greenwood quickly informed Halifax of the Polish concern, which, he added, the Labour Party considered justified. While Labour's suspicions mounted, Hitler's SS prepared the staging of a 'frontier incident', which Germany might then cite as justification for the planned invasion. On the following day, as dawn broke, a five-and-a-half-year darkness fell over Europe. Germany's territorial incursion and the bombing of open cities supplied Poland's allies with a clear *casus foederis* for an immediate declaration of war upon the aggressor. The Prime Minister apparently recognized this in his statement of 1 September to the House of Commons:

> The time has come when action rather than speech is required. 18 months ago in this House I prayed that the responsibility might not fall upon me to ask this country to accept the arbitrament of war. I feel that I may not be able to avoid that responsibility.

Yet Chamberlain was eager to try, though he was aware that only one peaceful solution remained – a suspension of German aggression and the withdrawal of her forces from Poland. To provide against the possibility of war, however, British forces were mobilized.

Arthur Greenwood expressed his party's conviction that the die had already been cast; he deprecated the loophole left by Chamberlain, reminding the Commons that Great Britain already stood honour bound to act at once. Reinforcing principle with practicality, he told the Prime Minister that to think Hitler would draw back was to build hopes upon sand. In this crisis, he deputized well for the ailing Attlee, expressing far better than Chamberlain those convictions with which Britain soon entered the war: '. . . however great the sufferings, however poignant the agony and whatever the sacrifice may be, I know in my heart that freedom and mankind's hope for the future cannot be quenched. I know that liberty will prevail.'[161]

That evening the Parliamentary Executive decided a most important matter: they unanimously resolved to refuse Chamberlain's invitation that several Labour leaders enter the government. The National Executive accepted this decision without discussion. Attlee later justified this action on two grounds: Labour felt no confidence in Chamberlain and his immediate associates; also they considered it advisable to have an alternative government available.[162] Chamberlain here reaped the bitter fruits of his poisoned relationship with the Loyal Opposition; Greenwood conveyed to him that decision early on 2 September; simultaneously he expressed shock and outrage at the failure of Britain and France to give any help whatever to the Poles, now in their second day of brave battle. Possibly to convey unequivocally the strength of its feeling, Labour agreed to the government's extension of conscription to those between eighteen and forty-one.

Meanwhile the British Cabinet resolved a course of action.

During the day, a considerable minority group within the Cabinet, including John Anderson and, somewhat surprisingly, John Simon, pressed upon Chamberlain their view that Germany should be presented with an ultimatum expiring that midnight.[163] Chamberlain, though 'anxious to bring things to a head',[164] encountered several complications. In the first place, Mussolini had on 31 August attempted to replay his Munich role by proposing an international conference on the Polish question; though Chamberlain did not ascribe altruistic motives to the Duce, he considered the proposal '. . . a perfectly genuine attempt to stop war . . .' Nonetheless the British government regarded the withdrawal of German troops a necessary precondition for any such conference, once the act of aggression had taken place.[165]

Chamberlain's delay in going to war has been explained in terms of the British and French belief that such a conference might be convened, even after such hope had been in fact dashed.[166] Yet such a desperate cloaking of the truth is not found in the relevant documents; rather, these lend credence to the orthodox explanation of British delay, namely Chamberlain's desire to co-ordinate his policy with the French, who persisted in thinking, late in the afternoon of 2 September, in terms of a forty-eight-hour notice to Germany. Citing the incompleteness of French measures of evacuation, Bonnet informed the British Foreign Office that '. . . it was impossible to give the French Ambassador [in Berlin] instructions for a midnight ultimatum'.[167] He promised however that the French government would decide upon the time limit later that evening.

In consequence, Chamberlain faced the Commons early in the evening of 2 September without having delivered an ultimatum to the German government. He stipulated that there could be no international conference without the withdrawal of German troops and announced that the British and French governments were communicating as to the limit of time within which Germany would have to agree to withdraw. He continued:

If the German Government should agree to withdraw their forces then H.M. Government would be willing to regard the position as being the same as it was before German forces crossed Polish frontiers. That is to say, the way would be open to discussion . . . on the understanding that the settlement arrived at would be one that safeguarded the vital interests of Poland and was secured by an international guarantee.[168]

311

Talk of such a conference, while Poland was actually being over-run, stung a House of Commons which had expected quite a different statement into a rare fury. As 'shocked, restive and resentful' MPs scented another Munich, Greenwood rose to reply for the Opposition. Robert Boothby, despairing of the government, shouted across the floor of the House to Labour's Deputy Leader, 'Speak for England'.[169] Hopes that a partisan retort would not follow were fulfilled: on the eve of Britain's involvement in the Second World War the Labour Party's spokesman did speak for England, responding to this appeal with patriotism and a sense of honour. Whether or not by turning on the government he might have succeeded in bringing them down,[170] Greenwood rather showed that England spoke with one voice on behalf of Poland.

Amid a House of Commons characterized by Chamberlain as '. . . out of hand, torn with suspicions, and ready . . . to believe the government guilty of any cowardice and treachery'[171] Greenwood stressed that he was deeply disturbed with developments: aggression was already thirty-eight hours old and the Anglo-Polish Pact dishonoured, in effect, for that period. Though he did not presume to judge the reasons for the delay, he inquired tellingly '. . . how long we are prepared to vacillate at a time when Britain and all that Britain stands for, and human civilisation, are in peril? To wait upon France would entail both loss of life and betrayal of national interest – and honour.'[172] Those Conservative MPs whom Dalton found 'red-faced and almost speechless with fury' at the Prime Minister's declaration could only welcome Greenwood's solemn warning that Chamberlain had better have something more definite to say on the next day.

A formidable portion of the Cabinet subsequently supplemented the heavy barrage of parliamentary opinion; Chamberlain, anxious, in the words of one of the dissident Ministers, '. . . to retrieve the impression he had made in the House', yielded to the combined entreaties and notified the French that a declaration of war would have to be presented to Parliament on the next day.[173] There was no holding-out until noon of 3 September: an hour earlier the British ultimatum expired and a state of war existed.

Hugh Dalton had kept vigil at the Foreign Office while the British Cabinet had met to determine that timing. As the meeting

312

broke up, Dalton sought out Halifax to warn him of the consequences in the House of Commons if the pledge to Poland were
not kept. The Foreign Secretary assured him: 'I quite understand. It has been very difficult. But it will be all right to-
morrow.'[174] Halifax recalled the details of his meeting 'a
prominent member of the Labour Party' somewhat differently:

As we passed in the passage, he, still in the House of Commons
atmosphere, said to me, 'Foreign Secretary, can you give me any hope?';
to which I replied, 'If you mean hope of war I think I can promise you a
certainty for to-morrow'; to which he in turn replied, 'Thank God'.[175]

One hopes the noble Earl did not mean to deprecate the behaviour
of the other House, for there was forged in the Commons on
2 September the determination and steadfastness of the British
nation which Winston Churchill was both to draw upon and
personify in the following years.

Dalton did not blaspheme in thanking God for the long-delayed
opportunity to right the European balance in 1939; for too long
aggression had gone unpunished. Millions were now to lay down
their lives, and of these surely some were conscious that they were
dying for the restoration of the rule of law among nations. Un-
principled concessions to the dictators could have led to the base
servitude of the European continent had not men like Dalton,
and Churchill, welcomed the chance to overthrow the ignoble
course of British foreign policy. Churchill, as usual, expressed
this sentiment more movingly than anyone else. At last in the
government, he noted his reaction to the declaration of war:

I felt a serenity of mind and was conscious of a kind of uplifted
detachment from human and personal affairs. The glory of old England,
peace-loving and ill-prepared as she was, but instant and fearless at the
call of honour, thrilled my being and seemed to lift our fate to those
spheres far removed from earthly facts and physical sensation.[176]

France, hesitant to the end, followed Britain's lead in a matter of
hours.

The long grinding struggle was joined. The last months of peace
had slipped by. Chamberlain remained in power another seven
months, until he had failed in war as in peace. On 3 September
1939 Labour's foreign and defence policies, too often at odds in
the past, fused into one aim – the winning of the war against

L

fascism. Throughout the 1930s, the Labour Party had moved slowly and haltingly toward the realization that such a war would be necessary, and this process of realization had been the dominant theme of their international policy. Now that theme had come to a grim climax, and war was at hand.

To their credit, the Labour Party had grasped this essential truth before the National Government.

Bibliographical essay

Since full bibliographical information is given in the initial citation of each of the sources used in the preparation of this book, another listing in the bibliography seems superfluous. Instead I would prefer to describe the types of materials available and indicate specifically the utility of sources or accounts in the study of Labour's international policy. Yet to describe the sources for Labour's policy without relating these to the major sources, primary and secondary, for a study of the British government's foreign policy, would be to narrow the context in which Labour's alternatives were offered. As I have attempted to avoid that in the text, I propose to comment upon the sources upon which I have based my account of government policy. Obviously I will not include all materials which I have used or the greater number which I have read, and I hope the reader will indulge me in my comments as well as my selectivity.

With the exception of the private papers of leading members of the Labour Party in the period discussed above, the major sources for Labour policy are printed. The *Labour Party Conference Reports* are invaluable, and not only for the verbatim Conference discussions, where policy made by party leaders had to earn the approbation of the delegates, but also because of the inclusion of several written reports each year submitted to Conference by those bodies to which authority had been delegated. Especially informative is the report of the National Executive Committee, which however seldom states adequately the minority point of view. With the leaders deferring to Conference for but a week in the year, the day-to-day enunciation of Labour's international policy is best studied in the *House of Commons Debates*, Fifth Series, vols 259–351. The turmoil of that debate produced revealing insights into the carefully masked differences among Labour's leaders concerning the nature of their policy, particularly in the years after 1935. Throughout the entire period, Labour was so inadequately represented in the House of Lords, both in terms of numbers – there were less than twenty Labour peers – and of effective leadership, that the debates there are nearly meaningless. As a supplement to the *Conference Reports*, the *Reports of Proceedings* of the Trades Union Congress serve nicely, often foreshadowing the debates of Conference; the forces of the Labour left were generally weaker here than in the party, we might add. The 1938 *Report of Proceedings* assumes special significance, since the party did not meet in Conference that year.

Pamphlets and leaflets issued by the Labour Party, whether ascribed to the party or to specific individuals, reflect official policy; grouped below by year are those which are of concern to the student of foreign or defence policy: 1932: *War and Socialism*. 1933: *The Communist Solar System*, a model for decade-long Executive attacks upon the concept of working with the Communists; *Hitlerism*, with a Foreword by Walter Citrine; *Labour's Foreign Policy*, written by Arthur Henderson, reviewing policies past, present and projected. 1934: *Fascism: The Enemy of the People; For Socialism and Peace*, a basic statement of Labour aims, primarily domestic but international as well; *Nazis, Nazism, Nazidom*. 1935: *The Case Against the 'National' Government*. 1936: *The Demand for Colonial Territories and Equality of Economic Opportunity*, a comprehensive examination of the economic grievances of the Fascist powers. 1937: *International Policy and Defence*, an important up-dating of Labour attitudes; *Labour's Immediate Programme*, establishing an order of priority for projects largely carried over from *For Socialism and Peace*. 1938: *Labour's Claim to Government*; *Labour and the Crisis in Foreign Policy*; *Labour and Defence: The Truth*; *Labour and the Popular Front*. 1939: *Unity: True or Sham?*, the Executive's case against Cripps.

A valuable, but limited, collection of unpublished material relating to official discussions of Labour Party policies is housed in Transport House, Smith Square. Under the aegis of the party's International Department, the Memoranda of the Advisory Committee on International Questions were prepared for general but 'expert' discussion by that body. The Committee, however, was not faced with the political implications of its policy recommendations and so was often more radical than the Executive to whom its reports were forwarded. Since this radicalism could take the form either of realism in foreign policy early in the decade or of ideas of appeasement more comprehensive even than Chamberlain's, these memoranda well depict the intra-party conflict in matters of international policy. Minutes and agenda for the period 1932–9 also are on file, providing a guide to the disputations of the ACIQ. Though the minutes do not reproduce the actual discussion, they normally identify the authors of the various memoranda and note the fate of the document. Such minutes and agenda also exist for the meetings of the National Executive Committee, although they were not made available to me. Now that a Labour government has reduced the fifty-year rule to thirty for state documents, the Labour Party ought to open its archives to scholars on no less favourable terms. Some other unprinted material of value is found in the archives in a collection, 'Documents on European situation since 1935'. William Gillies' 'The European Situation and Labour Policy' (September 1936) and an International Department memorandum on foreign policy and defence of 1937 are of decided significance.

Private papers of the principal Labour figures are not yet generally available. Hugh Dalton's diaries are being prepared for use at the London School of Economics, which also holds the Webb papers. Earl Attlee has stated that his papers for the period are few and unimportant; they are also unavailable. Alan Bullock used Ernest Bevin's private papers in compiling his biography, as did Michael Foot in portraying Aneurin Bevan; neither collection is yet accessible. One may only hope that future years will find these major, and other lesser, collections, passing into public hands.

Contemporary political tracts can prove most useful in any attempt to re-create the mood of the thirties. Clement Attlee's *The Labour Party in Perspective* (London, 1937) provides an official view of the role of the Opposition and the hopes of the shadow government which he led; that such ideas and hopes were not shared by the Labour left is apparent in Sir Stafford Cripps' *The Struggle for Peace* (London, 1936), an important source for views held by a vocal minority within the party. G.D.H.Cole's *The People's Front* (London, 1937) presents the most persuasive case made for a broad left coalition, characterized by a sense of political realities all too often lacking among popular front advocates. Though concerned primarily with domestic matters, John Strachey's *The Coming Struggle for Power* (London, 1933) must be taken into account by the student of foreign affairs because of its continuing influence upon the left. More accurate and moving at the same time than Strachey's analysis is George Orwell's *The Road to Wigan Pier* (London, 1937), which convincingly portrays the desperation which was all too often regarded as the lot of the poor in that troubled decade.

Memoirs and biographies abound for the period, although some are of little value. For the Labour Party, three works in particular stand out. Hugh Dalton's *The Fateful Years: Memoirs, 1931–1945* (London, 1957) is replete with 'inside' material drawn from his extensive and impassioned diaries for the period. Dalton's account sheds much light upon internal divisions and the decision-making mechanism of the party, but it must be used with care, because his assertions sometimes cannot be checked and his passions can degenerate into prejudices, e.g. his treatment of Cripps. His right-wing, pro-rearmament biases must be kept in mind. Alan Bullock's *The Life and Times of Ernest Bevin*, vol. I: *Trade Union Leader, 1881-1940* (London, 1960) offers neither the excitement nor the dangers of Dalton's memoirs. Bullock's assessment of the impact of international developments upon this influential trade union leader is not likely to be bettered. So too does Michael Foot fulfil the biographer's primary task of bringing his subject to life in *Aneurin Bevan*, vol. I: *1897-1945* (London, 1962), an exciting and well-written account; Foot is no less enthused about the causes Bevan espoused than was the fiery Welshman himself. Two other biographies approach the success of Bullock and Foot: Colin Cooke's *The Life of Richard Stafford Cripps* (London, 1957) draws upon Cripps' speeches, letters and *Tribune* articles to justify his actions throughout our period. Cooke's interpretation, which is not completely convincing, is also bedevilled by what was probably Cripps' own basic political weakness – dryness. Raymond Postgate's biography of his father-in-law, *The Life of George Lansbury* (London, 1951), is somewhat uncritical but essential to an understanding of the man and his course of action. Two other biographers were successful in their own times, but the subsequent publication of other studies have by this time lessened their importance. Mary Agnes Hamilton's *Arthur Henderson* (London, 1938), a sympathetic and lucid account, and *Remembering My Good Friends* (London, 1944), treating the personalities and policies of twentieth-century Labour leaders, are both worth the student's attention. Roy Jenkins' *Mr. Attlee: An Interim Biography* (London, 1948) is properly titled, though not without signs of Jenkins' talent for political biography. For our period Jenkins is more informative than Attlee himself, but then, he could hardly not be. Certain lesser figures, in or near the Labour Party, have been well served – generally too much so – in biographical treatments: Victoria de Bunsen, *Charles Roden Buxton: A Memoir* (London, 1948), John McNair, *James Maxton: Beloved Rebel* (London, 1955) and Kingsley Martin, *Harold Laski, 1893-1950: A Biographical Memoir* (London, 1953) may interest the reader of this book.

Labour autobiographies or memoirs yield rather less than the biographies. With the exception of Dalton's account and several which shed light upon the workings of the Labour left, there is little to recommend them. Taken together, Fenner Brockway's *Inside the Left: Thirty Years of Platform, Press, Prison and Parliament* (London, 1943), Jennie Lee's *This Great Journey* (New York–Toronto, 1942), J.T. Murphy's *New Horizons* (London, 1941) and John Paton's *Left Turn!*, vol. II (London, 1936) are an impressive collection of material dealing with the Independent Labour Party, the Socialist League and the Communist Party, and their relations to the Labour Party. Clement Attlee's *As It Happened* (London, 1954) is disappointingly meagre and clearly mistitled; though Francis Williams supplies leading questions to Attlee in his *A Prime Minister Remembers: The War and Post-War Memoirs of the Rt. Hon. Earl Attlee* (London, 1961), in a first chapter on the thirties Attlee does not respond. Matching him in his reticence is Lord Morrison's *Herbert Morrison: An Autobiography* (London, 1960). Though not a memoir in the strict sense, A. L. Rowse's *The End of an Epoch: Reflections on Contemporary History* (London, 1947) serves much the same purpose, by placing Rowse, a right-wing Labour parliamentary candidate throughout much of the period, in his own time. His particular criticism of the party leadership is a useful balance against the grievances voiced by the left wing. Yet another counterweight is Lord Citrine's *Men and Work: The Autobiography of Lord Citrine* (London, 1964) which is useful for the trade union point of view, but not nearly so useful as one might hope, given Citrine's penchant for precise written records.

Any student of the Labour Party will have to acknowledge his debt to the pioneering and sound scholarly efforts of G. D. H. Cole, particularly his *A History of the Labour Party since 1914* (London, 1948), clearly the most valuable secondary account yet available. As a compendium of factual information, Cole's *History* is without peer; at the same time, he retains a good measure of scholarly objectivity in dealing with the Executive's resistance to the various front movements which he actively supported in the 1930s. Ralph Miliband's *Parliamentary Socialism: A Study in the Politics of Labour* (London, 1961) is throughout coloured by a left-wing, activist bias; in his thoroughly researched criticism of Labour's parliamentary-centred course of action since its foundation as a party, Miliband builds a useful dissenting case. Robert E. Dowse's *Left in the Centre: The Independent Labour Party, 1893–1940* (London, 1966) may well stand as the last word on the subject.

For detailed treatment of specific topics covered above, William Rayburn Tucker's *The Attitude of the British Labour Party towards European and Collective Security Problems, 1920–1939* (Geneva, 1950) is of some use for the twenties, though Tucker wrote largely without benefit of memoir, biographical or unpublished materials; not surprisingly, his is a surface approach. Shorter but with such materials in hand is Henry Winkler's 'The Emergence of a Labor Foreign Policy in Great Britain, 1918–1929', *Journal of Modern History*, 27: 247–58 (September 1956); this will remain a valuable article until Professor Winkler supersedes it with his promised book-length study of Labour's foreign policy in the first post-war decade. Catherine Anne Cline's *Recruits to Labour: The British Labour Party, 1914–1931* (Syracuse, 1963) discusses the radicals who broke with the Liberal Party during the First World War and treats their attitudes towards socialism and foreign policy upon

319

joining the Labour Party. Roy Jenkins, *Pursuit of Progress: A critical analysis of the achievement and prospect of the Labour Party* (London, 1953) offers some temperate and incisive judgments on Labour's record in our period. Two unpublished manuscripts housed in the University of London Library are notable for their wealth of detail. The Ph.D. thesis of Samuel Davis, *The British Labour Party and British Foreign Policy, 1933–1939* (1950) is good for newspaper and periodical materials but naturally deficient in any other type of sources. The M.Sc. thesis of James Jupp, *The Left in Britain: 1931–1941* (1956) is an interesting examination of the radical wing of the Labour movement, with greater pretensions to statistical accuracy than are in fact possible.

Among journals, clearly the most valuable for an examination of Labour's policy is *The New Statesman and Nation*. In domestic policy, including the issue of a broad left coalition, the *New Statesman* was generally to the left of what the *Statesman* judged the unnecessarily timid leadership of the party; in foreign policy a wider measure of agreement prevailed. Yet as a responsible journal, the columns of the *New Statesman* were open to all types of Labour, or radical, opinion; the correspondence columns regularly featured intra-party conflict. 'Inside' information is often found in the column 'A London Diary' written by the editor, Kingsley Martin, who sought to entertain as well as enlighten. The editorial column proper, 'Comments', is both critical and well written. A selection from the weekly 'Diaries' is conveniently available in Kingsley Martin, *Critic's London Diary: From the New Statesman, 1931–1956* (London, 1960). Orthodox Labour opinion is reflected in the pages of *The Labour Magazine*, continued on a monthly basis from September 1933 forward as *Labour*. Published jointly by the Trades Union Congress and the Labour Party, *Labour* was at once glossier and less informative than its predecessor; in catering to a mass market, the editors permitted the quality of the published material to drop markedly. The trade union point of view advocated by Citrine and Bevin usually prevailed in the most important feature of *Labour*, a column of editorial comment entitled 'All the World Over'. Pieces critical of government policy were featured in the realm of international policy. *Political Quarterly* also deserves special note: it regularly printed longer articles dealing with topical problems written by such figures as Hugh Dalton, Harold Laski, R. H. S. Crossman, A. L. Rowse and Leonard Woolf; some of these articles achieved a lasting significance.

Among the newspapers, reaction to Labour's policies ranged from the constant support of the *Daily Herald*, then the daily voice of the party, with an editorial policy influenced by Ernest Bevin, and the general sympathies of the *News Chronicle*, to the savage criticisms of the *Morning*

Post, which delighted in exaggerated accounts of Labour's internal dissensions. Slightly to its left was *The Times*, no friend to Labour but more concerned with its pursuit of appeasement than with criticism of the Labour Party. It remains a mine of information about political proceedings in Great Britain. The *Observer* contained incisive political reporting, which was rarely favourable to Labour. Probably the best-balanced editorial commentary upon Labour's policies stemmed from the *Manchester Guardian*. The press-clipping files at Transport House enable the student to consult a wide range of press opinion, collected topically, thus affording him a convenient but not comprehensive survey of the press literature of the period.

In establishing the general context of international relations, within which the Labour Party offered its alternatives, one may now turn to various collections of documents which have been published for the inter-war period. Though the major series are not yet complete, a sufficient number of volumes have been published to indicate clearly the lines of national policy followed in the period. Of primary importance here are several series within the *Documents on British Foreign Policy* (HMSO, London). The Third Series, covering the months from March 1938 to the outbreak of war, is now complete, with an index. The Second Series, intended to survey the years from 1929 to 1938, is as yet incomplete, though eight volumes have appeared. The years 1935–8 still remain a documentary blank, one which ought to be filled with all deliberate speed. The massive burdens of the editorship of this series must be recognized; all scholars stand in great indebtedness to the efforts of E. L. Woodward and Rohan Butler, their successors and collaborators. The *Documents on German Foreign Policy* (Government Printing Office, Washington, D.C.), under the editorial supervision of Allied historians, offer much to the student of British history, particularly by way of comment upon British policies. Series D, dating from 1936 or 1937, depending on the topics involved, through 1941, is now complete in thirteen volumes, and five of the six volumes of Series C, dating from Hitler's accession to power through October 1936, have been published. Only the first several volumes in the projected French series, *Documents diplomatiques français, 1932–1939*, have yet appeared; the collection will be most welcome for the light thrown on Anglo-French relations. Of great use in connection with the Nazi-Soviet Non-Aggression Pact is the collection of documents edited by R. J. Sontag and J. S. Beddie, *Nazi-Soviet Relations, 1939–1941* (Department of State, Washington, D.C., 1948). Of much less interest because of its tendentious editing is *New Documents on the History of Munich* (The Ministry for Foreign Affairs of the Czechoslovak Republic and the

L*

Ministry for Foreign Affairs of the USSR, 1958), though it contains official government documents dealing with the Munich crisis.

Secondary accounts of decided use in dealing with inter-war diplomacy are G. M. Gathorne-Hardy, *A Short History of International Affairs, 1920–1939* (4th edition, London, 1950), very strong in contemporary sources, W. M. Jordan, *Great Britain, France, and the German Problem, 1918–1939* (London, 1943) and Arnold Wolfers, *Britain and France between Two Wars: Conflicting Strategies of Peace since Versailles* (New York, 1940). John Wheeler-Bennett made use of documents collected for use in the Nürnberg Trials to compose his *Munich: Prologue to Tragedy* (London, 1948), the general lines of which have only been confirmed by the subsequent publication of British and other German documents. Alan Bullock's superb biography *Hitler: A Study in Tyranny* (revised edition, London, 1964) is also a dispassionate examination of the course of international events; less successful in this regard but an important biography nonetheless is Sir Ivone Kirkpatrick's *Mussolini: Study of a Demagogue* (London, 1964). Also making use of the published documents is A. J. P. Taylor, whose controversial *The Origins of the Second World War* (New York, 1961), although misleading in several important respects, has much to recommend it. Taylor's treatment of Hitler as a master of diplomatic improvisation succeeds, though his dismissal of the Hossbach memorandum is not convincing. Taylor's account seems, however, mild by comparison to the deliberate distortions of history created by the fertile imagination of Andrew Rothstein, in his *The Munich Conspiracy* (London, 1958); several of his many errors have been cited in the footnotes.

Specific aspects of international relations in the 1930s have been treated by Reginald Bassett, *Democracy and Foreign Policy: A Case History, The Sino-Japanese Dispute, 1931–1933* (London, 1952), whose defence of the actions of the British government is open to strong objections, and Irving S. Friedman, *British Relations with China* (New York, 1940), a useful corrective. The agony of the Spanish Civil War is clear in Hugh Thomas' well-known work *The Spanish Civil War* (New York, 1961), which is republican in tone. Dante A. Puzzo, *Spain and the Great Powers* (New York, 1962) is useful in connection with the practice of non-intervention. Though I have not had the opportunity to examine it. George W. Baer's *The Coming of the Italian-Ethiopian War* (Cambridge, Mass., 1967) should meet the need for a comprehensive diplomatic history of that conflict. For events leading to the *Anschluss*, both Jürgen Gehl, *Austria, Germany and the Anschluss* (London, 1963) and Gordon Brook-Shepherd, *Anschluss: The Rape of Austria* (London, 1963) may profitably be consulted. Appeasement is dealt with severely in Lewis Namier's *Diplomatic Prelude, 1938–1939* (London, 1948) and in Martin Gilbert and Richard Gott, *The Appeasers* (London, 1963). A more formal diplomatic history of that practice can be found in Arthur H. Furnia, *The Diplomacy of Appeasement: Anglo-French Relations and the Prelude to World War II, 1931–1938* (Washington, D.C., 1960), which for all its documentation is a dull and disappointing work. Some of the conditions which produced sympathies for appeasement are clarified in R. B. McCallum's *Public Opinion and the Last Peace* (London, 1944). They too figure prominently in John F. Kennedy's *Why England Slept* (New York, 1940), a book which has merits beyond the author's subsequent fame; he is, however, mistaken in some respects.

On the domestic scene, a secondary account of considerable importance is Reginald Bassett's *Nineteen Thirty-One: Political Crisis* (London, 1958), which is comprehensive and in most matters convincing. Whether his rehabilitation of Ramsay MacDonald will stand depends upon the results of David Marquand's projected biography of that much-maligned figure. Adelaide Livingstone's *The Peace Ballot: The Official History* (London, 1935) is aptly titled and full of information; a number of essays in *The Baldwin Age*, edited by John Raymond (London, 1960) add colour to the period.

Autobiographies or memoirs by prominent political figures who were not members of the Labour Party can be utilized either as a critical commentary upon that party's actions or as a means of studying the policies of the National Government. Winston S. Churchill, *The Gathering Storm* (Boston, 1948) is critical of both, though the emphasis is upon the very real harm done by the men in power. His magisterial account will long be read. Anthony Eden, Earl of Avon, develops the most revealing 'inside' criticism of the policies of those administrations of which he was a prominent member, until his resignation early in 1938. *Facing the Dictators, 1923–1938* (Boston, 1962) must be carefully checked against Eden's own remarks in the *Parliamentary Debates*, for the judgments of Eden as memoirist do not always agree with those of Eden as involved participant. Consistent with his strong right-wing political views of the thirties is Leopold Amery's third volume of memoirs, *My Political Life: The Unforgiving Years, 1929–1940* (London, 1955), a detailed account of the period. Sir Samuel Hoare's *Nine Troubled Years* (London, 1954) is a thorough-going defence of the policies which Hoare had a hand in shaping; the rationale of appeasement is clearly spelled out, for Hoare does not beg the question. That cannot, alas, be said either for Sir John Simon's *Retrospect* (London, 1952) or the Earl of Halifax's *Fulness of Days* (London, 1957), both of which are disappointingly incomplete. For details of diplomacy presented in undiplomatic fashion, Lord Vansittart's *The Mist Procession*

(London, 1958) is a compelling indictment of the policies of Mac-Donald and Baldwin, though his pen was more often dipped in acid than was necessary. Valuable for a view of Baldwin is the major chronicle of Establishment goings-on, enthusiastically collected by an inveterate gossip and influential adviser, Thomas Jones, in *A Diary with Letters* (London, 1954). Another keeper of a diary, Harold Nicolson, was further from the levers of power than was Jones, but his *Diaries and Letters, 1930–1939* (New York, 1966) captures revealing details about the life and politics of the period. Far less revealing is Harold Macmillan's *Winds of Change, 1914–1939* (London, 1966) which finds Macmillan blown off course from the memoir which he began to write into a conventional historical account of the 1930s.

Biographies of Conservative politicians supplement these memoir accounts. Stanley Baldwin attracted the attention both of G. M. Young, whose *Stanley Baldwin* (London, 1952) is one of the strangest 'official' biographies ever written, admitting the justice of most of the charges brought against Baldwin, and A. W. Baldwin, *My Father: The True Story* (London, 1955), an account written in retort to Young. Keith Feiling's *The Life of Neville Chamberlain* (London, 1946) is an honest and objective approach to his subject, though the reader may well draw conclusions other than those of Feiling from the material which he prints. Ian Macleod's attempt to rehabilitate the Prime Minister, in his *Neville Chamberlain* (London, 1961) falls short of his goal. Halifax's disappointing memoirs are compensated for by the full and critical assessment *The Life of Lord Halifax*, written by the Earl of Birkenhead (Boston, 1966). John Evelyn Wrench has written an interesting account of *Geoffrey Dawson and Our Times* (London, 1955), treating Dawson's editorship of that paper and his close relations with the Conservative hierarchy. Those intertwining circles of the pre-war political Establishment are also the subject of A. L. Rowse's *Appeasement and All Souls* (London, 1961), misleadingly retitled in an American edition *Appeasement: A Study in Political Decline, 1933–1939* (New York, 1961). John Wheeler-Bennett's biography of *John Anderson: Viscount Waverley* (London, 1962) supplies new materials concerning Cabinet discussions in August–September 1939.

Notes

1 The roots of Labour's international policy

1 Quoted by Winston Churchill, *House of Commons Debates*, Fifth Series, vol. 330, 21 December 1937, col. 1830. (Hereafter cited as *H.C. Debs.*, by volume.)
2 For the latter contention, Henry R. Winkler, 'The Emergence of a Labor Foreign Policy in Great Britain, 1918–1929', *Journal of Modern History*, 27: 247 (September 1956).
3 *Ibid.*, p. 248.
4 W. M. Jordan, *Great Britain, France, and the German Problem, 1918–1939* (London, 1943), p. 40.
5 Winkler, 'Emergence', p. 249.
6 Ralph Miliband, *Parliamentary Socialism* (London, 1961), p. 45.
7 S. Maccoby, *English Radicalism: The End?* (London, 1961), pp. 561–2.
8 Quoted in Catherine Ann Cline, *Recruits to Labour, 1914–1931* (Syracuse, 1963), p. 74.
9 Winkler, 'Emergence', p. 252, who adds: '. . . even after the first wave of reaction to the post-war settlement had receded, the bulk of the trade-union leadership remained closer to the radicalism of the ILP and the UDC than to the moderation of colleagues such as J. R. Clynes and J. H. Thomas.'
10 R. B. McCallum, *Public Opinion and the Last Peace* (London, N.Y., 1944), pp. 52–3.
11 Jordan, *German Problem*, p. 40.
12 William R. Tucker, *The Attitude of the British Labour Party towards European and Collective Security Problems, 1920–1939* (Geneva, 1950), p. 55.
13 Cline, *Recruits*, p. 86.
14 Hugh Dalton, *Towards the Peace of Nations* (London, 1928), p. 46.
15 Winkler, 'Emergence', p. 253.

16 Arthur Henderson, *The League of Nations and Labour* (London, 1918), p. 5.

17 Winkler, 'Emergence', p. 248

18 Henry R. Winkler, 'Arthur Henderson', in Gordon Craig and Felix Gilbert, eds, *The Diplomats* (Princeton, 1953), p. 312.

19 Winkler, 'Emergence', p. 256.

20 Dalton, *Peace of Nations*, p. 211.

21 Jordan, *German Problem*, p. 207.

22 Quoted in Tucker, *Attitude*, p. 35.

23 Miliband, *Parliamentary Socialism*, p. 45.

24 Egon Wertheimer, *Portrait of the Labour Party* (London and New York, 1929), p. 158.

25 *Ibid.*, pp. 188–9.

26 Francis Williams, *Ernest Bevin* (London, 1952), p. 189.

27 Jordan, *German Problem*, p. 207.

28 *Labour Party Conference Report, 1926*, p. 256. (Hereafter cited as *LPCR*, by year.)

29 McCallum, *Public Opinion*, pp. 15–16.

30 *LPCR, 1926*, p. 257.

31 Arthur Henderson, *Consolidating World Peace* (Oxford, 1931), pp. 10–11.

32 Bertrand Russell, *Which Way to Peace?* (London, 1936), p. 8.

33 Arthur Ponsonby, 'Disarmament by Example', *Journal of the Royal Institute of International Affairs*, 7:227–8 (July 1928).

34 William P. Maddox, *Foreign Relations in British Labour Politics* (Cambridge, Mass., 1934), p. 58.

35 Winkler, 'Henderson', p. 333.

36 Alan Bullock, *The Life and Times of Ernest Bevin*, vol. I (London, 1960), 549.

37 G.D.H.Cole, *The People's Front* (London, 1937), p. 168.

38 Leonard Woolf, ed., *Revision of Treaties and Changes in International Law* (London, 1933), p. 17. Woolf maintains to this day the correctness of the strictures laid against Versailles by the Labour left, in his *Downhill All the Way* (New York, 1967), pp. 240–1, the fourth volume of his masterly autobiography.

39 Rolland A. Chaput, *Disarmament in British Foreign Policy* (London, 1935), p. 44.

40 Jordan, *German Problem*, p. 154.

41 Arnold Wolfers, *Britain and France between the Wars* (New York, 1940), p. 366.

2 Politics and policies of the opposition

1 Arthur Henderson was shattered beyond his powers of speech by MacDonald's action. (Mary Agnes Hamilton, *Arthur Henderson*, London 1938, p. 385.)
2 For a contemporary assessment of the likely consequences of these reductions, John Maynard Keynes, *Essays in Persuasion* (London, 1931), pp. 157–62.
3 Quoted in Keith Feiling, *The Life of Neville Chamberlain* (London, 1946), p. 191.
4 Bullock, *Bevin*, I, 478.
5 Quoted in Reginald Bassett, *1931: Political Crisis* (New York, 1958), p. 97, a fully documented account of these events, favourable to MacDonald's course of action.
6 E.g. Sidney Webb, who had commented: 'The General Council are pigs . . . they won't agree to any "cuts" of Unemployment insurance benefits or salaries or wages.' (Beatrice Webb, *Diary, 1924–1932*, London 1956, p. 281.)
7 Quoted in Bassett, *1931*, p. 187.
8 *LPCR, 1932*, p. 5.
9 *256 H.C. Debs.*, 8 September 1931, col. 25.
10 Hamilton, *Henderson*, pp. 385–6.
11 A further weakening of the pound in September underlay the British government's decision, on the 21st, to repeal the gold standard. Such an action, which that government had been formed to prevent, lessened their control of the House of Commons. A government supporter has commented: 'It was felt that the situation could only be regularised, and lasting confidence established, by a Government confirmed in full power by the votes of the people.' (Quoted in Harold Nicolson, *King George the Fifth*, London 1952, p. 490.)
12 *LPCR, 1931*, p. 155.
13 *Ibid.*, p. 205. Ironically he was a nephew of Beatrice Webb.
14 For the latter contention, Bassett, *1931*, p. 293.
15 Philip Snowden, *Autobiography*, vol. II (London, 1934), 956–7.
16 For the text of his speech, Bassett, *1931*, pp. 444–9.
17 Miliband, *Parliamentary Socialism*, p. 191.
18 *Trades Union Congress Report, 1931*, p. 405.
19 The fifty-two included five Independent Labour Party candidates and one independent Labour supporter; the Labour Party had, however, lost only one supporter in five (1·7 million from its 1929

poll of 8·3 million). For the last statement, Roy Jenkins, *Pursuit of Progress* (London, 1953), p. 60.

20 J. R. Clynes, *Memoirs, 1924–1937* (London, n.d.), p. 208.

21 Harold Laski, 'The Underlying Assumptions of the National Government', *Political Quarterly*, 5:22 (March 1934).

22 Sir Arthur Salter, *Security, Can We Retrieve It?* (London, 1939), p. 279.

23 Herbert, Lord Morrison, *An Autobiography* (London, 1960), pp. 131–2.

24 Clement Attlee, *The Labour Party in Perspective* (London, 1937), p. 60.

25 Miliband, *Parliamentary Socialism*, p. 15.

26 John Paton, *Left Turn* (London, 1936), p. 308. For recent accounts of the ILP position and decline, see Robert E. Dowse, *Left in the Centre: The Independent Labour Party, 1893–1940* (London, 1966) and, in a narrower framework, Arthur Marwick, *Clifford Allen: The Open Conspirator* (Edinburgh and London, 1964).

27 Paton, *Left Turn*, p. 386.

28 Fenner Brockway, *Inside the Left* (London, 1942), p. 240.

29 Only 452 of 635 ILP branches survived to the end of 1932; in the same period, membership declined from 16,773 to 11,092 and continued its downward spiral to 4,392 at the end of 1935. (Miliband, *Parliamentary Socialism*, p. 195, n. 3.)

30 The vote in favour of disaffiliation at the special ILP conference had been 241 to 142.

31 G. D. H. Cole, *A History of the Labour Party since 1914* (London, 1948), p. 282.

32 *Ibid.*, p. 225.

33 *Ibid.*, p. 284.

34 Bullock, *Bevin*, I, 515–16.

35 Author's interview of Lord Citrine, 19 July 1962.

36 J. T. Murphy, *New Horizons* (London, 1941), p. 310.

37 'Faith in socialism . . . can be and is elevated into a complete if somewhat vague system of domestic and international politics.' (E. J. Meehan, *The British Left Wing and Foreign Policy*, New Brunswick, N.J., 1960, p. 37.)

38 Hugh Dalton, *The Fateful Years, 1931–1945* (London, 1957), pp. 24–5.

39 *LPCR, 1932*, p. 204.

40 Dalton, *Fateful Years*, p. 31.

41 *LPCR, 1932*, p. 204 (Arthur Ponsonby, then Leader of the Opposition in the House of Lords).

42 'Leaders in Difficulty', *The Times*, 7 October 1932.

NOTES

43 Somewhat of a misnomer, until in 1937 the representatives of the Constituency Parties were elected solely by those parties rather than by the entire Conference.

44 305 *H.C. Debs.*, 22 October 1935, col. 38.

45 Hugh Dalton, *Hitler's War* (Harmondsworth, 1940), p. 32.

46 Reginald Bassett, *Democracy and Foreign Policy* (London, 1952), p. 551. Bassett grants to the directing bodies of the Labour movement outside Parliament 'tentative, contingent and conditional gestures' in that direction on two occasions, but he holds that nothing was done to follow up these gestures.

47 Robert H. Ferrell, 'The Mukden Incident: September 18–19, 1931', *Journal of Modern History*, 27:67, 69 (March 1955).

48 G. M. Gathorne-Hardy, *Short History of International Affairs, 1920–1939* (4th edition, London, 1950), pp. 316–17.

49 *Documents on British Foreign Policy, 1919–1939*, Second Series, vol. VIII, 745 (No. 603). (Hereafter cited as *DBFP.*) Unfortunately, the documents dealing with the period following the League's decision to dispatch a mission have as yet not been published.

50 Charles Loch Mowat, *Britain between the Wars, 1918–1940* (London, 1955), p. 421. Cf. Bassett's justification of Simon's action, on the grounds that such isolation of Japan would have entailed sanctions, which the United States was not prepared to accept (*Democracy*, p. 588). Thus the precise meaning of Simon's reply has long been disputed; perhaps the publication of the relevant British documents will settle the matter.

51 *DBFP*, 2s., VIII, 885 (No. 720).

52 *Ibid.*, p. 4 (No. 1; 8 January 1930).

53 260 *H.C. Debs.*, 25 November 1931, cols 460–4.

54 Irving Friedman, *British Relations with China* (N.Y., 1940), p. 29.

55 *LPCR, 1932*, p. 68.

56 *Idem.*

57 Manchuria and the deteriorating international situation were mentioned in a resolution, 'Disarmament and Peace', but the five speakers concentrated on the former topic. Bassett acknowledges the existence of this strongly worded warning, but he adds: 'The Parliamentary Labour Party did nothing to follow that up. Nor did the Labour Party outside Parliament.' (*Democracy*, p. 552.) This stricture, however, can apply only to the period preceding the issuance of the Lytton report, though Bassett does not note this important qualification.

58 270 *H.C. Debs.*, 10 November 1932, cols 526–8.

59 Reported in 'Comments', *New Statesman*, 4:714 (10 December, 1932).
60 Friedman, *British Relations*, p. 41.
61 *LPCR, 1933*, p. 51; the Parliamentary Labour Party had, however, advocated an arms embargo only upon Japan (*ibid.*, p. 150).
62 275 *H.C. Debs.*, 27 February 1933, col. 46.
63 Bassett, *Democracy*, p. 552, cites a telling passage from Lansbury's speech in the Commons on 25 June 1937, which supports such a contention.
64 275 *H.C. Debs.*, 27 February 1933, col. 59.
65 Arthur Henderson, *Labour's Foreign Policy* (London, 1933), p. 4.
66 284 *H.C. Debs.*, 21 December 1933, cols 1503, 1536.
67 Bassett, *Democracy*, p. 549. In maintaining that the Labour Party offered 'comparatively little criticism' of the British government's policy from 1931 to 1933, Bassett does not reveal his standards with regard to the amount of criticism; one can only hope they were not based upon vastly increased Parliamentary attention to foreign affairs later in the decade: such a comparison is meaningless.
68 299 *H.C. Debs.*, 11 March 1935, col. 89.
69 John, Viscount Simon, *Retrospect* (London, 1952), p. 191.
70 *LPCR, 1932*, p. 60 (May 1932).
71 See above, p. 14.
72 270 *H.C. Debs.*, 10 November 1932, col. 526.
73 289 *H.C. Debs.*, 18 May 1934, col. 2060.
74 John Wheeler-Bennett, *Pipe Dream of Peace* (N.Y., 1935), pp. 5–6.
75 Hamilton, *Henderson*, p. 260.
76 *DBFP*, 2s., III, 478–80 (No. 213, Enclosure; 15 July 1931).
77 *Ibid.*, pp. 483–6 (No. 215).
78 *Ibid.*, pp. 514–15 (No. 239).
79 'World Peace Can Be Won', *Labour Magazine*, 10: 440 (February 1932).
80 Wheeler-Bennett, *Pipe Dream*, p. 12.
81 Sir Samuel Hoare (Viscount Templewood), *Nine Troubled Years* (London, 1954), p. 125.
82 Robert, Viscount Cecil, *A Great Experiment* (London, 1941), p. 241.
83 'Editorial Notes', *Labour Magazine*, 11: 121 (July 1932).
84 *DBFP*, 2s., III, 559–60 (No. 252).
85 Quoted in Philip Noel-Baker, 'Disarmament', *International Affairs*, 13: 3 (January–February 1934).
86 *DBFP*, 2s., III, 583–5 (No. 264).
87 *Ibid.*, p. 589 (No. 270).
88 *Trades Union Congress Report, 1931*, pp. 241–3, 375.

89 *LPCR, 1931*, p. 184.
90 Philip Noel-Baker, 'The League of Nations', in John Raymond, ed., *The Baldwin Age* (London, 1960), p. 102.
91 262 *H.C. Debs.*, 8 March 1932, cols 1749–50.
92 *DBFP*, 2s., IV, 110–11 (No. 53).
93 *Ibid.*, pp. 163–4 (No. 89).
94 *Ibid.*, pp. 172–5 (No. 92).
95 *LPCR, 1932*, pp. 228, 229.
96 For the genesis of this body, Winkler, 'Emergence', pp. 254–5, and for enlightening comments about the quality and (somewhat disappointing) impact of its work by its secretary for nearly thirty years, Leonard Woolf, *Downhill*, pp. 221 and 238–40. One should add that membership on the ACIQ was open to all Labour MPs and 'experts' appointed by the National Executive. Attendance at its meetings in the 1930s varied normally from about six to twenty, chaired by C. R. Buxton. Its memoranda are unpublished, but this author was given access to them.
97 ACIQ Memorandum No. 428A.
98 270 *H.C. Debs.*, 10 November 1932, cols 626–8.
99 *Ibid.*, 10 November 1932, col. 546.
100 *DBFP*, 2s., IV, 297–8 (No. 186).
101 *Ibid.*, p. 372 (No. 218, Enclosure).
102 *Ibid.*, p. 535 (No. 306).
103 *Ibid.*, pp. 562–3 (Appendix IV).
104 *Documents on German Foreign Policy*, Series C, I, 187 (No. 103), 410 (No. 226) and 462 (No. 251). (Hereafter cited as *DGFP*.)
105 Wheeler-Bennett, *Pipe Dream*, p. 126.
106 *Ibid.*, p. 164.
107 *DBFP*, 2s., V, 466 (No. 293).
108 As late as 27 September, the British Councillor, Newton, had viewed 'with considerable reserve' the possibility that Germany would leave the conference and the League of Nations if her demands were not met. (*DBFP*, 2s., V, 642, No. 415.)
109 *DGFP*, C, I, 912–13 (No. 493) and 923–4 (No. 499).
110 *DBFP*, 2s., V, 660 (No. 431).
111 *Ibid.*, p. 671 (No. 443).
112 Wheeler-Bennett, *Pipe Dream*, p. 181.
113 Hamilton, *Henderson*, p. 432; Winkler contends that after 1932 Henderson's efforts at Geneva were carried on in 'a vacuum of unreality'. ('Henderson', p. 341.)
114 *DBFP*, 2s., VI, iii (Preface).
115 *Ibid.*, pp. 368–9 (No. 244).
116 Gathorne-Hardy, *International Affairs*, p. 356.

117 *DBFP*, 2s., VI, 300 (No. 195).
118 287 *H.C. Debs.*, 14 March 1934, col. 465.
119 J.L.Brierley, 'The League of Nations', in David Thomson, ed., *The New Cambridge Modern History*, vol. XII (Cambridge, 1960), 478–9.
120 Though evidence has been cited that the Labour government had been divided on the Protocol and might have hesitated to approve it. (R. W. Lyman, *The First Labour Government, 1924*, London 1957, p. 176.)
121 Wolfers, *Britain and France*, pp. 223–8.
122 Arthur Henderson, *Labour's Way to Peace* (London, 1935), pp. 34–5.
123 Dalton, *Peace of Nations*, p. 213.
124 Jenkins, *Pursuit of Progress*, p. 9.
125 *Trades Union Congress Report, 1932*, p. 359.
126 Norman Angell, *After All* (London, 1951), pp. 266–7.
127 ACIQ Memorandum No. 431A.
128 ACIQ Memorandum No. 433A (April 1933).

3   The menace of fascism

1 So Sir Horace Rumbold, British Ambassador in Berlin, had reported on 19 November 1932. (*DBFP*, 2s., IV, 82, No. 38.)
2 *LPCR, 1933*, p. 277 ('Democracy v. Dictatorship').
3 Joseph Compton, 'Down with Fascism', in the National Joint Council's *Hitlerism* (London, 1933), pp. 10–11.
4 Walter Citrine, *ibid.*, p. 7 ('Foreword').
5 Walter Citrine, 'In Defence of Freedom', *Labour Magazine*, 12:51–3, 103–5 and 150–2 (June, July, August 1933).
6 *LPCR, 1933*, p. 18.
7 Bullock, *Bevin*, I, 526–7.
8 E.g. Citrine's report 'Dictatorships and the Trade Union Movement', *Trades Union Congress Report, 1933*, pp. 425–35.
9 *DBFP*, 2s., V, 47–55 (No. 35).
10 276 *H.C. Debs.*, 23 March 1933, cols 609–10.
11 *Ibid.*, 13 April, col. 2742.
12 A.J.P.Taylor, *The Origins of the Second World War* (N.Y., 1961), p. 136. Taylor captures the error of such a position, shared by Liberals as well as Labour: 'They tried to distinguish between Germany and Hitler and insisted that, while Germany was right, Hitler was wrong. Unfortunately this was not a distinction which the Germans were willing to make.'

13 276 *H.C. Debs.*, 13 April 1933, cols 2765 and 2775 (Col. Wedgwood).
14 *DGFP*, C, I, 291 (No. 158).
15 *Ibid.*, p. 434 (No. 237).
16 280 *H.C. Debs.*, 5 July 1933, col. 347.
17 John Strachey, *The Coming Struggle for Power* (London, 1935), p. 384. Michael Foot regards this book as one of the most influential left documents of the decade (interview of 25 July 1962).
18 *Trades Union Congress Report, 1933*, p. 69 (A. G. Walkden).
19 Author's interview with Lord Citrine, 19 July 1962.
20 Miliband, *Parliamentary Socialism*, p. 205.
21 *LPCR, 1933*, p. 16.
22 Stephen Graubard, *British Labour and the Russian Revolution* (Cambridge, Mass., 1956), p. 181.
23 Bullock, *Bevin*, I, 522–3.
24 The Co-operative Party was affiliated to the Labour Party.
25 Paton, *Left Turn*, p. 402; Brockway, *Inside the Left*, ch. xxv.
26 Cole, *Labour Party*, p. 291.
27 Quoted in the Labour Party's *The Communist Solar System* (London, 1933), p. 3.
28 Miliband, *Parliamentary Socialism*, p. 214.
29 Storm Jameson, 'To a Labour Party Official', *Left News*, November 1934, cited by Neal Wood, *Communism and British Intellectuals* (N.Y., 1959), p. 107.
30 'Comments', *New Statesman*, 5:401 (1 April 1933).
31 'Critic' (Kingsley Martin), 'A London Diary', *New Statesman*, 6:379 (30 September 1933).
32 *Trades Union Congress Report, 1933*, pp. 432 and 324.
33 *Ibid.*, p. 328.
34 *LPCR, 1933*, p. 221.
35 Cole, *Labour Party*, p. 287.
36 *LPCR, 1933*, p. 159.
37 'Labour Party Conference', *Manchester Guardian*, 2 October 1933.
38 While Bevin is properly regarded as a spokesman for official Labour, he did not sit on the National Executive during the decade; he was, however, influential in the TUC General Council and the National Joint Council (later the National Council of Labour), as well as in the editorial content of the *Daily Herald*.
39 *LPCR, 1933*, p. 161.
40 Bullock, *Bevin*, I, 531.
41 Colin Cooke, *The Life of Richard Stafford Cripps* (London, 1957), pp. 141–2.

42 Frank Wise, first Chairman of the Socialist League, died shortly after the Hastings Conference.
43 The Labour Party, *War and Socialism* (London, 1932).
44 See ACIQ Memoranda Nos. 431A and 433A.
45 Arthur Henderson, *Labour's Foreign Policy* (London, 1933), pp. 12–16, 4.
46 *LPCR, 1933*, p. 186.
47 *Trades Union Congress Report, 1933*, pp. 302–4. See above pp. 43–4.
48 *LPCR, 1933*, p. 198.
49 Dalton, *Fateful Years*, p. 45.
50 'Comments', *New Statesman*, 6:402 (7 October 1933).
51 'Labour and War', *Manchester Guardian*, 11 October 1933.
52 Hoare, *Nine Troubled Years*, p. 126.
53 Cole, *Labour Party*, p. 288.
54 E.g. Hoare, *Troubled Years*, p. 126.
55 Winston S. Churchill, *The Gathering Storm* (Boston, 1948), p. 85.
56 McCallum, *Public Opinion*, pp. 177–80.
57 Cf. 'Comments', *New Statesman*, 6:503 (28 October 1933) with 'Critic' (Kingsley Martin), 'A London Diary', *ibid.*, p. 575.
58 281 *H.C. Debs.*, 13 November 1933, col. 613.
59 *LPCR, 1933*, p. 192.
60 See *The Times*: 'A Useful Lesson', 27 October 1933: 'By Elections', 24 October and 16 October 1933.
61 Dalton, *Fateful Years*, p. 47.
62 317 *H.C. Debs.*, 12 November 1936, col. 1144.
63 G. M. Young, *Stanley Baldwin* (London, 1952), pp. 229 and 177.
64 A. W. Baldwin, *My Father: The True Story* (London, 1955), p. 187.
65 C. G. Hancock, 'Correspondence', *The Times*, 27 October 1933.
66 By-election results are listed in *LPCR, 1935*, pp. 30–5. Note that in the comparative voting lists given on pp. 36–7 the 1931 Labour poll at Wentworth is mistakenly assigned to the Conservatives.
67 Adelaide Livingstone, *The Peace Ballot* (London, 1935), p. 7.
68 An implication explicitly stated by the Labour-affiliated *Daily Herald*, which on 25 March 1935 treated the Ballot as 'votes for peace'.
69 Gathorne-Hardy, *International Affairs*, p. 408.
70 Leopold Amery, *My Political Life*, vol. III (London, 1955), 160.
71 Cecil, *Great Experiment*, p. 257.
72 Livingstone, *Peace Ballot*, p. 51.
73 Churchill, *Gathering Storm*, p. 170.
74 *DGFP*, C, IV, 394 (No. 188).
75 *LPCR, 1935*, p. 156.

76 Statistics cited in John F. Kennedy, *Why England Slept* (N.Y., 1940), pp. 16, 235.
77 For the classic expression of that view on the part of the Foreign Secretary who had led Britain into that war, see Sir Edward Grey (Viscount Grey of Fallodon), *Twenty-five Years, 1892–1916* (N.Y., 1925), vol. II, 53.
78 262 *H.C. Debs.*, 8 March 1932, cols 1665–6. Labour's desire for a Ministry of Defence possessing full powers was not met until Churchill assumed such a role in May 1940.
79 275 *H.C. Debs.*, 9 March 1933, col. 1386.
80 *Ibid.*, 14 March 1933, col. 1926.
81 Samuel Davis, 'The British Labour Party and British Foreign Policy, 1933–1939', unpublished Ph.D. thesis (1950), p. 108, in the University of London Library.
82 281 *H.C. Debs.*, 7 November 1933, cols 79 and 80.
83 *Ibid.*, 13 November 1933, cols 700–2.
84 283 *H.C. Debs.*, 29 November 1933, cols 958 and 1018.
85 285 *H.C. Debs.*, 14 February 1934, col. 2000.
86 We may note here that Attlee's predominance in these debates does not stem from a disinclination on Lansbury's part to speak on military affairs, but from his frequent indispositions.
87 286 *H.C. Debs.*, 8 March 1934, cols 2046–8.
88 Churchill, *Gathering Storm*, pp. 112–13.
89 286 *H.C. Debs.*, 8 March 1934, col. 2078.
90 287 *H.C. Debs.*, 14 March 1934, cols 465–6.
91 292 *H.C. Debs.*, 30 July 1934, col. 2366; Churchill, *Gathering Storm*, p. 114. He misdates the government's proposal to 20 July.
92 292 *H.C. Debs.*, 30 July 1934, cols 2345, 2377 and 2426.
93 Bullock, *Bevin*, I, 550.
94 Dalton, *Fateful Years*, p. 53.
95 Gordon Brook-Shepherd, *Dollfuss* (London, 1961), pp. 138–40.
96 Bullock, *Bevin*, I, 546–7.
97 'All the World Over', *Labour*, 1:146 (March 1934).
98 *LPCR, 1934*, p. 245.
99 Brook-Shepherd, *Dollfuss*, pp. 135–6.
100 Gathorne-Hardy, *International Affairs*, pp. 374–6.
101 The Labour Party, *For Socialism and Peace* (London, 1934), p. 18 (pagination is from the 1938 edition).
102 *Trades Union Congress Report, 1934*, p. 322 (W. Monslow).
103 *Ibid.*, pp. 324 and 338.
104 Lord Citrine, *Men and Work: An Autobiography*, vol. I (London, 1964), 301.
105 *LPCR, 1934*, pp. 152 and 166 (E. S. More).

335

106 Dalton, *Fateful Years*, pp. 55–6.
107 *LPCR, 1934*, p. 157.
108 *Ibid.*, p. 176.
109 'The Labour Conference', *Manchester Guardian*, 1 October 1934.
110 Cf. Attlee's reaction to the Socialist League's foreign policy proposals, *LPCR, 1934*, pp. 174–5, with Morrison's rough handling of their domestic programme, pp. 163–4.
111 Not so, though Lansbury spoke only briefly, to no grave import; *LPCR, 1934*, p. 146.
112 Dalton, *Fateful Years*, p. 55.
113 R. H. S. Crossman, 'Some Elementary Principles of Socialist Foreign Policy', in G. E. Catlin, ed., *New Trends in Socialism* (London, 1935), pp. 25 and 28.
114 Labour Party, *For Socialism and Peace*, p. 36.
115 Cooke, *Cripps*, pp. 165–6.
116 In such a vein the *Manchester Guardian* commented: 'Every democratic institution understands the rule that when a man is a nuisance the best way to make him behave properly is to burden him with responsibility.' ('Two Conferences', 4 October 1934.)
117 *LPCR, 1934*, pp. 136 and 138.
118 *Ibid.*, pp. 138–9 and 140.
119 *Ibid.*, pp. 306 and 307.
120 Mowat, *Britain between the Wars*, p. 474.
121 *LPCR, 1934*, p. 308.
122 Mowat, *Britain between the Wars*, p. 475.
123 *Trades Union Congress Report, 1934*, pp. 142 and 249.
124 Quoted by Miliband, *Parliamentary Socialism*, p. 220.

4 Challenges external and internal

1 Brook-Shepherd, *Dollfuss*, p. 231. The British government was however informed by its Berlin embassy that Hitler was '. . . certainly in the dark about the Vienna "putsch".' (*DBFP*, 2s., VI, 887, No. 550, 31 July 1934.)
2 For the former point, Sir Ivone Kirkpatrick, *Mussolini: Study of a Demagogue* (London, 1964), p. 284; for the latter, Gathorne-Hardy, *International Affairs*, p. 391.
3 Hubert Cole, *Laval: A Biography* (N.Y., 1963), p. 55; Gathorne-Hardy, *International Affairs*, pp. 402–3.
4 Kirkpatrick, *Mussolini*, pp. 293–5, 297.
5 William C. Askew, 'The Secret Argeement between France and Italy on Ethiopia, January 1935', *Journal of Modern History*,

25:48 (March 1953); for the latter assertion, Gathorne-Hardy, *International Affairs*, p. 394.

6 Kirkpatrick, *Mussolini*, p. 287; cf. Askew's assertion that Laval's assurances of a free hand held for '. . . every question with the government of Abyssinia'. ('Secret Agreement', p. 48.)

7 The Earl of Avon (Anthony Eden), *Facing the Dictators* (Boston, 1962), p. 136.

8 *Ibid.*, p. 144.

9 *Statement Relating to Defence*, Cmd. 4822 (1935).

10 *DGFP*, C, III, 979–80 (No. 517). In his dispatch Neurath deleted the word 'tactless' from the draft (n. 1).

11 *Ibid.*, pp. 1015–16 (No. 539).

12 Eden, *Facing the Dictators*, p. 144.

13 *DGFP*, C, IV, 79–82 (No. 46).

14 Asserted by Simon, *Retrospect*, p. 204.

15 Robert, Lord Vansittart, *The Mist Procession* (London, 1958), p. 519.

16 Kirkpatrick, *Mussolini*, p. 291.

17 *DGFP*, C, III, 1067 (No. 555).

18 Gathorne-Hardy, *International Affairs*, p. 401.

19 D. C. Watt, 'The Anglo-German Naval Agreement of 1935: An Interim Judgment', *Journal of Modern History*, 28:165 (June 1956).

20 Feiling, *Chamberlain*, p. 258.

21 *DGFP*, C, IV, 277–81 (No. 141).

22 Hoare, *Troubled Years*, pp. 141–2; Watt, however, contends that the French reply, though delayed, was in the hands of the British government before the signature of the treaty. ('Naval Agreement', p. 170.)

23 Eden, *Facing the Dictators*, p. 258. Charging the British government with giving '. . . a disastrous impression of bad faith', Bullock too asserts that France and Italy had not been consulted. (Alan Bullock, *Hitler: A Study in Tyranny*, London 1959, p. 309.)

24 *DGFP*, C, III, 588 (No. 275).

25 Kirkpatrick, *Mussolini*, p. 298.

26 Eden, *Facing the Dictators*, pp. 257–8.

27 Churchill, *Gathering Storm*, p. 142.

28 *DGFP*, C, IV, 587 (No. 285).

29 Gathorne-Hardy, *International Affairs*, p. 408; Hoare's own extract (*Troubled Years*) significantly does not include the last sentence.

30 Hoare, *Troubled Years*, pp. 166 and 171.

31 Quoted in Mowat, *Britain between the Wars*, pp. 543–4.

32 *LPCR, 1935*, pp. 4 and 6.

33 ACIQ Memorandum No. 454B (March 1935).

34 ACIQ Memorandum No. 455A.
35 Simon, *Retrospect*, p. 204.
36 E.g. Addison, 302 *H.C. Debs.*, 22 May 1935, col. 430.
37 *Ibid.*, cols 2194 and 2209.
38 304 *H.C. Debs.*, 11 July 1935, col. 534.
39 ACIQ Memorandum No. 457A (July 1935).
40 *LPCR, 1935*, p. 12.
41 304 *H.C. Debs.*, 1 August 1935, cols 2894 and 2898.
42 Cooke, *Cripps*, pp. 124, 175.
43 Michael Foot, *Aneurin Bevan*, vol I (London, 1962), 210.
44 Bullock, *Bevin*, I, 558.
45 *Trades Union Congress Report, 1935*, pp. 346 and 349.
46 Bullock, *Bevin*, I, 564.
47 295 *H.C. Debs.*, 28 November 1934, col. 871.
48 *Ibid.*, 28 November 1934, col. 893.
49 299 *H.C. Debs.*, 11 March 1935, col. 35.
50 *Ibid.*, 11 March 1935, col. 78.
51 299 *H.C. Debs.*, 14 March 1935, col. 614.
52 295 *H.C. Debs.*, 28 November 1934, col. 926.
53 'Socialist M.P.s' "Musts" for Mr. Henderson', *Daily Mail*, 6 March 1935; 'Mr. Henderson Is Angry', *Daily Express*, 7 March 1935, reported that Henderson had met the PLP and 'told them where to get off'. The *Daily Herald* of that date reported that the PLP had unanimously agreed that Henderson should determine his own course. ('Mr. Henderson and Arms Conference'.)
54 E.g. Lansbury's speech, 299 *H.C. Debs.*, 21 March 1935, cols 1398–9.
55 301 *H.C. Debs.*, 2 May 1935, cols 673–4.
56 302 *H.C. Debs.*, 22 May 1935, col. 367.
57 Bullock, *Bevin*, I, 560.
58 Citrine, *Men and Work*, p. 350.
59 'Socialists and Bigger R.A.F.', *Morning Post*, 21 May 1935; 'Changing Front', *ibid.*, 22 May 1935.
60 'Surprise Decision of Labour', *The Times*, 23 May 1935.
61 304 *H.C. Debs.*, 11 July 1935, col. 538.
62 *Trades Union Congress Report, 1935*, p. 371.
63 Dalton, *Fateful Years*, p. 66.
64 *Ibid.*, pp. 66–7.
65 Quoted in 'Lord Ponsonby's Resignation', *The Times*, 19 September 1935.
66 Raymond Postgate, *The Life of George Lansbury* (London, 1951), p. 300.
67 'A Labour "Split",' *The Times*, 20 September 1935.
68 *Idem.*

69 'Political Speeches', *The Times*, 21 September 1935.
70 Postgate, *Lansbury*, pp. 299–300.
71 Citrine, *Men and Work*, p. 351.
72 Postgate, *Lansbury*, p. 300.
73 Bullock, *Bevin*, I, 562.
74 *Ibid.*, p. 562, n. 1.
75 Williams, *Bevin*, p. 197.
76 Dalton, *Fateful Years*, p. 63.
77 Quoted in Jürgen Gehl, *Austria, Germany and the Anschluss, 1931–1938* (London, 1963), p. 15.
78 *LPCR, 1935*, pp. 153–6.
79 *Ibid.*, p. 157.
80 Jenkins, *Pursuit of Progress*, p. 14.
81 Stafford Cripps, *The Struggle for Peace* (London, 1936), p. 61.
82 ACIQ Memorandum No. 433A (April 1933).
83 *LPCR, 1935*, p. 172.
84 *Ibid.*, pp. 160–1.
85 Postgate, *Lansbury*, p. 301.
86 *LPCR, 1935*, pp. 175–7.
87 'Critic' (Kingsley Martin), 'The Brighton Front', *New Statesman*, 10:438 (5 October 1935).
88 Williams, *Bevin*, p. 193.
89 Bullock, *Bevin*, I, 567.
90 'Taking' is reported in *LPCR, 1935* and in the *News Chronicle*; the *Observer* recorded the stronger term 'hawking' ('Labour Party Conference', 6 October 1935); Francis Williams uses the word 'trailing' (*Bevin*, p. 193).
91 *LPCR, 1935*, pp. 178–80.
92 Patricia Strauss, *Cripps – Advocate and Rebel* (London, 1943), p. 103.
93 Quoted in Postgate, *Lansbury*, p. 303.
94 Williams, *Bevin*, p. 196.
95 Postgate, *Lansbury*, p. 304.
96 Williams, *Bevin*, pp. 196–7; Bullock, *Bevin*, I, 570.
97 Quoted in Bullock, *Bevin*, I, 569.
98 Postgate, *Lansbury*, p. 304.
99 *LPCR, 1935*, p. 242.
100 *Ibid.*, pp. 196–201.
101 Elaine Windrich, *British Labour's Foreign Policy* (Stanford, 1952), pp. 131–2. Misdating Cripps' resignation to after the Conference, she misses the force of Bevin's argument to that body.
102 Foot, *Bevan*, I, 211.
103 'Cato', *Guilty Men* (London, 1940), p. 33. Co-authorship has also been attributed to Mervyn Jones.

104 Such a calculation was probably based on the fact that each constituency represented could cast 1,000 votes at the minimum; the assertion thus assumes nearly no trade union support. ('Labour Party Conference', *Observer*, 6 October 1935.)

105 Dalton, *Fateful Years*, p. 70.

106 Postgate, *Lansbury*, p. 304.

107 Roy Jenkins, *Mr. Attlee* (London, 1948), p. 162.

108 Gathorne-Hardy, *International Affairs*, pp. 410–11.

109 305 *H.C. Debs.*, 22 October 1935, col. 29.

110 *Ibid.*, 23 October 1935, cols 151–2.

111 *Ibid.*, 22 October 1935, col. 67.

112 *Ibid.*, 23 October 1935, col. 165.

113 *Ibid.*, 22 October 1935, col. 43.

114 One writes 'apparently' because until the publication of the relevant British documents we do not know precisely what information concerning British intentions Hoare conveyed to Mussolini late in September. For the German Foreign Minister's estimate, see *DGFP*, C, IV, 674–5 (No. 317).

115 305 *H.C. Debs.*, 23 October 1935, col. 458.

116 Mowat, *Britain between the Wars*, p. 556.

117 305 *H.C. Debs.*, 22 October 1935, cols 44–6.

118 Mowat, *Britain between the Wars*, p. 554.

119 'The Board of Trade production index for the first six months of 1935 showed that activity in every industry ... except mining exceeded the 1930 level.' (Dana A. McHenry, *His Majesty's Opposition*, Berkeley 1940, p. 184.)

120 *Ibid.*, p. 187. Attlee, Clynes, Greenwood and Morrison delivered the broadcast addresses.

121 Cited, *ibid.*, p. 186.

122 Cf. the strong dissent of Miliband, *Parliamentary Socialism*, pp. 227–9.

123 Eden, *Facing the Dictators*, p. 317.

124 *Ibid.*, pp. 321, 325 and 326.

125 Feiling, *Chamberlain*, pp. 268–9.

126 Quoted in Iain Macleod, *Neville Chamberlain* (London, 1961), p. 184.

127 Quoted in G.M. Young, *Stanley Baldwin* (London, 1952), p. 215.

128 'Cato', *Guilty Men*, pp. 36–7; Reginald Bassett, 'Telling the Truth to the People', *Cambridge Journal*, 2:84–95 (November 1948).

129 Churchill, *Gathering Storm*, p. 180.

130 Cole, *Labour Party*, p. 311, mistakenly adds David Grenfell to this list. Grenfell had sat in the 1931–5 Parliament and had played an active role in debate.

131 Dalton, *Fateful Years*, p. 75.
132 H. J. L[aski], 'Some Notes on the General Election', *New Statesman*, 10:805 (30 November 1935).
133 Churchill, *Gathering Storm*, p. 180.

5 The year of indecision

1 This paragraph is based upon Dalton, *Fateful Years*, pp. 79–83.
2 Bullock, *Bevin*, I, 572.
3 Eden, *Facing the Dictators*, p. 329.
4 Ciano asserts that Laval's pledge of French support for the Italian action in Abyssinia went beyond economic matters: '... the French were fully informed of our plans for territorial conquest.' (*Ciano's Diary*, edited and translated by Andreas Mayor, London 1952, p. 208.) See also above, pp. 85–6.
5 Eden, *Facing the Dictators*, pp. 331 and 334; in the latter contention he is quoting Hitler's interpreter, Dr Paul Schmidt.
6 Only on 5 December had Laval asked Hoare to stop in Paris for several hours (which became two days) on his way to a sorely needed holiday, in order to discuss the situation. The government supporter Harold Nicolson viewed the results as disgraceful: '... Sam Hoare was certified by his doctors as unfit for public business, and on his way to the sanitorium he stops off in Paris and allows Laval to do him down.' (Harold Nicolson, *Diaries and Letters, 1930–1939*, ed. by Nigel Nicolson, New York 1966, p. 232, 12 December 1935.)
7 Eden, *Facing the Dicators*, pp. 334–5.
8 307 *H.C. Debs.*, 5 December 1935, cols. 327–30.
9 *Ibid.*, 5 December 1935, cols. 330 and 346.
10 *Ibid.*, 5 December 1935, col. 426.
11 The terms might have been known earlier, if Mussolini's assertion that '... Baldwin was so absorbed in reading a detective story that for a whole Sunday afternoon he did not open the envelope containing the instructions about the Hoare-Laval plan' (quoted in *Ciano's Diary*, p. 8) has any basis in fact.
12 This paragraph is based upon Eden, *Facing the Dictators*, pp. 335–41.
13 Though controversy still surrounds the source of the leak, Laval is exculpated in two recent accounts (Hubert Cole, *Laval*, p. 74); Arthur Furnia, *The Diplomacy of Appeasement* (Washington, 1960), p. 175, n. 68. Cf. Gathorne-Hardy, *International Affairs*, p. 416.
14 307 *H.C. Debs.*, 10 December 1935, cols 718, 817 and 856.
15 Eden, *Facing the Dictators*, p. 344.

16 Hoare, *Troubled Years*, p. 183.
17 The expression is Baldwin's, quoted in Eden, *Facing the Dictators*, p. 335.
18 Feiling, *Chamberlain*, p. 274.
19 Hoare, *Troubled Years*, p. 185, where Baldwin's assurance is also recorded.
20 Eden, *Facing the Dictators*, p. 346.
21 John Evelyn Wrench, *Geoffrey Dawson and Our Times* (London, 1955), p. 326.
22 Hoare, *Troubled Years*, p. 187.
23 307 *H.C. Debs.*, 19 December 1935, col. 2018.
24 *DGFP*, C, IV, 905 (No. 458; his italics).
25 *Ibid.*, p. 924 (No. 465).
26 Henderson B. Braddick, 'The Hoare-Laval Pact: A Study in International Politics', *Review of Politics*, 24:342–64 (July 1962) treats the British effort as 'bluff', carried on for domestic political purposes.
27 Hoare, *Troubled Years*, p. 179.
28 Young, *Baldwin*, p. 217.
29 307 *H.C Debs.*, 19 December 1935, cols 2031–2 and 2035.
30 Hoare, *Troubled Years*, p. 188.
31 Quoted in Robert Boothby, *I Fight to Live* (London, 1947), pp. 204–5, from a conversation of March 1940.
32 Vansittart, *Mist Procession*, p. 529.
33 *DGFP*, C, IV, 923 (No. 465). Thus the German Ambassador reported the view of Lord Monsell, First Lord of the Admiralty, and, implicitly, Sir Ernle Chatfield, C.-in-C. of the British Fleet. It is interesting to note that those in charge of the Mediterranean Fleet '. . . had no fear whatever of the result of an encounter with the Italian Navy'. (Viscount Cunningham of Hyndhope, *A Sailor's Odyssey*, N.Y. 1951, p. 173.)
34 Eden, *Facing the Dictators*, p. 294.
35 307 *H.C. Debs.*, 19 December 1935, col. 2029.
36 *Ibid.*, 19 December 1935, cols 2067–70.
37 Foot, *Bevan*, I, 210.
38 'Vigilantes' (Konni Zilliacus), *Inquest on Peace* (London, 1935), p. 281.
39 Foot, *Bevan*, I, 212–13.
40 Eden, *Facing the Dictators*, p. 356.
41 *Ibid.*, p. 365.
42 309 *H.C. Debs.*, 24 February 1936, cols 68 and 77–80.
43 *Ibid.*, 24 February 1936, col. 113.
44 *Ibid.*, 24 February 1936, col. 150.
45 Eden, *Facing the Dictators*, p. 368.
46 *DGFP*, C, IV, 745 (No. 360).

47 E.g. *ibid.*, pp. 204–6 (No. 107, Enclosure) and 492–3 (No. 230, Enclosure).
48 *Ibid.*, p. 202 (No. 107); Bullock, *Hitler*, p. 312.
49 *DGFP*, C, IV, 1142 (No. 564).
50 Bullock, *Hitler*, p. 313.
51 As reported by the German Ambassador in Rome, *DGFP*, C, IV, 1143 (No. 564).
52 Eden, *Facing the Dictators*, pp. 375–6. This represented a considerable change in policy since 20 March 1933, when the British Military Attaché had stated in the German Foreign Office that '... not only British politicians but also British soldiers would not stand for any nonsense on this question [the demilitarized zone]. (*DGFP*, C, III, 1030, No. 547.)
53 *DGFP*, C, IV, 175 (No. 96).
54 Eden, *Facing the Dictators*, pp. 374–5.
55 *Ibid.*, p. 383.
56 *Ibid.*, p. 379.
57 *Ibid.*, p. 389.
58 *Ibid.*, p. 410.
59 310 *H.C. Debs.*, 26 March 1936, cols 1454–7.
60 *Ibid.*, 26 March 1935, cols 1457–8.
61 *Ibid.*, 26 March 1935, col. 1531.
62 *History of The Times, 1912–1948*, vol. II (London, 1952), 899.
63 'Is There A Way to Peace?', *New Statesman*, 11:372 (14 March 1936).
64 Quoted in Bullock, *Hitler*, p. 315.
65 Eden, *Facing the Dictators*, pp. 412–13.
66 310 *H.C. Debs.*, 26 March 1936, col. 1536.
67 Eden, *Facing the Dictators*, p. 424.
68 We might recall Hoare's specific citation of this possibility as one of the reasons impelling him to the settlement embodied in the Hoare-Laval Pact.
69 311 *H.C. Debs.*, 6 May 1936, cols 1717–18 and 1736.
70 E.g. Cranborne's comments, *ibid.*, 6 May 1936, col. 1838.
71 Eden, *Facing the Dictators*, p. 433.
72 Quoted in Feiling, *Chamberlain*, p. 296.
73 313 *H.C. Debs.*, 18 June 1936, cols 1201 and 1216.
74 *Ibid.*, 23 June 1936, cols 1714–15.
75 289 *H.C. Debs.*, 18 May 1934, col. 2139.
76 Hugh Thomas, *The Spanish Civil War* (N.Y., 1961); Dante A. Puzzo, *Spain and the Great Powers* (N.Y., 1962).
77 Thomas, *Spanish Civil War*, pp. 90–1; Puzzo, *Spain*, p. 21.
78 Puzzo, *Spain*, p. 37.

79 Quoted in Thomas, *Spanish Civil War*, p. 5.
80 Eden, *Facing the Dictators*, p. 439. Though the Spanish situation was not on the agenda, it came up indirectly, and 'Blum, Delbos, and Leger were clearly made to understand the negative attitude of the British Conservatives, who did not wish to take sides in the "faction fight" in Spain . . .' (Joel Colton, *Léon Blum: Humanist in Politics*, New York, 1966, p. 241.)
81 Thomas, *Spanish Civil War*, pp. 214 and 219, the latter quoting Blum.
82 For the latter gloss, James Joll, *Three Intellectuals in Politics* (N.Y., 1961), pp. 38–9; Colton, *Blum*, pp. 241–5, maintains that 'there is no doubt that he left London much disturbed over the official British climate of opinion and shaken in his determination to aid Spain even if he was not yet prepared to abandon his original intention'.
83 Eden, *Facing the Dictators*, p. 451.
84 Quoted in Thomas, *Spanish Civil War*, p. 234.
85 *Ibid.*, p. 258; Colton, accepting his subject's words at precisely face value, regards the allegation as 'unproved' (as technically it remains). Yet he admits that 'the British pressure was strong even if indirect'. (*Blum*, p. 241, n. 9; p. 242.) In a wider context, Puzzo asserts that 'British influence in the determination of French policy towards Spain was decisive . . . the chief architect of appeasement in Spain was Great Britain'. (*Spain*, p. 244.)
86 Colton notes that 'the idea of an international agreement on non-intervention seems to have originated with Léger and the permanent officials at the Quai d'Orsay'. (*Blum*, p. 247.)
87 Joll, *Three Intellectuals*, p. 39. Yet 'as soon as he abandoned the thought of resigning and accepted non-intervention as a policy, a change came over him. He began now to defend the non-intervention policy as though it were his from the very beginning – as the proper course of action both to aid the Spanish Republic and to prevent a general war.' (Colton, *Blum*, pp. 250–1.) This hardening of Blum's attitude seems the key to his subsequent denial of British pressures and his post-war acceptance of the entire blame for the ill-begotten policy; it certainly calls into question the value of Blum's testimony, though Colton relies on that testimony to minimize British pressures.
88 Eden, *Facing the Dictators*, pp. 451 and 458.
89 As the British Cabinet did not meet from the end of July to the beginning of September, policy was in fact made in the Foreign Office; Baldwin had nothing whatever to do with that policy. (*Ibid.*, p. 454.)

90 'Labour Party and Spain', *The Times*, 21 July 1936.
91 'British Worker and Spanish Worker', *The Times*, 28 July 1936.
92 Foot, *Bevan*, I, 221.
93 315 *H.C. Debs.*, 27 and 31 July 1936, cols 1196 and 1892.
94 Noting these absences at such a crucial time, 'Critic' (Kingsley Martin) commented: 'There is something almost fantastic in the quietism of English Labour ... The parallel with the German Social Democrats just before Hitler is unpleasantly close.' ('A London Diary', *New Statesman*, 12:245, 22 August 1936.)
95 Bullock, *Bevin*, I, 586–7.
96 Eden, *Facing the Dictators*, p. 455.
97 Citrine, *Men and Work*, p. 359. His account is misleading in suggesting that Labour opposed non-intervention from the first, which is not the case. Nor is it likely that the full meeting overruled the recommendation of the deputation, as Citrine's account implies.
98 *LPCR, 1936*, p. 29.
99 Dalton, *Fateful Years*, pp. 95–6.
100 *Trades Union Congress Report, 1936*, pp. 361–7.
101 Taylor, *Origins*, pp. 122–3.
102 *Trades Union Congress Report, 1936*, p. 379.
103 *DGFP*, Series D, III, 13 (No. 11; 25 July 1936).
104 Taylor, *Origins*, pp. 121–2.
105 'Non-Intervention', *New Statesman*, 12:180 (8 August 1936).
106 Wood, *Communism and British Intellectuals*, p. 56; Dalton, *Fateful Years*, p. 97.
107 'Trenches Across Europe', *New Statesman*, 12:148 (1 August 1936).
108 Foot, *Bevan*, I, 219.
109 Strauss, *Cripps*, p. 86.
110 Jennie Lee, *This Great Journey* (N.Y., 1942), p. 209.
111 307 *H.C. Debs.*, 6 December 1934, cols 511–12.
112 'Labour and the Arms Race', *New Statesman*, 11:252 (22 February 1936).
113 'The End of Sanctions', *New Statesman*, 11:1016–17 (27 June 1936).
114 Norman Angell, 'Collective Defence the Only Policy', *Labour*, 3:208 (May 1936).
115 Foot, *Bevan*, I, 196.
116 A. L. Rowse, *End of an Era* (London, 1947), p. 12.
117 307 *H.C. Debs.*, 19 December 1935, cols 2118–20.
118 308 *H.C. Debs.*, 14 February 1936, col. 1317.
119 309 *H.C. Debs.*, 9 March 1936, col. 1829.
120 'Labour and Defence', *The Times*, 26 February 1936.
121 Dalton, *Fateful Years*, p. 87.

122 'Socialist Party Split on Rearmament', *Morning Post*, 4 March 1936.

123 See 'Labour Council and Defence', *The Times*, 5 March 1936; 'Labour Critical of Defence White Paper', *Manchester Guardian*, 5 March 1936.

124 The General Council had taken the trouble to announce that no such approach had been made, reports to the contrary. ('Labour and Defence', *The Times*, 26 February 1936.)

125 Dalton, *Fateful Years*, p. 87.

126 Bullock, *Bevin*, I, 580.

127 309 *H.C. Debs.*, 9 March 1936, cols 1865 and 1851.

128 *Ibid.*, 10 March 1936, cols 2073 and 2079.

129 Quoted by John Bowle, *Viscount Samuel* (London, 1957), p. 299.

130 310 *H.C. Debs.*, 16 March 1936, col. 82.

131 312 *H.C. Debs.*, 21 May 1936, col. 1426. Conservative back benchers were generally critical of the appointment; e.g. Earl Winterton, a fervid Tory, regarded Inskip as an able man but held that his lack of administrative experience made the appointment 'fantastic'. (*Orders of the Day*, London 1953, p. 214.)

132 Lord Ismay, *The Memoirs of General Lord Ismay* (N.Y., 1960), p. 75.

133 313 *H.C. Debs.*, 23 June 1936, cols 1708-9, where Baldwin is quoted as well.

134 Dalton, *Fateful Years*, p. 90.

135 Quoted in 'Labour and Defence', *Manchester Guardian*, 25 July 1936.

136 Dalton, *Fateful Years*, p. 90.

137 Cf. division lists given in 315 *H.C. Debs.*, 20 July 1936, cols 195-6 with 201-2, cols 205-6 with 213-14 and see also *ibid.*, 27 July 1936, division lists in cols 1245-6, 1249-50 and 1253-4. The division list for Foreign Office Supply, cols 1217-18, establishes the presence of the eight in the Commons.

138 Attlee, *Labour Party in Perspective*, pp. 270-1.

139 William Gillies, 'The European Situation and Labour Policy', 1 September 1936 (unpublished).

140 *Trades Union Congress Report, 1936*, p. 358.

141 Dalton, *Fateful Years*, p. 30.

142 E.g. 'Socialists and Arms Policy', *Morning Post*, 19 September 1936; 'Foreign Policy and Rearmament', *The Times*, 19 September 1936.

143 'Labour and Arms', *Observer*, 20 September 1936. Oddly enough, this account implies that Dalton was one of the least resolute for rearmament, some distance behind Attlee and Morrison.

144 *LPCR, 1936*, pp. 182 and 184.
145 Dalton, *Fateful Years*, p. 103.
146 *LPCR, 1936*, pp. 193 and 194.
147 *Ibid.*, p. 203.
148 *Ibid.*, pp. 203–4.
149 Bullock, *Bevin*, I, 586; *LPCR, 1936*, p. 206.
150 Cole, *Labour Party*, pp. 324–5.
151 Foot, *Bevan*, I, 226.
152 Dalton, *Fateful Years*, p. 95.
153 Puzzo, *Spain*, pp. 61–6.
154 Thomas, *Spanish Civil War*, pp. 288–9; Puzzo, *Spain*, p. 83.
155 *LPCR, 1936*, pp. 169 and 170. In so asserting, Greenwood contradicted the traditional Labour argument that armaments manufacturers would sell to any country or faction to realize their profits.
156 *Ibid.*, p. 169.
157 *Ibid.*, pp. 179, 176, 177–8 and 173.
158 Foot, *Bevan*, I, 228; *LPCR, 1936*, p. 173.
159 *LPCR, 1936*, p. 213.
160 Foot, *Bevan*, I, 231. Both Dalton (*Fateful Years*, p. 99) and Bullock (*Bevin*, p. 587) err in asserting that Señora de Palencia was the famed Communist orator 'La Pasionaria'.
161 *LPCR, 1936*, p. 215.
162 *Ibid.*, p. 258.
163 Dalton, *Fateful Years*, p. 100.
164 *LPCR, 1936*, pp. 50 and 51.
165 *Ibid.*, p. 300.
166 Cole, *Labour Party*, p. 341.
167 Attlee's *Labour Party in Perspective* is an obvious exception, although he contemplated the formation of a front in the most dire circumstances.
168 Henry Pelling, *The British Communist Party* (London, 1958), p. 97; Wood, *Communism and British Intellectuals*, p. 60. See also Stuart Samuels, 'The Left Book Club', in *The Left-Wing Intellectuals Between the Wars, 1919–1939*, edited by Walter Laqueur and George Mosse (No. 2 of the *Journal of Contemporary History*).
169 *LPCR, 1936*, pp. 208 and 209 (Rhys Davies).
170 *Ibid.*, pp. 252 (F. Bingham) and 254.
171 These constitutional reforms were effected at the 1937 Conference.
172 Williams, *Bevin*, p. 202.
173 George Ridley, 'The Edinburgh Conference Examined', *Labour*, 4:66 (November 1936).
174 Lee, *Great Journey*, pp. 173–4.

175 Kingsley Martin, *Harold Laski* (London, 1953), pp. 105–6 (letter of 10 October 1936).
176 'A Party Adrift', *The Times*, 12 October 1936.

6   For Spain and rearmament

1 G.D.H.Cole, 'After Edinburgh', *New Statesman*, 12:580 (17 October 1936).
2 Hugh Dalton, 'More Thoughts on Edinburgh', *New Statesman*, 12:617–18 (24 October 1936).
3 'Correspondence', *New Statesman*, 12:665–6 (31 October 1936).
4 Dalton, *Fateful Years*, p. 114.
5 A.J.P.Taylor, 'Confusion on the Left', in Raymond, ed., *The Baldwin Era*, maintains that 'no one on the Left cared whom Edward VIII married, whether he married, when or how often'. (p. 179.)
6 Feiling, *Chamberlain*, p. 288.
7 Churchill, *Gathering Storm*, p. 217.
8 Dalton, *Fateful Years*, p. 111.
9 Robert Fraser, 'Hugh Dalton', *Labour*, 4:63 (November 1936).
10 Dalton, *Fateful Years*, p. 115.
11 Fraser, 'Dalton', p. 63.
12 Patricia Strauss, *Bevin & Co.* (N.Y., 1941), pp. 176–7.
13 For the latter assertion, Mary Agnes Hamilton, *Remembering My Good Friends* (London, 1944), p. 188.
14 Bullock, *Bevin*, I, 591.
15 *Ibid.*, p. 590.
16 Citrine, *Men and Work*, p. 239.
17 *Ibid.*, p. 68.
18 Bullock, *Bevin*, I, 591.
19 ACIQ Memorandum No. 473A.
20 Ibid., 'Note of Dissent'.
21 ACIQ Memorandum No. 479A.
22 ACIQ Memorandum No. 480 (May 1937).
23 Foot, *Bevan*, I, 251; author's interview of Michael Foot, 25 July 1962.
24 Foot, *Bevan*, I, 245.
25 *LPCR, 1937*, p. 270.
26 Foot, *Bevan*, I, 246.
27 Miliband, *Parliamentary Socialism*, pp. 233–4.
28 Bullock, *Bevin*, I, 596.
29 Dalton, *Fateful Years*, pp. 129 and 151, the latter quoting the *Manchester Guardian* of 15 February 1937.

30 Quoted by Davis, 'The British Labour Party and British Foreign Policy', p. 557.
31 G. D. H. Cole, *The People's Front* (London, 1937), p. 332; see also his *The Condition of Britain* (London, 1937), the latter co-authored with Margaret Cole.
32 *LPCR, 1937*, p. 27.
33 Cole, *Labour Party*, p. 349.
34 Lee, *Great Journey*, p. 286.
35 Fenner Brockway, *The Workers' Front* (London, 1938), p. 228.
36 *LPCR, 1937*, p. 27.
37 Attlee, *Labour Party in Perspective*, p. 124.
38 'The Disunited Front', *New Statesman*, 13:109 (23 January 1937).
39 Quoted in Thomas, *Spanish Civil War*, p. 310.
40 Argued by Puzzo, *Spain*, pp. 144–5.
41 *LPCR, 1937*, p. 7.
42 *Ibid.*, p. 164.
43 Strauss, *Bevin & Co.*, p. 125; Foot, *Bevan*, I, 237.
44 316 *H.C. Debs.*, 29 October 1937, col. 45.
45 E.g. *Trades Union Congress Report, 1936*, pp. 362–3.
46 316 *H.C. Debs.*, 29 October 1937, col. 58.
47 *DGFP*, D, III, 391 (No. 375; 4 July 1937).
48 Taylor, *Origins*, p. 121.
49 316 *H.C. Debs.*, 29 October 1936, cols 58–9.
50 318 *H.C. Debs.*, 1 December 1936, col. 1071 (Wise).
51 319 *H.C. Debs.*, 19 January 1937, cols 98–101 and 110–11.
52 E.g. Mussolini's instruction that '... *actual* withdrawal of the Italian volunteers was out of the question until the set-back at Guadalajara ... had been made good'. (Quoted in *DGFP*, D, III, 261, No. 238, 29 March 1937.)
53 Thomas, *Spanish Civil War*, p. 408; 322 *H.C. Debs.*, 14 April 1937, cols 1029–30.
54 *Ibid.*, 14 April 1937, cols. 1041–2 and 1053–4.
55 Thomas, *Spanish Civil War*, p. 410; 322 *H.C. Debs.*, 14 April 1937, col. 1142.
56 Thomas, *Spanish Civil War*, p. 410.
57 *Ibid.*, p. 411; after one further confrontation in which the Nationalists backed down, they made no further attempt to prevent British shipping from putting in to Bilbao.
58 322 *H.C. Debs.*, 20 April 1937, cols 1657 and 1661–2.
59 323 *H.C. Debs.*, 6 May 1937, col. 1361 (Wilkinson).
60 324 *H.C. Debs.*, 25 June 1937, cols 1546, 1551–2 and 1614.
61 326 *H.C. Debs.*, 15 July 1937, cols 1594–5 (Eden) and 1587–8 (Attlee).
62 *Ibid.*, 30 July 1937, cols 3533–4.

63 Cole, *Labour Party*, pp. 329–30.
64 *LPCR, 1937*, pp. 58–9.
65 E.g. Miliband, *Parliamentary Socialism*, p. 254, and Foot, *Bevan*, I, 253–5.
66 Feiling, *Chamberlain*, p. 291.
67 320 *H.C. Debs.*, 17 February 1937, cols 1206, 1219 and 1224.
68 *Ibid.*, 18 February 1937, col. 1407.
69 E.g. 321 *H.C. Debs.*, 11 March 1937, col. 1386 (Alexander).
70 324 *H.C. Debs.*, 25 May 1937, cols 286–7. See above, p. 70.
71 325 *H.C. Debs.*, 21 June 1937, col. 960.
72 E.g. Sinclair's remarks, 326 *H.C. Debs.*, 27 June 1937, col. 2899.
73 Dalton, *Fateful Years*, pp. 133–4.
74 'Socialists Split on Defence', *Daily Telegraph*, 4 March 1937; 'Labour Party and Defence', *The Times*, 22 July 1937.
75 Bullock, *Bevin*, I, 592–3; author's interview of Lord Citrine.
76 *Trades Union Congress Report, 1937*, p. 426.
77 Labour Party International Department, 'Memorandum on Foreign Policy and Defence' (n.d., 1937), p. 10.
78 Gillies' reference was to their Memorandum No. 479A (April 1937) which argued that the danger of war had decreased in the past six months, because both of British rearmament and the failure of German and Italian arms in Spain.
79 'Memorandum on Foreign Policy and Defence', pp. 9 and 10.
80 Dalton, *Fateful Years*, pp. 133 and 134–5.
81 326 *H.C. Debs.*, 27 July 1937, cols 3015–16, recorded the rare instance in which George Buchanan managed to vote against the Navy Estimates while at the same time acting as Teller.
82 Dalton, *Fateful Years*, p. 137.
83 Foot, *Bevan*, I, 264.
84 'Arms Race Splits Socialists', *Daily Express*, 22 July 1937; 'Labour Party and Defence', *The Times*, 22 July 1937; 'Labour's Annual Dilemma', *Manchester Guardian*, 22 July 1937.
85 'Critic', (Kingsley Martin), 'A London Diary', *New Statesman*, 14:175–6 (31 July 1937).
86 'A Rank and File Debate', *Morning Post*, 23 July 1937.
87 A point made by the late Hugh Gaitskell in an interview given the author on 17 July 1962.
88 *LPCR, 1937*, p. 207.
89 See ACIQ Memorandum No. 473A.
90 *LPCR, 1937*, p. 279.
91 Both Dalton (*Fateful Years*, p. 139) and Cole (*Labour Party*, p. 331) specify July, although the daily press did not comment until September.

92 National Council of Labour, *International Policy and Defence* (London, 1937). Despite his earlier assertion, Philip Noel-Baker remained a Labour MP after this sentiment was given official sanction.

93 Cole, *Labour Party*, p. 332.

94 See George Lansbury, *My Quest for Peace* (London, 1938).

95 Quoted in 'Labour's Rearmament Policy', *Manchester Guardian*, 20 September 1937.

96 'Strength for Peace', *Daily Herald*, 4 September 1937; 'Labour's Foreign Policy', *The Times*, 4 September, and the issues of the other papers for that date.

97 Bullock, *Bevin*, I, 593.

98 *Trades Union Congress Report, 1937*, pp. 406–7.

99 Dalton, *Fateful Years*, p. 141; *LPCR, 1937*, p. 138.

100 *LPCR, 1937*, pp. 195–6.

101 *Ibid.*, pp. 196, 201, 205 and 207.

102 Foot, *Bevan*, I, 265.

103 *LPCR, 1937*, pp. 208–9.

104 *Ibid.*, p. 211.

105 *Ibid.*, pp. 212, 214 and 215.

106 *Ibid.*, p. 157.

107 *Ibid.*, pp. 158–9.

108 E.g. Harold Laski, 'British Labour Comes to Life', *The Nation* (N.Y.), 165:559 (20 November 1937).

109 Dalton, *Fateful Years*, pp. 116–17.

110 One N.E.C. member, George Dallas, was in fact spared by this expansion; Joseph O'Toole was nonetheless defeated.

111 'Labour's Differences', *The Times*, 4 October 1937.

112 *LPCR, 1937*, p. 146.

113 Dalton, *Fateful Years*, p. 144.

114 *LPCR, 1937*, p. 154.

115 'Labour Looks Left', *The Times*, 11 October 1937; 'Comments', *New Statesman*, 14:591 (16 October 1937).

116 *LPCR, 1937*, pp. 234–5.

117 A. L. Rowse, 'The Present and Immediate Future of the Labour Party', *Political Quarterly*, 9:16 (January- March 1938).

118 *LPCR, 1937*, p. 140.

119 Gathorne-Hardy, *International Affairs*, pp. 327–31.

120 Eden, *Facing the Dictators*, pp. 593–4.

121 For this paragraph, *ibid.*, pp. 593–613.

122 Cordell Hull, *Memoirs* (2 vols, N.Y., 1948), I, 562.

123 Eden, *Facing the Dictators*, p. 616.

124 326 *H.C. Debs.*, 30 July 1937, col. 3539.

125 *LPCR, 1937*, p. 4.

126 327 *H.C. Debs.*, 21 October 1937, col. 75.
127 328 *H.C. Debs.*, 1 November 1937, col. 596.
128 Friedman, *British Relations*, p. 111.
129 Quoted, *ibid.*, p. 115, from Eden's speech of 21 December.
130 330 *H.C. Debs.*, 21 December 1937, col. 1883.
131 ACIQ Memorandum No. 470.
132 For the challenges, ACIQ Memoranda Nos 471 (November 1936) and 479A (April 1937); for Buxton's assertion, No. 482.
133 ACIQ Memoranda Nos 483 and 483A (November 1937).
134 ACIQ Memorandum No. 475 (January 1937).
135 *LPCR, 1939*, p. 5.

7   'A far away country . . .'

1 Eden, *Facing the Dictators*, p. viii.
2 Herbert Tracey, ' "Mr. President": First World Disarmament Conference', *Labour Magazine*, 10:436 (February 1932).
3 'All the World Over', *Labour*, 1 : 2 (September 1933).
4 Kennedy, *Why England Slept*, p. 157.
5 The Labour Party, *The Demand for Colonial Territories and Equality of Economic Opportunity* (London, 1936).
6 'A Talk with Hitler', *New Statesman*, 14:865 (27 November 1937).
7 *LPCR, 1937*, p. 207.
8 Bullock, *Bevin*, I, 624.
9 Victoria de Bunsen, *Charles Roden Buxton* (London, 1948), p. 157.
10 310 *H.C. Debs.*, 26 March 1936, col. 1446.
11 Harold Laski, *The Labour Party, the War and the Future* (London, 1940), p. 3.
12 Eden, *Facing the Dictators*, p. 501.
13 Hitler's first year in power had reminded him of the old aggressive Wilhelmian Germany, '. . . instigating, suggesting, encouraging bloodshed and assassination, for her old selfish aggrandizement and pride'. (Macleod, *Chamberlain*, p. 206.)
14 Feiling, *Chamberlain*, p. 329.
15 Chamberlain opened informal conversations with the Italian Ambassador, Grandi, quite on his own. (*Ibid.*, p. 330.)
16 *Ibid.*, p. 331.
17 Churchill subsequently wrote that the Nyon Conference offered 'a proof of how powerful the combined influence of Britain and France, if expressed with conviction and a readiness to use force, would have been upon the mood and policy of the Dictators'. (*Gathering Storm*, p. 248.)

18 Feiling, *Chamberlain*, pp. 332–3 (diary entry of 26 November). The meeting, initially scheduled for Berlin, was shifted to Berchtesgaden at Hitler's behest; Eden, who was far from keen on the entire project, warned against the change of venue, arguing that '... it is essential to avoid giving the impression of our being in pursuit of the German Chancellor'. (*Facing the Dictators*, p. 578.)

19 Bullock, *Hitler*, pp. 336–9, sketches the contents of the 'Hossbach Memorandum'. Cf. Taylor, *Origins*, pp. 131–4.

20 Eden, *Facing the Dictators*, pp. 625 and 627.

21 *Ibid.*, pp. 661–2. Grandi reported that Chamberlain, '... in addressing his questions directly to me, expected from me – this was obvious – nothing more nor less than those details and definite answers which were useful to him as ammunition against Eden'. (*Ciano's Diplomatic Papers*, ed. by Malcolm Muggeridge, London 1948, pp. 175–6.)

22 332 *H.C. Debs.*, 21 February 1938, col. 49; for Chamberlain's narrowing of the issue, col. 63.

23 *Ibid.*, 21 February 1938, cols 51–2.

24 *Ibid.*, 21 February 1938, cols 65 and 72.

25 *Ibid.*, 21 February 1938, col. 112 (Griffiths).

26 *Ibid.*, 22 February 1938, cols 219, 213, 227 and 229.

27 *Ibid.*, 22 February 1938, col. 310.

28 The Labour Party, *Labour and the Crisis in Foreign Policy* (London, 1938), p. 3.

29 Feiling, *Chamberlain*, p. 339; Churchill had cautioned Eden that he should not allow personal feelings of friendship for his late colleagues to hamper his doing full justice to his own views. (Eden, *Facing the Dictators*, p. 679.)

30 Foot, *Bevan*, I, 272.

31 '... I had firmly resolved that it would never come to that. One cannot sacrifice many lives to save a few – especially when the eventual outcome of such a contest was not even doubtful, as in our case.' (Kurt von Schuschnigg, *Austrian Requiem*, N.Y. 1946, p. 44). See also Bullock, *Hitler*, pp. 385–7.

32 For Eden's account, *Facing the Dictators*, pp. 655–84; cf. Gordon Brook-Shepherd, *Anschluss: The Rape of Austria* (London, 1963), p. 187.

33 E.g. Bellenger's reminder to the government that '... the integrity and independence of Austria are declared objects of British policy...' (331 *H.C. Debs.*, 16 February 1938, col. 1862.)

34 332 *H.C. Debs.*, 2 March 1938, cols 1246 and 1248.

35 333 *H.C. Debs.*, 14 March 1938, col. 52.

36 The point is forcefully made by Brook-Shepherd, *Anschluss*,

pp. 89–92. Eden confirms the Austrian Government's '. . . playing down of the odious truth' concerning Hitler's pressure upon Schuschnigg. (The Earl of Avon [Anthony Eden], *The Reckoning*, Boston 1965, p. 7.)

37 333 *H.C. Debs.*, 14 March 1938, cols 54 and 55.

38 Churchill, *Gathering Storm*, p. 272.

39 See the remarks of A.V. Alexander, 333 *H.C. Debs.*, 14 March 1938, cols 152–3.

40 *Ibid.*, 24 March 1938, cols 1402–6; he had remarked four days earlier that 'you have only to look at the map to see that nothing we or France could do could possibly save Czechoslovakia from being overrun by the Germans, if they wanted to do it'. (Feiling, *Chamberlain*, p. 347.) This strategic concept was quietly abandoned in 1939, when Britain guaranteed Poland.

41 333 *H.C. Debs.*, 24 March 1938, col. 1421.

42 Feiling, *Chamberlain*, pp. 341–2.

43 Gathorne-Hardy, *International Affairs*, pp. 457–9.

44 335 *H.C. Debs.*, 2 May 1938, cols 545, 547 and 645.

45 Macleod, *Chamberlain*, pp. 119–20.

46 328 *H.C. Debs.*, 26 October 1937, col. 21; 27 October 1937, cols 197 and 89 (Greenwood).

47 330 *H.C. Debs.*, 21 December 1937, col. 1831.

48 332 *H.C. Debs.*, 7 March 1938, col. 1564; the Labour amendment is cited, col. 1567.

49 *Ibid.*, 7 March 1938, col. 1660.

50 333 *H.C. Debs.*, 15 March 1938, cols 254–5.

51 *LPCR, 1939*, p. 138; 333 *H.C. Debs.*, 15 March 1938, col. 335.

52 Dalton, *Fateful Years*, p. 165.

53 *Idem.*

54 Churchill, *Gathering Storm*, p. 232.

55 335 *H.C. Debs.*, 12 May 1938, cols 1763 and 1792.

56 Dalton, *Fateful Years*, p. 166.

57 336 *H.C. Debs.*, 25 May 1938, col. 1255.

58 Quoted in Dalton, *Fateful Years*, p. 169.

59 Quoted, *ibid.*, p. 170.

60 *Ibid.*, p. 171, for Dalton's admission that some credit for substantial improvements in the strength and equipment of the RAF must go to Swinton's slowly maturing programmes.

61 *Ibid.*, p. 208.

62 Cole, *The People's Front*, p. 103.

63 Cole, *Labour Party*, pp. 352–3.

64 Foot, *Bevan*, I, 279, n. 1.

65 Quoted in Cooke, *Cripps*, p. 197, from *Tribune* of 14 June 1938.

66 Dalton's account fails to note the role played either by *Reynolds'*
News or the *News Chronicle*; even more tellingly, he fails to mention
Spain at all after 1937. (Foot, *Bevan*, I, 277, n. 1.) Citrine too
subsequently found himself compelled by exigencies of space to
omit a chapter dealing with the Spanish Civil War (*Men and Work*,
p. 10).

67 Foot describes as 'ludicrous falsehoods' Dalton's allegations,
'... designed to bolster Dalton's other charge that Cripps was
concerned with a publicity stunt for himself; that he ran *Tribune*
as a paper dedicated to "the worship of One Leader, the projection
of his Unique Personality and the promotion of his Personal
Policy".' (*Bevan*, I, 277, n. 1.) Dalton's rancour may well have
run this deep, but surely he had political intentions in mind as well
– even after the fact.

68 Quoted, *ibid.*, p. 279.

69 James Jupp, 'The Left in Britain: 1931 to 1941', unpublished
M Sc. thesis (1956), in the University of London Library, pp. 555–64.

70 *LPCR, 1939*, p. 43.

71 The Labour Party, *Labour and the Popular Front* (London, 1938),
p. 5.

72 Foot, *Bevan*, I, 278–9.

73 'Labour and Europe's Troubles', *Reynolds' News*, 31 July 1938.

74 Cole, *Labour Party*, p. 356.

75 Hugh Dalton, 'Some Impressions of Czechoslovakia', *New Statesman*, 9:709 (18 May 1935).

76 Hugh Dalton, 'England and Europe', *Contemporary Review*,
148:129–37 (August 1935).

77 ACIQ Memorandum No. 490A. This argument has in fact become
the principal component of Conservative apologetics dealing with
Munich.

78 ACIQ Memorandum No. 494 (May 1938).

79 Lord Noel-Buxton, 'England and Germany', *Contemporary
Review*, 153:8 (January 1938).

80 Churchill, *Gathering Storm*, pp. 273–4.

81 *DBFP*, 3s., I, 85–6 (No. 106, Enclosure).

82 The British Military Attaché to the Berlin Embassy discredited the
Czech reports and so, implicitly, Hitler's involvement, on 24 May.
(*DBFP*, 3s., I, 380–1, No. 316, Enclosure.)

83 Bullock, *Hitler*, pp. 408–9.

84 Wheeler-Bennett regards this situation as '... an example of successful powers terrified at their own success ...' almost without
parallel. (*Munich: Prologue to Tragedy*, London 1948, pp. 62–3.)

85 338 *H.C. Debs.*, 26 July 1938, col. 2960.

86 *Ibid.*, 26 July 1938, cols 2969–70. Eden is critical even of the principle of the mission, because the British government thereby '... committed themselves to meditation without undertaking to uphold the result'. (*The Reckoning*, p. 28).

87 338 *H.C. Debs.*, 26 July 1938, cols 2969–70.

88 Dalton, *Fateful Years*, p. 173.

89 *LPCR, 1939*, pp. 13–14.

90 *Ibid.*, p. 14; the last sentence, garbled there, is taken from the text printed in 'Clear Warning to Germany', *Manchester Guardian*, 8 September 1938. Andrew Rothstein, in a book (*The Munich Conspiracy*, London 1958) critical of the actions of every country except Soviet Russia in the Czech crisis, flaws the British Labour Party for refusing, until this declaration, to give whole-hearted support to the Czechoslovaks, e.g. by giving qualified approval to the Runciman Mission. This approval fostered the impression that 'Runciman might be used for some purpose *other* than that of intimidating Czechoslovakia' (p. 211). Rothstein's criticism of the Labour Party hinges upon his assumption that the party's leaders should have seen that Chamberlain was not looking toward settlement of Sudeten grievances through some form of autonomy, but rather favoured dismemberment. As Chamberlain did not decide to intervene directly until 13 September, Rothstein demands that Labour anticipate that decision and act accordingly.

91 Wheeler-Bennett, *Munich*, pp. 90–1.

92 *Trades Union Congress Report, 1938*, p. 372; 'Parliament and the Crisis', *Daily Telegraph*, 14 September 1938. Halifax, however, used the Labour manifesto in an attempt to bring Hitler to recognize that war could result if he failed to negotiate on the basis of the proposals recently put forth by the Czech government. (*DBFP*, 3s., II, 277–8, No. 815.)

93 *Ibid.*, p. 314 (No. 862). Chamberlain had, however, considered the possibility of such a trip as early as 30 August (n. 1).

94 *Ibid.*, p. 310 (No. 855); see also Nos. 852, 857 and 861. Rothstein at this point indicts the Labour Party for granting Chamberlain a '... blank cheque, given him in advance, and in full knowledge of his previous policy ...' (p. 214) to proceed to his fateful meeting with Hitler at Berchtesgaden by Attlee's approval of that journey '... in Parliament on September 14 ...' (p. 213). The House of Commons in fact did not sit from 29 July to 28 September. This central flaw concerning a supposed blank cheque vitiates much of his argument.

95 Feiling, *Chamberlain*, p. 365.

96 280 *H.C. Debs.*, 5 July 1933, col. 359.

97 This paragraph is based upon Dalton, *Fateful Years*, pp. 176–83, and Citrine, *Men and Work*, pp. 361–6. One discrepancy is Dalton's omission of Citrine's comment to Chamberlain that '. . the preponderance of opinion on the National Council of Labour was that he had done the right thing' in going to see Hitler.

98 Citrine, *Men and Work*, p. 365. That this possibility may not have seemed far-fetched to Chamberlain is indicated by his biographer's assertion that the Prime Minister returned thinking that '. . . he [Hitler] could not be long-lived in this state of hysteria . . .' (Feiling, *Chamberlain*, p. 365.)

99 *LPCR, 1939*, p. 15. The role of Labour's Leader in the deliberations of the National Council of Labour is enigmatic. Citrine complains about the lack of guidance supplied by Attlee: 'He was referred to by my colleagues on the General Council as "Clam Attlee" and worthily he sustained the reputation.' (p. 367.)

100 *LPCR, 1939*, p. 15.

101 E.g. *DBFP*, 3s., II, nos 973, 991, 998, and 1007.

102 *Ibid.*, p. 450 (No. 1007).

103 Dalton, *Fateful Years*, p. 185.

104 *LPCR, 1939*, p. 16.

105 Dalton, *Fateful Years*, p. 188. Halifax talked to Eden in virtually these terms on 11 October. (Eden, *The Reckoning*, p. 42.)

106 *DBFP*, 3s., II, 465 (No. 1033). Ivone Kirkpatrick, who made these British notes, elsewhere quotes the German: 'Es tut mir leid, aber das geht nicht mehr.' (*The Inner Circle: Memoirs*, London 1959, p. 115.) A better translation is: 'I'm sorry, but they [the proposals] will no longer do.'

107 *Idem.*

108 *DBFP*, 3s., II, 473 (No. 1033).

109 Bullock, *Hitler*, p. 420.

110 *DBFP*, 3s., II, 519 (No. 1092) and 541–2 (No. 1097).

111 Rothstein's censure of the Labour Party's agreement at this time with Chamberlain that the terms themselves were no longer a subject of dispute (p. 217) ignores the continuing readiness of the Czech government to abide by the Anglo-French proposals.

112 Dalton, *Fateful Years*, pp. 197–8.

113 Bullock, *Hitler*, p. 426; *DBFP*, 3s., II, 565–6 (No. 1129).

114 Quoted by Feiling, *Chamberlain*, p. 372.

115 *DBFP*, 3s., II, 578 (No. 1144).

116 *Ibid.*, p. 587 (No. 1158).

117 *Ibid.*, pp. 587–8 (No. 1159).

118 For Chamberlain's significant omissions, see Wheeler-Bennett, *Munich*, p. 169, n. 3.

NOTES

119 Dunglass subsequently became the Earl of Home and ultimately Sir Alec Douglas-Home. Curiously, this information was not conveyed to Chamberlain until 4.15, though the Foreign Office had received word from Berlin a full hour earlier (see *DBFP*, 3s., II, 593–4, No. 1174).

120 Subsequently he informed Benes that '. . . I shall have the interests of Czechoslovakia fully in mind . . .' (*ibid.*, p. 599, No. 1184).

121 Feiling, *Chamberlain*, p. 374; 339 *H.C. Debs.*, 28 September 1938, col. 28. By ignoring the latter part of Attlee's statement, Rothstein is able to revert to his pet metaphor, Labour's giving to Chamberlain 'a blank cheque' to do as he wished. (*The Munich Conspiracy*, p. 217.)

122 339 *H.C. Debs.*, 28 September 1938, col. 28.

123 *Nicolson: Diaries and Letters, 1930–1939*, p. 371.

124 *Ibid.*, p. 371, n. 1; Wheeler-Bennett, *Munich*, p. 170; Eden, *The Reckoning*, p. 33.

125 'Eleventh Hour Peace Move', *The Times*, 29 September 1939; 'The Scene in Commons', *Manchester Guardian*, same day.

126 *LPCR, 1939*, p. 251 (Noel-Baker).

127 *Ibid.*, p. 18.

128 The judgment of Chamberlain's authorized biographer: Feiling, *Chamberlain*, p. 375.

129 *DBFP*, 3s., II, 640 (No. 1228, Appendix). The text of the agreement is given, *ibid.*, pp. 627–9 (No. 1224).

130 Chamberlain's own description, *ibid.*, p. 504 (No. 1073).

131 Gathorne-Hardy, *International Affairs*, p. 474.

132 Alfred Duff Cooper, *Old Men Forget* (N.Y., 1954), p. 246; 339 *H.C. Debs.*, 3 October 1938, col. 45.

133 339 *H.C. Debs.*, 3 October 1938, col. 52.

134 *Ibid.*, 3 October 1938, col. 56.

135 *Ibid.*, 3 October 1938, col. 58 and 4 October, col. 357. Despite Attlee's speech, A.J.P.Taylor maintains that Labour used the moral argument against Munich that '. . . the frontiers of existing states were sacred and that each state could behave as it liked within its own borders.' This defence of 'legitimacy' Taylor regards as a strange and ineffective argument for the British left to use in 1938. Even stranger is Taylor's presentation of Labour's position! (*Origins*, p. 184.)

136 Harold Macmillan traces the establishment of two distinct groupings among the Conservative dissenters to the summer of 1938. Both the Churchill faction and the larger Eden grouping were concerned with the prospects for Chamberlain's foreign policy. Macmillan '. . . acted in a sense as a link between the two bodies',

and Churchill and Eden remained in close contact as well. (*Winds of Change, 1914–1939*, London 1966, pp. 548–9.)

137 Dalton, *Fateful Years*, p. 185.
138 *Ibid.*, p. 199.
139 339 *H.C. Debs.*, 4 October 1938, cols 351, 353–5.
140 Churchill, *Gathering Storm*, pp. 326–8; such a charge seems quite irrelevant unless one is prepared to argue that Chamberlain agreed to the Munich terms because of the parlous state of British defences rather than to secure 'peace in our time'. Churchill, however, does not subscribe to that view; thus he apparently argues that the Labour Party, because of past errors, had no right to maintain a correct policy in the fall of 1938. Eden, we should note, voices the same irrelevant criticism of Labour. (*The Reckoning*, p. 4.)
141 339 *H.C. Debs.*, 6 October 1938, col. 548.
142 For this incident, Dalton, *Fateful Years*, pp. 200–3.
143 *Ibid.*, pp. 199–203, by far the fullest account of the negotiations; Eden offers nothing, and Macmillan (*Winds of Change*, pp. 568–9) serves only to confirm Dalton's memory.
144 Francis Williams, *A Prime Minister Remembers* (London, 1961), p. 20.
145 Ivor Davies, *Trial by Ballot* (London, 1950), pp. 144–5.
146 Amery, *Political Life*, III, 298–9.
147 Wheeler-Bennett, *Munich*, p. 184. Nicolas Mansergh, *Survey of British Commonwealth Affairs: Problems of External Policy* (London, 1952), shows this opposition in great detail but concludes that Chamberlain's policy owed little or nothing to Dominion inspiration. (p. 439.)
148 For this incident, Dalton, *Fateful Years*, p. 189.
149 Wheeler-Bennett, *Munich*, p. 106, Rothstein, *Munich Conspiracy*, ch. viii, and The Ministry for Foreign Affairs of the Czechoslovak Republic and The Ministry for Foreign Affairs of the USSR, *New Documents on the History of Munich* (Prague, 1958), Preface, argue – the latter two tendentiously – that Russia was prepared to defend Czechoslovakia. Cf. Langer and Gleason, *Challenge to Isolation*, ch. iii, and Henry L. Roberts, 'Maxim Litvinov', in *The Diplomats*, p. 376.
150 William R. Shirer, *The Rise and Fall of the Third Reich* (New York, 1960), p. 413; for a negative assessment of this possibility, John Wheeler-Bennett, *The Nemesis of Power* (New York, 1954), pp. 420–4.
151 Dalton, *Fateful Years*, p. 204.
152 Wheeler-Bennett, *Munich*, p. 435.

153 For affirmative opinions, Churchill, *Gathering Storm*, pp. 336–9, and Amery, *Political Life*, III, 289–92; for expert military advice to the contrary, *Time Unguarded: The Ironside Diaries, 1937–1940*, edited by Col. Roderick Macleod and Denis Kelly (New York, 1962), pp. 61–2, and the views of Lord Trenchard, quoted in Wheeler-Bennett, *Munich*, p. 435.

154 Kennedy, *Why England Slept*, p. 191. He and Hoare (*Troubled Years*, pp. 332–6) miss the point that in 1938 the striking range of the Luftwaffe was only 300 miles; thus the danger of air attack was not comparable to that of 1940, when the attack came at much closer range.

155 Cf. the strongest statement of the case for the 'historical facts' of British rearmament in the 'year of grace', in vivid contrast to the 'highly conjectural' advantages allegedly lost to Britain through failure to fight in 1938: Macleod, *Chamberlain*, p. 266.

8 The last months of peace

1 Foot, *Bevan*, I, 286.
2 Cooke, *Cripps*, p. 231.
3 Although scheduled to meet in two weeks' time, the NEC agreed to this special meeting, despite what they subsequently characterized as 'the preemptory character of this demand'. (*LPCR, 1939*, p. 48.)
4 Quoted in Foot, *Bevan*, I, 287.
5 Cooke, *Cripps*, p. 231.
6 Dalton, *Fateful Years*, p. 210. In defence of Cripps' action, we must note that he had informed the Executive that he considered it his right to circulate the memorandum if they rejected it; when, a year earlier, Cripps had offered a similar proposal, the Executive had circularized to the affiliated organizations a full statement of the majority position, while Cripps' views went undefended. In 1939, he was looking to his own interests – and those of his proposal.
7 For an incisive discussion of Cripps' 'Anglican conscience', which dictated this refusal to compromise, see David Marquand, 'Sir Stafford Cripps', in *Age of Austerity*, edited by Michael Sissons and Philip French (London, 1963), pp. 177–8.
8 Dalton, *Fateful Years*, p. 211.
9 *LPCR, 1939*, p. 46; Dalton, *Fateful Years*, p. 212. Pritt would have voted against expulsion had he been able to attend.
10 The Labour Party, *Unity: True or Sham?* (London, 1939), p. 5.
11 Cooke, *Cripps*, p. 235.
12 *Unity: True or Sham?*

13 R. H. S. Crossman, 'Sir Stafford and the Younger Generation', *New Statesman*, 17:118 (28 January 1939).

14 'A Plea for Compromise', *New Statesman*, 17:413 (18 March 1939).

15 Foot, *Bevan*, I, 288–9.

16 Quoted, *ibid.*, p. 289.

17 Quoted in Dalton, *Fateful Years*, p. 214.

18 We look in vain for an explanation of the use of this technique by either Cripps' or Bevan's biographer.

19 Foot, *Bevan*, I, 288.

20 *LPCR, 1939*, pp. 49 and 51.

21 Dalton, *Fateful Years*, p. 217; Foot, *Bevan*, I, 291 ignores the separate decisions in claiming that the majority for expulsion was only two, when in fact the majority was ten.

22 Quoted in Strauss, *Cripps*, p. 121.

23 Cooke, *Cripps*, p. 236.

24 *Ibid.*, p. 242.

25 Jenkins, *Attlee*, p. 209.

26 Marquand, 'Cripps', pp. 179–80.

27 For Chamberlain's remarks, 340 *H.C. Debs.*, 2 November 1938, col. 321. Halifax privately expressed the government's reasoning: 'If we fail to take what is probably our last chance of bringing the Agreement into force . . . Mussolini will be likely finally to conclude that we are not in fact at all anxious to resume normal Anglo-Italian friendship; and Berlin–Rome Axis will be proportionally strengthened.' (*DBFP*, 3s., III, 344, No. 358, 27 October 1938.)

28 *Ibid.*, p. 345 (No. 360).

29 340 *H.C. Debs.*, 2 November 1938, cols 217 and 321.

30 342 *H.C. Debs.*, 19 December 1938, cols 2511 and 2523. When autonomy was granted to Slovakia in November 1938, the country's name was transmogrified, in a manner symbolic of the internal division forced upon her, to Czecho-Slovakia. This distinction is observed throughout this chapter.

31 *Ibid.*, 19 December 1938, cols 2525–6.

32 343 *H.C. Debs.*, 31 January 1939, cols 69 and 79.

33 Puzzo, *Spain and the Great Powers*, p. 200.

34 Thomas, *Spanish Civil War*, p. 583.

35 Feiling, *Chamberlain*, p. 393.

36 344 *H.C. Debs.*, 28 February 1939, cols 1099 and 1105–6.

37 E.g. George Strauss, still within Labour ranks, insisted: 'If there were real non-intervention, if the British Government really stood by its principles and either insisted on the withdrawal of the foreign help which General Franco has, or else restored to the central Government in Spain its proper rights, the central Government

would very soon be able to drive General Franco from the shores of Spain.' (*Ibid.*, 28 February 1939, cols 1119 – Chamberlain – and 1160.)

38 Thomas, *Spanish Civil War*, p. 584.
39 *DBFP*, 3s., III, 379 (No. 397; 3 December) and 387 (No. 403; 6 December).
40 343 *H.C. Debs.*, 7 February 1939, cols 797–803, 824–5.
41 Feiling, *Chamberlain*, p. 396.
42 Wheeler-Bennett, *Munich*, pp. 329–30.
43 Bullock, *Hitler*, pp. 433, 438–9. Without entering into the controversy recently provoked by A.J.P.Taylor's revisionist account of the diplomacy of 1939, I will generally follow the orthodox version, typified by Bullock; Taylor makes a number of interesting and valid points, several of which are incorporated in my account.
44 Bullock, *Hitler*, p. 445. Taylor apparently expects that Hacha should have known that Hitler's threat to bomb Prague was 'the most casual of Hitler's many improvisations ... the German air fields were shrouded in fog'. (*Origins*, p. 202.) Fog is not, however, a permanent meteorological condition.
45 345 *H.C. Debs.*, 14 March 1939, col. 223.
46 Wheeler-Bennett, *Munich*, p. 352.
47 345 *H.C. Debs.*, 15 March 1939, col. 437.
48 For these criticisms, *ibid.*, 15 March 1939, cols 443, 449 and 545.
49 *Ibid.*, 15 March 1939, cols 460–2.
50 *Ibid.*, 16 March 1939, col. 613; Wheeler-Bennett, *Munich*, p. 355. Neither Wheeler-Bennett nor Halifax's biographers, however, indicate the process by which the Foreign Secretary moved from his statement on the afternoon of 15 March, couched in the terms of appeasement and clearly preconcerted with Chamberlain's statement (112 *H.L. Debs.*, cols 214–18; 345 *H.C. Debs.*, cols 435–40), to his subsequent resolute advice.
51 Quoted in Feiling, *Chamberlain*, pp. 400 and 403.
52 345 *H.C. Debs.*, 3 April 1939, col. 2481. Greenwood deliberately chose to speak about mutual aid, because he recognized that the Conservatives did not like the term 'collective security'. The important matter was the inclusion of Russia, no matter what the arrangement was called.
53 Dalton, *Fateful Years*, p. 230.
54 The leader is excerpted, *ibid.*, p. 239, n. 1; see also pp. 242–3.
55 See Gilbert and Gott, *Appeasers*, pts. three and four, and Taylor, *Origins*, p. 199.
56 348 *H.C. Debs.*, 8 June 1939, cols 644–5 (Burgin) and 664–5.
57 344 *H.C. Debs.*, 8 March 1939, col. 2271.

58 Dalton, *Fateful Years*, p. 175.
59 Eden, *The Reckoning*, p. 61; the same mark is made against the Liberals, we should add.
60 336 *H.C.Debs.*, 30 May 1938, col. 1778.
61 *Ibid.*, 30 May 1938, col. 1790. Obviously the quotation was not direct.
62 The Labour Party, *Labour's Claim to Government* (London, 1938), p. 8.
63 John Wheeler-Bennett, *John Anderson, Viscount Waverley* (London, 1962), pp. 213–14.
64 Cole, *Labour Party*, p. 362.
65 342 *H.C. Debs.*, 6 December 1938, cols 1038, 1045–6, 1050 and 1124. That the force of Labour's argument against conscription was lost even upon those who were willing to give the party a hearing is apparent in Macmillan's comment: 'By some strange aberration, British Socialists still regarded the obligation of military service, applicable to the whole nation, as undemocratic.' (*Winds of Change*, p. 594.)
66 *LPCR, 1939*, p. 22.
67 342 *H.C. Debs.*, 20 December 1938, cols 2744 – Greenwood – and 2766.
68 Foot, *Bevan*, I, 284.
69 Bullock, *Bevin*, I, 636.
70 *LPCR, 1939*, pp. 20 and 22.
71 342 *H.C. Debs.*, 20 December 1938, col. 2818; *LPCR, 1939*, p. 20.
72 *DBFP*, 3s., IV, 489 (No. 507; 23 March 1939).
73 *DBFP*, 3s., V, 251–2 (No. 227; 20 April 1939).
74 Wheeler-Bennett, *Munich*, p. 380, n. 1; Feiling, *Chamberlain*, p. 405.
75 Quoted in R. J. Minney, *The Private Papers of Hore-Belisha* (London, 1960), p. 196.
76 346 *H.C. Debs.*, 26 April 1939, cols 1151–4 and 1155.
77 *Ibid.*, 27 April 1939, cols 1345–6, 1349 and 1352.
78 *Nicolson: Diaries, 1930–1939*, p. 400.
79 346 *H.C. Debs.*, 27 April 1939, col. 1372.
80 *Ibid.*, 27 April 1939, cols 1352–61.
81 Bullock, *Bevin*, I, 637.
82 Foot, *Bevan*, I, 294.
83 So reported the British Ambassador in Paris, with specific reference to MM. Delbos and Blum. (*DBFP*, 3s., V, 356, No. 303; 28 April.) Blum himself wrote in *Le Populaire* on 27 April: 'I do not hesitate to state to my Labour comrades my deepest conviction that at the

very moment at which I write, conscription in England is one of the capital acts upon which the peace of the world hangs.' (Colton, *Blum*, p. 321.)

84 Dalton, *Fateful Years*, p. 250.

85 Clement Attlee, *As It Happened* (London, 1954), p. 104; in making the latter remark, Attlee added that 'it's not always a good idea to change your system approaching war', but one would think that recruitment is certainly one system which should be changed in such a situation! (Williams, *A Prime Minister Remembers*, pp. 18–19.)

86 Jenkins, *Attlee*, p. 200.

87 R.H.S.Crossman, 'Labour and Compulsory Military Service', *Political Quarterly*, 10:309–21 (July–September 1939).

88 Bullock, *Bevin*, I, 638.

89 For once, however, Miliband does not raise this argument, because he regards Labour's opposition to conscription as 'profoundly mistaken'. (*Parliamentary Socialism*, p. 265.)

90 *LPCR, 1939*, pp. 226 and 228.

91 Dalton's implication, *Fateful Years*, p. 218; *LPCR, 1939*, p. 230.

92 Dalton, *Fateful Years*, p. 219.

93 R.H.S.Crossman, 'Labour Lays a Ghost', *New Statesman*, 17:849 (3 June 1939).

94 *LPCR, 1939*, p. 293.

95 Cooke, *Cripps*, pp. 240–1.

96 Dalton, *Fateful Years*, p. 245.

97 For Perth's warnings, *DBFP*, 3s., V, 117 (Nos. 68 and 69; 3 April); for Italian assurances, *ibid.*, pp. 125 (No. 77; 6 April) and 129 (No. 83; 7 April).

98 346 *H.C. Debs.*, 13 April 1939, cols 13–14, 16–17 and 20–1.

99 *LPCR, 1939*, pp. 240–1.

100 *Ibid.*, p. 247.

101 *Ibid.*, p. 282.

102 *Ibid.*, p. 284.

103 *Ibid.*, p. 250.

104 *Ibid.*, p. 285 (A.F.Seares).

105 *Ibid.*, p. 330.

106 Quoted in 'Labour Movement and Crisis', *Manchester Guardian*, 22 March 1939.

107 346 *H.C. Debs.*, 3 April 1939, cols 130 and 136.

108 Wheeler-Bennett, *Munich*, p. 394.

109 *DBFP*, 3s., V, 206 (No. 170) and 228–9 (No. 201).

110 *Ibid.*, p. 252 (No. 229; 20 April 1939).

111 *Ibid.*, pp. 267 (No. 247; 21 April 1939) and 451 (No. 398; 6 May 1939).
112 347 *H.C. Debs.*, 19 May 1939, col. 1821.
113 *Ibid.*, 19 May 1939, cols 1837 and 1847.
114 *LPCR, 1939*, p. 240.
115 Eden, *The Reckoning*, p. 63.
116 Feiling, *Chamberlain*, p. 403.
117 *DBFP*, 3s., V, 8 (No. 1).
118 Wheeler-Bennett, *Munich*, p. 389.
119 Graubard, *British Labour and the Russian Revolution*, pp. 291–2.
120 Dalton, *Fateful Years*, p. 249; Churchill, *Gathering Storm*, pp. 362–5.
121 *DBFP*, 3s., V, 679–80 (No. 624; 25 May) and 753 (No. 697; 2 June).
122 348 *H.C. Debs.*, 7 June 1939, cols 400–1.
123 On 8 June, the French Ambassador in London canvassed the possibility of sending some distinguished personage to Moscow to carry on the negotiations, but Cadogan of the Foreign Office presented to him – unfortunately he did not record them for posterity – the arguments which weighed against such a mission. (*DBFP*, 3s., VI, 4, No. 3.)
124 Wheeler-Bennett, *Munich*, p. 404.
125 E.g. Wrench's description of his own feelings, in *Dawson and Our Times*, p. 392, n. 1.
126 Lord Strang, *Britain in World Affairs* (London, 1961), p. 326. Such knowledge does not, however, undercut Taylor's assertion that 'the British . . . did not anticipate a deal between Moscow and Berlin.' (*Origins*, p. 231.)
127 Halifax summarized the British position in this regard on 12 July: '. . . a claim to interpret and pass judgment upon the actions of an independent State is one to which H.M.G. could not possibly be a party.' (*DBFP*, 3s., VI, 333, No. 298.)
128 For this altogether strange – and diplomatically unorthodox – incident, see Ivan Maisky, *Who Helped Hitler?* (London, 1964), p. 165.
129 Sir Lewis Namier, *Diplomatic Prelude, 1938–1939* (London, 1948), p. 202. Namier contrasts this leisurely procedure with Ribbentrop's hurried flight to Moscow on 23 August, when he took an entourage of thirty-two in a Focke-Wulf Condor.
130 *DBFP*, 3s., VI, 674 (No. 638).
131 350 *H.C. Debs.*, 31 July 1939, cols 2012 and 2020.
132 Chamberlain's attitude earlier in the month was noted by General Ironside in his diary for 10 July: 'Chamberlain said that it seemed

impossible to come to an understanding with Russia. Did I think it was right? I told him that though it was much against the grain, it was the only thing we could do. Chamberlain ejaculated "The only thing we cannot do".' (*Time Unguarded*, p. 78.)

133 350 *H.C. Debs.*, 2 August 1939, cols 2428 and 2454.

134 *Ibid.*, 2 August 1939, cols 2512–13; see also col. 2474 (Reed).

135 Department of State, United States, *Nazi-Soviet Relations, 1939–1941*, edited by R. J. Sontag and J. S. Beddie (Washington, 1948), p. 34 (27 July 1939).

136 *Ibid.*, pp. 36 and 39–41.

137 *DBFP*, 3s., VI, 591–2 (No. 539).

138 *Nazi-Soviet Relations*, p. 50.

139 *Ibid.*, pp. 58 (16 August 1939) and 66–7 (20 August).

140 Sir Lewis Namier, astute student of the negotiations, spelled out the reasons why Britain could not agree to cede the border countries to Russia, even as a sphere of interest: 'This Germany could do, but not the artificers of the post-1918 settlement, of the League of Nations, and finally of the guarantee treaties of March–April 1939 (to accept a *fait accompli* was a different matter). Through an alliance with Britain and France, Russia could not even hope to recover the territories east of the Curzon Line which the verdict of the Principal Allied and Associated Powers had originally assigned to her.' (*Diplomatic Prelude*, p. xvi.)

141 The Earl of Halifax, *Fulness of Days* (London, 1957), p. 207.

142 George Kennan, *Russia and the West under Lenin and Stalin* (Boston, 1961), p. 328.

143 Taylor's arguments are developed in *Origins*, pp. 230–47; it is well worth keeping in mind his reminder that the lack of evidence for the internal workings of Soviet policy forces all historians to conjecture, whether they work from outward appearances or personal prejudices.

144 Stalin's foremost biographer believes that the Russian leader was long undecided and that he made up his mind only on 19 August. Thus, Stalin's April proposals to the western powers he considers genuine, though only one aspect of a dual diplomacy – it was the 'utterly discouraging' Allied replies which caused Stalin to believe that he should expect nothing but obstruction and affront from London and Paris. (Isaac Deutscher, *Stalin: A Political Biography*, London and New York 1949, pp. 431–7.)

145 Churchill, *Gathering Storm*, p. 365.

146 The different versions of Hitler's remarks quoted in Wheeler-Bennett, *Munich*, pp. 414–15, and Bullock, *Hitler*, pp. 482–3, agree both on this point and on the probable time of the invasion,

26 August. Interestingly, the Foreign Office learned of Hitler's intention on 25 August. (*DBFP*, 3s., VII, 258–9, No. 314, Enclosure.) Chamberlain must surely have been informed of the lurid details of Hitler's intentions, including his assertion: 'I have but one worry, namely that Chamberlain or some other pig of a fellow ("Saukerl") will come at the last moment with proposals or with ratting ("Umfall").' The Prime Minister's subsequent negotiations seem perverse in this light.

147 Quoted in Wheeler-Bennett, *Munich*, p. 417, n. 1.

148 *DBFP*, 3s., VII, 127 (No. 145). This declaration originated in the Foreign Office, in a draft submitted by Halifax to the Prime Minister on 19 August. (*Ibid*., p. 82, No. 83, Enclosure.)

149 *LPCR, 1940*, p. 8.

150 Dalton, *Fateful Years*, p. 260; incredibly, this telegram was received at the Foreign Office on 18 August but not handled by the responsible (Central) Department until four days later! (*DBFP*, 3s., VII, 41–2, No. 41.)

151 'In This United', *Daily Herald*, 24 August 1939.

152 351 *H.C. Debs*., 24 August 1939, col. 5.

153 In a similar fashion, the British role in the Far Eastern dispute need not concern us; for the student of appeasement as practised by Chamberlain's government it is of greater concern.

154 351 *H.C. Debs*., 24 August 1939, col. 20.

155 *Ibid*., 24 August 1939, cols 58–9.

156 'This is the Hour', *Daily Herald*, 25 August 1939.

157 351 *H.C. Debs*., 29 August 1939, col. 116.

158 Dalton, *Fateful Years*, p. 259.

159 *LPCR, 1939*, p. 17.

160 Dalton, *Fateful Years*, p. 261.

161 351 *H.C. Debs*., 1 September 1939, cols 126–7, 135.

162 Dalton, *Fateful Years*, p. 264; Attlee, *As It Happened*, p. 105.

163 Wheeler-Bennett, *Anderson*, pp. 230–1.

164 By his own testimony, quoted in Feiling, *Chamberlain*, p. 416.

165 For a Foreign Office Minute on the diplomacy pertaining to the Italian proposal, see *DBFP*, 3s., VII, 530–1 (No. 749).

166 Taylor maintains: 'Hitler had initially replied to Mussolini that, if invited to a conference, he would give his answer at mid-day on 3 September. Therefore Bonnet, and Chamberlain with him, strove desperately to postpone a declaration of war until after that time, even though the Italians no longer intended to invite Hitler or anyone else.' (*Origins*, p. 171.)

167 *DBFP*, 3s., VII, 513–14 (No. 718).

168 351 *H.C. Debs*., 2 September 1939, col. 281.

169 The remark is attested to by many witnesses, and traditionally ascribed to Leo Amery, though it was not recorded in the *House of Commons Debates*. Harold Nicolson, however, credited Robert Boothby, who recently confirmed the accuracy of Nicolson's observation. (*Diaries, 1930–1939*, p. 419.) Cf. Amery's account: 'I dreaded a purely partisan speech, and called out to him across the floor of the House 'Speak for England'. (*Political Life*, III, 324.)

170 The possibility is suggested by Hore-Belisha, who commented that Greenwood acted 'with great patriotism and statesmanship' (Minney, *Hore-Belisha*, p. 226.)

171 Quoted in Feiling, *Chamberlain*, p. 416.

172 351 *H.C. Debs.*, 2 September 1939, cols 282–3.

173 Minney, *Hore-Belisha*, p. 227; *DBFP*, 3s., VII, 524–6 (Nos 740 and 741).

174 Dalton, *Fateful Years*, p. 267.

175 Halifax, *Fulness of Days*, p. 210. Ivone Kirkpatrick contributes yet another incident to Dalton's vigil: 'He [Dalton] asked me how things were going and I told him that it seemed by no means certain that the French would consent to enter the war. I inquired if in that event the Labour Party would favour our declaring war alone. He replied that he did not know, and I told him firmly that unless we went to war we were sunk.' (*Inner Circle*, pp. 143–4.) Such a reversal of roles hardly corresponds to the temper of the Labour Party, evidenced in Parliament.

176 Churchill, *Gathering Storm*, p. 409.

Index

Hacha, President, 274
Haile Selassie, Emperor, 85, 135
Halifax, Lord, 219, 223, 244, 249,
270, 276, 290, 294, 296, 299, 300,
309, 313
Hamilton, Mary Agnes, 108
Hastings, 55
Henderson, Arthur, 3, 5, 6, 7, 10,
11, 18, 20, 25, 26, 32, 35, 36, 37,
39, 40, 41, 42, 43, 58, 59, 60, 77,
78, 96, 102, 215
Henderson, Arthur (junior), 129
Henderson, Nevile, 305
Henlein, Konrad, 237, 241
Herriot, Edouard, 36, 140
Hicks, George, 113, 144, 162, 241,
283
Hitler, Adolf, 12, 21, 39, 41, 46, 47,
48, 49, 50, 51, 52, 56, 59, 64, 70,
73, 76, 83, 84, 86, 87, 88, 90, 92,
95, 97, 101, 126, 130, 131, 132,
133, 134, 136, 141, 145, 146, 151,
152, 160, 161, 163, 166, 185, 194,
216, 217, 219, 223, 224, 239, 240,
242, 243, 244, 245, 246, 247, 248,
249, 250, 251, 252, 257, 258, 259,
271, 273, 274, 276, 283, 294, 295,
296, 298, 299, 300, 301, 302, 303,
305, 306, 307, 308, 309, 310
Hitlerism, 47, 48, 49
Hoare, Sir Samuel, 35, 60, 90, 92,
95, 98, 112, 113, 120, 121, 123,
124, 125, 126, 127, 128, 153, 185,
274, 298
Hoare-Laval Pact, 122, 123, 124,
125, 126, 127, 128, 149, 151
Holland, 73, 283
Hong Kong, 29
Hoover, President, 36
Hoover, Plan, the, 36, 37
Hore-Belisha, Leslie, 283, 284, 286
House of Commons, 3, 18, 19, 21,
25, 26, 27, 32, 33, 37, 38, 49, 62,
63, 70, 79, 82, 91, 95, 96, 99, 112,
117, 120, 121, 122, 124, 126, 127,
129, 132, 133, 135, 151, 152, 155,
156, 160, 175, 177, 185, 187, 189,
195, 210, 218, 220, 221, 223, 229,

236, 239, 241, 247, 249, 250, 253,
258, 272, 273, 276, 277, 279, 281,
284, 293, 298, 299, 301, 306, 308,
310, 311, 312, 313
Howard, Peter, 110
Hull, Cordell, 209
Hungary, 275
hunger marches, 53

Ilford, 65
Ilford Record, 65
Independent Labour Party, 4, 8, 9,
22, 23, 24, 36, 51, 52, 80, 168,
177, 179, 180, 181, 195
imperialism, 2, 4, 8, 9, 12, 45, 62,
92, 93, 94, 103, 110, 127, 128, 149,
165, 201, 215, 217, 357
Inskip, Sir Thomas, 154, 191, 280
intellectuals, 24, 25, 56, 57, 81, 167,
170, 269
International Brigade, 266
internationalism, 2, 4, 6, 7, 8, 43,
91, 137, 201, 217
International Policy and Defence,
197, 198, 199, 200
international police force, 74, 91
Italy, 58, 61, 73, 81, 84, 85, 86, 87,
88, 91, 92, 93, 94, 95, 102, 109,
111, 112, 113, 119, 120, 121, 122,
126, 127, 129, 134, 135, 136, 137,
138, 142, 144, 154, 161, 162, 174,
182, 183, 185, 187, 193, 197, 210,
212, 217, 218, 220, 226, 227, 239,
247, 269, 270, 271, 273, 287, 290

Jameson, Storm, 53
Japan, 27, 29, 30, 31, 32, 33, 34, 44,
45, 58, 59, 61, 68, 76, 77, 88, 92,
154, 163, 174, 197, 207, 208, 209,
210, 211, 212, 213
Jenkins, Arthur, 195
Jenkins, Roy, vii, 268
Johnston, Tom, 117
Jones, Morgan, 95, 142, 240

Kellogg-Briand Pact, 9, 28, 30,
62
Kennan, George, 303

N